MARQUETTE SLAVIC STUDIES

V

SLOVAKIA

A Political History: 1918-1950

SLOVAKIA

A Political History: 1918-1950

BY JOSEPH A. MIKUS, J.D.

Member of the Slovak Institute, Cleveland, Ohio

Revised and Implemented Edition
Translated from the French by Kathryn Day Wyatt
and Joseph A. Mikus

THE MARQUETTE UNIVERSITY PRESS

MILWAUKEE   1963   WISCONSIN

Library of Congress Catalog Card Number: 63-13803

© Copyright, 1963, Marquette University Press, Milwaukee, Wis.

MANUFACTURED IN THE UNITED STATES OF AMERICA

DEDICATION

To the Rt. Rev. Theodore G. Kojis, Abbot
President of the Slovak Institute, Cleveland, Ohio

and

In memory of the Rev. John J. Lach, Pastor
Parish of the Immaculate Conception, Whiting, Indiana

For their generosity in promoting
Slovak culture

Foreword to the English Edition

This work, first published in 1955 in Paris under the title *La Slovaquie dans le drame de l'Europe,* deals with the political development of that country between 1918 and 1950. This span of time, representing a heartbreaking drama in European history, can be subdivided into three acts: World War I and its aftermath; the period between World War I and World War II; World War II and its consequences. While many books have been written on the involvement and performance of the protagonists on the European political stage of that time, little is known concerning the role, less important of course, but no less thrilling, of smaller European nations.

In the present volume the author describes the impersonation of Slovakia. This rather small, but one of the oldest Central European countries, had then to steer its course first between the Scylla and Charybdis of the Magyar and Czech patronage and later on of German and Soviet imperialism. Now, in fact, it seems submerged by the Communist flood. These four basic determinants, as should be expected, have caused tensions and prompted reactions, producing at the same time turning points in the Slovak national development. This explains why the Slovak question has been mostly analyzed as a marginal problem of the interests of Slovakia's neighbors. No wonder, therefore, that historical facts and events of that nation have frequently been misinterpreted.

Here is a book in English outlining within an articulate system Slovakia's political history in that crucial period as viewed by an American of Slovak descent. To the reader it makes available a number of hitherto unknown documents. It stresses the deeper sense of that country's history: its ambition to be free of foreign attempts at domination and to fulfill its destiny as a free political unit within a larger Central European, or simply, European federative framework.

Pluralist federalism is thus the basic philosophy which animated the author in writing this volume. States, in his opinion, are mechanical power constructions. Nations instead are organic units of a future order of Mankind. This self-confident conformity of Slovak national aspirations with the long range objectives of Mankind confers on the work a so-to-say transhistorical value.

Slovakia's freedom thus becomes one of the high postulates of European justice and international order.

The book is being published by the Slavic Institute of Marquette University as a contribution to the understanding of the tangled area commonly referred to as East-Central Europe.

January 10, 1963   ROMAN SMAL-STOCKI
Milwaukee, Wisconsin   Director, Slavic Institute
                                     Marquette University

Foreword to the French Edition

The fate of Slovakia, which was a State in the ninth century and which was afterward absorbed by the Hungarians and then by the Czechs, is a typical living illustration of the tragic destiny of small European nations joined with others within larger states. Mr. Mikus gives us an example of this in stirring pages.

History is a great lady whom some slander and others disdain; she is often disfigured by those who dress her in sham clothing. A history of Slovakia, accordingly as it is written by a Slovak, a Hungarian, or a Czech, is presented in a different, indeed even opposite manner; in each case there are supporting documents and the claim not only to objectivity but to Truth.

I should like to take the opportunity in the foreword to this important book on Slovakia to draw attention to the serious political problem of multinational states.

Since the Revolution of 1789, politicians and ideologists—the two are sometimes confused—have not ceased to proclaim *urbi et orbi* that peoples have the right to self-determination. How many revolutions have been fought to the sound of this refrain? How many sovereigns have been dethroned in the name of this allegedly liberal maxim? How many wars have been started with this as a pretext? But also how many treaties have been weakened for not having recognized this principle? How many times has the peace been disturbed because agreements made from this point of view have not been respected?

The adversaries of composite empires in the process of dismemberment, to hasten the same in the hope of profiting thereby, have always made the greatest promises for the future to the various component members of the union. Once the collapse is accomplished and peace has come; once the new political edifices are in position and dominated by political, religious, or social influences; then one perceives that the bait used only led to traps or cages where one is now bound, and the freedoms hoped for vanished.

In wars of coalition, it is the strongest conqueror who speaks as master and settles the problems in sympathy with a certain number of political and economic interests which are most often convenient for him. If one adds to that the plots and friendships which allow some men to make their ideas and ambitions triumph; if one takes into consideration the more or less hidden influences, hatreds, or religious or antireligious sectarianism, one will understand that the part reserved for the peoples' preferences, wishes, demands, or even merely their rights, is very slight.

What people has ever really independently determined its own way of life according to its own tastes?

When one gets to the bottom of the problem, one must again ask in what manner the peoples could express their opinion and make it triumph. Let us not speak of plebiscites or referenda, for there never has been one that has not been falsified in one way or another. Otherwise one would not have seen sovereigns dethroned who had been voted in by plebiscites a few months before.

I shall perhaps be told that there are parliamentary representations speaking in the name of the nation. But in the case of groups of peoples, the so-called parliamentary representations exist for the most part only after the signing of agreements regulating the fate of the nation in question, which fate is decided beforehand by self-appointed politicians often having no right to speak validly in the name of a whole nation.

Then again, to what extent are a nation's members of Parliament, even if they have been regularly elected by a real majority, independent and honest enough to discuss the interests and rights of country or nation with a view only to the common good and national interest?

In short, admitted all this to be united under the best conditions, in the case of compounded states certain parliamentary representations are most often themselves only ineffective minorities even if they are able to act.

All the efforts of the governments that dominate the disparate elements of these countries aim at trying to kill the national consciousness of the elements in question. The efforts toward assimilation or fusion all rest on force, constraint, and vexations. When it is a matter of populations a bit retarded from the standpoint of material civilization, attempts are even made at times to keep them in a sort of subserviency so that they will be less dangerous.

When the measure is full to overflowing and the nationalities revolt, one crushes them and puts down the uprising with abominable ferocity. By fire, sword, and blood one shows them the will of the strongest to reduce to silence—to death if need be—voices which would be tempted to denounce before the whole world the injustice which these minorities suffer from century to century.

Aspirations toward freedom become crimes of treason vis-à-vis the power which does you the honor to oppress you.

Bodies can be tortured, hands bound, tongues torn out, mouths gagged—but the soul of a people is not killed. The soul of peoples is transmitted from generation to generation in as mysterious and impalpable a manner as the soul of our children with the life that we give them.

What adds to the horror of the treatment inflicted on small nations is the hypocrisy displayed by the ruling governments. Laws are voted but never put into operation. Liberties are granted in principle but always refused in reality. Instruments of propaganda are flaunted to the outside world, but as quickly shut up in an iron closet only to remain there as a dead letter for the country on the inside.

As the consciousness of forming a national community subsists in spite of everything, resists all anguish, rises above all pain and is transmitted unceasingly, clandestine resistance is organized and perfected. At times it shows signs of its existence; it always maintains a secret state of rebellion which waits only for an opportunity to manifest itself.

But insurrection either succeeds and for the moment triumphs (complete and enduring success is very rare), or at the first signs of agitation, mass deportations and extermination, as methodical as ferocious, try to bring to their senses those who wanted to shake off the oppressive domination. In this case the dread of the police brings calm and resignation.

Why must the great European nations make themselves—why have they made themselves—accomplices of such crimes through cowardice, political friendship with the oppressors, sectarianism, or by reason of various interests that are often of low if not sordid inspiration and means!

Many examples of all these facts relating to Slovakia are to be found in Mr. Mikus' book. Analogous ones could be cited for all of Central Europe and even for the Soviet Union.

Such are the dealings—for they are not only recent—which throughout the centuries kept Slovakia from becoming again the free and independent State desired by the Slovaks. But the sufferings of this people continue and are more frightful since Communism has enslaved them and all of Central Europe.

Among the tyrannical methods practiced today in order to stifle within the Slovak soul all that could help in a resurrection is religious persecution.

The Catholicism which in the life and history of Slovakia holds a position as great as in Poland, which was always the symbol and leaven of national unity, this same Catholicism is today hunted down: priests and laic are imprisoned, rights trampled under foot, schools secularized, Catholic civil servants eliminated, associations forbidden and dissolved, goods confiscated. But in addition, as in all the countries behind the Iron Curtain, there were and still are attempts to dominate the Church and create a sort of Red Caesar-Papism. Every way has been used to undermine the people's confidence in the Holy See, to provoke dissentment between the episcopate and the clergy on one hand, the clergy and the faithful on the other. A thousand vexatious interferences have been invented. Propaganda favoring apostate priests has been used in order to create a certain popularity for them. Accusations of immorality were brought against those who remained loyal. Ecclesiastical celibacy was criticized. The Church was likened to capitalism in order to discredit it in the eyes of the people. All the devices were and are good. An alleged governmental "Catholic Action" was created. Falsehoods were invented, the State deified.

Since the Church is persecuted, bound, chased from the cathedrals and all its organizations, it has only one refuge: souls. But there, it is out of reach. For it becomes more strengthened and intensified, and gives evidence of a still stronger resistance as the attacks become harder and more demoniac.

With different nuances and varying degrees, the methods of procedure, the aims, the ambitions are the same in all the countries behind the Iron Curtain. Everywhere there is a death battle between atheistic communism and Christianity, for they are absolutely incompatible. Communism is for the moment apparently triumphant in Central Europe. But the Church has from her Founder the promise of eternity. The Cross will triumph sooner or later over the Sickle and Hammer. Oppressed nations will find freedom again, and from the spiritual point of view enslaved peoples will again have the right to self-determination. But it is indispensable that the systems which will be built on the ruins of communist regimes have at the base of their structure a respect for contracts, freely given adherence, assured freedoms, national individualities revived and in full bloom for the greatest mutual benefit of the populations united in a federated Europe.

PAUL LESOURD

Professor at the Catholic University in Paris.

Preface

*Nations are moral persons that have
their own life. . . . A people struck from
the political map of Europe subsists in
spite of the indifference of governments.*
                    Jules Cambon, *The Diplomatist*

The peoples of the Western world generally know little about
Slovakia, and the little that they know is unfortunately laden with
errors. From two sides, as a matter of fact, an effort has been
made with the same zeal to obscure Slovakia's image.

It was Magyar "political science" which, before 1914, first
tried to put the resources of erudition into the service of politics.
Political science is a tractable child. It cannot refuse anything to
politicians. It was a matter of proving that for Slovakia, "a poor,
retarded, passive country, and strictly speaking without history,"
there could be no better fate than submission to the Magyar State.
Hungarian historians indulged in deformations of reality and half-
truths which were fitting to such conclusive proof.

Meanwhile between the two wars, Czech "political science"
ensured relief. Conceiving an alleged unity of language and culture, it invented the myth of a "Czechoslovak" nationality. Czech
historians and linguists, among others, attempted to dissolve
Slovak individuality in an artificial community and furnish arguments to the politicians responsible for the new State: Masaryk
and Beneš.

The "political science" of the Western nations fell into step.
Instead of going to the sources, as would have been proper, it
preferred to take the easy way and utilize Czech and Magyar
works. One of the most typical cases is that of the French historian, Ernest Denis. Friend of the Czechs, he showed his sympathy
for them by the monumental work, *La Bohème après la Mon-
tagne Blanche*. Won over by Beneš during World War I to the
idea of a Czecho-Slovakia under Czech leadership, this historian
became the instrument of a policy. His book, *La Question d'Autriche: les Slovaques*,[1] in spite of some positive aspects, cannot
be taken as the basis for an impartial study of the problem.

The Magyars who for reasons only too obvious had not been
able to establish a criterion of ethnical relationship with the

[1] Paris, 1917.

Slovaks, were more or less frankly addicted to the notion of a guardian people—race of "lords" consecrated by nature to the guidance of other men. It is this same state of mind that, in 1919, actuated Mr. Guy de Roquencourt, to write in a pleasantly playful tone in a Swiss review[2] written in French the lines later quoted. Mr. de Roquencourt, ill-satisfied with the new reorganization of Central Europe, simply suggested that national consciousness in Slovakia was of foreign inspiration and that the common man, absorbed enough by the care of making his barley and potatoes grow well, would have never thought of it by himself. He wrote:

> Never having formed a State nor organic province for ten centuries, the Slovaks, like blissful people, have no history other than that of their own local backwashes. Without national consciousness, they did not even know that they were profoundly unfortunate until the day when apostles who came from beyond the mountains informed them that freed from the Magyars' yoke, they were called to high destinies which, it seems, are in the process of being fulfilled. Today national consciousness has been born in them. But the Slovaks are profoundly different from their Czech congeners, at least for the greater part, for more than half are more nearly like the Pole or the Ruthenian than the Czech; they are very much mixed with Magyar and German elements, which form bourgeois and intellectuals among them; therefore no one can know if their eventual new establishment within the heart of a Czecho-Slovak State will long be to their liking. Great disappointments probably await the "great power" led by Mr. Masaryk.

Everything considered, it is not surprising—but it is regrettable —that definitions of Slovakia like the following are to be found in French and Western dictionaries and manuals: "A very closed country, long subjected to tyrannical domination, very much retarded, without large cities, Slovakia corresponds to the expanded part of the Carpathians of the north. . . ." or "The Slovaks lead a patriarchal life under the direction of their Catholic priests. . . ."[3] or again

> "The Slovaks (three to six million Czechs) have acclaimed the Union, but they have not arrived at the same

[2] "La question slovaque," extract from *La Revue Politique Internationale*, Lausanne XXXVI (January-February, 1919), 80.

[3] Allix, Leyritz and Merlier, *Géographie pour l'enseignement secondaire* (Paris: 1926), p. 202.

stage of civilization: they are peasants, shepherds, for the great part illiterate, over whom the clergy is all-powerful."[4]

Before World War I, Slovakia was undoubtedly at a rather retarded stage of material civilization, although its people were quick of mind and avid for education. But does one realize the degree of servitude to which the Slovaks have been held for long centuries? "What contempt did the Magyars have," writes Mr. Aulneau, "for this people relegated to the rank of serfs and against whom they exercised every violence to dominate them the better."[5] In short, the treatment consisted of depriving these enslaved peoples of education and in general of everything that makes for civilization, in order to keep them in a primitive state, and of course to keep them enslaved because they were primitive. A strange vicious circle.

As for the indisputable role of the clergy in the national movement, one can understand if one considers that the priests—offspring of the people—were the only ones to enjoy the freedom necessary for any public activity. Lawyers, professors, journalists, in short, all the intellectuals were more or less dependent on foreign regimes.

It goes without saying—so natural is it—that each time a patriotic act was evidenced in Slovakia, instead of seeking its really deep causes, the government preferred to attribute a foreign origin to it, thereby justifying the most bloody repressions. Already at the time of the Magyars, especially after 1848, Slovak movements were, in the eyes of the Hungarian government, only manifestations of budding Slavism. During the Czecho-Slovak regime, it was for the government of Prague a question of troubles of evident Magyar inspiration. In Aulneau's book, we read:

> Magyar propaganda attempts further to create a Slovak nationalist movement by stirring up religious divisions and by separating the Slovaks, ardent Catholics, from the Czech freethinkers.[6]

The contemporary phase is much more complex still. We are too close to the events of the last war for political passions not to cloud the opinions of certain Czech writers on Slovakia's attitude during the period when it dared to set out upon a different road from that of the Czechs.

[4] L. Genet, Précis d'Histoire Contemporaine, 1919-1930 (Paris: 1936), p. 208.
[5] J. Aulneau, Histoire de l'Europe Centrale (Paris: 1926).
[6] Ibid. p. 482.

Quite recently, communist historians have claimed to interpret Slovak history in the light of "scientific socialism." Attention can be drawn, among others, to Gustáv Husák, former President of the Board of Commissioners of Bratislava, whose book, *Battle for the Future*,[7] constitutes a falsification of Slovak history that is not less dangerous than the preceding ones.

Finally, many Western "observers" or "fellow travellers," lending themselves to suggestions of the Communists of Prague, propagate at the present time erroneous information on the action of the Slovaks' heroically resisting the ascendancy of bolshevism.

Any foreigner wishing to take up the study of the question will therefore have to beware of treatises on Slovak history written by Magyars, Czechs, or Communists. He will find it indispensable to refer to national authors: Frank Sasínek, Julius Botto, Jozef Škultéty, Daniel Rapant and František Hrušovský, or to the sources.

We shall try, in calling constantly upon firsthand documents for help, to shed some light on the political events of Slovakia in one of the most dramatic and at the same time one of the most confused periods of its history.

Washington, D.C.   J. A. MIKUS
July, 1953

---

[7] To facilitate the reading and understanding of the text, the titles of works written in Slavic languages (Slovak, Czech, etc.) to which I refer are translated into English. Their title in the original language is indicated in the bibliography at the end of the book.

Contents

CONCLUSION:
FOR A FREE SLOVAKIA IN
A FEDERATED EUROPE

EPILOGUE TO THE ENGLISH EDITION
APPENDICES:

THE IDEA OF THE SLOVAK STATE
THROUGHOUT HISTORY

> *The Slovaks have unflinchingly trav-*
> *ersed centuries of distress when adversity*
> *bore down on them. Their unshakeable*
> *constancy is sufficient to make us believe*
> *in their future.*
>
> Ernest Denis, *Les Slovaques*

Central Europe is a complicated place, a zone of quicksands on the European continent where living forces dispute constantly for power. It happens that for a certain time one of the statisms under discussion succeeds in dominating these forces completely, but the latter in turn always end up by affirming themselves.

In Western Europe, it is currently thought that this cyclic process as it were is a chaotic phenomenon inherent in the "oriental" or "Balkan" mentality of the peoples who live in that region. This opinion is false, for this region has its laws of evolution and even its constants which it is indispensable to know and understand.

Whereas in the states of Western Europe the sociological, political, and juridical notions are in harmony and are nearly one and the same, in Central Europe they are juxtaposed and entangled one with the other. Whoever wishes to understand the problems of this part of Europe must begin by studying its sociological physiognomy, the raw material without which he could not grapple with the political aspects. It is therefore necessary for him to become initiated into the geography, races, religions, languages, and psychology of all the peoples who have asserted themselves there throughout the centuries. Only then will he be able to go on to the study of the political phenomena, that is to say, the collective individualities animated by one will, the result of a common culture which confers upon the still unconscious masses—"the people" in the strict sense of the word—a personality within the compass of political ontology. It is the consciousness of a common destiny and the desire to attain to a common end which are the essential criteria of the nation.

Central Europe presents serious political problems precisely because it is made up of numerous nations each with its own aspirations and each savagely attached to its destiny. Their individualities, which have asserted themselves by constant struggles throughout the centuries, have strengthened their physical, psychological, and moral characteristics—their character—to such a point that today there can be no question about their ever going backward. They have been transformed into ethnical and ethical organisms that think and act in a manner all their own. Bound to a concrete geographical position, they have become just so many active forces, each of which has a physiognomy different from that of its neighbors. They sprang up biologically by forming united communities of the same will and with inner reactions and outward manifestations peculiar to them alone. The final goal of such organic communities is to become established in the form of an entity, distinguished by an organized power, a technical superstructure, an autonomous statute—in short, to raise itself to the dignity of a state.[1]

Seen from this angle, juridical reality is only a special form of a nation's organization. While the sociological element and the political criterion form the substance of any state organization, the juridical qualification is only its formal attribute. Considered as substance, the nation constitutes a value that is superior to the state. The state is to the nation what the receptacle is to wine. This natural superiority of substance over form, which gives the deepest meaning to the nations' right to self-determination, is of paramount importance for the appreciation of the real value of multi-national states, such as those which did exist or still do exist within the confines of Central Europe. Austria-Hungary, Czecho-Slovakia and Yugoslavia are typical examples. Such states have some prospects of enduring politically only if they result from a spontaneous will of all the nations which form them. On the other hand, if one of these succeeds in getting hold of the power to the detriment of the others, imposing itself by force or ruse on the other nations of the heterogeneous state, the latter is then unquestionably lost.

The political history of Central Europe is in reality only that of an incessant struggle between individual nationalities seeking to recover or preserve their juridical status and soul-less statisms, masking ambitions of conquest of the strongest nationalism. And

---

[1] Harold Laski speaks of the separatist character of nationalities. See *A Grammar of Politics* (London: 1948), p. 220.

here it is a matter of the struggle for liberty and democracy against international feudalism. It is also a question of the struggle for victory of sociological, political, and juridical elements, and consolidation of the national idea within the limits of the international community.

If one wishes to avoid the errors of the past, one must be realistic and recognize in each nation—a fundamental element of Central Europe—its juridical individuality. In forming multi-national states the map of Europe can indeed be simplified, but a problem which is now a century old cannot be solved.

The idea of the Slovak State is derived from this organic conception of nations as natural units of the international community.

We shall see how this supreme idea has acted upon the evolution of the Slovak nation, how it has spurred on its effort, and how, after a short-lived concreteness in the Middle Ages, this idea had to brave foreign political concepts which claimed the right to make it disappear in order to substitute for it.

Finally, we shall see how in spite of all the ups and downs of history this idea lives on and constitutes a moral force, more living now than ever before, incessantly taking its inspiration from the universal principle of liberty.

Great-Moravia

A Slovak State, known throughout European history by the name of Great-Moravia, existed from the ninth century. It is even interesting to note that this State was the first political unity in Central Europe. The Slovaks, established on the confines of the Slavic and Germanic worlds, were constantly threatened by the encroachments of their neighbors. The common danger among the little isolated principalities gave birth to the idea of grouping themselves together. The first sovereigns of this State were Princes Pribina, Mojmír, Ratislav, King Svätopluk (870-894), and his son Mojmír II (894-907).

In the first half of the ninth century, Great-Moravia was converted to Christianity. One can still see a church at Nitra that was erected in 833; it is today embodied within the ensemble of the cathedral. This was the first Christian church in Central Europe. A mission from Byzantium intensified the evangelization of the country. At the invitation of Prince Rastislav, St. Cyril and St. Methodius preached throughout all Slovakia from 863 on.

The Slovak State had at that time a first-rate international position. It maintained relations with the Holy See and the neighboring empires. In 879, Svätopluk sent a delegation of priests and noblemen to Pope John VIII who granted important privileges to the Slovak State.

Great-Moravia temporarily even ruled the territories of Bohemia which it had conquered by force of arms; but the Czech Prince Spytihněv in 895 allied himself in Regensburg to the Germanic King Arnulf and became an instrument in his policy against the Slovak ruler.[2]

The Slovak princes carried on relations with Byzantium, whose allies they were, against the Bulgar-Turkish coalition. Their prosperity suddenly came to an end at the beginning of the tenth century. In 907, a coalition grouping Magyars and Germans inflicted upon them the disastrous defeat of Bratislava. The Slovak State disappeared at that time, absorbed by its more powerful Magyar adversary. Nevertheless, nothing could ever efface the memory of Great-Moravia and its glorious sovereigns.

Today, if the Slovaks still claim Great-Moravia, it is not for the mere luxury of evoking the memory of a brilliant past, rather it is to satisfy the same thirst for liberty which animated their ancestors.

Upper Hungary

Integrated within the kingdom of Saint-Stephen, Slovakia constituted in the eleventh and twelfth centuries an administrative principality forming the appanage of the heir to the throne. It was called Upper Hungary.

Like a flash of light in the long night of the Middle Ages, the idea of the Slovak State reappeared in the twelfth century in the political work of Duke Matúš Čák de Trenčín (1296-1321). Profiting by the struggles of various pretenders to the throne of Hungary, he organized Slovakia under the scepter of his personal power, apart from any interference from the crown of Saint-Stephen, finally taken away by Charles of Anjou. Ernest Denis in his work, *La Question d'Autriche: les Slovaques,* reports the facts in this wise:

> It is certain that Matúš Čák grouped almost the whole of Slovakia under his power and exercised for a quarter of a century an authority that was well-nigh absolute. The little State that he had formed had of necessity a Slavic character. The poets who later celebrated in Matúš Čák the hero of liberty reborn certainly falsify history in giving

[2] See: František Hrušovský, *The Slovak Princes* (Scranton, Pa.: 1949), p. 244.

him intentions that he never had; but without knowing or wishing it, by the very reason that he separated himself from the rest of Hungary and reassembled the Slovak counties under a common rule, he revived the idea of primitive independence. It is certain that he leaned on the popular classes for support, and they rewarded him for his understanding by their grateful remembrance of him.[3]

The centuries that followed are marked in Hungary by numerous peasant revolts against the *adscriptio glaebae,* an institution of Hungarian public law as codified in *Tripartitum Opus Juris Consuetudinarii Regni Hungariae* of 1514 by Stephen Werböczy. It made of peasants serfs *(rustici, coloni)* of large landed properties. These were class struggles, and struggles for individual liberty rather than political revolts of a national tendency. Here the Magyar, Croatian, or Rumanian peasant too was enslaved in the same manner as the Slovak within the confines of this heterogeneous Kingdom. These rebellions fill the whole beginning of modern times.

At this time, Latin was the official language in Hungary. It was accessible only to a minority: those politically or intellectually privileged. Among the masses only the different mother tongues were known: Magyar, Croatian, Rumanian, Slovak, etc.

Toward the end of the eighteenth century, a profound change took place in the lethargical state of the different nationalities of the Danube space. The enlightened despotism of Joseph II, who wished to impose Germanism more strongly, entailed a violent reaction of all national collectivities. The French Revolution kindled the mind with the idea of liberty and gave an irresistible impulsion to the soporific peoples. Animated henceforth by the ideal of their liberation, they vowed a deep interest in their language and literature. Their cult of all the elements of national life is the very expression of this awakening.

In Slovakia it is Anton Bernolák (1762-1813) who has the merit of having codified the spoken language. He fashioned an important dictionary and grammar, thus facilitating the divulgence of modern ideas among the people. It is to this initiative that the Slovaks owe the definitive strengthening of their national unity.

The Slovak ethnical element could thus evolve clearly into a nationality distinct from its neighbors: Magyars, Poles, and Czechs. Literature ensures Slovakia, in the Slavic world and all

[3] Ernest Denis, *La Question d'Autriche: les Slovaques* (Paris: 1917), p. 118.

of Europe, the physiognomy of a nation. It has contributed greatly to the formation of a common consciousness and a single heart. It has served to fashion the national soul.

Prepared thus, the Slovak collectivity was able for the first time in the modern period to manifest its political will. The Declaration of Liptovský Sv. Mikuláš of May 10, 1848, is the first confrontation of national reality with the policy of the Magyars in the Hungary of that time. Its contents remained a program of burning urgency for the Slovak policy for the next ninety years. Many were the revendications that the Slovaks presented at that time; such were, afterward, their political and social postulates in all their struggles against foreign dominations up to the re-establishment of the Slovak Republic: the federative reform of the Hapsburg monarchy, the equality of rights with the other nationalities, a Diet formed by a National Council, the official recognition of Slovak as a language of administration, the opening of Slovak primary and secondary schools and a national university and polytechnical school, the right to possess a flag as symbol of the Slovak fatherland, a national guard with a suitable supreme command as military expression of the national will, universal suffrage, liberty of the press, and the ascription to the peasants of the lands which they held by only a precarious title.

Building upon this political will of the Slovak nation, Ľudovít Štúr (1815-1856), the first Slovak leader to have a European culture and stature, inserted Slovakia as a special political unit in his conception of the Slavic world, and presented to the Congress of all the Slavs who met in Prague in June, 1848, a resolution on the necessity of reorganizing the monarchy in the federative sense.[4]

To battle for liberty and honor is a proof that one is capable of having a proper political will. Thus the insurrection of Jozef Miloslav Hurban in September, 1848, against Budapest, expressed the lively aspiration of the Slovak community for freedom. At a huge mass rally, on September 19, 1848, at Myjava, Štúr proclaimed nothing less than the political independence of Slovakia and invited the whole nation to rise against the Budapest government. The essential point of his speech was as follows:

> On this solemn occasion we declare ourselves independent of the Magyars; we decline all obedience to the Magyar nation, to its government and ministries. And whosoever within the scope of our power shall continue in

[4] F. Bokes, *History of the Slovaks and Slovakia* (Bratislava: 1946), p. 173.

xxviii

some union with them, we shall regard as an enemy of and traitor to our nation; consequently, he shall not escape deserved punishment.[5]

By its importance, the uprising showed this people to be conscious of its own capabilities, ready to defend, arms in hand, its interests and its very existence. Slovakia was therefore a unity which obeyed its own destiny and sought its own place in the current politics of its time and even outside the constitutional bounds of Hungary.

The uprising of 1848 has still another meaning. It was a conscious opposition to the schemings of Kossuth, aiming at the separation of Hungary from the Hapsburg Empire and its transformation into a purely nationalistic Magyar State. The Slovak uprising led by Štúr, Hurban, and Hodža was not, as one might believe, an armed intervention of the Slovak people in favor of the centralism of Vienna. It had as its objective the creation of a Danubian federation.

The same aspirations inspired the petitions which were presented on March 20, 1849, to Emperor Francis-Joseph at Olomouc by a delegation of twenty-eight members, presided over by Canon Jozef Kozáček; then on April 13, 1849, to the government of Vienna by Hurban, Štúr, and Michal Miloslav Hodža.

A little later, Štúr did not hesitate to take another step forward by formulating the rights of the Slovaks to their national existence. In his work of 1856, *Das Slawenthum und die Welt der Zukunft*,[6] he says virtually:

> In order to insure a development in our life and win in world history a place which would be in accordance with the qualities of our spirit and strength, we must free ourselves once and for all from the foreign yoke that is crushing us and gain political independence. For an enslaved nation whose hands are tied and whose mind is stunned is under a constant menace to perish sooner or later.

[5] Daniel Rapant, *The Slovak Uprising 1848-1849*, II-1, (Turčiansky Sv. Martin: 1950), p. 163.

[6] *Das Slaventhum und die Welt der Zukunft* (Bratislava: 1931), p. 162. It is interesting to note that it has been impossible to date to publish this book in Slovak. Štúr wrote the original in German and later had a translation made in Russian which was published in two editions: Moscow: 1867, and St. Petersburg: 1909. A Slovak publication was impossible during the Hungarian regime, because it was considered too Pan-Slavic; impossible again during the First Czecho-Slovak Republic because in it Štúr demands Slovakia's independence; and again impossible during the Slovak State because Štúr was anti-German and the prepared edition had to be withdrawn at the insistence of the German Minister at Bratislava; nor, yet, today can we have a Slovak publication because Štúr was an anti-communist.

On February 2, 1861, Jozef Miloslav Hurban presented the
Minister of the Interior at Vienna with a memorandum which
summarized the principal demands expressed by the Slovaks in
1849.

But a greater importance must be granted the *Memorandum
of the Slovak Nation* of June 7, 1861, which was drawn up and
voted by a meeting of political leaders and delegates from Slovak
cities and towns at Turčiansky Sv. Martin, and afterward presented to the Parliament of Hungary. This memorandum, which
called for the recognition of a "Slovak region," marks another
event in the history of the idea of a Slovak State. This region,
which was to comprise the whole population of the Slovak language of Upper Hungary, was to constitute an autonomous territory having its own administration, courts, schools, and cultural
institutions. Therein expressed is the modern idea of the proportionate representation of the Slovaks in the central services of
Hungary.

This important document brings to light the ensemble of problems set by the diverse nationalities of the Kingdom. It shows the
Slovaks to be perfectly conscious of the danger created by Magyar statism which persisted in assimilating non-Magyar nationalities. The Slovaks here declared that their interests were bound up
with the Rumanians, Serbs, Croats, and Carpathian Ruthenians
—all menaced like themselves.

The epoch of *Matica Slovenská* (1863-1874),[7] called by the
writer Konštantín Čulen "the time of hopes and disillusions,"[8] was,
in a way, the national *Sturm und Drang*. It was at that time that
the Slovaks succeeded in coming out from the abyss "of historical
nonentity"[9] where they had been since the fall of Great-Moravia,
and not only declaring their existence, but also manifesting their
culture and their spiritual life—in a word, their consciousness
of forming a national community politically mature and disci-
plined. During these few years, the Slovak people was able to
show its own physiognomy and give free rein to its historical
ambitions. It had its newspapers, books, schools, cultural institutions, national associations, political meetings, all of which were
symbols of a live national organism and a conscious political evo-

---

[7] Slovak Institute of Sciences and Arts, founded by the Bishop of Banská
Bystrica, Štefan Moyses, and destined to spread Slovak culture and literature.
[8] Konštantín Čulen, *The Years of Slovak Hopes and Disillusions* (Bratislava:
1932).
[9] S. H. Vajanský, *Complete Works* (Turčiansky Sv. Martin: 1912), XI, 222.

lution. It was, in short, the maturation period of the cells and fibers that would constitute, in the struggle which was to follow, the nerves and muscles of the national body.

After the Austro-Hungarian Compromise in 1867, the Slovaks were left completely to the mercy of Budapest. A policy of pitiless Magyarization was begun with a view to transforming the heterogeneous kingdom of Saint-Stephen into a purely Magyar State. An instrument of propaganda only, a hypocritical law on the nationalities and their rights was voted at Budapest in 1868. Politically the Slovaks, bound hand and foot, were given up to Magyar bureaucracy. In 1874, the *Matica Slovenská* was dissolved and in 1875, the last three Slovak *gymnasia* were closed in Turčiansky Sv. Martin, Kláštor pod Znievom, and Revúca. From then on, there remained in Slovakia only Magyar secondary schools where the professors had the right to teach in the Magyar language alone.

This period thus marks a distinct regression in national life. Bound as it was, the nation could no longer breathe. The "end of century" spirit crept into the Slovak community.

The Congress of Nationalities (Rumanian, Slovak, and Serbian) which met August 19, 1895, in Budapest, denounced vigorously, however, the policy of the government that reserved all the important public offices for the Magyars alone at a time when the latter were not even representative of half the total population of the kingdom. "It is only the ensemble of the nationalities of Hungary that one has a right to identify with the State," declared the Congress,[10] and it demanded universal suffrage and representation of the different nationalities in Parliament.

In 1896, the government organized the festivities for the State's first millenium, with the evident pretention of proving to the world that Hungary was a purely Magyar State. It seems that nothing could oppose this attitude, since the Magyars alone had the right to express themselves. Yet the Rumanians, Slovaks, and Serbs again came together to protest against this inexact presentation of reality and again demand equal rights for all nationalities. Their protests brought no improvement.

[10] It is curious to note that after 1918, the term "Hungary" was kept to designate the national Magyar State. As a matter of fact, former Hungary included, besides the Magyars, the Slovaks and the Carpathian Ruthenians, Serbs, Croats, Rumanians, and Germans. The Trianon Treaty reduced historical Hungary to the ethnical Magyar territory. It would therefore be logical to call the new State "Magyaria" (See *Foreign Relations of the U.S.*, I, Washington [1942], 348, 387) or "Magyarland," a term that would translate its Magyar name, which is "Magyarország."

In Slovakia the people, not letting themselves be discouraged by these successive setbacks, began to reorganize their forces for a final act of rebellion. At the beginning of the twentieth century, they were led by two men endowed with large vision for the political future: Svetozár Hurban Vajanský and Andrej Hlinka.

These two men were predestined by their personal daring and moral integrity as well as their uncompromising national feeling, to become the leaders of their generation. Thus it was not just by chance that their destinies crossed in the Magyar prison of Szeged. Their sufferings and sacrifices for the Slovak cause are a tribute to the idea of justice, a tribute which increases the moral capital of the nation and enriches its history.

Vajanský was a political writer as well as a poet who, astride the two centuries and at the time of national passivity and Hlasist[11] deviation, saw with surprising prescience the political consequences that the existence of the Slovak nation implied. His unshakeable certitude and firm faith in the historical mission of the Slovak people became apparent from the following statement:

> We are an ethnical group regularly introduced into the community of nations, forming an entity of itself, effectively existent, essential, real; endowed with all the qualifications, all the criteria of an autochthonous nation with its own territory, personality, language, customs, ethnographical boundaries, history, merits, sacrifices, its loyalty tried and tested in war and peace. We are at once a nationality and a nation recognized by the throne and by law, a nation having not only its duties but also its rights.[12]

And farther on:

> If there is no doubt whatsoever that only mass deportation, extermination by sword, poison, fire, water, dynamite, perpetrated methodically and pitilessly, could wipe the Slovak nation from the surface of the earth, a crime for which nobody, for material and moral reasons—of this we are fully convinced—can make himself guilty, we can understand neither this postponement of a reasonable solution to our national question nor this persistent wish to weaken the Slovak nationality by partisan actions.[13]

[11] *Hlas* was a monthly periodical published for the first time in 1898 by a group of Slovak Protestant intellectuals and free thinkers, among whom was Vavro Srobár who, confronted with the danger that Magyarization constituted, preached the necessity of the Slovaks' fusion with the Czechs.

[12] Vajanský, *Complete Works*, XI, 280-81.

[13] *Ibid.*, p. 282.

In the elections held for the Parliament of Hungary in 1905, the Slovaks presented 13 candidates of whom, because of great Magyar pressure, only Ferko Skyčák and Milan Hodža were victorious. The same year Ferko Skyčák, who had been elected as a candidate on the list of the Hungarian Populist party, abandoned this group and founded the Slovak Populist party. Andrej Hlinka became then an active campaigner for its candidates.

In consequence of a political crisis, Parliament was to be dissolved and new elections held in 1906. From the 18 Slovak candidates only seven were elected: six on the program of the Slovak Populist party and one on that of the Slovak National party.

A massacre which took place at Černová in 1907,[14] contributed largely afterward to making the Slovak question—until then a simple matter of Magyar subprefects—a problem for the European conscience. At the moment when the Dreyfus affair in France was causing governments to fall, the dead of Černová inspired writers and made the voices of Björnsterne Björnson, Leo Tolstoi, Seton Watson and others, rise up against the cruelty of Budapest.

This event threw a harsh light on the internal problems of the Austro-Hungarian monarchy and contributed to the creation of the psychosis of catastrophe which had spread about over the years preceding World War I.

Thus, although they have been juridically absorbed for a thousand years by foreign statism, the Slovaks have none the less subsisted, as much a special sociological element as a distinct political force. The Slovak people, united by their language and traditions, has given proof throughout the centuries of an historical individuality animated by the constant desire of liberating itself from its oppressors.

---

[14] The village of Černová which at that time had just built a church, wanted it to be consecrated by Andrej Hlinka, a native of the village. Monsignor Párvy, a Magyar bishop of the Slovak diocese of Spiš, opposed it because he saw in Hlinka Slovak patriot. Profiting by the moment when Hlinka was on a trip to Moravia, the Bishop chose a loyal priest of the regime to consecrate the church. The Sunday when the latter wished to enter the village, accompanied by the subprefect and a group of gendarmes, the populace prevented his carriage from passing. The subprefect then gave the order to fire. There were fourteen killed and sixty wounded.

PART I

CZECHO-SLOVAKIA

History is a world court for individuals and nations.

T. G. Masaryk, *The New Europe*

AT THE CLOSE of World War I, six States, among which was Czecho-Slovakia, arose from the debris of Austria-Hungary.

Inspired by the modern principle of the right of peoples to self-determination, Czecho-Slovakia was introduced into the international community under the patronage of the Entente. Presided over by T. G. Masaryk, a person who was already enjoying an incontestable prestige in the West, the new Republic could aspire to a long and great future.

The Slovaks, represented in the struggle for liberation by General M. R. Štefánik, henceforth a legendary hero, as well as by their emigrants in America, saw in this new State the realization of all their aspirations.

Now, in spite of an apparently irreproachable Constitution and well-ordered economic and financial systems, Czecho-Slovakia was to collapse in a manner as surprising as it was dramatic after only twenty years of existence. Unlike a number of Czech and foreign political writers who, trying not to touch upon painful realities, confined themselves to an analysis of the Constitution and the political institutions—in short, the façade of Czecho-Slovakia—we propose to outline here the history of the precarious existence of this State. We shall emphasize the contradiction that existed incessantly between its creative principle and its implementation, the constant disagreements that resulted from the opposition of its internal forces and the divergencies between the theory and acts of its statesmen. In fact, if one does not know the Slovak and German problems, vices hidden from the new State of 1918, it is impossible to understand the disintegration of the Czecho-Slovakia of 1938, and still less the events that were later to unfold in Slovakia.

The causes which were to decide the fate of Czecho-Slovakia can be reduced to four: the mistakes of the policy of Prague after World War I, the right of the Slovaks to self-determination, the progressive breaking down of the League of Nations and the Central European security system, and finally, the question of German minority in Czech countries. Whereas the first and last two of these causes led the Czecho-Slovak State to Munich, where, according to the well-known expression of Mr. Beneš, it received its death blow, the second gave it its finishing stroke on March 14, 1939.

Federation, the Creative Principle of the Czecho-Slovak State

During World War I, three solutions to the Slovak problem were envisioned:[1] an independent Slovakia,[2] Slovakia as a State-member of a federated Austria-Hungary, and the union of Slovakia with the Czech countries. All things considered, it was the latter solution which was adopted, being recognized at that time by the majority of Slovaks as the most reasonable.

The idea of a Czecho-Slovak State rested on the future political union of two Slav nations equally oppressed under the Austro-Hungarian regime: the Czech and Slovak nations. Its essential aim was the combining of the efforts of these two peoples with a view to the avoidance of any foreign oppression in the future. This State was therefore conceived as dualistic, having to be made up of two ethnical elements whose relationship would be expressed by a formula showing absolute equality.

All the important political agreements which were concluded between the Slovak and Czech emigrants stipulated that the future State would have federal organization; among others, the Cleveland and Pittsburgh agreements were explicit on this subject.

Thus the Cleveland Agreement, which was concluded October 25, 1915, between the Czech National Alliance and the Slovak League of America, stipulated that the federative union of the Czech and Slovak peoples would assure the complete

---

[1] See: T. G. Masaryk, *The Making of a State* (New York: 1927), pp. 221-23.
[2] Historical Section of the Foreign Office, *Slovakia* (London: 1920), p. 22.
   "In the extreme section of the Nationalists the proposal has been put forward for the establishment of a separate Slovak State which would include the whole north-west of Hungary, and would comprise some two to two and a half million inhabitants; and it is this party also which insists upon the differences between the Slovak and Czech languages."

autonomy of both.[3] This agreement received the adherence of
T. G. Masaryk, then president of the National Czecho-Slovak
Council in Paris. As for the Pittsburgh Agreement, signed May
30, 1918, by the representatives of the Slovak League on one hand
and the Czech National Alliance as well as the Union of
Czech Catholics on the other, it foresaw that the Czecho-Slovak
State should rest on the equality of the two nations that were
prepared to set it up. As regards Slovakia, the following stipula-
tion is found:

> Slovakia shall have its own administration, its own par-
> liament, and its own courts. The Slovak language shall be
> the official language in the schools, in governmental offices,
> and in public life generally.

With his signature, T. G. Masaryk, the designated president of
the future State, had taken cognizance of this.

All these dispositions were, furthermore, as much in con-
formance with the federative aspirations of the Czechs (Palacký,
Rieger, and even Masaryk and Beneš before 1914) and Slovaks
(Štúr, Francisci, Moyses, Paulíny-Tóth, Daxner, Vajanský) in
the time of Austria-Hungary as with the general policy of the
Allied Powers; for on January 8, 1918, President Woodrow Wil-
son set forth the following principle in his "Program for World
Peace" as outlined in his famous Fourteen Points:

> The peoples of Austria-Hungary, whose place among
> the nations we wish to see safeguarded and assured, should
> be accorded the freest opportunity of autonomous de-
> velopment (Point 10).

On October 19, 1918, Juriga, one of the two Slovak deputies
in the Budapest Parliament, made a statement declaring that the
Slovaks henceforth had the right to decide freely on their own
political destiny as well as their relationship with the other free
nations. He made it clear that it would be up to the Slovak
National Council to define this right and to send a delegation to
the Peace Conference at the end of the war to defend it.

Therefore, it was under the federative aspect that the idea
of the Czecho-Slovak State was accredited with the great Allied
Powers.

In an official note dated May 20, 1919, addressed to the Supreme Council of the Paris Peace Conference, Mr. Beneš stated:

[3] Peter P. Yurchak, *The Slovaks, Their History and Traditions* (Whiting,
Ind.: 1946), p. 210.

"Czecho-Slovakia will have an extremely liberal regime analogous to Switzerland's."

The Conference took cognizance of this note just as it did of the oral statements made in this connection by Mr. Beneš, and D. H. Miller reproduced all these assurances in his work, *My Diary*, in these terms:

> The Czecho-Slovak government intends to organize the State, accepting as the basis of the national laws the principles applied by the Constitution of the Swiss Republic, and thus make of the Czecho-Slovak Republic a sort of Switzerland.[4]

It must also be noted that in the documents presented to the Allies, Mr. Beneš had the term "Czecho-Slovakia" written with hyphen, a fact which implied the recognition of the dual character of the State.[5] Besides, he leaned on the Cleveland and Pittsburgh Agreements to convince the Allies of the Slovaks' wish to constitute a common State with the Czechs.

The plan of giving a federative structure to the Czecho-Slovak State appears, although in a less clear-cut manner, even in the treaty that the principal Allied and Associated Powers concluded with Czecho-Slovakia at Saint-Germain-en-Laye on September 10, 1919. This document contains, in effect, the conditions according to which these powers were prepared to confirm their recognition of Czecho-Slovakia and confer upon it international juridical personality. While the statement of the aims pointed to certain political realities, the main body contained the fundamental principles to which the internal policy of the new State would have to conform. Thus one can read in the preamble of this treaty that

> . . . the peoples of Bohemia, Moravia and a part of Silesia, just as the people of Slovakia, decided of their own will to become united, and did in fact unite by a permanent union, with the aim of establishing a single, sovereign and independent State under the title of the Czecho-Slovak Republic;

that "the Ruthenian people to the south of the Carpathians adhered to this union"; and that Czecho-Slovakia, to whom the United States of America, the British Empire, France, Italy, and Japan have just confirmed their recognition "as a member of the

---

[4] D. H. Miller, *My Diary at the Conference of Paris* (New York: 1924), XIII, 16.
[5] Cf. Dr. Stephen Osuský, *Beneš and Slovakia* (London: 1943), p. 20.

sovereign and independent nations," desires "to make its institutions conform to the principles of liberty and justice and to give a sure guarantee of it to the inhabitants of the territories over which it has assumed sovereignty."

The stipulations accepted by the Czecho-Slovak government are inserted in two chapters, of which the first has reference to the whole population in general, and the second to the particular position of Sub-Carpathian Ruthenia. One reads there especially:

> Czecho-Slovakia agrees to grant to all inhabitants full and complete protection of their life and liberty without distinction of birth, nationality, language, race or religion (Art. 2).

And also:

> All the Czecho-Slovak nationals shall be equal in the eyes of the law and shall enjoy the same civil and political rights, without distinction of race, language or religion (Art. 7, par. 1).

Furthermore, this treaty ensured those citizens not speaking Czech the freedom of using their own language in the courts (Art. 7, par. 4) and assured their children of instruction in that language (Art. 9, par. 1).

By the same treaty,

> Czecho-Slovakia pledged itself to organize the territory of the Ruthenians to the south of the Carpathians within the boundaries fixed by the principal Allied and Associated Powers under the form of an autonomous unit within the Czecho-Slovak State, provided with the greatest autonomy compatible with the unity of the Czecho-Slovak State (Art. 10).

The Ruthenians were to be under the jurisdiction of officials chosen from their own population (Art. 12) and they were to have "fair representation" in the Prague Parliament (Art. 13).

Article 14, paragraph 2, of the Saint-Germain Treaty stipulated that

> . . . every member of the Council of the League of Nations would have the right to bring to the Council's attention any infringement or danger of infringement on any one of these obligations (those which were assumed by Czecho-Slovakia).

All the obligations incurred by the new Czecho-Slovak State allowed the following affirmations: (1) that the Slovaks united

themselves to the Czechs of their own free will to form a common
State, thus making use of the right of peoples to self-determination;[6] (2) that the degree of union between Slovaks and Czechs
was to be determined by the free decision of the two nations;[7]
(3) that the character of the Czecho-Slovak State, dual at first
by reason of the nature of its constituent elements, became tripartite by the inclusion of Sub-Carpathian Ruthenia; (4) lastly,
that the Slovak nationality and language, like all the other non-
Czech nationalities and languages, were to enjoy in Czecho-
Slovakia an international guaranty.

The Inconsistencies of the Czech Democracy

> *With centralization, you have apoplexy
> at the center and paralysis at the extremi-
> ties.*
>   Lamennais

THE "CZECHOSLOVAK" NATION

Messrs. Masaryk and Beneš deliberately altered the original
conception of the Czecho-Slovak State. Although they had succeeded in destroying Austria-Hungary in the name of the principle of nationalities, they practiced in Czecho-Slovakia a policy
of denationalization toward the Slovaks identical with the one
of which the Magyars had been guilty. Instead of a federative
State they organized a centralized one. They disfigured in their
policy the famous definition of Abraham Lincoln's democracy:
"The government of the people, by the people and for the people."
Having sanctioned by law the fiction of a "Czechoslovak" nation,
they established a regime which, in reality, was to be the domination of the more numerous Czechs over the Slovaks. For Beneš,
the Slovaks were "Czechoslovaks" and the Czechoslovaks, Czechs.[8]

---

[6] "The Slovaks entered Czecho-Slovakia as free and equal partners of the
Czechs," states Mr. Bohdan Chudoba, a Czech deputy, in his article,
"Czechoslovakia, a Study in Disintegration," *Thought*, XXV (March,
1950), 88.

[7] Masaryk and Beneš stated in the Declaration of Independence drawn up
in Paris, October 18, 1918, that the "definitive decision as to the Constitution itself was in line with the representatives legally elected by the
liberated and united people."

[8] "The Czecho-Slovaks, or just simply the Czechs, are made up of two
elements: seven million Czechs in Bohemia, Moravia, and Silesia, and
three million Slovaks inhabiting northern Hungary, from the confluence
of the Moravia and the Danube to the Upper Tisza. These two branches
of the same nation have the same civilization, the same language, and
the same history." E. Beneš, *Détruisez l'Autriche–Hongrie!* (Paris, 1916),
p. 5.

By this simplification, he hoped to eliminate the Slovaks as political partners of the Czechs. In the case of one State and two nations, he knew that fundamental laws should be the result of an agreement between both. If there were only "one nation," he thought, public law would be "spontaneously" proclaimed by a simple majority.

The Prague government was in no wise in a hurry to grant autonomy to the Slovaks, as Masaryk had promised them in the Pittsburgh Agreement,[9] nor to the Carpathian Ruthenians who had received their guarantee by the Saint-German Treaty. Power considerations led *it* to put into practice a policy of assimilation vis-à-vis the Slovaks and Ruthenians. The Czechs, who numbered only seven and a half million in a State having fourteen million inhabitants, realized the weakness of their position. In order to increase their majority in comparison with the 3,123,448 Germans and 747,096 Magyars, they decided to assimilate the Slovaks. The Prague government undertook to realize its policy of "unification" in Slovakia on political, cultural, economic, and social planes.

POLITICAL STATISM

The Declaration of Turčiansky Sv. Martin—The Czecho-Slovak Republic was proclaimed October 28, 1918, in Prague by the "Czechoslovak" National Committee, a temporary government of which V. Šrobár, a Slovak, participated. Now, the signature of Šrobár at the bottom of this very important document was politically and juridically of no value whatsoever. In fact, the person himself, who was then on a trip to Prague to gather information, was in no wise qualified to sign anything for

[9] Masaryk, for whom the question was embarrassing, could not do otherwise than minimize its importance:

"The other weighty consequence lay in the negotiations at Pittsburgh between Czechs and Slovaks. There, on June 30, I signed the Convention [the 'Czechoslovak Convention'—not a Treaty] between the Slovaks and the Czechs of America. It was concluded in order to appease a small Slovak faction which was dreaming of God knows what sort of independence for Slovakia, since the ideas of some Russian Slavophils, and of Štúr and Hurban-Vajansky, had taken root even among the American Slovaks. Therefore, Czechs and Slovaks agreed upon the Convention which demanded for Slovakia an autonomous administration, a Diet, and Courts of Law. I signed the Convention unhesitatingly as a local understanding between American Czechs and Slovaks upon the policy they were prepared to advocate. The other signatories were mainly American citizens, only two of them being non-Americans, though further signatures were afterwards added without authorization." Masaryk, *The Making of a State*, pp. 220-22.

Slovakia, since he had received no mandate for such. F. Bokes, a contemporary Slovak historian who could not be charged with anti-Czech feelings, points out correctly that the National Slovak Council, a revolutionary organ of Slovakia, was not set up until October 30, 1918, the day of the Turčiansky Sv. Martin Declaration—that is, two days later.[10]

If this Czech anticipation of the Slovak National Council's decision, which constitutes a *captatio benevolentiae* on the part of Prague toward the representative Slovak organ, was without importance as far as the birth of the Czecho-Slovak State was concerned, it was however to have a widespread repercussion on the political structure of the whole State. As a matter of fact, Mr. Šrobár was one of the "Hlasistes," a defeatist group of the Slovak intelligentsia.[11] Being but a pawn on the political chessboard of Prague, this former student of Charles University had been carefully chosen by the Czechs with an eye to imposing on Slovakia a unified "Czechoslovak" State, a strictly centralized and predominantly Czech State.

A gathering of Slovak political leaders, formed into a National Slovak Council on October 30, 1918, at Turčiansky Sv. Martin, accepted the principle of union with the Czechs. Nevertheless the Turčiansky Sv. Martin Declaration constitutes a debatable document since it was falsified in letter and spirit.

In what do these two falsifications consist?

There can be no doubt that the Slovaks, having made up their minds to break with the Magyars "such an ill-matched marriage," as Hlinka put it, were animated by the desire to assure themselves of the greatest liberty possible within the compass of the new State still in formation. They also wished for an autonomous status, as the Americans of Slovak descent had expressed it in the Pittsburgh Agreement. Having come together at Turčiansky Sv. Martin, they sought formal action to manifest this wish for which they were going to be responsible in the eyes of history. Whereas in Paris Mr. Beneš was at work assuring the Allies that Czecho-Slovakia, as heterogeneous as Austria-Hungary had formerly been, would be organized after the pattern of Switzerland, that is to say under the federative form, his confidential agents of "Hlasiste" leanings (A. Štefánek, M. Ivanka, I. Dérer, F. Houdek, and others) employed all means to persuade the as-

[10] F. Bokes, *History of the Slovaks and Slovakia*, p. 362.
[11] See note 11 to the Introduction.

sembly of Turčiansky Sv. Martin that the Allies would give their consent to the separation of Slovakia from Hungary only on condition that the assembly would declare that ethnically and culturally the Slovak nation was an integral part of the "Czecho-Slovak" nation.

A discussion of this point was begun at that time, for excepting the "Hlasistes," all those who participated in the session felt that such a declaration was destined to distort the reality of the independent existence of the Slovak nation. Nevertheless, their horror at Hungary's past was such, and their credulity vis-à-vis the Czechs—their "nearest Slavic brothers"—so strong that they finally yielded and signed their declaration without realizing how skillfully Beneš was going to make use of such a falsification. Hlinka himself signed this evident fiction against which he afterward had to struggle until his last breath.[12] The point in question in the declaration is conceived as follows: "The Slovak nation is a part of the Czecho-Slovak nation united as much from the linguistic as the cultural and historical point of view."

Now, it was not in order to snatch the Slovaks from the claws of the Magyars that Mr. Beneš needed this declaration. He really had designs that were much more remote. From that moment on, he dreamed of a centralized State and it is with this constitutional centralization in mind that he needed the formal consent of the Slovaks.

Without the preceding explanations it would be impossible to understand this confused document by which a nation declared itself to be part of another nation whose existence would be sought in history in vain.

In the final passage of the declaration, the signers, as if they had wanted to make up for the fault committed, stated precisely their aspirations for the future:

> We are persuaded that the Slovak people, laborious and intelligent, who, in spite of the unheard-of oppression to which they have been submitted, have been able to attain a high degree of national culture, not only will not be excluded from the benefits resulting from the peace and community of nations, but will also be granted the possibility of developing along the lines of their own character in order to be able to contribute, in proportion to their own strength, to the progress of Humanity.

[12] "We were mad! We helped the Czechs to dupe Europe!" Hlinka acknowledged years afterward in the Parliament of Prague.

The Turčiansky Sv. Martin Declaration was again the object of new intrigues. Mr. Milan Hodža, another "Hlasiste," was to make a slight alteration destined to weaken considerably the position of the Slovaks within the compass of the new State. This document contained, in effect, a clause by the terms of which the Slovak National Council reserved the right to send a special delegation to the Peace Conference in Paris to ask for an international guarantee of Slovak autonomy within the bounds of the Czecho-Slovak State. On the evening of October 30, 1918, when all the signers had left Turčiansky Sv. Martin, Mr. Hodža, who had come from Budapest, read the declaration which was already at the printer's and quite simply struck out this clause.

Hodža seems to have acted on his own initiative, pushed into this course by political ambition. It is noteworthy that for a long time he had been a partisan of a Danubian federation. As it was impossible up to the last moment—the Hapsburg monarchy not being completely lost, nor the existence of Czecho-Slovakia completely assured—to foresee what the outcome of the war would be, he had to play a double game to insure for himself a political role in either event. In October, 1918, while keeping contact with certain Czech deputies in Vienna, he flirted in Budapest with statesmen who were partisans of an Austro-Hungarian federation: the Prime Minister of Hungary, Mr. Wekerle and Mr. Kristóffy.[13] When the Czechs learned of this duplicity, Mr. Rašín, an important member of the Czech *maffia*, declared that Prague would have a rope in store for Hodža as soon as Czecho-Slovakia was established.

Informed by his friends of what was awaiting him, Hodža, after the proclamation of the Czecho-Slovak State, October 28, at Prague, had to redeem himself by concessions made at the expense of the Slovak nation. Through this bargaining, he believed

[13] M. V. Šrobár, an orthodox "Czechoslovak" who was a colleague of Hodža in the Slovak Agrarian party, subjected his opportunism of that time to the severest of criticisms:

"Dr. Hodža, according to the testimony of trustworthy persons, was working at the same time in the opposing camp, that is to say, with Czech deputies who were undermining the monarchy and preparing the Czecho-Slovak State. Of course, Mr. Hodža did not want the monarchy upheld at any price. He merely wanted to secure his future. He had to win no matter what happened. Thus his aid to Kristóffy was nothing other than a political 'alibi.' If the Magyars won, he would say: 'I was with you.' And if the Czechs won, he would say: 'I was one of you.' In both cases he had trustworthy witnesses."

Dr. Vavro Šrobár, *Slovakia Liberated* (Prague: 1928), I, 96.

he could be sure of an office in the government of the new State, and possibly be delegated by the Czechs to the Paris Conference over the head of the Slovak National Council.

When the signers of the Turčiansky Sv. Martin Declaration knew that it had been falsified by Hodža, they were very indignant and protested energetically but in vain. They demanded the original declaration in order to be able to exact the carrying out of the clause concerning the Slovak delegation to Paris, but they were never able to obtain it. It had mysteriously disappeared.[14]

These modifications of the Declaration of Turčiansky Sv. Martin helped Mr. Beneš to realize his political plans. Thus Slovakia was considered by the Czechs as a conquered country. Scarcely formed as yet, Czecho-Slovakia was immediately torn by a desperate struggle which was never to cease—that of the Slovaks against Czech imperialism. In internal legislation the word "Czecho-Slovakia" was soon transformed into "Czechoslovakia." The State's politically constitutive acts, to which Mr. Beneš had not hesitated to refer at the time of the Peace Conference—the Cleveland and Pittsburg Agreements—were qualified in the wink of an eye as "false," devoid of any value.

Meanwhile, on December 12, 1918, Mr. Šrobár was sent to Slovakia equipped with "full powers" from the central government and put at the head of a puppet autonomous government appointed by Prague. Generals, "Czechoslovak" legionnaires, and tens of thousands of Czech civil servants were soon to follow him. Thus Šrobár imposed a "Czech peace" on a people who were cherishing illusions of liberty.

After voting for the union of Slovakia with Czechia, the Slovak National Council was dissolved by Prague.

The Revolutionary Assembly—As soon as the game had been won with the Allies, Masaryk and Beneš had to consolidate their power within the new State. They accomplished this by relying upon some Slovak "collaborators" without any mandate. To "represent" Slovakia in the Czecho-Slovak Revolutionary Assembly, the Czech political circles, at the proposal of Mr. Šrobár, chose persons indicated by Prague and who had no real representative stamp on them whatsoever. Out of 270 seats, not only did they give but 54 to the Slovaks (who, given the number of their population, ought to have had more than 70), but they even included

[14] Bokes, *History of the Slovaks and Slovakia*, p. 364.

among the "Slovak representatives" a dozen authentic Czechs such as Messrs. Beneš, Pilát, Hálek, Záruba-Pfeffermann, Kolísek, Rotnágl, Cholek, Miss Alice Masaryková, the President's daughter, and others.

A member of this Assembly who was later to become the archbishop of Nitra, Msgr. Karol Kmeťko, wrote the following on this Byzantine policy of Prague's:

> In all, there are 40 Slovak deputies. (With Dr. Šrobár, there were 41!) Out of these 40 deputies, the Catholics number ten and the Protestants 30, although Slovakia is made up of 80 per cent Catholics and only 20 per cent Protestants.[15] This proportion becomes still more astonishing if one considers how many of these ten deputies are members of the Slovak Populist party and how many of them are against us. It must be stated that the Catholic Slovaks have within the Parliament of Prague only four deputies determined to defend their deeply religious sentiments and their Christian convictions.[16]

The Supreme Administrative Court of the Republic, called upon to express itself on the manner in which the Czecho-Slovak State had been born, did not hesitate to give in a sentence rendered on April 14, 1919, the following explanation: "Slovakia was annexed to the Czecho-Slovak State as a consequence of its occupation by armed Czecho-Slovak forces." Gliding over the lapidary contradictions of this judgment, the Supreme Administrative Court adopted this "Hrad"[17] opinion without lifting an eyebrow.

A. Hlinka then became in Slovakia the very symbol of resistance to Prague's domination. He decided to attend the Paris Peace Conference, there to plead the cause of Slovakia before the international Areopagus. Unable to obtain his Czecho-Slovak passport, he secretly crossed the Polish border and from there, provided with a Polish passport, made his way to Paris. There, in September, 1919, he presented a memorandum by which he made an appeal for aid from the Allies and solicited for Slovakia a controlled international status within the new State.[18] De-

---

[15] Actually there were about 16 per cent Protestants, the remainder being Uniats.
[16] Quoted in the book of Karol Sidor, *The Slovaks on the Floor of the Parliament of Prague* (Bratislava: 1943), I, 36.
[17] B. Mirkine-Guetzevitch, jurist though he may be, does not hesitate to make a bold plunge into politics when he says: "But there is in Prague a 'Château policy' (Hrad, the President's residence) which has its adversaries, but which is essential to the greatest good of the State." B. Mirkine-Guetzevitch, *La Tchécoslovaquie* (Paris: 1930), p. 30.
[18] *Aide-Mémoire des Slovaques à la Conférence de la Paix* (Paris: 1919).

nounced by Mr. Beneš as an agent in the Hapsburgs' service, Hlinka was turned out by the French police. Back in Slovakia, this authentic representative of the Slovak people was, in spite of his parliamentary immunity, taken by night in a police truck to Mirov in Moravia, where for six months he was imprisoned as punishment for his audacity.[19]

The Constitution of February 29, 1920—The final wording of the Constitution was discussed in the Prague Parliament without the presence of the Germans, Magyars, Carpathian Ruthenians and with numerous Slovak figureheads. On February 19, 1920, the six Catholic Slovak representatives[20] of that time, to mark their disagreement with the conformist attitude of the "Slovak Parliamentary club," put a motion before the Constitutional Committee which stated that the vote for such a constitution would not prevent them from persevering in their struggle for autonomy and a legislative Diet of Slovakia.[21]

The fundamental act of the Czecho-Slovak State was thereafter voted on February 29, not by a Constituent Assembly freely elected by the people, but by a Revolutionary one. Instead of having general elections, as would have been normal in a truly democratic country, Messrs. Masaryk and Beneš, through deputies whom they had appointed, had a constitution voted, founded on the fictitious existence of a united "Czechoslovak" nation; this move deprived the Slovak nation of its political and juridical individuality and, as a matter of fact, assured the Czechs of the exclusive direction of the State.

Although the preamble of the Constitution claimed in highflown formulas the right of peoples to self-determination,[22] Messrs. Masaryk and Beneš found it quite natural, by means of go-between straw men of their choosing, to deprive the Slovak nation of the right which had been clearly guaranteed by international treaties.[23]

---

[19] Cf. Karol Sidor, *Meditazioni di Hlinka à Mirov* (Città dell Vaticano: 1942).

[20] Jozef Buday, Karol Kmeťko, Ján Koválik, Štefan Onderčo, Josef Sivák, Florián Tománek.

[21] Cf. Sidor, *The Slovaks on the Floor of the Parliament of Prague*, p. 101.

[22] "We, the Czechoslovak nation, proclaim at the same time that we want to make all efforts so that this Constitution and all the laws of our country be applied in the spirit of our history as in the spirit of the modern principles contained in the keynote: self-determination, for we intend to belong to the community of nations as a civilized, peace-loving, democratic, and progressive member." J. Hoetzel and V. Joachim, *La Constitution de la République Tchécoslovaque* (Prague: 1920), p. 21.

[23] This method of procedure did not, however, prevent Mr. Masaryk from

When the Slovak deputy, F. Juriga, with the United States as example, besought in vain a federative, therefore more democratic, constitution in the Prague Parliament, he was interrupted by Václav Brouček, a Czech member of that body, with the observation: "That may be good for North America, but not for us, my dear colleague!"[24] From that moment on, all the Slovaks who dared speak of the existence of two nations and write the term "Czecho-Slovakia" with a hyphen became suspect of separatism and plots against the integrality and security of the State.

Conceived in terms of individual liberalism and copied after the parliamentary institutions of France (the existence of two chambers and separation of powers), the Constitution of 1920 was in fact only an ingenious sleight-of-hand whose duplicity would remain one of its characteristic features until the end. Nonetheless it arrested the attention of Mr. B. Mirkine-Guetzevitch, who termed it "a perfect example of a rigorously democratic structure, as much by its general principles as by the over-all institutions of public law."[25] This specialist on European constitutions between the two World Wars was entirely satisfied to laud its "static aspect" without concerning himself with its dynamic character, that is, without knowing "if this Constitution penetrated into political life completely or only in part."[26]

Speaking about the lack of political realities behind this Constitution and the precipitation with which it had been adopted by the Revolutionary Assembly, Ferdinand Peroutka, a Czech political writer, commented on it in his work *The Building of the State* with the following comparison:

> The Czechoslovak Constitution is similar to an artificial park established in one night on an empty square. It was necessary to bring trees and turfs of grass and then wait to

qualifying the Slovak "deputies" in the Parliament of Prague as "legal" representatives of the people:
"In the [Pittsburgh] Convention it was laid down that the details of the Slovak political problem would be settled by the legal representatives of the Slovak people themselves, just as I subsequently made it clear that our Declaration of Independence was only a sketch of the future Constitution, and that the Constitution itself would be finally determined by the legal representatives of the people. And so it was [sic!]. The Constitution was adopted by the Slovaks as well as by the Czechs. The legal representatives of Slovakia thus expressed themselves in favor of complete union, and the oath sworn upon the Constitution binds the Slovaks, the Czechs and me too." Masaryk, *The Making of a State*, p. 221.
[24] Sidor, *The Slovaks on the Floor of the Parliament of Prague*, p. 105.
[25] Mirkine-Guetzevitch, *La Tchécoslovaquie*, p. 19.
[26] *Ibid.*, p. 19.

see whether they would throw out roots or not. The nation had not a living constitutional tradition to rely upon. The Czechoslovak Constitution has a double origin: the inspiration from foreign examples and the compromise among political parties. Allegedly, a constitution has to be like a coat individually tailored to order. But who would have been able to compute at that time the measurements of the political body of the Czechoslovak nation?[27]

The authoritarian nature of the fundamental act of the Czecho-Slovak State was very adequately described by Emanuel Radl, Professor of Charles University in Prague. This Czech political philosopher said:

The Constitution of Czechoslovakia is an expression of the absolutist principle of the right of war (revolution). A committee had been established during the First World War which continued its activity even after the War and which was a self-appointed executive body of the victorious nation. The German and Magyar population were considered as defeated in war, and the laws were simply dictated to them. Neither directly nor indirectly were these minorities asked how their relations should be regulated in respect to the State. Absolutism was predominating in such a degree that the Government attempted to intervene in Church affairs without any regard for the Church's interests. State interests held primacy and were decisive: Germans, Magyars and the Catholic Church were considered as enemies of the State and consequently the Government was of the opinion that State power should prevail upon them.[28]

Therefore, the ethical and political authority of this Constitution was nil as much with the Slovaks as with the minorities. And the provisions it contained on the autonomy of Sub-Carpathian Ruthenia were as so many dead letters until 1938.

As long as the Revolutionary Assembly lasted, except for Milan R. Štefánik—one of the founders of the State, whose plane was tragically brought down May 4, 1919, by a Czecho anti-aircraft battery of Bratislava—the following Slovaks were members of the government of Prague: Mr. Vavro Šrobár, an Agrarian, the Minister of Public Health; Mr. Fedor Houdek, a Protestant and Agrarian, the Minister of Supplies; and Mr. Milan Hodža, a Protestant and Agrarian, the Minister of Unification.

[27] Quoted in Sidor, *The Slovaks on the Floor of the Parliament of Prague,* p. 161.
[28] Emanuel Rádl, *War Between Czechs and Germans* (Prague: 1928).

The First Legislature—At the expiration of the mandate of the Revolutionary Assembly, the Czechs, in order to attain their ends, attempted to divide the Slovak people. To disintegrate more easily this deeply religious population, they set up in Slovakia the multiform system of political parties, with an especially leftist tendency. Slovak figureheads helped them to realize this task. A host of Czech civil servants acted as "yeast in the dough," and their mission was to shake up the "ignorant and benighted masses" and inculcate "culture, a progressive spirit, and modern political ideas."

Thus, in the elections of April, 1920, the Social-Democracy constituted the first Czech political "gift" to the Slovak people. The Czech Agrarian party with its president, Mr. Švehla, made sure of the close collaboration of Mr. Hodža, head of the Slovak Agrarians. Paid for and organized by the general secretariats of the Czech political parties, a feverish agitation began its reign among the Slovak people, who became the stake of all sorts of political adventurers. The Slovak Populist party, weakened by Hlinka's imprisonment, collaborated in the interest of Catholicism with the Czech Populist party of Monsignor Šrámek. The results of the elections of April 18, 1920, were the following: the Social-Democrats obtained twenty-three mandates, the Hodža Agrarians twelve and the Hlinka Populists twelve. Besides, there were still one German and nine Magyar deputies in Slovakia.

The result of these elections led by Mr. Karel Kramář, head of the Czech National-Democratic party, to make the following confession in the Parliament of Prague on November 4, 1920: "We have committed a grave sin. We must face it squarely. The contribution we have made to Slovakia is the most odious thing we have: party politics."[29]

Hlinka was liberated only after he had been re-elected deputy in April, 1920. Having taken command of the Populist party, he slated the autonomy of Slovakia in his platform.

In his commentary on the elections of April, 1920, Ferdinand Juriga, a deputy of the Slovak Populist party, declared on June 10, 1920, on behalf of his colleagues in the Prague Parliament:

> We do not consider the elections of April 18 and 20 as a free expression of the Slovak people. They involved non-Slovak soldiers, non-Slovak officials and other non-Slovak factors. A terrifying censorship of the press, an arbitrary

[29] Sidor, *The Slovaks on the Floor of the Parliament of Prague*, p. 162.

imprisoning of our people and leaders prevented this act from being an expression of the free will of our population.[30]

Mention must here be made of the way in which the Czech democracy was interpreting the principle of equality of citizens by the Law on Elections. While the Constitution introduced a system rigidly unified and centralistic for the whole of the Republic, the numbers of voters necessary for the election of one deputy was fixed at 43,840 in the Czech lands, 53,384 in Slovakia, and not less than 78,538 in Sub-Carpathian Ruthenia. This information was reported in *Pravda,* Bratislava, October 16, 1954 (Michal Dzvornik, "Electoral practice in Czechoslovakia before Munich").

The political terrorism employed against the Slovak Populist Party did not cease after the elections. On October 10, 1920, this party held a political gathering in Námestovo during which Czech soldiers shot with a machinegun into the crowd killing two peasants.[31]

In October, 1920, six Social-Democratic deputies left their party to found a Communist one. So it was that a Jew (Taussik), two Magyars (Borovszky and Surányi) and a Czech (Svétlik), aided by two Slovaks, became the apostles of communism in Slovakia.

On November 26, 1921, the deputies of the Slovak Populist party, deceived by the Czech Populists, ceased definitively all collaboration with them, a fact which led Monsignor Šrámek, a Czech Catholic dignitary who did not hesitate to support Beneš' assimilatory policy with respect to the Slovaks, to say to Hlinka: "You will see us in Slovakia again!" This threat was to be realized during the second legislature.

As early as January 25, 1922, the Slovak Populist party, under the firm leadership of A. Hlinka, presented in the Prague Parliament its first project of law, outlined by deputy Ľudovít Labaj, aiming at the constitutional reform of the Republic. This project can be summed up in the following way:

Slovakia will have its own Diet and government. The legislative body will be formed by 61 deputies. Elections into the Slovak Diet will be held in conformity with the Czecho-Slovak electoral law of February 29, 1920. The jurisdiction of the Diet of Slovakia will embrace the affairs of national education, de-

[30] *Ibid.,* pp. 143-44.
[31] *Ibid.,* pp. 163-65.

nominations, commerce, justice, agriculture, public works, social welfare and finances to provide for the needs of the regional administration.

The Slovak government, formed by these departments, will be appointed by the President of the Republic from among Slovak personalities. This executive body will be empowered to appoint officials and employees. The executive power in Slovakia will belong to the Slovak government as regards the laws which would be voted by the Czecho-Slovak Parliament, as well as those which would be passed by the Diet of Slovakia. The Slovak government will be responsible to the Diet of Slovakia. Laws enacted by the Central Parliament will be without validity in Slovakia if rejected by the majority of two-thirds of the members of the Diet of Slovakia.

Common issues incumbent on the Central Parliament will be: the president, the army, foreign affairs, and communications, with a corresponding common budget. One-third of all officials in the common governmental departments in Prague and in foreign service will be Slovaks. Under a common Czecho-Slovak command, Slovakia will have its own army units located on its own territory.

To be valid in Slovakia, acts of the President will need the signature of the Slovak competent Minister.[32]

Even though this project of law found a sufficient quotient of signatures among the deputies, the presidium of the Prague Parliament on advice of the government never submitted it for discussion. Pigeonholed in the files, it constitutes, however, an evident proof of how different, with respect to the Constitution of 1920, was the standpoint of the Slovak Populist party on what should have been the position of Slovakia within the Republic.

Assembled at its convention on August 3, 1922, at Žilina, the Slovak Populist party adopted in the presence of all its representatives, senators, and 560 delegates a memorandum addressed to the civilized world giving expression to the bitterness and deception which the policy of Prague caused the Slovak nation. This pathetic document cites Czech statesmen on trial before the whole world accusing them of the violation of the letter and spirit of the Pittsburgh Pact and the St. Germain Treaty.

[32] *Ibid.*, pp. 186-87.

Protesting against the assertions of the Prague government that the status of Slovakia is simply a question of the internal administration of the Republic, the memorandum states: "The Slovak problem is of international relevance, interesting by its political and military implications the whole of Europe."

The memorandum read:

> In demanding autonomy, we desire moreover that a Slovak National Assembly should be able to deliberate without being exposed to any external influence and come to an agreement with the brotherly Czech nation concerning the fundamental question of our common State: What should be the mutual relations of these two nations?[33]

It is interesting to note that during the first years of the Czecho-Slovak State, the Communists, wanting to exploit the Slovak people's desire for independence, went one better than the autonomist platform of the Hlinka party. Mr. Gottwald, at that time Communist deputy, in a brochure titled: *Slovakia is Hungry*,[34] made a pronouncement on this matter in terms not at all favorable to Czecho-Slovak political unity. According to him, Hlinka's Populist party had engaged in "a struggle which, under cover of autonomy, was to kill the right of secession of the Slovak people...."[35]

During the first legislature the following Slovak politicians were part of the Prague government: Mr. Ivan Dérer, a Social-Democrat successively Minister for the Administration of Slovakia and Minister of Unification; Mr. Ivan Marković, a Social-Democrat, Minister of National Defense; Mr. Vavro Šrobár,

---

[33] *Cri de détresse. Adresse au monde civilisé par un pays condamné à mort, par une nation se débattant dans l'agonie* (Vienna: 1922).

[34] Klement Gottwald, *Slovakia is Hungry* (Bratislava: 1925).

[35] This policy was inspired by the following motion which was voted by the Fifth Congress of the Komintern in June, 1924:

1) The Congress states that there is not a Czechoslovak nation: the Czechoslovak State, outside of the Czech nationality, comprises Slovaks, Germans, Hungarians, Ukrainians, and Poles;

2) The Congress deems necessary that the Communist party of Czechoslovakia, as regards these national minorities, proclaim and set into practice the right of self-determination of peoples, up to and including the right to separate.

"The Communist party of Czechoslovakia in particular will have to uphold the Slovaks' struggle for independence while seeking always to protect this movement from the influence of the Nationalist bourgeoisie and tie it up with the common struggle of laborers against capital."

See: *Le cinquième congrès de l'internationale communiste. Rapport de l'Executif.* (Paris: 1924), p. 432.

Minister of Unification, later Minister of Public Education; Mr. Martin Mičura, Minister for the Administration of Slovakia; Mr. Vladimir Fajnor, an Agrarian, Minister of Unification; Mr. Milan Hodža, Minister of Agriculture; Mr. Jozef Kállay, Minister for the Administration of Slovakia.

Of all these persons, Mičura alone was a Catholic.

The Second Legislature—The second elections took place on November 15, 1925. According to the electoral law, Slovakia should have had sixty-one deputies. However, four of the Slovak mandates were allotted to candidates of the Czech parties who had presented themselves in the electoral districts of Bohemia and Moravia. Four Czechs became officeholders.

The Hlinka party then became the first Slovak party with twenty-three deputies. Discounting the Magyar, German, and Communist electors—the latter had sworn their allegiance to Moscow—it represented the majority of the ethnic Slovak population. Then came Hodža's Agrarian party with twelve deputies, the Communist party with eight, the Social-Democratic party with two, the Czech Populist party of Šrámek with one deputy, the Magyar National party with five, and finally the Magyar Christian Socialist party with four deputies.

The infiltration cells of Slovak public life set up by the Czech parties constituted the fundamental method of the policy of division and weakening that Prague was practicing in Slovakia. Revolutionary Marxism, Progressist Socialism, "Czechoslovak" Catholicism, Czech National Democracy, Czech National-Socialism; all these tendencies were destined to trouble the mind of the Slovak people, Christian and national, in order to bring them more easily under obedience to the policy of Prague. The Czech parties spent considerable sums for their activities in Slovakia. Thus, the election of one or two deputies necessitated the creation of regional secretariats that no one came to consult, newspapers that no one read, the organization of meetings that, except for a few Czech civil servants, no one attended.

In 1927, the Czechs saw that they were obliged to make a few concessions. At the insistence of the Hlinka party, the Parliament of Prague voted a law on the administrative reorganization according to which the State was divided into four regions: Bohemia, Moravia-Silesia, Slovakia, and Sub-Carpathian Ruthenia. Thus Slovakia became at least a bureucratic unit, a fact which was going to permit it slowly to prepare the *cadres* of its civil servants. This law made the provision that there would be a president at the head of the administration of each country. Named by the government, he would be aided in his task by a regional assembly which, proportionate to the size of the country, would number from fifty to one-hundred and twenty members. Two-thirds of the latter would be elected by the people and one-third appointed by the government. As B. Mirkine-Guetzevitch justly recognizes, "this last disposition was keenly criticized as an artificial means of assuring the authority of the central power." He also said:

> In general, if the autonomous powers conferred on the assemblies in the regions and districts appear to be considerable enough, especially from the French point of view, the control of the civil service by the State seems to have to be rather close.[36]

Aside from this concession, Prague resolutely opposed any Slovak attempt at division of legislative and executive power. The political tension between Prague and Bratislava therefore continued to increase.

Just about the same persons represented Slovakia in the government as before: Messrs. Hodža, Ivan Dérer, Jozef Kállay and Juraj Slávik. On January 15, 1927, however, when the Hlinka party entered the government, Monsignor Tiso became the Minister of Public Health and his colleague, Marko Gažík, the Minister of Unification. Mr. L'udovít Labaj was to succeed him. But, on October 8, 1929, the Hlinka party left the government and remained in the opposition until the end of the Republic.

The Third Legislature—The elections of October 27, 1929, had the following results: the Slovak Populist party, eighteen deputies, the Agrarian party, twelve; the Social-Democrat party, four; the National-Socialist party, two; the Czech Populist party, one; the National Democratic party, one; the Artisans' party, one; the Razus National party, one—totalling forty deputies. Besides, fourteen mandates were divided between the Communist party and the Magyar and German minorities.

The decrease in the number of deputies falling to the Slovak Populist party indicates that Slovakia's population was not content with the party's compromising with the government. Therefore, the Populists had to concentrate their effort once more on the problem of granting home rule for Slovakia. Karol Mederly, a legal expert and one of the party's representatives in the Prague

[36] Mirkine-Guetzevitch, *La Tchécoslovaquie* p. 54.

Parliament, was given the job of preparing a new project of law. Known as the project of Andrej Hlinka and Associates, the draft was presented on May 8, 1930 to the Parliament as print No. 425/III. This proposal intended to extend to Slovakia, by a constitutional law, the provisions of Article 3 of the Constitution of February 29, 1920, which dealt with the autonomous position of Sub-Carpathian Ruthenia.

According to this second project, Slovakia would have had its own Diet like the one that had been stipulated for Ruthenia. This legislative body would be competent to enact laws regarding language, education, religion, local administration, and justice as well as other particular matters that the laws of the Czecho-Slovak Republic would confer on it. Laws enacted by the Diet of Slovakia, to which the President of the Republic had given his consent, would be promulgated in a special collection of laws and signed by the Governor of Slovakia.

In the National Assembly of Czecho-Slovakia the Slovak land would be represented by a proportional number of deputies and senators in accordance with the respective Czecho-Slovak electoral laws. A governor appointed by the president of the Republic on the proposal of the central government, would stand at the head of the Slovak administration. The governor would be accountable even before the Diet of Slovakia.

State officials in Slovakia would be chosen, as far as possible, from the native population.

Though more modest in its design and implications than the first project, the second one had the same fate. It has never been put on the agenda of the National Assembly.

In 1933, following political changes in Germany, there was a considerable increase in Hungary in the revisionist campaign directed against Slovakia. Some Czech newspapers and journalists, in view of the perspective of a German menace, started flirting with the idea of appeasing Hungary by the cession of a part of Slovakia's territory. Did not Beneš appease the Poles by the cession of the northern part of the Slovak counties of Orava and Spiš, when in 1920 they got angry with the Czechs because of their occupation of the Těšín coal mines? In order to prevent any political adjustment between Prague and Budapest at the expense of Slovakia, the club of the Slovak Populist deputies presented to the Prague Parliament, on April 26, 1933, the following resolution:

Aware of the unshakable will of the Slovaks to live as a distinct nation on the historical territory of the Slovak land, inherited from their forefathers, the representatives of the Slovak nation in the Czecho-Slovak National Assembly solemnly proclaim:

We definitely oppose any effort to mutilate the frontiers of the Slovak land, stressing not only the integrality of the Slovak historical territory but even the wholeness of the Slovak nation. This nation will never admit that a part of it be separated and attributed to any state. The unified Slovak nation wishes to take part in its own national development as any other member of the community of civilized nations.

Conscious of our ethnic distinctness we cannot but claim for ourselves the exclusive right of decision upon our territorial and national integrality. With respect to the present constitutional position of Slovakia, this right can be vested only in a Slovak National Council.[37]

Even though by such a declaration the Slovak Populist party took a strong position in favor of Czecho-Slovakia, T. G. Masaryk and E. Beneš remained unimpressed by the claims for home rule in Slovakia.

The same persons in the Agrarian and Social-Democratic parties remained perpetually "cabinetable." Politically, therefore, Slovakia was attached to the Czech countries by minority parties. For reasons of propaganda, Beneš always kept a few Slovak opportunists in the government, but he continued to care just as little about the gulf which kept ever widening and deepening between the Slovak people and the government of Prague.

The Fourth Legislature—In the elections of 1935, the antidemocratic policy of Prague vis-à-vis Slovakia as well as Sub-Carpathian Ruthenia had a new opportunity to make itself manifest. The number of parliamentary representatives was far from corresponding to the number of inhabitants of Slovakia and also to the figure set by the electoral law. Of course the decrease in Slovak participation profited the Czechs. The statistics of the countries of the Republic and their deputies in Prague were actually the following:[38]

---

[37] Sidor, *The Slovaks on the Floor of the Parliament of Prague*, II, 72.
[38] See "Interpellation of Deputy Martin Sokol of October 29, 1937," in K. Čulen, *Czechs and Slovaks in the Administration of the Czecho-Slovak Republic* (Bratislava: 1944), pp. 114-16.

Countries	Population 1930	Per-centage	Corresponding number of deputies	Number of mandates	
				According to the law	According to the elections
Bohemia	7,109,376	48.8	146	160	162
Moravia-Silesia	3,563,010	24.3	73	70	71
Slovakia	3,329,793	22.8	69	61	58
Sub-Carpathian-Ruthenia	725,357	4.1	12	9	9

Slovakia underwent an analogous decrease in the number of its senators.

To give an idea of the inequality in Czecho-Slovakia, it is enough to state that Sub-Carpathian Ruthenia, for its 12,000 square kilometers and 725,357 inhabitants, had only nine deputies in the Parliament of Prague, whereas the electoral district of Prague, with a population scarcely greater, had forty-five for itself alone.[39]

All these electoral figures, however, could do nothing against the Slovak Autonomist movement that was gaining ground. In the elections of May 19, 1935, the Autonomist coalition obtained twenty-two seats in the Parliament, while the Agrarian party had only twelve, the Communist party six, the remaining mandates being divided among the other small parties. In spite of this result, Slovakia for the most part remained in the opposition. The dissatisfaction created by the general policy of Prague was greater and greater.

The Slovaks did not weary of asking that the Pittsburgh Agreement be incorporated into the Constitution. In 1935, after Masaryk's resignation, the Autonomist party voted for Beneš' election to the Presidency of the Republic in the hope that he would respect the promises made to Monsignor Tiso, then Vice-President of the Populist party, relative to the autonomous regime in Slovakia.

M. Beneš, however, was in no hurry. Only one year later, in 1936, because of the constant worsening of the international position of Czecho-Slovakia, Milan Hodža, the new Prime Minister, started negotiations with the Slovak Populists in the hopes of winning their participation in the government. Monsignor Jozef Tiso, Karol Mederly, and Martin Sokol were negotiators for their party.

[39] Hoetzel and Joachim, *La Constitution de la République Tchécoslovaque*, p. 11.

Their claims were summed up under two headings. The first one included requests of constitutional character: the recognition of the legal individuality of the Slovak nation, a legislative Diet in the sense of the Pittsburgh Agreement, the recognition of Slovak as the official language in Slovakia, and a Ministry for Slovakia. The second category listed 32 points aiming at the abolition of the discriminatory policy of Prague vis-à-vis Slovakia in the field of public administration, culture, the school system, social welfare, unemployment, public finances, taxation, foreign commerce, agriculture, justice, civil service, price regulations.[40]

Beneš, confident in the Soviet Alliance, remained unyielding.

In the summer of 1938, the Sudeten German problem started boiling in Czecho-Slovakia. It was in such an atmosphere that the deputies and senators of the Slovak Populist party adopted, on September 19, 1938, a Manifesto which read as follows:

Calling upon the right of self-determination of the Slovak nation we firmly demand:

1) that the individuality of the Slovak nation and language be fully recognized by public law;

2) that the Slovak question be definitively, and without delay, resolved according to the stipulations of the Pittsburgh Agreement and our last project of law demanding a legislative Diet for Slovakia.

Having ignored the Slovak problem for twenty years, Beneš finally had to take cognizance of it under very dramatic conditions. One week before the Munich Conference, on September 22, 1938, he had his proposal for its solution delivered to the leaders of the Populist party. But even that document is characteristic of the way his mind worked. Compelled *in extremis* to recognize the Slovak nation as a distinct political factor, he asked *per contra* the negotiators of the Populist party to recognize the existence of a "Czechoslovak nation" in the ethnical sense of the word and thus support the infinitesimal Protestant Slovak minority (Dérer) that claimed kinship with such a nation.[41] No longer able to defend the thesis of a single "Czechoslovak" nation, he bargained to become the advocate of an absurd triple one (Czechs, Slovaks and "Czechoslovaks"), rather than resign himself to the recognition of a dualistic state.

---

[40] Sidor, *The Slovaks on the Floor of the Parliament of Prague*, II, 169.
[41] E. Beneš, *Où vont les Slaves?* (Paris: 1948), p. 278.

It is also fitting to note that a separate census was not made
of the Slovaks the two times a census was taken during the
"Czechoslovak" Republic in 1921 and 1930. Officially, therefore,
their existence was unknown.[42] It had been possible to know the
exact importance of the Slovak minority in Hungary, whereas it
became impossible to know the number of Slovaks in the Republic.

This ingenious prestidigitation in the case of Mr. Beneš expressed his relativist concept of politics, morals, and law all at
the same time. For him, as Mr. Osuský said, politics was made
up of 90 per cent tactics and 10 per cent principles.[43]

EFFORT TOWARD CULTURAL ASSIMILATION

To attempt to justify the invasion of Czech teachers and professors who had overrun Slovakia, Mr. Ripka did not hesitate to
declare that half the Slovaks were illiterate.[44] Thus he tried to
defend before the Western world the deplorable policy of the
government of Prague; but other Czechs, who were not speaking
for the outside, were more honest. Thus it was that the *České
Slovo*, the official organ of Mr. Beneš' Czech National-Socialist
party, disclosed the aims of the cultural policy of Prague in 1929:

> There is something more than individual interests that
> keeps the Czechs in Slovakia: the laying of the foundation
> of the Czechoslovak . . . union, so that by constant contact
> and influence there would finally arise the unified Czecho-
> slovak nation—one in spirit and in tongue. . . .[45]

The Law Regarding the Use of the Language—The State Act
No. 126 of February 29, 1920, on the use of the language in the
administration and teaching, stated that in principle the Slovak
language should be used in public life in Slovakia; but the Czech
officials, civil servants, and professors interpreted this decision
in such wise as to make a rule of the exception. In Slovakia, all
the printed matter of the public administration and schools was
drawn up in Czech, as were the bulletins of the University of

---

[42] According to the census of 1921, the Republic numbered 8,760,957
"Czechoslovaks" besides Germans, Magyars, Ruthenians, Poles, Rumanians, Tziganes, etc., but not one Slovak. The census taken in 1930 according to the same criterion numbered 9,688,770 "Czechoslovaks."

[43] See Osusky, *Beneš and Slovakia*, p. 16.

[44] "These two provinces (Slovakia and Sub-Carpathian Ruthenia) did not
awaken to an independent life until 1918, at a time when the majority
of their population was illiterate and backward both in their political
and national consciousness." Dr. Hubert Ripka, *Munich: Before and After*,
(London: 1939), p. 244.

[45] See: Osuský, *Beneš and Slovakia*, (back fly-leaf of book).

Bratislava and the notices in public gardens and tourist resorts. These simple facts provoked a lively indignation among the Slovaks.

Higher Education—Under the Hungarian regime there was a university in Slovakia—Elizabeth University—with a Law School at Bratislava, and a School of Mines and Forestry at Banská Štiavnica. The instruction was given in Magyar.

The Czecho-Slovak regime began by suppressing the School of Mines and Forestry under the pretext that there was the same kind of school at Příbram in Bohemia and that it had to suffice for the whole of the Republic. As for the University at Bratislava, which the Slovaks were impatient to own ultimately, it was given the name of "Comenius University"—in honor of a great Czech teacher of the Renaissance, a foreigner in Slovakia—and it immediately became the high instrument of the planned assimilation of the Slovaks "in spirit as in language."

Although L'udovit Štúr, the most authentic interpreter of Slovak spiritual and ethnical individuality, had written around 1850: "The Czechs are of different roots than ours; their history does not concern us, for we have no part in it,"[46] Professor Václav Chaloupecký of the University of Bratislava attempted to inculcate into his students a unitary conception of "Czechoslovak history," a fact which nonetheless did not prevent him from terming the Slovak nation "bastard."

Professor Albert Pražák became the mouthpiece for "Czechoslovak integration" on the literary plane. He searched the works of each Slovak writer for the spirit of such and such a Czech literary period and was determined to prove that the Slovak poets and novelists were just simply imitators of Czech writers.

Mr. Václav Vážny tried to bring Czech and Slovak grammar together. For him, Czech and Slovak were but two forms of the "Czechoslovak" language. This grammarian in the service of politics, thanks to powerful support from the Slovak Centralists, even succeeded in getting himself made president of the Linguistic Commission of the Slovak Institute of Sciences and Arts, the *Matica slovenská*. Vážny also was able to impose his unitarian interpretations upon this Commission which in turn printed them in the official dictionary of the Slovak language that this Institute was publishing. This tendentious scholar was

[46] Dr. Milan Hodža, *The Czecho-Slovak Schism* (Turčiansky Sv. Martin: 1920), p. 189.

dropped from office only in 1932, by an assembly boiling with anger and spurred on by Hlinka in person.

In the Law School, Professor Zdeněk Peška assumed the task of defending the centralist legislation of the "Czechoslovak" State. His antifederative theories and his interpretation on the use of the Czech language in the administration and in education won for him numerous hostile student demonstrations.

The political make-up and behavior of the teaching personnel of the Comenius University of Bratislava were such that it became a third Czech university rather than the first Slovak university as illustrated by the fact that on October 6, 1938, fifty-six of its professors were Czech and twenty-four were Slovak. Instead of encouraging the Slovak students to seek out university careers, the Czech professors regarded Comenius University as their fief, a stronghold of Czech "culture" and "learning."

Another proof of the policy of discrimination with respect to the Slovaks, as it was practiced by the Ministry of Public Education in Prague, manifested itself in the distribution of scholarships destined to facilitate attendance of students at foreign universities. It was unfair to Slovak students, who were always put on short allowance. To supplement the inadequacies of these allocations, the Executive Committee of the Regional Administration of Slovakia decided to create special scholarships for the students of the University of Bratislava. Now, within the very bosom of this structure, the influence of the Czech professors was so strong that in 1931-32, for instance, out of the five students of the Law School of Bratislava who received scholarships, three were Czechs.

In spite of the professors' efforts and the spirit of their teaching, Slovak youth was in large part federalist. Prague therefore vehemently opposed the opening of a School of Natural Sciences as well as a Polytechnic School in Slovakia. Whereas the German minority had a complete university and a Polytechnic School, the Slovaks, constitutive elements of the State, had to be contented with a fragmentary university which included only the School of Arts and Sciences, and the Law and Medical Schools. Later, however, Schools of both Catholic and Protestant Theology were added.

It was only at the very end of the First Republic that Prague ceded to the increasingly energetic demands of Slovakia and opened a Polytechnic School at Košice. But Slovakia was still deprived of a School of Business Administration as well as a Conservatory of Music.

Secondary Education—The secondary schools constituted another instrument of assimilation in Slovakia.

The programs of secondary education provided for Slovakia the "Czechoslovak" language and for Bohemia, Moravia, and Silesia the Czech language. This arrangement made it possible for Czech professors to teach Czech grammar and literature in Slovakia without any reciprocity for Slovak. The scholarly libraries acquired quantities of Czech books but neglected Slovak works. While the secondary schools in Slovakia were called "Czechoslovak," the same establishments in the former Austrian sections were called just simply "Czech."

On February 22, 1926, a delegation from the Association of Slovak Professors presented to the Minister of Public Education in Prague, Mr. Srdínko, a memorandum[47] expressing their grievances and wishes on the subject of the education of the Slovak, as well as the material plight of Slovak professors, who were always outstripped and eclipsed by their Czech colleagues.

From a total of 932 professors in secondary education in Slovakia, there were, on October 1, 1938, 523 Czechs and 345 Slovaks, the remainder belonging to the other nationalities of the Republic. At the same period there were 33 Czechs and 25 Slovaks as directors of the *gymnasia* and teachers' colleges.[48]

The vocational schools in Slovakia before October 6, 1938, numbered 53 directors, 79 professors and 368 teachers of Slovak nationality; and 57 directors, 148 professors and 385 teachers of Czech nationality.

Even in elementary education it was found that along side of 8,234 Slovak teachers there were 2,054 Czech.[49]

The Czech educators were not the only ones to consider themselves missionaries of Czech culture in Slovakia; all the civil servants, even the most modest, were imbued with the seriousness of the task incumbent upon them. Judge, customs officer, gendarme, *Sokol*,[50] janitor—all were equally convinced of the importance of their mission as "bearers of culture (Kulturträger) and progress to the clerical and backward country" which, to their way of thinking, was Slovakia.

---

[47] Čulen, *Czechs and Slovaks in the Administration of the Czecho-Slovak Republic*, p. 166.
[48] *Ibid.*, p. 164.
[49] *Ibid.*, p. 166.
[50] Member of a sporting association.

ECONOMIC DISCRIMINATION

Industry—Within the bounds of Hungary, Slovakia was the most highly industrialized region. In the economy of the old Kingdom, it had the same place as Czechia in Austrian economy. Thanks to its forests, it had the greatest production of cellulose in Central Europe (Žilina, Ružomberok). Copper mines were exploited at Krompachy, silver mines at Banská Štiavnica, iron at Podbrezová and coal at Handlová. Slovakia also produced sugar, alcohol, and chemicals. It possessed a half dozen glass factories.

When Slovakia had changed its political compass, it was found to have keen competition from the Czech countries, which were more industrialized. Determined to favor their industry, the Czechs set about suppressing Slovak enterprises one after the other: the extraction of copper was stopped and glass-making disappeared almost completely. Their economic policy consisted in slowly reducing Slovakia to an exclusively agricultural production.

In the report which Mr. Viliam Široký, chairman of the Slovak Communist party, presented at the end of May, 1949, to the Nineteenth Congress of the Communist party at Prague, he provided statistics on the industrial evolution of the country throughout the First Czecho-Slovak Republic. In 1913, according to him, Slovak industry employed 92,000 workmen, a figure which represented at that time 17 per cent of the population. After its union with Czechia, the prewar rising tendency ceased to exist in Slovakia. In 1927, industry employed only 80,000 workmen. During the ten years following, the increasing industrialization of Czecho-Slovakia was scarcely felt in Slovakia, since in 1937 the number of its workmen rose to only 104,915.[51]

One can see, therefore, from the economic point of view, that "Czechoslovak" unity presented only disadvantages for Slovakia. The result of this policy, as William Diamond notes, was that "In the period 1934-37, 91.5 per cent of the total industrial employment of the country occurred in Czech lands."[52]

The Agrarian Policy—The Czechs also used the agrarian reform to affirm their economic position in Slovakia.

A French observer of Slovakia of that time, Mr. Darras, while defending the policy of the government of Prague, is obliged to

[51] See *Pravda*, Bratislava, (May 29, 1949).
[52] William Diamond, *Czechoslovakia between East and West* (London: 1947), p. 172.

admit that "too many parcels of good land, instead of being divided among the peasants, have served to form, under the name of *zbytkové statky,* a new agrarian middle class."[53]

These "residue-estates," made up, as Mr. Darras himself explains, of the parts of large estates which had not been distributed among the peasants, included the principal dwelling and farm buildings of these properties. These holdings were used to further the political ends of the Czech Agrarian party which utilized them either to settle the Czechs in the south of Slovakia or to reward the Slovaks disposed to support the centralist policy of the government in Slovakia. Thus there arose a privileged class, the *zbytkári,* resembling somewhat the class of the old *zemani* of the Hungarian feudal system. While these last had received their goods as recompense for their services in the army, the former received them for their services in politics.

Finance—From the financial point of view, the country fell completely under the Czechs' control. The largest Czech banks (Živnobanka, Legiobanka, Moravská banka) founded an important system of branches in Slovakia. It is fitting to note here that Slovak industry, extorted from Magyar finance to become in large part the property of Czech banks, paid its taxes through the intermediary of the headquarters in Prague, a fact which showed the total amount of taxes paid by Slovakia to be a considerably lower figure than what it was in reality. Slovak economy was thus absorbed by Czech finance, and Mr. Darras has depicted the Czecho-Slovak financial "cooperation" in 1930 in the following oversimplified manner:

> As for the few Slovak banks, of which the most important was the *Slovenská banka,* they soon came into intimate liaison with the great credit establishments of Prague, so that still nowhere to this day is the union between the two parts of the Republic as perfect as in the financial domain.[54]

The Procedure of the Administration—Discriminations were introduced into all branches of economic life. Here are a few examples: the tax on the transportation of merchandise in Slovakia was for a long time 5 per cent higher for freight and 7 per cent higher for express than the corresponding tax in Czech lands. The tariffs by rail in Slovakia, per ton and per kilometer, were

[53] M. Darras, "Onze ans de vie indépendante en Slovaquie," *Le Monde Slave,* Paris, (May-June, 1930), p. 177.
[54] *Ibid.,* p. 181.

110 per cent higher, and the tariffs on parcels were five times more than those in force in Czechia.[55]

The decree No. 424 of July 1, 1931, of the Ministry of Finance was equally significant, for it fixed the stamp duty on dispatch notes of commercial accounts at eight crowns in Slovakia, but at only five in Czech countries.[56]

The price policy was not less discriminatory. Calculated at the Stock Exchange of Prague, the price of wheat, for instance, in Slovakia and in Sub-Carpathian Ruthenia had to be subject to the discount of the shipping charges, a situation which obliged the peasants in the eastern part of the Republic to sell their produce at prices considerably lower than the rates in force in Czech countries.

The Policy of Investments—A policy of investments very unfavorable to Slovakia was the cause of frequent bitter criticisms on the part of Slovak deputies. Stigmatizing this, Monsignor Tiso declared, March 20, 1931, at the tribune of the Parliament of Prague that, because of the discriminatory tariffs, Slovakia had suffered a loss of half a billion crowns since the beginning of the existence of the Czecho-Slovak State; that until the end of December, 1925, the government had given 168 million crowns for the construction of electric power plants in the Czech countries, whereas it had not constructed any in Slovakia; that they had harnessed 241 kilometers of rivers in Czechia, but not any in Slovakia; that they had spent 77 million crowns for the harnessing of torrential streams in Czechia while they had spent only two million for the same purpose in Slovakia; that the damming of the Moldau and the Elbe in Bohemia had cost the State a billion and a half crowns, while for similar works on the Váh in Slovakia, they had just merely opened a credit for 28 million crowns.[57]

In the fall of 1933, Mr. Rázus, a Slovak Protestant Autonomist deputy, brought to the attention of the Parliament that from the sum of three billion, 380 million crowns which had been appropriated to encourage urban construction in the Republic, Slovakia had benefited by only 100 millions, and that in the bargain

[55] See: Interpellation of the Slovak Deputy Martin Sokol at the Parliament of Prague, March 27, 1937.
[56] Čulen, *Czechs and Slovaks in the Administration of the Czecho-Slovak Republic*, p. 47.
[57] Quoted in Konštantín Čulen, *Biography of Msgr. Tiso* (Scranton: Pa.: 1947), pp. 89-90.

60 per cent of this allocation had been paid to Czechs residing in Slovakia.

The same method of procedure was employed with regard to the use of the "funds for the improvement" of agriculture. Out of one billion, 780 million crowns, Slovakia and Sub-Carpathian Ruthenia were given, from 1919 to 1930, the modest sum of 127 millions, the balance having been allocated to Czech countries.[58]

State Provision Orders—The policy of State controlled ordering constitutes a grievous chapter in Slovak economic life. The Czecho-Slovak State had got in the habit of ordering for the army and administration stationed in Slovakia, either from firms in Bohemia or Moravia, or from Czech dealers residing in Slovakia. Numerous petitions were presented by Slovak Autonomist deputies to the Parliament of Prague with an eye to obtaining a just ruling on this score. Their efforts were always in vain. Although proclaiming itself "Czechoslovak," the Republic of Mr. Beneš stubbornly persisted until the end in this "Czech first" policy.

Slovakia's "Liabilities" Balance Sheet—On October 20, 1933, shortly after an unprecedented political fiasco suffered by the government on the occasion of a fête commemorating the Slovak Prince Pribina at Nitra,[59] Prime Minister Malypetr delivered an address to the Parliament of Prague in which, desiring to bring out Slovakia's ingratitude, he indicated the sum total of the latter's alleged financial indebtedness to the State treasury. He said among other things that from 1919 to 1932 the deposits of Slovakia to the State's funds had mounted to 14,015,392,549 crowns, while it had drawn out 15,647,581,084 crowns and that consequently its liabilities were one billion, 632 million crowns.

The government saw such a happy defense of its policy in Mr. Malypetr's speech that they had it posted in all of Slovakia. However, it must be added that the figures given were purely fictitious. As a matter of fact, Mr. Hodža himself, although a member of the Agrarian party, as was Mr. Malypetr, criticized them in a speech given at Liptovský Sv. Mikuláš.

In fact, separate economic statistics were never set up for the different countries integrated in the Republic. The political economy of the government of Prague in Slovakia and Sub-Carpathian Ruthenia for twenty years allowed no efficacious check whatsoever on the part of the Slovak deputies. Since the administration

[58] *Ibid.*, p. 100.
[59] See later, p. 46.

of finance had been centralized in Prague, the different countries did not appear in the publications of the Bureau of Statistics, and Prague still vehemently opposed the establishment of statistics that would have allowed bringing to the public eye the assets and liabilities of each country in the Republic.

The *Otto Commercial Encyclopaedia* defines the economic relationship of Czechia and Slovakia frankly and simply as follows: "Slovakia will be our colony. It is a mistake to think that a colonial power could not be next to the metropolitan area. Example: Siberia in relation to Russia."[60]

And, as a matter of fact, during the twenty years that the First Czecho-Slovak Republic lasted, the Czechs succeeded in realizing the economic subjection and impoverishment of Slovakia. Whereas in 1930 the bank deposits in Czechia rose to 45,366 million crowns (4,250 crowns per capita) and in Slovakia to 4,020 million crowns[61] (1,200 crowns per capita), toward the end of Czecho-Slovakia they reached nearly 50 billion crowns in Czechia and only 5 billion in Slovakia.

This inequality was far from being the result of the economic situation of Slovakia under the Hungarian regime, as certain Czech economists would have it. It was the result of a policy of pauperism which suited Prague's general designs very well, for it greatly reduced Slovak resistance to the Czech efforts at assimilation.[62] One of the best proofs of this policy is brought out in a text of Mr. Ripka destined to illustrate the "progressist" characteristic of Czechia in contrast to the "backward" eastern part of the Republic:

> Even after Munich, the crippled Czech countries raised 75 per cent of the grain production. The remainder was in

---

[60] *Otto Commercial Encyclopaedia.* II, 1217.
[61] *Slovák*, Bratislava, (1931), Nos. 32-34.
[62] C. A. Macartney, *Problems of the Danube Basin* (Cambridge: 1942), p. 122.
  "On the other hand, most of them (the Slovaks) also found themselves unable to accept the Peace Conference thesis of a unitary Czechoslovak nation. Some of them felt this to mean, in practice, domination by the economically and socially stronger Czechs, and they reacted in the form of a flamboyant Slovak nationalism which was a main reason for the absence of revolt with which they accepted the dissolution of the Czechoslovak State."

Slovakia and Sub-Carpathian Ruthenia. Some 80 per cent of all industrial enterprises were in the Czech countries, 17 per cent in Slovakia and 3 per cent in Sub-Carpathian Russia. About seven-eighths of the production capacity were in the Czech districts, while only one-eighth was in Slovakia and Sub-Carpathian Russia. The share of Slovakia in the national income was about a tenth of the whole. The taxation and consumption capacity of the Slovaks and Ruthenes was incomparably lower than that of the Czechs. Out of all capital savings, which were estimated at about 58 billion crowns in the old Czechoslovakia and about 38 billion in the post-Munich Republic, about 90 per cent was in the Czech districts and 10 per cent in Slovakia. The Czech countries thus represented about 85 to 90 per cent of the whole economic power of the State even after the Munich Agreement.[63]

SOCIAL INJUSTICE

The Czechs in Slovakia—There had been a very great number of Czechs in Austrian bureaucracy. They had the reputation for docility and they felt as much at home in Vienna, Galicia, or Bosnia-Herzegovina as in Prague. After the dismemberment of the Austro-Hungarian Monarchy, many had returned to Czechia, a much smaller area, thus creating a considerable bureaucratic surplus. The government consequently used Slovakia and Sub-Carpathian Ruthenia as an outlet for them. This explains the fact that as early as 1921 there were 71,733 Czechs in Slovakia.[64]

Among them, there was a great number of adventurers and civil servants transferred for disciplinary reasons. This disturbing element had no interest in the religious and national feelings of the Slovak population.[65]

"I am convinced," said Karel Kálal, a Czech writer known as a defender of "Czechoslovak" unity, "that we have sent into Slovakia 80 per cent decent people,"[66] which was as much as to say that 20 per cent were not.

A certain Czech intelligence officer's report which was found in the archives of the government at Prague, contains the following passage:

[63] Ripka, *Munich: Before and After*, pp. 244-245.
[64] E. Čapek, "The Slovak Nation up to 1918," *Nové Čechy*, (June 28, 1928).
[65] It is from this time that we date the following little Slovak song:

Čech nám berie vieru,	The Czechs take from us
Reč i karieru	Our faith, language and careers
A Svätých na poli	And the Sokols destroy
Rúcajú Sokoli.	Our saints in the fields.

[66] M. Kálal, *In Pursuit of an Idea: The Czechoslovak Problem* (Prague: 1928), p. 238.

In 1920, the Minister of the Interior, Černý, arrives in Sub-Carpathian Ruthenia. At Mukačevo, he is greeted by Prefect Slavík, Sub-prefect Kozler, Head of that administrative district, Dr. Klíma, and Chief-of-police Švacha. The local inhabitants had already expressed their opinion on these State representatives,[67] so an ironical smile is to be seen on each face, a smile that we do not understand. State machinery works more slowly than the judgment of the people. But our eyes are soon opened: Prefect Slavík, Sub-prefect Kozler, District-head Klíma, Chief-of-police Švacha—all soon had to appear in court for dishonesty duly proved and have their offices taken from them.[68]

A similar report could have been made on what was going on in Slovakia. In an article on Czech activity in Slovakia the newspaper *Moravsko-Slezský denník*[69] published the following passage:

> From Bohemia and Moravia have come numerous grasping individuals seeking personal gain in Slovakia. . . . The Slovaks' hatred of these unprincipled intruders has spread over the entire Czech nation.

Prague not only flooded Slovakia with Czech civil servants, but it also discriminated unjustifiably in the remunerations it accorded.

The government of Prague instituted a special indemnity known as "slovenská výhoda" (Slovak allowance) for Czech civil servants in Slovakia. Thus they gave them, as a residence and travel indemnity, a sort of bonus for their political activity. These bonuses put Slovak civil servants on a notably inferior status. Whereas a Slovak official of the ninth class earned 7,450 crowns a year, his Czech colleague received 24,117 for exactly the same work.[70]

In December, 1937, the deputies of the Populist party presented Mr. Hodža with an interpellation on the subject of "colonial supplement" given Czech civil servants going to Slovakia for their duties. While the latter received a supplement of thirty crowns a day, Slovak civil servants going to Czechia received no indemnity whatsoever.[71]

[67] All the Czechs.
[68] Čulen, *Czechs and Slovaks in the Administration of the Czecho-Slovak Republic*, p. 56.
[69] *Moravsko-Slezský denník*, No. 259, 1920.
[70] Čulen, *Czechs and Slovaks in the Administration of the Czecho-Slovak Republic*, p. 45.
[71] *Ibid.*, p. 48.

Many foreign authors have been misled by Czech interpretations of problems relating to Slovakia at that time. Thus with regards to the Czech civil servants detailed in Slovakia, S. Harrison Thomson adopts Prague's point of view when he writes: "It was the intention of the government that the Czechs should be withdrawn as soon as competent Slovaks could be trained to displace them."[72] Now this statement is far from reflecting the truth, and facts are called upon to belie it. The Slovak Student Union stated as a matter of fact that there were three thousand unemployed intellectuals in Slovakia in 1934,[73] whereas no Czech civil servant had been sent back to Bohemia.

Statistics of the personnel of the Directorate of railroads in Bratislava and Košice give the following figures for 1925: of 5,134 engineers and other employees, 90 per cent were Czechs; of 12,355 subordinate agents, 60 per cent were Czechs; and of 16,025 manual workers, 30 per cent were Czechs.[74]

On June 16, 1938, the newspaper *Národnie Noviny*, organ of the Slovak National party of the Autonomist Rázus, published an article by Dr. Pošvár stating that there were at that time 120,926 Czechs in Slovakia.[75] These formed the closely knitted cells of the administrative and public life of the country. Since there were many bachelors, this figure represented 20,541 high officials of the Slovak administration and about 20,000 occupied in private activities.[76]

There is no doubt that the arrival of the Czechs in Slovakia helped greatly to aggravate the most serious of the Slovak social problems of modern times: the emigration problem.

The policy carried on by former Hungary had obliged about a million Slovaks to leave for foreign parts between 1850 and 1918. The Czech policy was to be attended by the same consequences. The following table gives, in figures and percentages,

[72] S. Harrison Thomson, *Czechoslovakia in European History* (Princeton: 1944), p. 292.
[73] *Slovenský denník*, Bratislava, (October 28, 1934).
[74] Čulen, *Czechs and Slovaks in the Administration of the Czecho-Slovak Republic*, p. 70.
[75] *Ibid.*, p. 88.
[76] *Ibid.*, p. 215. The following anecdote illustrates this fact: during a debate in the Prague Senate, a Czech senator, wishing to make fun of the Autonomist senator, J. Durčanský, whom he obviously considered a "primitive" peasant, asked him: "Tell us, my dear colleagues, the difference between autonomy and the automobile." The one questioned, endowed with sturdy good sense, replied: "Autonomy is an automobile which would bring back 120,000 Czechs from Slovakia to Prague!"

the importance of Slovak emigration in proportion to the whole
of the Republic.

TOTAL EMIGRATION			
Year	For the Republic	For Slovakia	Percentage
1920	34,942	13,373	38.2
1921	35,212	15,023	42.6
1922	39,459	16,737	42.4
1923	32,341	16,596	51.3
1924	54,273	35,202	64.8
1925	19,350	8,715	45.0
1926	26,129	14,409	55.0
1927	23,596	12,053	51.0
1928	24,540	13,544	55.1
1929	30,715	19,401	63.1
1930	26,893	17,832	62.1
1931	9,845	4,753	48.5
1932	5,343	2,364	44.2
1933	4,831	3,132	64.8
1934	5,065	3,016	59.5
1935	5,686	3,707	65.1
1936	7,201	4,831	67.0
1937	14,772	8,595	58.1
Total	400,193	213,283	54.3

This mass emigration, however, did not succeed in absorbing
all the unemployed of Slovakia whose number, varying according
to the degree of economic depression, was often great. Thus in
1934 there were 140,000.

Slovaks in the Central Administration—Another deplorable
aspect of the life shared by Czechs and Slovaks was the condition under which Slovaks were admitted to the central administration of the State.

As Slovakia represented 23 per cent of the Republic's population, it would have seemed logical—as the competitive system
was not generally used—to reserve for Slovaks 23 per cent of the
positions in the central administration. Now the statistics for the
Slovak civil servants during the twentieth and last year of the
Czecho-Slovak Republic show the following:[77]

	Slovaks		*Civil Servants*
The Parliament of Prague	1	out of	224
Service of the Chief of State	3		96
Presidency of the Council	9		153
Ministries:			
Foreign Affairs	33		1,246
Interior	2		386

[77] Čulen, *Biography of Msgr. Tiso,* p. 250.

	Slovaks		Civil Servants
Justice	12	out of	143
Unification	6		51
National Defense	6		1,300
Generals	1		139
Industry: civil servants	4		417
Agriculture	11		391
Post Offices	7		305
Communications	9		1,006
Public Works	4		82
Commerce	1		322
Social Welfare	4		397
Public Health	6		182
Finance	12		630

Therefore, there were 131 Slovaks out of 7,470 civil servants working in 17 services of the central administration, that is 1.7 per cent of the total, while there should have been approximately 1,700.

Of the 318,981,000 crowns representing the sum total of the salaries paid annually to the civil servants of the Republic, the Slovaks received only 3,614,000, that is 1.1 per cent. If the 23 per cent proportion had been respected, the Slovak civil servants would have received 73,000,000 crowns annually.[78]

EXCEPTIONAL LEGISLATION

Czecho-Slovakia was a State with a standard of living relatively higher than other Central European countries. This prosperity can be explained by the fact that it inherited the biggest share of the former Austro-Hungarian industry, the Czech lands themselves having taken over more than 60 per cent of the whole capacity of that Empire. Some Western political writers, accustomed to see prosperity coupled with democracy, frequently expressed the opinion that the Republic of T. G. Masaryk was a living example of democracy. Yet this judgment is based rather on appearances than on political realities. In its external outlook and classical wording, the document known as "Constitution of Czechoslovakia" seems indeed to be charged with a high-minded spirit. Many articles in it sound like a paraphrase of the American Constitution. Translated into foreign languages, this document is still to be found in libraries of universities and governmental departments.

[78] Čulen, *Czechs and Slovaks in the Administration of the Czecho-Slovak Republic*, p. 209.

Having for all practical purposes identified themselves with the State, the Czechs however soon felt the need for an exceptional legislation to keep the dissatisfied Slovaks, Ruthenes, Germans, Magyars, and Poles under control. Since the international position of the Republic was from the beginning far from being consolidated, the Czechs availed themselves of the two attempts of former Emperor Charles IV to take over power in Hungary in 1921, as well as the rise of Magyar revisionism and later on of naziism, to strengthen the regime against "internal and external enemies." They managed to do it in subsequent legislation, by which the Constitution was going to be emptied of its legal meaning, and its provisions converted into pure Platonic norms.

Six weeks after approving the Constitution, the legal experts of the new Republic had a law passed by the Czech majority of the Parliament known as the Special Powers Act. No. 300, of April 14, 1920. It wisely states that in time of war or whenever events occur that seriously jeopardize State integrality, its republican form, its Constitution or public order, extraordinary measures can be taken for their protection. These measures may provisionally limit or abolish the freedoms granted by the Constitution in its articles: 107, on personal freedom; 112, the inviolability of the domicile; 113, freedom of the press, meeting, and association; and 116, freedom of correspondence. It was, of course, up to the government to decide in the form of a decree, whether the situation foreseen by the law, *casus legis*, really existed or not.

The first legislature became famous for having voted *the Law on the Protection of the Republic*. In effect, the Slovak problem became the Republic's chronic illness that the passive resistance of the minorities only aggravated. The Czech statesmen then decided to maintain the unity of the "Czechoslovak" nation and public order by more efficient means. On March 19, 1923, they had law No. 50/1923 voted by their parliamentary majority, and made it known henceforth as the Law on the Protection of the Republic. This law legalized political justice. In addition to the punishment of habitual crimes perpetrated against the State's security (high treason, plots against the territorial integrity of the State, intelligence with the enemy or with agents of a foreign power, the disclosure of State secrets, etc.), it made the constitutional liberties illusory by prohibiting any criticism of the regime. The idea was simple: whoever should dare to criticize a fellow citizen because of his nationality, religion, or lack of religion could be brought before the court under the charge of disturbing the peace or stirring up rebellion. By this means, Prague desired to protect the Czech civil servants in Slovakia, Ruthenia, and the Sudeten regions who were everlastingly provoking people by their lack of tact with respect to national or religious feelings.

All legalistic and political traps of the Law on the Protection of the Republic were displayed during the so-called Tuka trial in 1929. Vojtech Tuka, Professor of International Law and Legal Philosophy at Magyar University in Pécs prior to 1918, being of Slovak descent, became a member of the Prague Parliament on the ticket of the Slovak Populist party in 1925. On October 5, 1929, he was sentenced for alleged treason to fifteen years' imprisonment by the Regional Tribunal in Bratislava. Although pronounced that day at one o'clock in the afternoon by the aforementioned court, the sentence had already been divulged by the Prague morning press. The public prosecutor cited as chief witness against Tuka a certain Christina Schram from Vienna, who later admitted that she had been engaged for this testimony by the Czech Military Attaché in Vienna through one of his agents, Gustáv Vályi-Weiner, and had received money for that service. All top secret documents about this concocted political trial were found in the papers of President Masaryk after the collapse of the Republic in 1939.

The aforementioned Special Powers Act of 1920 was amended and the arbitrary power of the government strengthened by Act No. 125 of July 10, 1933. The main provisions of this laconic law may be summed up in the following way: In time of war or whenever within or on the State frontiers, events should seriously jeopardize State integrality, its democratic-republican form, its Constitution, or its peace and order, . . . the State Security Office can, without a judge's writ, order letters and other sendings to be confiscated or opened (Art. 7), associations to be put under control or their activity suspended (Art. 8), meetings in places of public traffic forbidden (Art. 9) and the publication of papers limited or, if need be, suspended (Art. 10).

On October 25, 1933, the Prague Parliament adopted law No. 201 concerning the suspension of activities and the dissolution of political parties. Article 1 reads:

> If the activity of a political party seriously endangers the independence, constitutional unity, integrality, democratic-republican form or security of the Czechoslovak

Republic, the Executive is empowered to suspend the activity of such a party or dissolve it.

All associations or groups, civic or economic, connected with the prohibited party could also be submitted to State control or suspended (Art. 3). Upon decision of the corresponding district office, the adherents of a party whose activity had been suspended may be ousted from their domicile, put under police supervision, or be subjected to the censorship of all communications (Art. 7).

In 1936, the political atmosphere in Czecho-Slovakia was getting more tense by reason of Germany's growing military menace. A cloud of fear overshadowed the Republic. The Prague Parliament then passed bill No. 131 of May 13, 1936, known as the State Defense Act, which in view of the approaching storm was to strengthen considerably the arbitrary powers of the Executive. Making the Administration responsible for an early and adequate readiness in building up the State defense, the act defined the latter term in the following way:

> Under State defense, aside from the military and economic, are included all measures designed to cope with any and all threats to the Czechoslovak Republic's sovereignty, independence, integrality, constitutional unity, democratic-republican form and security as well as an attack against them.

Chapter 3 of this act established the category of enterprises important for the defense of the State. Article 9, point 1, provides that the holder of such an enterprise has to be reliable from the point of view of State security. Point 9 of the same Article defines an "unreliable person" as follows:

> From the point of view of State security all persons are to be considered as unreliable about whom there are justified reasons to believe that they would use their position in a spirit incompatible with the State Defense Act: namely, those who have developed or are developing an activity directed against the sovereignty, independence, integrality, constitutional unity, democratic-republican form and security of the Czechoslovak Republic or against the defense of the State; those who are inciting or seducing others for such activities; who extol, consent or contribute to such activities; who were members of the political party which was officially forbidden for anti-State activities after this act had come into force; or who are suspect of having connections with other politically unreliable persons or with a foreign power.

All this exceptional legislation, like Damocles' sword, was menacing non-Czech nationalities, parties, and citizens. The State Defense Act had practically put the loyalty of all Sudeten Germans into question. The legal system of Czecho-Slovakia, instead of protecting the citizen irrespective of his nationality, was sanctioning the privileged position of the ruling class. Even at the time when the State structure might have been strengthened only by putting into practice the principle of equal justice for all nationalities, Czech statesmen thought to enlarge the power of the Czech bureaucracy and police. Such a policy could not help becoming tragic for this multi-national State. For the stronger the government's control over other nationalities, the weaker was the idea of the State. The driving of the federationist movement in Slovakia, Sub-Carpathian Ruthenia, and Sudeten German territory into extremism and illegality, the branding of their adherents as law breakers, the censuring of their press and confiscating of their books,[79] the forbidding of their meetings, the limiting of their human rights in general caused in Czecho-Slovakia tensions of such a force that their explosion was only a question of time.

Paraphrasing a sentence of Sallust (*Nam imperium facile his artibus retinetur quibus initio partum est. Bellum Catilinae,* Cap. 2), T. G. Masaryk would vainly declare that states remain alive because of the ideas which gave them birth. The Czecho-Slovak State, conceived along federative lines and attempting to subsist by centralism was soon to come to a crisis.

Slovakia Demands Self-Determination

The right of peoples to self-determination has been one of the greatest principles of the twentieth century. No infringements can succeed in altering its value.

It is certainly not the liberty of a few weak nations that could threaten the political equilibrium of the world, as is assumed in simplistic manner by certain political authors desirous of avoiding the "Balkanization" of Europe.

Self-determination as a directing principle, both national and international, is becoming more and more victoriously established in spite of all the difficulties opposing its realization. It is this principle which constitutes indisputably in our present-day era the real criterion of political ontology. The historic grandeur of this

[79] The first edition of *Biography of Msgr. Andrej Hlinka* by Karol Sidor, published during the Presidency of T. G. Masaryk in 1934 in Bratislava, was confiscated while the second one was censured at 34 different places.

motivating force consists in the abolition of international feudalism subjugating certain little nations to the imperialism of more
powerful ones. F. Palacký, the celebrated Czech historian, recognizes the historical significance of this in the following statement:

> The right of nations springs from a genuine natural
> law; no people in the world has the right to ask that, for
> his own good, his neighbor should sacrifice himself; no
> one is obliged to deny himself or sacrifice himself for the
> good of his neighbor. Nature knows no people made for
> dominating, no people for serving.[80]

While World War I was still going on, Masaryk also con-
vincingly defended the principle of the liberty of little nations:

> Political independence is a vital need for an enlightened,
> civilized nation. Even in the most civilized states politi-
> cally dependent nations have been oppressed and ex-
> ploited economically and socially. . . . The greatest Polish
> poets gave a very penetrating analysis of the constant
> revolutionary sentiment of an oppressed enlightened na-
> tion. Mickiewicz summarized it in the words: "The only
> weapon of a serf is treason. . . ." National autonomy hon-
> estly carried out, recognition of language rights in schools,
> public offices, and parliament, may be sufficient in certain
> cases, especially for national minorities, but it is not suf-
> ficient for national majorities and nations who by sheer
> violence were deprived of their independence and are
> striving to regain it.[81]

In fact, a nation without a state is like a body without a backbone. In the words of Macartney, "the state is really the organized expression of the nation without which the latter can have
only a passive and shameful existence."[82]

The liberation of oppressed nations also bears universal
weight. Theoretically, Masaryk was of the opinion that it is nations that effect the mission of all humanity. He expressed it thus:

> Between nationality and internationality there is no an-
> tagonism; on the contrary, there is agreement: nations are
> natural organs of humanity. Humanity is not supernational,
> it is the organization of individual nations. If, therefore,
> individual nations struggle for their independence and at-
> tempt to break up states of which they have heretofore

[80] Letter from F. Palacký to the *Vorparlament* of Frankfurt in 1848. See
Beneš, *Où vont les Slaves?* p. 266.
[81] T. G. Masaryk, *The New Europe* (London: 1918), pp. 27-28.
[82] C. A. Macartney, *National State and National Minorities* (London: 1934),
p. 102.

been parts, that is not a fight against internationality and humanity; rather, it is a fight against aggressors who misuse states for the purpose of leveling them and enforcing political uniformity. Humanity does not tend to uniformity, but to unity; it will be a liberation of nations which will make possible the organic association, the federation of nations, of Europe, and all mankind.[83]

Mr. Beneš, himself a theorist of "democracy," could see in the "definitive crystallization of the principle of nationalities in nation states" only "the march toward democratization."[84]

All Masaryk's and Beneš' enthusiasm for the political liberation of small nations was inspired, of course, by the Czechs' struggle against Austrian domination. Before all Europe they buttressed their aspirations to liberty with a universal principle. Yet, once Czecho-Slovakia was admitted to the European concert, the Czechs contested the Slovaks' right to avail themselves of the same principle. From apostles of liberty they too then became oppressors.

Just as Moses stayed the waters of the Red Sea to permit the Jews' passage, so did Mr. Beneš want to block evolution to allow the Czechs a pure and simple domination of Slovakia. For him the World War had marked "the crowning of the struggle for the full application of the principle of nationalities in Europe."[85] In other words, a nation which had not attained its own political stature after World War I was to be forever deprived of the right to gain it.

In contrast, an English professor, E. H. Carr, speaking without bias about the problem, admits that the national principle is valid, even in opposition to Czecho-Slovakia. He expressed himself on this subject as follows:

> The order established at the close of World War I could in no case be considered final and definitive. The right of peoples to self-determination has become a summons to a constant secession. The movement which dismembered Austria-Hungary and created Yougoslavia and

---

[83] Masaryk, *The New Europe*, p. 26.
[84] "We understand how the Magyar State also should have trouble in accepting the inevitable evolution of Europe and the definitive crystalization of the principle of nationalities in national states such as they present themselves in the present phase of the evolution of the national idea and of the march of Central Europe toward democratization." E. Beneš, "Address to the Slovaks on the Present and Future of Our Nation," made on December 7, 1933, at Nové Zámky, *Le Monde Slave*, Paris, (February, 1934), p. 63.
[85] *Ibid.*, p. 27.

Czecho-Slovakia was to continue along lines that had to lead to the disintegration of Yougoslavia and Czecho-Slovakia. Once the premises of nationalism are admitted, its evolution has become natural, legitimate, and impossible to stop.[86]

For a long time Europe did not know of this contradiction which existed in Masaryk and Beneš between theory and practice and all this Machiavellianism veiled in words. Not being a minority in the sense of the international treaties, it was not possible for the Slovaks to have recourse at Geneva to the protection provided for minorities; and on the inside the "Law for the Protection of the Republic"—a Draconian expression of Czech legitimism—constantly stifled their voice. Whereas Germany succeeded in making a real European question of the problem of the Sudeten Germans, the Slovak problem remained a purely inside matter for Prague—until Munich—answerable only to censure, the police, and the State courts.

None of these efforts succeeded in preventing the abyss from becoming deeper and in making "Czechoslovak" unity wholly illusory.

The festivities of Pribina, which were organized August 15, 1933, on the occasion of the eleven-hundredth anniversary of the founding of the first Christian church at Nitra, showed the strength of Slovak national feeling and the powerlessness of centralism.

The government of Prague, in order to take the initiative away from Slovak Catholics, organized the fêtes and hoped that they would be the occasion of a demonstration of Slovak loyalty to Czecho-Slovakia. It took good care not to invite Hlinka, head of the biggest Slovak party then in opposition to Prague, for it was feared that he would take advantage of it to recall the glorious past of the Slovaks and rouse their national feeling. Now the members of the government as well as the ecclesiastical dignitaries were settled in the gallery and speeches were in full swing when Hlinka, perceived among the crowd into which he had slipped, became the object of a veritable ovation. Suddenly thousands of voices rose above the official orators' to demand Hlinka. How were silence and order to be restored? Finally Hodža recommended that Hlinka be invited to speak. He even held out his hand to help the old orator get up to the gallery.

[86] E. H. Carr, *Nationalism and After* (London, 1945), p. 30.

Then, before 150,000 wildly enthusiastic people, Hlinka pronounced in a tone at first calm and cool, then more and more ardent and excited, one of the greatest discourses of his life. The spectators listened to him in recollected silence. The representatives of the government, humiliated, left the gallery, and the foreigners present tried to get an explanation of what had taken place.

The Slovaks had indeed shown their loyalty, but not the kind for which Prague had hoped.

The Czechs, in spite of all reminders, remained entirely closed to the Slovak question. Therefore, Monsignor Tiso, at that time Vice-Chairman of the Populist party, in his speech of December 1, 1936, felt it once more necessary to mention the grave European events that were in preparation and clearly expressed the unshakable will of the nation to vindicate its imprescriptible rights. He specifically said:

> In consideration of the events that are being enacted here and abroad, I declare that the Slovak people, a national individuality, look upon themselves as the titular sovereign of the historical territory of the Slovak country, recognized by Public Law today. This right they claim pursuant to their best criterion and they will put it to the best use in the future at all times, for and against all.

During the years which followed, Hlinka adopted an attitude that could leave no doubt about his ideas on Czecho-Slovak relations. At the session of the Populist party's executive committee, March 24, 1938, he stated: "The year 1938 will have the same importance for us as the year 1918. Events must not surprise us."

During the summer of 1938, a delegation of the Slovak League of America, with Mr. Peter Hletko as Chairman, went to Slovakia by way of Poland to avoid having to stop first in Prague. They brought with them the original copy of the Pittsburgh Agreement which guaranteed the autonomy of Slovakia.

To commemorate the twentieth anniversary of the signing of this document, the Populist party organized a demonstration at Bratislava, on June 5, during which Mr. Hletko and Monsignor Hlinka displayed before the eyes of the assembled 100,000 people this Slovak charter, which Masaryk had signed, but later denied. This great political day gave the old Slovak national leader his last opportunity to hold the public spellbound.[87]

---

[87] He was to die August 16 of the same year.

After this demonstration, the foreign press agents surrounded Hlinka and asked him: "Isn't it really independence that you want?" And he replied with a rhetorical question: "Is there a nation in the world that does not want to be independent?"

Led on by this idea, he made known his logical conclusions in an interview with the correspondent of the *Corriere della Sera.* In the June 6, 1938 issue, this important Italian newspaper expressed Slovakia's dilemma in the headline: "Complete autonomy or divorce from the Czechs?" Hlinka then said literally: "If it is possible, we shall remain with the Czechs. Otherwise we shall be obliged to go our own way, for we have no desire to live in bondage."

That was a serious warning and the Hlinka party put it into a slogan, a true appeal to the right of people to self-determination: "The Slovak people want to live, were it even at the price of the existence of the Czecho-Slovak Republic."

On September 21, 1938, in a speech given at Treviso, Mussolini rightly interpreted the Czecho-Slovak crisis in this manner:

> If Czechoslovakia finds herself today in what might be called a "delicate situation," it is because she was—one may already say "was," and I shall tell you why directly—not just Czechoslovakia, but "Czecho-Germano-Polono-Magyaro-Rutheno-Rumano-Slovakia," and I would emphasize, now that this problem is before us, it should be solved in a general manner.[88]

Masaryk and Beneš had proclaimed toward the close of World War I:

> We no longer want to be part of a State whose existence is not justified and which, refusing to accept the essential principles of a reorganization of the modern world, remains a purely artificial political structure. . . .[89]

If the Slovaks had continued to defend the principle of the Czecho-Slovak State even after their twenty years' experience in common with the Czechs, they would thus have committed an act of political masochism.

The Spanish philosopher, Manuel Garcia Morente, said:

> For an historical person or quasi-person, no act can assume historical importance whose definition or ideological tenor is in fundamental contradiction to the essential be-

---

[88] Ripka, *Munich: Before and After,* p. 117.
[89] The Declaration of Independence by the Czecho-Slovak Provisory government in Paris, October 18, 1918.

ing and nature of his own national and individual personality. . . . That is why fidelity to one's own nature can
never be anachronistic.[90]

Struggling for their liberty the Slovaks assumed an attitude
in conformity at the same time with world development and the
intimate law of their innermost national being and historical
effort.

The Progressive Downfall of the
Czecho-Slovak Security System

> *The European system built after the war
> had been constantly weakening for sev-
> eral years; in the last three years it has
> changed fundamentally.*
> E. Beneš, in his resignation speech of
> October 5, 1938.

Beneš, who was intimately acquainted with all the inside
weaknesses of Czecho-Slovakia, was clever enough to link the
fate of this heterogeneous State with the general system of European security. Since the regime, in its inner workings, depended
only on the Czechs, the lack of stability had to be supplemented
by a system of collective security ingeniously reinforced by a
few bilateral or multilateral pacts. That, in brief, was the essential task of the foreign policy of Czecho-Slovakia. Beneš desper-
ately defended collective security which alone could preserve
the life of a fragile creation suffering from internal maladies and
exposed to innumerable external dangers. However, while pretending to be enthusiastic on the subject of the League of Nations, he did not really believe in its effectiveness. That is why
he was the first one in Europe who did not hesitate to contradict
the principle of collective security. This he did in 1920-1921
by making himself the promoter of a regional security organization: the Little Entente. The same reasons motivated the Friendship and Consultation Treaty which was made between Czecho-
Slovakia and France in 1924.

"Finally in 1925," to quote B. Mirkine-Guetzevitch, "Locarno
and the apparent progress in European consolidation tended
more and more to file the disappearance of the Czechoslovak
State with the Utopias."[91]

[90] Manuel Garcia Morente, *Ideas para una filosofia de la historia de España*
(Madrid: 1943), pp. 90-91.
[91] Mirkine-Guetzevitch, *La Tchécoslovaquie*, p. 49.

Soon, however, the apparently clear sky of Czecho-Slovakia's political position would begin to cloud over. Germany, which had joined the League of Nations in 1926 in order to contend for equality of rights, attained its end thanks to the Big Five's Declaration of 1932. Then, profiting by their rank as full-fledged members of the League of Nations, Germany and Italy plunged headlong into schemes directed against this institution. On March 18, 1933, Mussolini proposed a Four-Power Pact to Mr. Ramsay MacDonald and Sir John Simon, Prime Minister and Secretary of Foreign Affairs of the British cabinet respectively, during their visit to Rome. This document had as its aim the super-position on the League of Nations of a directory of four great powers and the strengthening of Germany's and Italy's position in the European political system. There is no doubt that the idea of such a pact was to weaken the position of the little states neighboring on Germany and Italy. Although it was signed on July 15, 1933, the Pact never became operative; it could not be ratified because of the opposition effected by the public in Great Britain and France. Although torpedoed, this attempt dealt a palpable blow to the prestige of the League of Nations.

Less than a year later, on October 14, 1933, Germany withdrew from the Disarmament Conference and the League of Nations. In so doing, it rejected the policy of European cooperation and set out on the pursuit of its own interests.

From that time on, Hitler's chief worry was armament and the re-establishment of the political power of the Reich. The solidarity of all the great powers as well as the comparable increase in their total military strength could alone have checked Germany's imperialistic designs. But at that time, the policy of France and Great Britain was far from being prompted by any such ends.

On March 16, 1935, Germany again brought obligatory military service into force. The British government sent Berlin a Platonic note of protestation without having got together beforehand with France. A little later, Sir Simon and Mr. Eden made their way to Berlin to have a talk with Hitler. Before these English statesmen, he rejected the collective security system, reaffirmed the decision made on general military service and announced to the winds an equal footing with Great Britain in aviation.[92]

---

[92] Winston S. Churchill, *The Second World War*, Vol. I: *The Gathering Storm* (Boston: 1948), p. 132.

As for France, it took the matter before the Council of the League of Nations, which in turn condemned Germany's unilateral measures by recommending penalties for its "having endangered the peace of Europe."

All these developments could have no other effect than to spur Mr. Beneš on to seek out new support, and his interest this time turned to the Soviet Union. The result was a mutual aid treaty that was signed on May 16, 1935 and ratified a short time later when Beneš was in Moscow.

On June 18, 1935, Great Britain surprised Europe by concluding a naval agreement with Germany without having informed the other signers of the Versailles Treaty. Thereby, Germany agreed to maintain the tonnage of its fleet at a third of Britain's. This agreement was actually nothing more than a regularizing by Great Britain of German violations of the treaty's military clauses.

On October 3, 1935, Mussolini, the political partner of Hitler, had Italian troops sent into Ethiopia. This flagrant violation of the territorial integrity of a State-member of the League of Nations, ascertained by the Committee of Six on October 7 and 10, ought to have resulted in punitive sanctions by all members against the aggressor. On November 18, these penalties were actually voted by the League of Nations. One of them was to be the embargo on gasoline. Mussolini stated that he would consider its application as an act of war. In order to avoid danger, they then decided at Geneva that this point would have to be re-examined.

On December 5, Sir Samuel Hoare, British Secretary of Foreign Affairs, reaffirmed the determination of His Majesty's government to fulfill the obligations of the Covenant of the League of Nations. All the other member-States did likewise. However, eight days later, December 13, the press published some Laval-Hoare proposals destined to settle the dispute; they offered Italy not only economic but also territorial concessions, and obviously at the expense of Ethiopia. It was the policy of *appeasement* that won out. Mussolini was winning the game. The punitive measures against Italy were ultimately abandoned July 15, 1936.

Just as the Japanese occupation of Manchuria in 1931, that of Ethiopia by Italy in 1935 dealt a sad blow to the League of Nations' political system. It was clearly to be seen that new forces had sprung up which would not reform but completely destroy the construction of Versailles.

The powerlessness of the League of Nations that had been shown in the case of Ethiopia was a temptation for Hitler to repeat Mussolini's "stroke." On March 7, 1936, he did indeed denounce the Pact of Locarno and had the demilitarized zone of Rhineland "symbolically" occupied.[93] No one stirred. That day the Covenant of the League of Nations, the Briand-Kellogg Pact, and that of Locarno were definitely filed away in the archives of European pacifism. It is then that Beneš himself caught sight of the spectre of Munich.[94]

The year 1938 would see the fate of Austria sealed. This country, whose Prime Minister Dollfuss had been assassinated by the Nazis on July 25, 1934 for having opposed the plots of the nazi minority directed from Berlin, was condemned to drown in the National-Socialist tide. On July 11, 1936, Hitler had already imposed on Schuschnigg an agreement which opened the gate to the influence of Berlin in Austria. Next, while Hitler was pretending to become disinterested, his substitute, Rudolph Hess, led a conspiracy against the Schuschnigg government. This game could end in nothing save Germany's total absorption of Austria. However, the system of European security was already dead. On March 14, 1938, once the deed had been done, Mr. Neville Chamberlain proclaimed in the House of Commons that they had to consider "as chimerical any idea of being able to go save the victim."[95]

France at that moment was replacing the Chautemps government with Mr. Blum's; thus it was not in a position to make more than a symbolic gesture of protestation.

There is no doubt that Germany, by re-establishing its military strength, had destroyed in Central Europe any influence of the Western political system. Since the Czecho-Slovakia of Beneš was "a Russian air base and an Anglo-French military makeweight in event of war"[96] with Germany, it was this country against which Germany was expected to direct its play.

Now the prospects that the Western statesmen had to offer Prague were not in the least encouraging. In the course of the debates that followed Hitler's occupation of Austria, Mr. Chamberlain had declared in the Commons that "one could not deceive the weak little nations by letting them hold on to the idea

[93] *Ibid.*, p. 195.
[94] E. Beneš, *Memoirs* (London: 1954), p. 13.
[95] Compton Mackenzie, *Dr. Beneš* (London: 1946), p. 186.
[96] Churchill, *The Gathering Storm*, p. 280.

that they could be protected by the League of Nations against an aggression."[97] And on March 21, 1938, the new parliamentary secretary of the Ministry of Labor, Mr. A. T. Lennox-Boyd, developed this idea as far as to say: "Great Britain has no longer any interest in Czecho-Slovakia."[98]

This attitude of the Western democracies assured Hitler that they would not intervene in favor of Czecho-Slovakia. He began therefore to effect military preparations. Speaking of this question in the Reichstag on January 30, 1939, he confessed: "On May 28 (1938), I first ordered military action prepared against this State for October 2; secondly, I ordered our defense organizations in the West to be accelerated and increased."[99]

Realizing the seriousness of developments in Czecho-Slovakia, Churchill recommended in a letter of August 31, 1938, to Halifax[100] that with the support of Roosevelt a note be prepared in common with the British, French, and Russian governments on the Sudeten question, to be sent to Germany. The three governments, however, never succeeded in adopting a common attitude. Even during the days preceding the critical events, they remained divided. On September 10, Mr. Bonnet, French Minister of Foreign Affairs, asked Sir Phipps, Great Britain's Ambassador in Paris, what the attitude of His Majesty's government would be if Hitler attacked Czecho-Slovakia. The British government's reply, made to Mr. Bonnet September 12, was in substance the same as the one given Mr. Cambon in 1914 by Mr. Grey:

> . . . as far as it is possible for me to furnish an answer at present to Mr. Bonnet's question, I can say that, although His Majesty's government can never allow France's security to be threatened, it is impossible for it to be specific as to the character and date of its future action under circumstances which cannot possibly be foreseen today.[101]

Under these conditions France was unable to fulfill the obligations which issued from the Friendship Treaty with Czecho-Slovakia. France evaluated this treaty as one of the elements of the European security system; and in accordance with the French Government's opinion which prevailed during the crisis of 1939,

[97] Mackenzie, *Dr. Beneš*, p. 187.
[98] *Ibid.*, p. 187.
[99] *Redes des Führers und Reichskanzler Adolf Hitler vor dem Reichstag am 30, Januar, 1939.* (Berlin: 1939).
[100] Churchill, *The Gathering Storm*, p. 293.
[101] G. Bonnet, *De Washington au Quai d'Orsay* (Geneva: 1946), pp. 360-61.

it would have been senseless to make one isolated wheel turn when the whole machine had collapsed.

Such was the approximate attitude of Czecho-Slovakia's allies also in the Little Entente.

Speaking in the Assembly of the League of Nations, September 21, 1938, about the German threat to Czecho-Slovakia, Mr. Litvinov made the following statement:

> Only two days ago the Czech government asked my government if the Soviet Union, within the compass of Soviet-Czech aid, would give Czecho-Slovakia effective and immediate assistance in case France, faithful to its agreement, would give similar aid. My government plainly replied in the affirmative.
>
> It is not our fault if they have not carried out our proposal. Unfortunately, other measures were adopted which could not help leading to a capitulation whose consequences will sooner or later become disastrous. We are not acting in the spirit of the Covenant of the League if we avoid a problematical war today only to have as a certainty a general war tomorrow, especially when it is done to satisfy the appetite of insatiable aggressors and at the price of the destruction or mutilation of sovereign states.

The liquidation of Czecho-Slovakia was a consequence of the spirit of appeasement that dominated Western policy from 1933 on, and the understandable distrust that the democracies had vis-à-vis the Soviet Union.

Sudeten Germans: Achilles' Heel of the Republic

Owing to Mr. Beneš' competency at the Paris Peace Conference in 1919, two completely opposite principles were put into practice for determining the frontiers of Czecho-Slovakia: the historical principle in Czech countries and the principle of nationalities in Slovakia. They took their stand on the ethnical criterion to destroy the historical unity that Austria-Hungary was. On the other hand, this same criterion was totally put aside in the case of Bohemia-Moravia-Silesia. If applied to these countries it would in fact have led to the separation of the border regions of the Sudetes from Czechia and the assignment of the same to defeated Germany along with the 3,123,448 Germans living there. For strategic and economic reasons special treatment was reserved for Czech countries.

The German minority of the Sudetes, like the other minorities of Czecho-Slovakia, benefited by the protection of the League of Nations under the terms of the treaty dealing with the recognition of the new State and the protection of the minorities, signed at Saint-Germain-en-Laye on September 10, 1919 by the principal Allied and Associated Powers.[102] The guarantee of the League of Nations is provided for in the following terms:

> Czecho-Slovakia agrees that, as far as the stipulations of chapters I and II affect persons belonging to minorities in race, religion or language, these stipulations constitute international obligations and will be placed under the guarantee of the League of Nations. . . . (Art. 14, par. 1)

Despite these assurances the political leaders of the Sudeten Germans never admitted as definitive the solution that had been adopted. Mr. Lodgman, Chairman of the German parliamentary group, stated on June 1, 1920, in the Parliament of Prague:

> The Germans of Bohemia, Moravia, Silesia, and Slovakia never expressed the wish to become united with the Czechs and form with them the Czecho-Slovak Republic. That is why they will never cease to claim the right of self-determination and they will consider it as the supreme principle of all their activities and their attitude toward the said Republic.[103]

The Sudeten Germans were soon to strengthen their opposition with regard to the Republic and energetically resist the constant effort of Czech expansion in the German regions. In order to weaken and break up the strength of the Sudeten Germans, Prague had several means at its disposal: economic measures, the school system, the administration, grants to Czech frontiersmen, etc. The government unfortunately used them in such manner as to arouse German nationalism. Instead of seeking grounds for mutual understanding, it poured oil onto the flames. This explains why the Germans proceeded without delay from passive resistance to open opposition.

As long as the Western political system fully protected Czecho-Slovakia, Mr. Beneš succeeded in winning to its cause some persons of the German Agrarian, Christian-Social, and Social-Democratic parties, which were only a fraction of the German minority: Messrs. Mayer-Harting, Spina, Jaksch, and Dr. Czech. Some of these parties were even represented in the gov-

[102] See certain stipulations of this treaty above, page 4.
[103] Sidor, *The Slovaks on the Floor of the Parliament of Prague*, I, p. 135.

ernment. But between 1933 and 1938, with the progressive un-obtrusiveness of the Western democracies in the Danubian sector, the German minority became the Achilles' heel of this heterogeneous State. In conformity with its racial theory (*Ein Volk, ein Reich, ein Führer!*) Nazi Germany began to busy itself with the Sudeten Germans.

In the last elections of the First Republic on May 19, 1936, the German party of the Sudetes, of Nazi tendency, obtained forty-four seats in the Parliament of Prague. It actually became the strongest political party of the Czecho-Slovak State.

Among the documents which poured into the Nuremberg trial was found a note written by Mr. Hoszbach relating a conference that Hitler had on November 5, 1937 with his closest collaborators in the Chancellery of the Reich. During the course of it, he broadly exposed his theory of vital space and his plans for the expansion of German power into eastern Europe with Austria and Czecho-Slovakia as the first objectives. These two countries were to serve him afterward as bridgeheads for his conquest of other countries.[104] The German party of the Sudetes was to play in this evolution the role of a powerful fifth column of the Third Reich.

Hitler made his intentions known with respect to the Germans of Austria and Czecho-Slovakia in the declaration which he made in the Reichstag on February 20, 1938:

"Over ten million Germans," he said, "live in two of the states adjoining our frontier." It was the duty of Germany to protect those fellow Germans and secure to them "general freedom, personal, political, and ideological."[105]

When Hitler occupied Austria in March, 1938, he envisioned "liquidating" Czecho-Slovakia under pretext of defending the German minority of the Sudetes. On April 21, 1938, he exposed to Keitel the substance of the "Green Plan" of attack, and he gave his final orders on June 18.[106] The attack was to be carried out by five armies made up of thirty-seven divisions. According to documents from the archives of the German government, Hitler planned in 1938 to have Mr. Ernst Eisenlohr assassinated in order to provoke the conflict. Eisenlohr was his own Minister

[104] *Judgment of the International Military Tribunal for the Trial of German Major War Criminals,* Nuremberg, September 30 and October 1, 1946. Presented by the Secretary of State for Foreign Affairs to Parliament by Command of His Majesty. (London: 1946), p. 19.
[105] Churchill, *The Gathering Storm,* p. 280.
[106] *Ibid.,* p. 290.

Plenipotentiary at Prague. In conformance with these plans, Konrad Henlein, leader of the Sudeten German party in Bohemia, stirred up agitation among the Sudetes at the same time against the government of Prague. On April 24, 1938, in a discourse delivered at Karlsbad, he formulated in eight points the demands of the German minority:

1. A statute had to be obtained for the Sudeten Germans granting them complete national and political equality with the Czechs.

2. As a guarantee of this equality, the Sudeten Germans would be recognized as a national entity with public law within the compass of the Czecho-Slovak Republic.

3. The German regions within the State would be officially determined and recognized.

4. These regions would have autonomous government.

5. Every Sudeten German residing outside German regions would enjoy legal protection because of the special statute for Sudeten Germans.

6. The injustices inflicted upon Sudeten Germans since 1918 would end, and the damages that had been done them would have reparation.

7. The principle of "German regions, German officials" would be applied.

8. The freedom of choice for the Germans and the freedom of adherence to the National-Socialist political philosophy would be fully recognized.

During a visit to London on May 13, Henlein proposed the following solution to Churchill:

> There should be a central Parliament in Prague which should have control of foreign policy, defense, finance, and communications. All parties should be entitled to express their views there, and the government would act on majority decisions. . . . The Sudeten German regions, and possibly the other minority districts, should enjoy local autonomy; that is to say, they should have their own town and county councils, and a Diet in which matters of common regional concern could be debated within definitely delimited frontiers.[107]

In short, it was a program of federative reform whose realization Mr. Beneš had promised at the Paris Peace Conference in 1919.

[107] *Ibid.*, pp. 285-86.

Nearly twenty years later, France and Great Britain had realized that unfulfilled demands of the nationalities in Czecho-
Slovakia was a problem involving the very existence of that State.
Therefore, on May 7, i.e., two weeks after Henlein's Karlsbad
speech, Messrs. de Lacroix and Newton, Ministers Plenipotentiary of the Paris and London governments in Prague, called on
the Czecho-Slovak Foreign Minister Kamil Krofta "to express the
hope that the Czech Government will go to the furthest limit in
order to settle the question."[108]

At Tábor on May 20, 1938, the day of the first Czecho-Slovak
mobilization, Mr. Beneš, speaking of the demands of the nationalities, recognized his negligence and omissions, stating in fact:
"We must not repeat the mistakes of the past."

Meanwhile the government had set about studying a "statute
of nationalities" destined to give satisfaction to the Germans. As
the work drew out and the situation became more and more tense,
the British government decided, in July, to send Lord Runciman
to Prague to play the role of "conciliator and mediator." On August 3, 1938, when he had only just arrived, Germany began to
mass its troops at the western border of Czecho-Slovakia. In spite
of the tense political atmosphere, Mr. Beneš was not inclined to
give in. After the Germans had rejected a first, then a second
plan—having judged both insufficient—the government in collaboration with Lord Runciman drew up a third, which allowed
regional autonomy for the Germans. This plan, approved by Lord
Halifax, was nevertheless again rejected by Hitler. So there was
nothing left for Prague to do except present a fourth plan. This
one was practically a capitulation. It allowed all the demands
formulated by Henlein at Karlsbad except the eighth point regarding Nazi philosophy. In addition, the government granted
credit to the Sudetes for 700 million crowns.

On September 7, while the Germans were studying these new
propositions, the *London Times* published an editorial whose
main passage ran as follows:

> If the Sudetens now ask for more than the Czech gov-
> ernment are ready to give in their latest set of proposals,
> it can only be inferred that the Germans are going beyond
> the mere removal of disabilities for those who do not find
> themselves at ease within the Czechoslovak Republic. In
> that case it might be worth while for the Czechoslovak
> government to consider whether they should exclude alto-

[108] *Ibid.*, p. 285.

gether the project, which has found favour in some quarters, of making Czechoslovakia a more homogeneous State by the cession of that fringe of alien populations who are contiguous to the nation to which they are united by race.

This article was followed by other "feeler" articles that advocated the detachment of Sudetenland, or at least a plebiscite. These writings were said to be of "officious" inspiration.[109]

Then clashes took place between Germans and Czechs. On September 12, Hitler made a violent speech against Mr. Beneš. At the same time, he came forth with threats aimed at Western statesmen:

> The Reich will no longer permit continued oppression of three and a half million Germans, and I pray foreign statesmen to be convinced that this is not just mere talk. . . . In case the democracies are persuaded that they must by all means protect those oppressing the Germans, serious consequences will ensue.[110]

This speech heartily encouraged the Sudeten Germans. On September 12 and 13, 1938, two dozen people were killed in free-for-alls. The Czecho-Slovak government could do nothing but proclaim martial law in the German regions. On September 14, negotiations with Henlein were broken off. On September 15, Henlein went to Germany and stated that same day on the Leipzig radio that the Sudeten Germans were only waiting to be incorporated into the Reich (*Heim ins Reich!*).

The same day, Chamberlain took a plane for Berchtesgaden where he met Hitler. The problem was then put squarely: Germany was asking for the annexation of the Sudetes.

On September 17, Chamberlain returned to London and called his government together. Lord Runciman was already back and presented his report. Its tenor was the following:

> I have been left with the impression that Czechoslovak rule in the Sudeten areas for the last twenty years has been marked by tactlessness, lack of understanding, petty intolerance and discrimination, to a point where the resentment of the German population was inevitably moving in the direction of revolt. The Sudeten Germans felt, too, that in the past they had been given many promises

---

[109] Ministère des Affaires de Etrangères de l'U.R.S.S., *Documents et Matériaux se rapportant à la veille de la Deuxième Guerre mondiale* (Moscow: 1946), II, 158.
[110] Roger Céré, *Chronologie du Conflit mondial: 1935-1945*, (Paris: 1945), p. 99.

by the Czechoslovak government, but that little or no action had followed these promises. . . .[111]

Lord Runciman recommended a "policy of immediate and energetic action," that is to say "the transfer to Germany of regions comprising 75 per cent Germans."

After twenty years during which the great powers had abandoned to the mercy of the Czechs the minorities as well as the Slovaks and the Ruthenians, London suddenly remembered the rights of self-determination. Mr. Churchill specified that the impression of a wrong to be righted was such that "even the mood appeared of championing the weak man against the Czech bully."[112]

In the course of a meeting that was held in London on September 18, Messrs. Daladier, Bonnet, and Chamberlain sought a solution which, according to Chamberlain's statement in the House of Commons, "would not bring about an European war, and therefore a solution which would not automatically compel France to take action, in accordance with her obligations."[113]

Consequently on September 19, a note was given Mr. Beneš by Messrs. Newton and de Lacroix saying that the regions comprising a majority of Germans ought to be given to Germany, whether directly or as the result of a plebiscite. But Mr. Beneš feared a plebiscite, for the Slovaks could have demanded one too, creating a situation which would have brought about the end of the Republic. He made himself recalcitrant to such a degree that the two governments were obliged to approach him again on the night of September 21, this time putting onto the government of Prague the whole responsibility for the events which would follow. On September 22, Chamberlain had another interview with Hitler at Godesberg. Hitler turned out to be more demanding than he was the first time. To Hitler's demands which were now piling up, Prague replied with general mobilization. At the request of Roosevelt and Mussolini, Hitler then agreed to a conference of the Big Four.

This conference, which took place on September 29 and 30 in Munich, took from Czech countries the regions having a German majority. Neither France nor Great Britain attempted to oppose the principle of self-determination to be applied to

[111] *The British White Paper* Cmd. 5847.
[112] Churchill, *The Gathering Storm*, p. 301.
[113] Mackenzie, *Dr. Beneš*, p. 206.

3,325,000 Germans. Thus Germany took from the Czechs the privilege that had been granted them by the Versailles Treaty. This was a terrible defeat for Mr. Beneš, as much international in nature as it was internal.

Responsibilities

> *Self-determination is not a mere phrase.*
> *It is an imperative principle which states-*
> *men will henceforth ignore at their peril.*
> Woodrow Wilson

A prominent person of the Slovak Renaissance period, Ján Francisci, said in 1843: "Our national parent stock is quite different in its language, customs and mission from the Czechs' and essentially it forms a unity within itself."

For Ľudovít Štúr it was their "foreign mentality" (*cudzota ducha*) that made the Czechs so different from the Slovaks.[114]

Michal Miloslav Hodža, speaking of Czechs and Slovaks, pronounced a sentence which was to remain famous: "We even feel with our mind, whereas you Czechs even reason with your heart."

Given the indisputable difference in the two mentalities, it was natural that the thoughts and actions of the Czechs in Slovakia and their whole policy should produce a violent psychological shock within the population.

When the Magyars engaged in open and pitiless strife to realize their policy of assimilation of the Slovaks, the latter could have no illusions about the exact intentions of their partners.

To arrive at the same end as the Magyars, the Czechs in return simulated love, brotherly feelings, assistance to the weak, while at the same time claiming for their solicitude progress in the common State. Their actions proved that they sought their own interests. They avoided an out and out fight, but they only multiplied the more their indirect and underhanded connivings destined to tear down the fortress of Slovak national individuality.

For Mr. Beneš it was the "State reason" which called for the assimilation of the Slovaks.[115] In his opinion the ethnical "Czecho-

---

[114] Hodža, *The Czecho-Slovak Schism*, p. 141.
[115] It was only years later that the Czechs frankly acknowledged their mistakes:

> "We have to admit that the whole evolution stimulated by the juridical structure of the State aimed at the assimilation of the Slovaks. Centralism was the obvious mistake of the First Republic."

Nová Svoboda, a Czech review dated February 23, 1946.

slovak" union was a "biological necessity"[116] for the Czechs. This is how he expressed the idea:

> Do the people here at home understand, in Bohemia and Slovakia, and do they understand here in Slovakia especially that the present-day task for the Czechs and Slovaks is to complete definitively the historical evolution which has led to the unification of our country and other nations of Central Europe; to form themselves into one strong, united, numerically powerful national body which can in the future hold out against any attacks by nations already fully formed from the national point of view?[117]

For Mr. Beneš the Slovaks' mission in the Republic was the regeneration of the Czechs by Slovak blood. He did not fear saying it in a straightforward manner:

> The Czechs, that part of the nation which is nearest Western culture, which is impregnated with the urban, industrial, and technical civilization of the modern world, need to be regenerated by the afflux of new national strength. This the Slovaks alone will be able to give to the whole nation in the years to come; for they are, on the national trunk, the young branch full of vitality, extremely rich in biological strength, in spontaneous, popular cultural force. . . . They have no right to shirk this task.[118]

Mr. Beneš knew very well that to render justice to the different elements of Czecho-Slovakia, the Slovaks included, would have meant the end of the State. Thus, he cautioned the Slovaks against autonomy:

> Let each Slovak think only of all the consequences—administrative, economic, cultural, national—in the same degree; let him reflect for only a moment, and then let him wonder if he wants thus to wound mortally the Czech and Slovak element of this State and the State itself; let him consider what would be for this country the meaning of the formula: "Slovakia to the Slovaks," "German territories to the Germans," "Magyar lands to the Magyars."[119]

Thus the application of the principle of justice of the Roman law *suum cuique* would have meant the end of the Czecho-Slovak State. For Mr. Beneš such an eventuality was by all means to be avoided.

[116] Beneš, "Address to the Slovaks . . ." p. 40.
[117] *Ibid.*, p. 34.
[118] *Ibid.*, p. 41.
[119] *Ibid.*, p. 49.

The same reasoning can be found coming from Mr. Ripka's pen:

> The Autonomists' demand was, in fact, to be exclusive master in a house which was built mainly (sic!) by the efforts of the Czechs.[120]

Mr. Beneš saw in the Czecho-Slovak State only the continuation of the Kingdom of Bohemia. This particularistic conception was vigorously denounced by his very close collaborator, Mr. Stephen Osuský, who wrote these lines:

> Alas, in his soul Dr. Beneš is a disguised Czech racist. Though he helped to found the Czechoslovak Republic, he remains a Czech racist, who sees in Czechoslovakia only an expansion of the Czech Kingdom, which annexed Slovakia and Carpatho-Ruthenia and made provinces out of them. True, this cannot be professed before the Western democracies. That is why he worshipped the Western European democratic institutions and professed democratic sentiments which he used as an alibi to conceal his own Czech soul and so destroyed the very purpose which he wanted to serve.[121]

President Masaryk, who also called himself a democrat, was a partisan of the assimilation of the Slovaks. This great "humanist" posed as the defender of "the rights of man," but the idea of sacrificing the Slovak nation entirely to the Czech policy seemed quite natural to him. Certainly Masaryk was not a partisan of open violence. He was for a violence given in doses, wittingly graded and spread over several decades.

L. Genet, after having put the question: "Could Czecho-Slovakia be changed from a centralist to a federative State?" replied in the following manner: "Masaryk was hostile to it; it has too many nationalities. The patient old man was counting on time."[122]

Overt double-dealing characterizes the Czech political regime. Democratic verbalism sought to hide a dictatorial regime as well as it could. Mr. Beneš knew how to wield at times the pen of the "democratic" writer, brimming with ideas likely to please the credulous and badly informed West; at other times he held the whip of the feudal lord determined to break any political opposition by force, if not by ruse or intrigue. It is precisely the

---

[120] Ripka, *Munich: Before and After*, p. 258.
[121] Osuský, *Beneš and Slovakia*, p. 19.
[122] Genet, *Précis d'Histoire contemporaine, 1919-1939*, p. 208.

absolute lack of honesty in the Czechs which envenomed the Czecho-Slovak relations from the beginning.

Mr. Ripka himself, an incomparable dialectic spirit, cannot deny the mistakes that were made by Prague in Slovakia:

> Hatred of the Czechs, which was deliberately fostered for years by the Slovak Autonomists, had many causes. Much harm was undoubtedly done by the shortsighted bureaucratic policy of centralization pursued in Prague, and also by the somewhat tactless behavior of some of the Czechs employed in Slovakia, who did not appreciate sufficiently the susceptibilities of the Slovaks. . . .[123]

But Mr. Ripka is clever enough to catch his own ball: "The solution of the so-called Slovak problem is not federation, but the decentralization of administrative power."[124] In other words the Slovak problem, as far as Mr. Ripka was concerned, did not exist as a national one. For him it was simply a regional problem like the Moravian one, for instance.

After having accepted the idea of a State in common with the Czechs, Slovakia was brutally driven into the gearing of a Centralist machine. It was trampled under foot for twenty years and no one, neither inside nor abroad, wanted to hear its aspirations and grievances. If for Masaryk the Czech question was of European range,[125] the Slovak question was for him only an internal problem of State, that is to say Czech. After establishing a parliamentary system and a centralized government for the whole Republic, the Czech statesmen by means of Czech governmental and parliamentary majority drove the Slovaks into the opposition. Before the Western democratic world, Messrs. Beneš and Ripka spent a long time in reducing the Slovaks to a mere political party, to a small fraction of the "Czechoslovak" nation. "If the Slovaks prefer to remain in the opposition," they said, "it is their democratic right, for the option for any political party's passing into the opposition is the very quintessence of democracy."

While largely shared with Hitler, Mr. Beneš' responsibility in Munich does not remain any the less evident. Political wisdom would have dictated granting to the Sudeten Germans at the opportune moment reasonable concessions within the compass of the Czecho-Slovak State which was foreign to them. Mr.

---

[123] Ripka, *Munich: Before and After,* p. 257.
[124] *Ibid.,* p. 394.
[125] T. G. Masaryk, *The Czech Question* (Prague: 1908), p. 253.

Beneš, who had never been disposed to attack this problem, thus gave the Sudeten Germans a ready-to-hand pretext to be thrown into the arms of Hitler.

Since their own natural manifestations had been strangled by Prague's "stepmother" policy, important regions of the Republic had become spiritually detached from it long before Munich.

Instead of formulating and applying a statute of nationalities from the beginning, Czecho-Slovakia put the question off until the last minute, when any solution had become impossible.

From the external point of view, one can say that Czecho-Slovakia by its very nature was the most vulnerable and the most fragile State that had come out of the Versailles system. Its artificial geographical character and its excessively elongated shape took from it any resistance to lateral or longitudinal pressures.

In order to protect this sickly creation, Masaryk and Beneš insisted from the beginning that Czecho-Slovakia's mission was to resist Germanism. They hoped that this way of looking at things would assure the consent of the democratic powers for the policy of Czech statism vis-à-vis the Slovaks, Ruthenians, and the minorities. The West unfortunately lent itself readily to this way of thinking and contributed particularly to the development of a grandeur complex in the Czechs. These latter had long cherished the hope that the European importance of the strategic position of the quadrangle of Bohemia would constitute a determining factor in their defense system in case of conflict with Germany.

One notes with regret that never was one voice lifted in the League of Nations to defend the rights of the Slovaks and Ruthenians against the "great European" that some wanted to see in the person of Dr. Beneš.[126] Quite the contrary. It was the favors lavished by the great powers on the Czecho-Slovak Republic and its leaders that allowed this State to maintain itself on the waves of European policy. The European system and the special instruments created by Beneš were for a long time the lid to a basket of crabs. As long as the lid was solid, the centrifugal forces of this heterogeneous State were never taken seriously. As soon as the lid was lifted these living forces broke out immediately.

Czecho-Slovakia virtually died in Munich, although its death throes had to be prolonged until March, 1939.

---

[126] See: L. Eisenmann, *Un grand Européen: Edouard Beneš* (Paris: 1934).

Part II

THE SLOVAK REPUBLIC

Malo periculosam libertatem quam tutum servitium.

By the Munich Agreement of the European Big Four Slovakia was condemned to transfer to Hungary the southern zone settled by Magyars. Faced with the threat of mutilation, the country reacted healthily in knitting the national unity more closely together. The numerous parties of the former system resulting from Prague's policy of *divide et impera* were spontaneously abandoned by their leaders and replaced by a gathering together of all Slovaks of good will. The amputation decided upon by Vienna was painful but not fatal for the country.

One knows that long before Munich an overwhelming majority of the Slovak population had already withdrawn its adherence not only to Mr. Beneš' political regime but to the Czecho-Slovak State itself.

After the annexation of Sudetenland by Germany, the Slovaks had the painful impression of being attached to a dead body. This situation was unendurable and a change was psychologically inevitable. Doubtless Germany stimulated the evolution from the external point of view. On Hitler's chessboard the plays had already been made as early as 1937. Confronted with his decision to liquidate Czecho-Slovakia, would an attitude of the Slovaks' fidelity to the State which they no longer considered theirs have changed the march of events? Surely no one would dare reply in the affirmative. Thus the Slovak Republic became established as the irremediable result of an evolution at once internal and external.

Although assailed by innumerable political, cultural, economic, and other problems, the Slovak State got a firm footing on the internal plane and in a large measure on the external plane also. Later, during World War II, in spite of the strong pressure exerted by Berlin, it could remain practically neutral in the conflict which brought together Germany and the Western Powers. Finally, although it had not taken part in the campaign against the Soviet Union except in a symbolic manner, it was pitilessly crushed in 1945 by the Red Army.

The Birth of the Slovak State

October 6, 1938—Under international pressure, Prague had to make up its mind to take care of the Slovak problem. On September 22, 1938, in the course of the crisis brought on by the German question, Mr. Beneš, after many postponements and three modifications, finally had the text of a plan of solution put into the hands of Monsignor Tiso, Vice-President of the Populist party in Bratislava.[1]

On September 24, the executive committee of this party, meeting in the Slovak capital, accepted Mr. Beneš' plan as the basis for negotiations.

After Munich, however, when the structure of the Czecho-Slovak State was beginning to fall apart, Mr. Beneš abdicated from office on October 5, 1938.[2] The Slovaks of all political parties realized then that the center of gravity of their problem resided in Slovakia and nowhere else. In the meantime, Monsignor Tiso had called the executive committee of the Populist party in session to be held on October 5 and 6 at Žilina. In the invitation published by the press he emphasized that "the Slovak nation demanded the right to decide its own fate."

This aroused the attention of other parties, which immediately sent their own representatives. And after having recognized, in a common deliberation, the failure of Mr. Beneš' policy,

---

[1] Beneš,*Où vont les Slaves?* p. 277.

[2] The following ideas can be pointed out in Beneš' Farewell Broadcast of October 5, 1938, showing the complete self-effacement of the latter when confronted by Hitler:

> All will be judged in due course by history and history will give a just verdict. . . . In these circumstances I think it is advisable that the new developments and the new European collaboration should not be disturbed from our side through the fact that the personal position of its leading representative apparently constitutes an obstacle to this development. . . . I am by conviction a democrat. I believe I am acting rightly in leaving so that our State and Nation can develop quietly and undisturbed in the new atmosphere and adapt itself to the new conditions. . . . Our State has had a special structure from the nationality standpoint. Now conditions will change greatly. . . . We shall have a national State as in one sense the development of the principle of nationality indicates. . . . This will provide the State with a great and new source of activity and a strong moral basis which it has not possessed hitherto. . . . It is necessary above all to come to an agreement with the Slovaks. . . . Today it is not this or that concession which is of importance. Give way to one another wherever necessary. Beneš *Memoirs*, pp. 292-94.

the deputies of the parties having the "Czechoslovak" program as basis adhered spontaneously and unreservedly to the program of the Populist party by actually merging with it. A manifesto was drafted and adopted by six parties, the said manifesto fixing the position of Slovakia after Munich. The important part is here given:

> The Munich Agreement of the Big Four has profoundly changed the State-controlled relations and political dealings in Central Europe. We Slovaks as a nation unto ourselves, who have been living for centuries on Slovak territory, are asserting our claim to the right of self-determination by asking for an international guaranteee for the indivisibility of our national unity as well as the territory which we inhabit. We want to be able in the future to determine freely both our national life and our State system. We want to live on friendly terms with all the nations that surround us and contribute in a Christian spirit to the solution of the problems that arise in Central Europe.

The representatives of the political parties assembled then passed a resolution in terms of which:

> "government and executive power in Slovakia should repose in a Slovak government," composed of five ministers, the following matters only being considered as the concern of the whole State: the activities of the ministries of foreign affairs and national defense, the administration of the national debt and the issue of loans for purposes interesting the whole State; the five Slovak ministers should at the same time be members of the central government in Prague.[3]

The resolution concluded by stating specific instructions:

> We ask that the Vice-President of the Slovak Populist party, Dr. Jozef Tiso, as Prime Minister designated by us, be instructed immediately to form, in agreement with the parties listed below, the first Slovak government, which will have to comprise a chairman and four ministers; he is further instructed to propose that the President of the Republic consent to his nomination.[4]

That very evening Monsignor Tiso telephoned this decision to Prague in emphasizing the wish of this assembly to establish an autonomous regime in Slovakia at once.

---

[3] Ripka, *Munich: Before and After*, pp. 241-42.
[4] This resolution was signed by the representatives of the Agrarian party (Hodža), the Artisans' party, the National Socialist party (Beneš), the Hlinka party, the National Slovak party (Rázus), and the Fascist group (Ivák).

The Carpathian Ruthenians, likewise disappointed in their hopes by the policy of Prague, acted in the same manner.

The government of Prague, over which General Sýrový presided as successor to Mr. Hodža who had vacated his seat September 23, 1938, was in a difficult position. The Rumanian government advised moderation, pointing out that according to information Hungary was preparing mobilization against Czecho-Slovakia.[5]

This intervention, more than any other consideration, pushed General Sýrový into accepting unreservedly the demands of the Manifesto of Žilina. Thus it was that on October 7, Slovakia established itself as an autonomous State.[6] Prague named Monsignor Tiso as Prime Minister of the Slovak government, of which Messrs. Durčansky, Černák, Teplánsky, and Lichner became members.[7]

On November 8, Monsignor Tiso organized "the Sunday of Slovak fraternity and unity." In a speech which he delivered on that occasion he stated:

> The Slovak nation has become unified in the spirit of Bernolák, Štúr, Moyses, and Kuzmány, in the spirit of Hlinka and Rázus. Class differences have ceased. We have before us a united nation. Let us forget everything that divided us in the past and let us all unite loyally in the work for a better future for Slovakia and the nation.

On November 19, the diminished Parliament of Prague ratified the autonomy of Slovakia and Sub-Carpathian Ruthenia by a 144 to 25 vote (the minority representing the Czech communists). The Czecho-Slovak State then became a trio. A law having the character of a provisory constitution proclaimed the creation of three member-States, Czechia, Slovakia, and Carpathian Ukraine as basic elements of the Federation.

Changes in Slovakia and Carpathian Ukraine were carried on by two constitutional acts of similar wording adopted the same day. The constitutional acts on the autonomy of the Slovak land was published under No. 299 in the Collection of Laws and Decrees of the Republic, according to which the official name of

---

[5] According to the testimony of Professor Karvaš at the Tiso trial. See Čulen, *Biography of Msgr. Tiso,* p. 398.

[6] *Dictionnaire Diplomatique* IV (Paris: Académie Diplomatique Internationale).

[7] The latter two had been deputies of the former Agrarian party of Dr. Milan Hodža.

the federal State of Czecho-Slovakia is written with a hyphen. Its preamble reads as follows:

> The National Assembly, considering that the Czecho-Slovak Republic originated in the convergent and sovereign will of the two nations endowed with equal rights; that in the Pittsburgh Pact and other similar agreements and declarations of domestic and international relevance the Slovak nation was granted entire autonomy, and in the effort to bring about a reconciliation between the Slovaks and the Czechs in the spirit of the Žilina Agreement, has adopted the following act:

Chapter 1, containing general provisions, proclaimed the land of Slovakia an autonomous part of the Czecho-Slovak Republic. Under terms of the act Slovak was adopted as the language of offices and schools in the territory of Slovakia. Citizens of Czech nationality, however, as well as administrative offices, tribunals, territorial authorities, and other public organs of the Czech-Moravian Land, could use the Czech language in dealing with public organs and agencies in Slovakia. Linguistic rights of national minorities (German and Magyar) as granted by the Treaty of St. Germain remained unchanged. The law enacted a particular "regional domicile" for Slovakia's native population, based on the domicile right in a community of Slovakia.

Chapter 2 dealt with the division of jurisdiction between the Czecho-Slovak federal Parliament and the Diet of Slovakia. The powers of the federal Parliament extending over the territory of the whole State were specified by a detailed enumeration. They embraced the following matters: the Constitution, foreign relations in a political and economic sense, national defense, provisions concerning State citizenship, immigration, emigration, passports; money, measures and weights systems; patents, trade samples and trade-mark protection; geodetic and cartographic service; communications (railroads, telegraphs and telephones); posts and postal savings and checking service; common budget (common debts and loans); customs, taxes, excises, and fees to cover common expenditures; revenues of monopolies and enterprises under federal management (except for forests and mines whose exploitation pertained to the respective land); legal provisions destined to ensure equal conditions in enterprises for the whole Republic.

Under the consent of the Diet of Slovakia other questions could be transferred over to the competence of the federal Par-

liament. This provision means that the presumption of general
jurisdiction was vested in the legislative organs of the member-
states, while the jurisdiction of the federal Parliament and government resulted from the delegation consented by those states.
The federal Parliament was constituted by the full assembly of
the legislative bodies of the three member-States, like the former
delegations of the *Reichsrat* in Vienna. The federal government
was made up of eminent Czech and Slovak leaders. To change
the Constitution, elect the president of the federation, and give
a vote of confidence to the federal government, the votes of three
delegations had to be cast separately, each one requiring a three-
fourth majority (curial system). The right to veto thus prevented
any one delegation from being put in the minority by a coalition
of the two other States.

After the new constitutional law was passed, the central government was changed. Mr. Karol Sidor became Minister of State
in the federal government. Furthermore, on December 16, 1938,
the Slovak government sent its representatives to the ministries
in charge of affairs in common: Mr. Zvrškovec to Foreign Affairs, Mr. Haššík to Defense and Mr. Hrnčár to Finance.

The new political and constitutional situation of Slovakia was
approved by 97 per cent of the population at the time of the elections, December 18, 1938, which took place according to the
Czecho-Slovak electoral law. The Parliament of Bratislava[8] which
resulted met for the first time on January 18, 1939.

Had this federative pattern been honestly put into effect at
the beginning, the future of Czecho-Slovakia might have been
assured. In 1938, unfortunately, it was destined to fulfill no other
purpose than to delay the final death throes of that State. The
Second Republic was to be in fact only an interlude of a few
months.

The Arbitration of Vienna—The Munich Agreement opened
the question of the Slovak-Magyar and the Czecho-Slovak-Polish
frontiers. It was decided that in principle these problems would
be regulated by agreement of the interested governments. Besides, supplement No. 2 contained the following provision:

> The heads of the Big Four governments declare that
> if the problem of Polish and Hungarian minorities in
> Czecho-Slovakia is not settled in three months by an agree-
> ment of the governments concerned, this problem will be

[8]Sixty-three deputies, including two Germans and one Magyar.

the subject of another meeting of the government heads of the Four Powers today assembled.

Following Munich the Western Powers completely abandoned Central Europe to its fate. Although the Big Four had become equal guarantors of the decisions made, France and Great Britain later withdrew from the political evolution in this sector. The arbitration of Vienna was the dramatic proof of their effacement.

The Czecho-Slovak and Magyar delegations, meeting on October 9 at Komárno, reached no positive conclusion in spite of the fact that their discussions lasted several days.

The Munich Agreement proclaimed that a new boundary line to be drawn between Hungary and Slovakia was to take into account the ethnical principle. Mr. Kánya, Hungarian Minister of Foreign Affairs, insisted that the question be decided on the basis of an ethnological map dated 1910, the year when Magyarization had reached its culminating point. Under these conditions certain regions that were almost entirely Slovak were to be again subject to Hungary.[9]

The Czecho-Slovak delegation desiring to give evidence of its good will had the cities of Slovenské Nové Mesto and Šahy evacuated immediately. Notwithstanding, the Magyar delegation formulated exorbitant demands: Bratislava, Nitra, and Košice were to be again subject to Hungary, and a referendum was to decide whether the rest of the Slovak population wished to be subject to the crown of Saint-Stephen or not. This solution was not acceptable to the Slovaks. The disagreement should normally have been decided by the powers that signed the Munich Agreement. Now the disappointment provoked by the weakness that France and Great Britain had evidenced at Munich was such that the government of Prague, to the great satisfaction of Budapest, put the final solution in the exclusive hands of Germany and Italy. The result of the arbitration of Vienna, so deplorable for Slovakia, must undoubtedly be attributed to the absence of France and Great Britain. Ciano protected the Magyars while Ribbentrop, not at all interested in defending Prague's counter-project, did not realize that his indifference on this point was going to strike the Slovak people a cruel blow.

Slovakia had to cede to Hungary eight whole districts (Stará Ďala, Feledínce, Královský Chlumec, Komárno, Košice, Parkán,

[9] Frantisek Hrušovský, *Geschichte der Slowakei* (Bratislava: 1942), pp. 190-91.

Dunajská Streda, and Železovce) and parts of twenty other districts (Bratislava, Galanta, Modrý Kamen, Veľké Kapušany, Košice, Krupina, Levice, Lučenec, Michalovce, Moldava nad Bodvou, Nitra, Revúca, Rožnava, Rimavská Sobota, Šala nad Váhom, Šamorín, Tornala, Trebišov, Vráble, and Nové Zamky).

A total of 10,309 square kilometers with 853,670 inhabitants were transferred by Slovakia to Hungary. Among them were, according to 1930 statistics 503,980 Magyars; 26,157 Jews; 272,145 Slovaks; 1,825 Ruthenians. The result of the arbitration of Vienna was the following: it left 57,913 Magyars in Slovakia, but it increased the Slovaks in Hungary from 180,000 to 452,145, that is to say, nearly eight times as many as there were Magyars in Slovakia.

Sub-Carpathian Ruthenia for its part had to give up to the Magyars 1,618 square kilometers with 190,768 inhabitants.

After the sentence, Monsignor Tiso, in the presence of the "illustrious" arbiters, Ribbentrop and Ciano, could not help protesting such an arbitrary decision.

In response, Ribbentrop addressed these few words of consolation to him: "Munich saved the Slovaks from the catastrophe of a total dismemberment of their country."[10]

The grievous task of making the terms of the Vienna Arbitrament known to the country fell to Monsignor Tiso:

> The destiny of the nation was placed in our hands at the moment when twenty years of erroneous policy had brought the State to a total decomposition on an international as well as internal plane. The Slovak government could save for the nation only what still remained to be saved. . . . We can only bow our heads and go back to our work, but no one can prevent us from declaring to the world that the Slovak nation has just been the victim of a great injustice.[11]

The psychological shock of these events was terrible, but it strengthened the feeling of the Slovak people's destiny which was soon to be reduced to the formula: "A smaller Slovakia, but our own!"

On November 10, 1938, the instinct of public safety led the groups who had signed the Manifesto of Žilina to merge into a single party: the National Union.

---

[10] Ripka, *Munich: Before and After,* p. 505.
[11] Čulen, *Biography of Msgr. Tiso,* pp. 223-24.

Never had the Slovaks felt themselves so politically abandoned as at that moment. They paid dearly for the mistakes accumulated over the years by Mr. Beneš' foreign policy. As a matter of fact, the Germans recognized afterward that at Vienna Slovakia had been the victim of German vengeance against Prague.

The German-Magyar Plots Against Slovakia—After the victory of Munich, Germany was no less determined than before to liquidate Czecho-Slovakia. According to the Nuremberg documents, Hitler's general directions countersigned by Keitel were given to the army whose next mission was reduced to the two laconic sentences following: "Liquidation of what remained of Czecho-Slovakia. Possibility of overthrowing Czecho-Slovakia in case its policy should become hostile to Germany."[12]

Mr. Dirksen, German Ambassador to London, passing through Berlin at the end of February and beginning of March, 1939, noted in a report that "there was a strengthening of rumors according to which relations with Czecho-Slovakia would grow worse in March, a situation which would make necessary instantaneous intervention by the Germans.[13]

Now if the Germans had resolved purely and simply to incorporate Czechia into their territory, they had only a vague idea of the most suitable manner of liquidating Slovakia and Sub-Carpathian Ruthenia. They were aware of Hungary's and Poland's ambition to have a common border line,[14] but they did not know to what length they wanted to extend it. The abandonment of Slovakia and Sub-Carpathian Ruthenia to Hungary was the more possible because the Budapest government was insisting in this wise in Berlin. The judgment rendered by the Nuremberg Tribunal contains an interesting passage on this score:

> On March 4, 1938, the accused Ribbentrop wrote to the accused Keitel on the subject of a suggestion which the Hungarian Minister to Berlin had made to him, by virtue of which the aims of an eventual war against Czecho-

---

[12] *Judgment of . . . War Criminals,* p. 19.

[13] Ministère des Affaires Etrangères de l'URSS: *Documents et Matériaux . . . de la Deuxième Guerre Mondiale,* II, 171.

[14] Mr. Beck, Minister of Foreign Affairs from Poland, declared, for instance: "The Polish Government knows of Hungary's aspirations to recover Sub-Carpathian Ruthenia and to create a common frontier with Poland. As long as the Hungarian Government pursues a policy to that end, it can count on the goodwill and support of Poland and on her complete sympathy." Quoted in Ripka, *Munich: Before and After,* p. 310.

Slovakia should be discussed between the German and Magyar armies. In the course of this letter Ribbentrop stated: "I have the most serious doubts on the subject of the timeliness of such negotiations. In case we should discuss with Hungary the aims of an eventual war against Czecho-Slovakia, we would run the risk of the other side's being likewise informed."[15]

The visit which Horthy, Imrédy, Kánya, and Raatz made to Hitler on August 21-26, 1938, was motivated by Hungarian preoccupations on the fate of Slovakia. Its aim is clearly expressed in the journal of General Jodl:

> Visit to Germany of the Hungarian Regent, accompanied by the Prime Minister, the Minister of Foreign Affairs, and the Minister of War, von Raatz. They arrived with the idea that in the course of a great war, after a few years and with the help of German troops, the old State of Hungary can be reestablished.[16]

An official report of the German Minister of Foreign Affairs contains this passage on the subject of the Hungarian statesmen's visit:

> Kánya has pulled himself together and has said that the military situation of Hungary was much better, that its country would be ready as far as armament was concerned to take part in the conflict as early as October 1 of this year (1938).[17]

This is how Churchill describes Horthy's visit:

> . . . Hitler had been very reserved in his attitude. Although he talked long with the Hungarian Regent on the afternoon of August 23, he did not reveal to him the date of his intended move against Czechoslovakia. He himself did not know the time. Whoever wanted to join the meal would have to share in the cooking as well.[18]

While awaiting the succession of events, the Magyar troops were massed together along the Slovak border. Between November 2, 1938, and January 12, 1939, Hungary provoked twenty-two border incidents.[19] Those of Slanec (December 19), Šurany (the

---

[15] *Judgement . . . of War Criminals*, p. 19.
[16] *The Trial of German Major War Criminals: Proceedings of the International Military Tribunal Sitting in Nuremberg, Germany.* II.: December 3-December 14, 1945. Published Under the Authority of H. M. Attorney General. London: 1946. p. 5.
[17] *Ibid.*, p. 15.
[18] Churchill, *The Gathering Storm*, pp. 323-24.
[19] See: Ripka, *Munich: Before and After*, pp. 506-8.

end of December), Munkáč, Ceha (the beginning of January) and Bervinkoš (January 10) found many echoes in the press in the Danube countries. Perpetrated by military and civil groups, their purpose was to provoke a political tension calculated to justify an armed attack and, should the occasion arise, the occupation of Slovakia. During this time the Magyar press was preparing public opinion for the events which were to follow. "The historic role of Hungary," Mr. Tibor Eckhardt wrote in the *Magyar Nemzet*, "is the organization of the Danube basin. Hungary will never give up the Carpathians that make up its natural boundary."[20]

On January 12, 1939, the Hungarian government consented, however, to the creation of a "neutral" zone to be prohibited to any armed person on either side of the border line.

In February the Magyars unleashed an intensive propaganda for the annexation of Slovakia by Hungary. In certain regions of Slovakia they distributed tracts representing a kneeling Slovak praying to God for "the return" to Hungary and ending with: "Long live Horthy!"[21]

Before March 13, 1939, Berlin was faced with the following alternative in regard to the Slovak question: either Slovakia would declare its independence and become Germany's ally, or else it would refuse—an act which would be one reason for the Reich's leaving Hungary's hands free to reconquer the former territory of the crown of Saint-Stephen. Hitler never ceased plotting in Budapest. As early as February, 1938, Dr. Edmund Veesenmayer, who was later to become Minister Plenipotentiary of the Third Reich in Budapest, informed Slovak politicians that Hungary was considering March 15 to attack Slovak territory. He did not forget to add that only the Declaration of Independence could ward off Hungarian intervention.

Now Germany was to reckon with intangible factors—an inevitability in all politics.

Facing the uncertainty of the turn that events would take in Slovakia, Hitler let the Magyar government know before March 13 that the time had come to be prepared to realize their territorial aspirations in Slovakia. Among the documents of the Nuremberg trial there is a telegram from Horthy, filled with joy and gratitude for this suggestion:

---

[20] *Magyar Nemzet* (Budapest: January 1, 1939).
[21] Johann Oscar Petreas, *Die Slowakei im Umbruch* (Turčiansky Sv. Martin: 1941), p. 136.

Your Excellency—my sincere thanks. I can hardly tell you how happy I am because this Head Water Region[22]— I dislike using big words—is of vital importance to the life of Hungary. In spite of the fact that our recruits have only been serving for five weeks, we are going into this affair with eager enthusiasm. The dispositions have already been made. On Thursday, the 16th of this month, a frontier incident will take place which will be followed by the big blow on Saturday. I shall never forget this proof of friendship, and your Excellency may rely on my unshakable gratitude at all times. Your devoted friend: Horthy.[23]

The German-Czech Plots Against Slovakia—In spite of the constitutional reform, Czecho-Slovak relations grew worse after Munich. Slovakia bore with difficulty the loss, through the fault of Prague's policy, of nearly a million inhabitants and the fertile regions of the south. In another way, Prague frowned upon the progressive organization of Slovakia as a member-state of the Czecho-Slovako-Ruthenian Federation. When the government of Bratislava sent nine thousand Czech civil servants from Slovakia into Bohemia, the Czechs considered this act as a national affront and not as the reparation of an injustice.

All these circumstances could only increase the clashes which continued to occur between the two nations. A discourse that Mr. A. Mach pronounced at Rišňovce February 5, 1939, and in which he declared that Slovakia was on the way to complete independence, added more fuel to the fire. How could Mach's declaration be explained?

Munich's status quo, in spite of the guarantee of its four signers, was to appear to many European statesmen as provisory. Churchill expressed himself clearly on this subject. In the speech that he delivered on October 5, 1938 in the House of Commons, he said:

All is over. Silent, mournful, abandoned, broken, Czechoslovakia recedes into the darkness. . . . I venture to think that in the future the Czechoslovak State cannot be maintained as an independent entity. I think you will find that in a period of time, which may be measured by years, but may be measured only by months, Czechoslovakia will be engulfed in the nazi regime. . . .[24]

[22] Allegorical expression to designate Slovakia and Carpathian Ukraine.
[23] Peter de Mendelssohn, *The Nuremberg Documents, Some Aspects of German War Policy, 1939-45* (London: 1946), p. 97.
[24] MacKenzie, *Dr. Beneš,* p. 242.

As a matter of fact, with its frontiers unprotected and its lines of communication cut, it was no more than the caricature of an independent State. The Slovaks, too, realizing that the liquidation of what remained of Czechoslovakia was inevitable, fiercely objected to sharing the fate of Bohemia. Through their ambiguous policy during the preceding twenty years, the Czechs owed their misfortunes to themselves. The majority of the Slovak people, who had been practically excluded from the government for twenty years, felt free of all responsibility and went their own way. The Czechs, crushed by Munich and perfectly well aware of the fate that was in store for them, became hypersensitive and suspicious and could no longer control their fears on the subject of the political evolution of Slovakia. Nor did the events in Sub-Carpathian Ruthenia give them any satisfaction. That is why on March 6, Mr. Hacha, who had been elected President of the Republic on November 30, 1938, recalled Mr. Julian Révay, Minister of the Interior, and immediately constituted a new government with Monsignor Augustin Vološín (Prime Minister, Minister of Education and Justice), the Czech General Lev Prchala (Interior, Finance and Communications), and Mr. Kločurák (Economy).[25]

To this distrust was added a subtle play directed by Berlin which was going to interfere with Czecho-Slovak relations. In this way, for instance, did *Gauleiter* Bürckel put the government of Bratislava on guard against the Czechs, claiming that the latter were preparing an armed intervention in Slovakia to abolish its autonomous status.

However, on March 7, Mr. Seyss-Inquart, *Reichsstatthalter* of Vienna, informed Mr. Sidor in a private interview in Bratislava that Hitler had decided to intervene in Czecho-Slovakia. He indicated to him that the Slovaks could not get along except by setting up an independent State.[26]

Furthermore, Mr. Hencke, German Chargé d' Affaires in Prague, encouraged the Czechs to use a strong hand with respect to Slovakia. On March 9, 1939, he was formally requested by Berlin to "reveal" to the Czech governmental circles a conspiracy being formed in Bratislava which would aim at the proclamation of independence.[27] The Prague government naturally nibbled at the bait.

[25] See: Ripka, *Munich: Before and After,* p. 364.
[26] See: *The Slovak Republic [A Symposium]* (Scranton, Pa.: 1949), p. 46.
[27] Germany's game was clearly proved during the collaboration proceedings

The Czech Coup d'Etat in Slovakia—The evening of March 9, 1939, the President of the Republic, Mr. Hácha, proceeded to the dissolution of the Slovak government of Monsignor Tiso and deputized two members, Messrs. Sivák and Teplánsky, to carry on. At the same time, the Czech Generals, Homola, Commander of the army corps of Banská Bystrica, and Vojta, Commander of the army corps of Bratislava, received orders to ensure security in Slovakia. They began by proclaiming marshal law in the country. During the day of March 10, they arrested several hundred Slovaks who were partisans of the federative regime. Monsignor Tiso was confined to a convent in Bratislava, while the others, including Minister Černák and Mr. Tuka, were taken to Moravia by the police and Czech tactical units and shut up at Brno in the Spielberg prison, celebrated by Silvio Pellico's stay there in Metternich's days. Others were incarcerated in the military prison at Olomouc and at Blansko.

The Prague radio announced on the morning of March 10: "Anyone who tells you that the German Reich wishes to separate Slovakia from the Czecho-Slovak State is a lying adventurer." Mr. Ripka later acknowledged:

> These words were not chosen for a propagandist purpose, but accorded with the opinion of the Prague government. It can be readily understood that before deciding upon its intervention in Slovakia, Prague had endeavored to ascertain the attitude of Berlin. From the replies made by the German Chargé d' Affaires in Prague, the Czech government assumed that Berlin regarded the whole dispute with the Slovak government as "an internal matter" of Czecho-Slovakia and that it had no objections to the measures which Prague proposed to adopt against the Slovak separatists.[28]

Sir Neville Henderson, then Ambassador of Great Britain in Berlin, had to acknowledge as a good observer that the Czech politicians:

brought against the members of the Protectorate government of Bohemia and Moravia in Prague, where Mr. Kalfus, former Minister of Finance, and Mr. Masarík, former head of the cabinet of the Minister of Foreign Affairs in Prague, testified to this effect, January 22-24, 1947. Even at Monsignor Tiso's trial in Bratislava, the attorney, J. Šujan, in the bill of indictment that he pronounced on March 13, 1947, had to state: "In Prague, blind and credulous politicians received from the nazi conspirators false protestations according to which they would not oppose Czech military intervention in Slovakia."

[28] Ripka, *Munich: Before and After*, p. 366.

. . . were incredibly shortsighted and domineering in their treatment of the Slovaks. . . .[29] . . . On March 10, the Czech President dismissed the Slovak Prime Minister, Father Tiso, occupied Bratislava with Czech troops and gendarmerie, and forcibly installed another government there. . . . The chance was too good a one for Hitler's opportunism to let slide. . . .[30] My warnings to M. Mastny[31] that his government was playing Hitler's game for him and that its folly would end in disaster . . . fell on deaf ears. . . . The Czech government persisted in its obstinacy. . . .[32]

Mr. Sidor, Minister of State in Prague, having learned the news from the lips of President Hacha, returned to Bratislava the evening of March 10. The next day he learned that Mr. Hacha had just appointed him President of the new Slovak government. To avoid disorder and an anti-Czech rebellion, although he was bound up with Monsignor Tiso, he made it known by a a statement on the Bratislava radio that he was accepting this office.

In spite of officious German interventions in Bratislava, "as late as March 11, it was officially denied by Berlin that any hostile action was being prepared against Czecho-Slovakia."[33] That only encouraged the Czechs.

The following night *Reichsstatthalter* Seyss-Inquart, accompanied by *Gauleiter* Bürckel and Mr. Keppler of the Ministry of Foreign Affairs in Berlin, went to Mr. Sidor in Bratislava to tell him that the time had come to declare independence. "Certainly," replied Sidor, "independence is also in my program. But, as regards its preparation and the opportune time for its realization, I reserve myself absolute liberty."[34] Hitler's envoys had to leave without obtaining any results.

On Mr. Sidor's refusal, Hitler called Monsignor Tiso to Berlin the morning of March 13 to enlighten him on the international aspect of the Slovak problem in Central Europe. The Sidor government and the presidency of the Union National party thought it impossible for Monsignor Tito to refuse such an invitation. The latter went then to Berlin accompanied by Deputy Štefan Danihel; Minister Ďurčanský joined them in Vienna.

[29] Sir Neville Henderson, *Failure of a Mission: Berlin 1937-1939* (New York: 1940), p. 210.
[30] *Ibid.*, p. 209.
[31] The last minister plenipotentiary from Czecho-Slovakia to Berlin.
[32] Henderson, *Failure of a Mission,* pp. 210-11.
[33] Ripka, *Munich: Before and After*, p. 373.
[34] Čulen, *The Biography of Msgr. Tiso*, p. 233.

Monsignor Tiso in Berlin, March 13, 1939—In Berlin Monsignor Tiso first had an interview with von Ribbentrop, then with Hitler.

The Chancellery of the Reich drew up an official report of Monsignor Tiso's conversation with Hitler on March 13, 1939, which is recorded in the documents of the Nuremberg trial; its tenor is as follows:

> The Czechs, Hitler told Tiso, were violating the Munich Agreement and were behaving in a provocative manner intolerable to Germany. At Munich, Germany had solved the Czech question according to her *Weltanschauung*, but if this solution had not produced results, Germany had decided absolutely to pursue it to its conclusion, without consideration for this ideological principle. The attitude of Slovakia was also a disappointment to him. In the past year, the Führer had to face the difficult decision of whether or not to permit Hungary to occupy Slovakia. He had been under a wrong impression as he had of course believed that Slovakia wished to be annexed to Hungary. This error was caused by the fact that Slovakia was farther away from Germany and by the importance of the more serious problems which then overshadowed this question. It was only in the crisis that the Führer was dissuaded from this opinion. It was then that he first noted that Slovakia wished to conduct her own affairs.
>
> Now he had permitted Monsignor Tiso to come here in order to make his position clear in a very short time. Germany had no interests east of the Carpathian mountains. It was indifferent to him what happened there. The question was whether Slovakia wished to conduct her own affairs or not. He did not wish for anything from Slovakia. But he wanted to secure final confirmation as to what Slovakia really wanted. He did not wish that reproaches should come from Hungary that he was preserving something which did not wish to be preserved at all. He took a liberal view of unrest and demonstrations in general, but in this connection, unrest was only an outward indication of internal instability. He would not tolerate it and he had for that reason permitted Tiso to come in order to hear his decision. It was not a question of days but of hours. He had stated at the time that if Slovakia wished to make herself independent, he would support this endeavor and even guarantee it. He would stand by his word as long as Slovakia made it clear that she desired independence. If she hesitated or did not wish to dissolve her connection with Prague, he would leave the destiny of Slovakia to the mercy of events for which he was no longer responsible.

Hitler then asked Ribbentrop whether he had anything
to add, and Ribbentrop repeated that a decision must be
made within hours and not days. He showed the Führer
a message he had just received which reported Hungarian
troop movements on the Slovak frontiers.[35] The Führer
read this report, mentioned it to Tiso and expressed the
hope that Slovakia would soon make her decision.[36]

Monsignor Tiso found himself in a very difficult situation.
The German statesmen wanted him to proclaim Slovakia's independence at once on the Berlin radio. A Slovak text already
prepared had been put into his hands. He categorically refused
this solution. In order that Slovak independence should not later
be considered the result of a personal convention between himself and Hitler, the decision had to be made by the Parliament
of Bratislava itself. By telephone from Berlin, Monsignor Tiso
therefore besought President Hacha to call the Slovak deputies
together for the next day in Bratislava. His request was granted.

The Declaration of Independence, March 14, 1939—According to the record of the meetings of the Bratislava Parliament,
Monsignor Tiso presented the following account, March 14,
1939:[37]

> Gentlemen, after the dramatic events which took place
> in Bratislava and Slovakia the nights of March 12 and 13,
> I was invited by the Chancellor of the Reich, Adolf Hitler,
> to go to Berlin. After receiving his invitation in the night,
> I went at once to Bratislava to consult some of my col-
> leagues there. During an interview with the important
> political persons who could be brought together hastily,
> it was decided that I should accept the invitation by
> reason of the seriousness of the interests at stake. In con-
> formance with this decision, I made my way to Berlin
> where I arrived Monday evening.[38]
>
> I am going to give you a very detailed report of this
> trip, dry, without recourse to any rhetoric, inspired by the
> sole desire to throw light on these historical events and
> all the factors which we have to take into consideration in
> our present deliberation.
>
> I was received in Berlin with all the honors due a sov-
> ereign of a free State. Immediately after my arrival, I was
> given an audience by the Reich's Minister of Foreign Af-

---

[35] Mendelssohn, *The Nuremberg Documents*, pp. 97-98.
[36] Undoubtedly this concerns the telegram that Mr. Horthy, Regent of
Hungary, sent on the subject of Slovakia, March 13, to Hitler. See
above, p. 77.
[37] Čulen, *Biography of Msgr. Tiso*, pp. 237-43.
[38] Monsignor Tiso was accompanied by Minister F. Durčanský.

fairs Ribbentrop. According to the notes that I took on this conversation, I am going to attempt to reproduce it for you in broad outline as faithfully as possible.

The Minister of Foreign Affairs, Ribbentrop, connected our conversation to our discussions previously held in Munich and Vienna. He remarked at the same time that he was perfectly well aware that the arbitration of Vienna had left us with bitter memories and that in spite of all his good will the town of Košice had been taken from us to be given to the Magyars. But he noted that Germany had tried to do everything possible in Slovakia's interest and that it would have done still more if it had been better informed on the Slovak nation. "Unfortunately," continued Ribbentrop, "you were not known in the world, and we had only fragmentary information on you. I did what I could in relying on the most recent information gathered. I think that you will recognize yourselves that I tried to have a favorable attitude toward you. Some time has passed since then. We have again brought it to the attention of Minister Chvalkovský[39] that the spirit of Beneš continues to reign in Bohemia. We carefully explained to him what was impelling us to express ourselves in this way and we informed him that the Munich Accord had not been concluded so that Beneš' spirit should continue to live on and get the upper hand, but rather in the hope of seeing it disappear more and more definitely. We have to record three events that took place these days and that, like bewitched rocks, weigh inexorably on our present policy without our being able to put them aside.

"First of all it is the military dictatorship established in the Carpathian Ukraine[40] which proves that Beneš' spirit, that of the old regime, is not on its way out, but that on the contrary it is striving to strengthen its position. To this must be added the forceful stroke in Bratislava which proves that the old regime is again trying to take root, strengthening its foundations and turning its political power into account to realize the hopes in which it delights.

"To these two points we must still add the treatment inflicted on our minorities in Czech countries—a fact that we cannot ignore. This treatment is a proof that the old spirit is not dead, that it dominates, and that it has clung on to the hope that its day could very well dawn again.

"The Slovak government that has been named recently we do not recognize; we consider as legal only the government to which the Parliament gave its unanimous vote of confidence on February 23. Today still, it is the only legal

[39] Chvalkovský was Minister of Foreign Affairs of Czecho-Slovakia after Munich.
[40] March 6, 1939.

representative of the Slovak nation. The arrangement made by the President of the Republic was unconstitutional. Our jurists examined not only the constitution, but also the Act that has reference to delegation of full powers and they were convinced that the President of the Republic had no right to dissolve the government without a preliminary vote of the Diet refusing it its confidence. What happened afterwards during the military intervention fully proves that this former spirit is sufficiently strongly felt. Events were precipitated in accelerated rhythm, and we are not in a position to say what the result will be if the Slovaks do not state clearly and quickly enough that they are not identified with this regime and the Czech nation. I do not wish to be a prophet, but everyone can understand that, following events happening at such a rate of speed, you are going to find yourselves in exactly the same situation as in Munich. There you passed for 'Czechoslovaks' by reason of our ignorance on your score, because you were living in the same State and because we consider every state as a unit. We cannot make war on the one who holds the Slovak territory in its power. That does not concern us. It would not be our business to go drive out for you the one who would invade your territory. We know that the Slovaks are a peace-loving and hardworking nation. We find, and we have proof of it, that you want to live in peace with us and we are grateful to you for it."

After this statement, I ventured a remark by which I attempted to make a résumé of the deepest meaning of all these arguments. I mentioned a governmental declaration read in this same Diet on February 21, and I emphasized the fact that it was founded on the following idea: The Slovak nation is in the process of building its State, its new State, its Slovak State.[41] This is proof that the national idea is alive, that the Slovak consciousness is active, that it is organizing the administration of the State to testify to its wish to live in its own manner according to the ethnical principle which today is a problem of world interest. I stated next, concerning our life in common with the Czechs, what I had already asserted on several occasions to some Germans of consequence, that we would take no initiative to liquidate the Republic, but that we would seek the opportune moment for our separation if we once saw that the course of events was taking a more favorable turn for us.

Whereupon my interlocutor observed: "Why this hesitation?"

[41] Monsignor Tiso is speaking here of the Slovak State as a member of the Czecho-Slovako-Ruthenian Federation established November 19, 1938.

I remarked that it did not come from any lack in national feeling or lack of desire to have our own State, but from the fact that our population is not very well informed about events. Our people could not, so to speak, disregard the persons who would be at the origin of the Slovak State and the circumstances in which it would be created.

Our national community would bitterly resent the difficulties which would ensue from the beginning and would not fail to reproach us for being the cause. On the other hand, if our people see that events are taking place in such fashion that we have only one single way out, that of independence, each Slovak will then accept it as an inevitable thing. Having grown wise by the evolution, he will even be able to consent to certain sacrifices, because he will know that he had no choice.

Ribbentrop replied that he understood this point of view. After which we were taken to the Chancellor of the Reich, Adolf Hitler, in the new rooms of the Chancellery, where the usual military honors were extended us. Besides my colleague Ďurčanský and myself, two generals and two diplomats were present at this audience.

The Chancellor opened the conversation in these terms: "I took the liberty of asking you to come to see me in order to talk to you and clear up the situation." After this introduction, he evoked the events of October in these words: "I have solved the problem which claimed attention at that time in the hope that our kind and loyal conduct vis-à-vis the Czechs would make them change their system in the territories which were left to them and that we would have respectively no bitter experience. Our hopes have not been realized. We are today in the presence of new experiences and complications which are not solely limited to our neighborly relations, but which have repercussions in the whole world. We have neither spilled blood nor assimilated foreigners, and we shall not permit bloodshed in the future. The German people have their *Wirtschaftsraum,* in which no one can set an obstacle. However, I must say that the Germans are being pushed around in the Czech countries where grows the hope for a turn in events and the reestablishment of the old regime. This hope is being reinforced and is often manifested in a vulgar manner. Problems are invented, plots are woven with foreign countries, and questions that are out of context in the present situation are raised with the sole purpose of stirring up hopes of a prospective change and a rapid return to the former state of things. In Europe we no longer need a firebrand for war. We can destroy it and we shall disperse it so that not a single trace of it will remain. In Prague there is only the question

of domination and many plans are made in this direction. This is the explanation of the events that took
place in Brno.[42] The Germans there say that they will no
longer suffer what the Czechs do to them. The Czechs in
turn call forth elements of disorder. There is always a constant seething there which threatens peace and order. Europe itself is menaced by it, and I, for one, do not permit
Europe's peace to be threatened. I am disappointed not
only in the Czechs, but also in the Slovaks. I must admit
that I did not know this problem in the former Republic. I
was not concerned with it. Only our representative from
Vienna explained it a bit, and it is on the basis of these explanations that I was convinced that the Slovak nation
wants to live, that it is carrying on a national struggle. That
is why, in spite of this incomplete information, I resolved to
undertake its defense. Otherwise, things would have happened differently as far as you are concerned. Because of
you the Magyars have become my enemies. I said to them:
'You can utter no claim on the Slovaks or the land which
they inhabit except in the case where they would manifest by a plebiscite their wish to belong to Hungary. Since
they want to have a life of their own and since they are
making statements of this sort, you can have no claim on
them.' The Magyar lords got angry, and I, pursuing the
same principle, see that even in Bratislava it is always the
old spirit that rules. The recently established government
is a proof of it. We do not want the Slovaks, but we shall
not help them if they themselves do not show sufficiently
that they want to live an independent life, with all the
consequences pertaining thereto. I shall be wary in the future of saying to the Magyars that Slovakia does not concern them, and that I am interested in its defense."

I realized that that is where the knot of the problem
is and that there is where the danger lies. Then Hitler read
me a report according to which the Magyars plan to occupy the Slovak territory in the days to come. A definite
position must be adopted regarding that.

"But *blitzschnell!*" (with lightning speed!) added Hitler.
"It must be proclaimed that the Slovak nation has its own
State, its own territory, and that anybody will be prevented from invading Slovak territory and subjugating its
inhabitants. There is no time to lose. It is not a question
of days, but of hours. That is why we want to solve, and
we will solve this question *blitzschnell*, as German interests demand in Europe. I do not want to make myself anyone's enemy. Henceforth I shall defend only my own according to ethnical principles. But whoever wants to live
according to his national character falls under the protec-

---

[42] Violent frays between Germans and Czechs had taken place in this city.

tion of this principle. After all it is on this point that you must decide *blitzschnell* as I have already said."

After this exposition made by Monsignor Tiso behind closed doors, the fifty-seven deputies from the Slovak Parliament voted unanimously for independence.

Three-quarters of an hour later the same Parliament voted the following law:

Article 1. The Slovak land declared itself an independent State. The Diet of the Slovak land is transformed into a Parliament of the Slovak State.

Article 2. Until the adoption of the Constitution of the Slovak State, the executive power is entrusted to the government named by the Presidency of the Parliament.

Article 3. All the laws, decrees and dispositions valid up to the present continue in force with the changes resulting from the fact of the existence of the independent Slovak State.

Article 4. By means of decrees, the government is instructed to take all measures necessary for the maintenance of order and the protection of the interests of the Slovak State.

Article 5. This law goes into effect this very day and it devolves upon the government to enforce it.

The following persons comprised the government which was afterward named by the Presidency of the Parliament: the Prime Minister, Dr. Jozef Tiso; Vice-Premier, Dr. Vojtech Tuka; Foreign Affairs, Dr. Ferdinand Ďurčanský, Interior, Karol Sidor; National Defense, Lieutenant-Colonel Ferdinand Čatloš; Public Education, Jozef Sivák; Economy, Dr. Gejza Medrický; Finance, Dr. Mikuláš Pružinský; Communications and Public Works, Julius Stano; Justice, Dr. Gejza Fritz.

By vote of the law quoted above, did the Slovak Parliament, born of the Czecho-Slovak electoral system, violate "European solidarity?"

In European politics between the two World Wars there was no moral principle whatsoever. The often contradictory interests of the Great Powers were by far predominant. At that time the West did not hesitate to collaborate closely with Mr. Beneš, organizer of a padded totalitarian regime in Czecho-Slovakia, or with King Alexander, the dictator of Yugoslavia; nor did it hesitate in establishing relations with Mussolini, Stalin, and Hitler. In the eyes of the Slovaks, Croates, Slovenes, Ukrainians, Bielorussians, and Armenians, this attitude of the Western Pow-

ers actually compromised the very idea of democracy, Dominique
Changeur said:

> In 1938, Slovakia had chosen its moment badly. But
> by what right could the great democracies reproach a
> people for this error, a people whose very existence had
> been denied? In the name of what peace? In the name of
> what liberty? In the name of what intangible principles?[43]

Hurled from the top of Taygetus by the democracies in times
of peace, the Slovaks could do nothing but choose their own
road in order to safeguard their existence at the time of the international crisis of 1938-39.

It remains to be seen therefore if Slovakia, in its separation
from Czechia, contributed to the strengthening of Germany's
military position. The answer can only be in the negative, for the
pure and simple occupation of Czecho-Slovakia by Germany
would have been infinitely preferable to Hitler. Indeed, he would
have had at his disposal a corridor through Slovakia and Sub-
Carpathian Ruthenia uninterrupted as far as Rumania. This
would have facilitated his immediate seizure of Hungary and
assured a formidable operations base to eastern Europe. As it
was, with Slovakia independent, the political and economic frontier of the Third Reich stopped sixty kilometers from Vienna.

The Reactions of the West in Face of the Events in Slovakia—
It is known that the signers of the Munich Agreement had become the guarantors of Czecho-Slovakia's integrity. This guarantee was to become operative, according to the government of
London, only ". . . in the event . . . of an act of unprovoked aggression. . . ."[44]

On March 13, 1939, in the House of Commons, Mr. Atlee put
the following question to Mr. Chamberlain, British Prime Minister:

> Is it proved that certain influences came to light in
> view of the separation of Slovakia from the rest of Czecho-
> Slovakia; and is our government obliged, in conformity
> with the guarantees that it gave by the Munich Agreement,
> to become directly interested in everything that concerns
> the inviolability of the rest of the Czecho-Slovak State?

Mr. Chamberlain replied: "Without full information I should
not like to pronounce any opinion on the first point of the ques-

[43] "Qu'est-ce que la Slovaquie?" in *Sources* Paris, (November, 1950).
[44] Churchill, *The Gathering Storm*, p. 343.

tion. Supposing that the case does come up, it will not draw us into applying the guarantee."

This attitude of London was confirmed by the German Ambassador in Great Britain, Mr. Dirksen, in the report that he sent to Berlin:

> When about March 12, the conflict broke out between Czechia and Slovakia—following a change of cabinet provoked by Prague in Slovakia—the English press did not show a very keen interest in the events. The secession of Slovakia was calmly received in its turn; the press declared almost unanimously that these events did not concern Great Britain.[45]

On March 15, 1939, Mr. Chamberlain, in announcing to the Commons Germany's occupation of Czechia, stated that this event did not establish a case necessitating the application of the guarantee given in Munich to Czecho-Slovakia:

> That remained our position (the obligation to keep the guarantee) until yesterday. But the position has altered since the Slovak Diet declared the independence of Slovakia. The effect of this declaration put an end by internal disruption to the State whose frontiers we had proposed to guarantee, and His Majesty's government cannot accordingly hold themselves bound by this obligation.[46]

There is a document proving that the United States itself did not consider that the situation created by the birth of the Slovak State was contrary to law. It is the letter in which President F. D. Roosevelt replied to Mr. Beneš' telegram of March 16, 1939, protesting in the name "of the Czecho-Slovak people" Germany's violation of Czecho-Slovakia's integrity.

Mr. Roosevelt's reply to Beneš, dated March 27, 1939, follows:[47]

> I have received your telegram of March 16th, 1939, regarding the tragic events of last week in Central Europe. I have followed these happenings with deep concern. While the Government of the United States has observed that the provinces of Bohemia and Moravia have been occupied by German military authorities and are now under the de facto administration of German authorities, it has not recognized the legal status of that situation. I need hardly add that I deeply sympathize with the Czecho-

---

[45] *Ministère des Affaires Etrangères de l'URSS: Documents et Matériaux . . . de la Deuxième Guerre Mondiale*, II, 172.
[46] Churchill, *The Gathering Storm*, p. 343.
[47] Beneš, *Memoirs*, p. 102.

slovak people in the unfortunate circumstances in which for the time being they find themselves. Very sincerely yours, Franklin D. Roosevelt.

It is clear that President Roosevelt distinctly separated the case of Slovakia from that of the Czech countries.

Before entering the war, the United States therefore gave proof of its neutrality with respect to the Slovak Republic. The general attitude of the West was about the same. At the time of the breaking up of the political equilibrium of Europe, there was a general stampede.

As for the Czechs, their attitude toward the Slovak State was intolerant from the beginning. Offended and jealous, they reasoned as did the old envious farmer: "If my house burns, my neighbor has not the right to do what he can to save his own." Was it not Mr. Beneš who long before was disloyal to the idea of the Czecho-Slovak State as a common house where two Slav nations would dwell on an equal footing, and who had substituted for it "the idea of the Czech racist State"?[48] The Slovaks with their instinct of self-preservation, in striving to save what they could of their national patrimony, did what any other nation would have done in their place.

Recognition of the Slovak State—Slovakia was recognized first by its neighbors: Poland (March 15, 1939), Hungary (March 16, 1939), and Germany (March 16, 1939). Hungary and Poland thus showed that they preferred to see the Slovak territory neutralized rather than be part of a rival "Czechoslovak" State. The constitutive or allied countries of the Axis recognized it next: Italy (April 11, 1939), Japan (June 1, 1939), Manchukuo (June 1, 1939), Rumania (August 18, 1939), Bulgaria (November 16, 1939), Finland (July 25, 1940), Croatia and Nationalist China of Nanking (July 1, 1941).

Among the neutral countries, the following recognized Slovakia: The Holy See (March 25, 1939), Switzerland (April 19, 1939), Spain (April 25, 1939), Sweden (July 26, 1939), Lithuania (November 11, 1939), Estonia (April 11, 1940), Latvia (April 13, 1940), and Vichy France (April 25, 1942).

Slovakia was also recognized by a number of States that struggled against the powers of the Tripartite Pact and that later became members of the United Nations: Poland, Liberia (May 12, 1939), Ecuador (May 17, 1939), Costa Rica (May 24, 1939),

[48] Osuský, *Beneš and Slovakia*, p. 21.

Yugoslavia (June 8, 1939), the U.S.S.R. (September 16, 1939), and the Netherlands (April 15, 1940).

In every case it was a question of recognizing it *de jure.* An incomplete recognition, called *de facto,* was granted Slovakia by France (July 14, 1939), Belgium (July 14, 1939), and Great Britain (May 4, 1939).[49]

The letter that the British Consul of Bratislava, Mr. Pares, addressed on May 4, 1939, to the Slovak Minister of Foreign Affairs, Mr. Ďurčanský, was worded thus:

> Your Excellency: On the instruction of the Secretary of State for Foreign Affairs, I have the honor to inform you that His Majesty's government in the United Kingdom proposes to appoint me as Consul for Slovakia with residence at Bratislava.
>
> Pending preparation of my commission I have the honor to request provisional recognition by the Slovak government of myself as His Majesty's Consul for Slovakia.
>
> I avail myself of this opportunity to express to your Excellency the assurance of my highest consideration. Pares, M.P., H.M., Consul.

The United States of America never made any statement recognizing Slovakia even *de facto.*

However, it is probable that Slovakia's international juridical status would have been entirely consolidated if the war had not completely thrown the political situation into confusion in Europe. One indisputable fact remains: twenty-seven States, of which the majority prior to World War II, recognized the international personality of Slovakia.

The Constitution

The legislative body did not delay giving the country a constitution. It was voted unanimously on July 21, 1939. Its preamble began with the following declaration:

"Having been protected by Providence, the Slovak nation has maintained itself for centuries in the space which was reserved for it, and with the help of Almighty God it has organized into a free State."

The preamble next disclosed that the mission of the Slovak State was to unite, in conformity with natural law, all the moral

[49] These facts are taken from the *Aide-Mémoire sur l'existence de la République Slovaque et sur la nécessité de conclure le Traité de Paix avec elle.* (Paris: 1946), pp. 14-15.

and economic forces of the people into a Christian and national community. In this community the State was to reduce social divergencies as much as possible, as well as oppose the interests of classes and groups. Executor of social justice and protector of the general well-being in harmonious oneness, it was, through its political and moral efforts, to attain to the highest degree of prosperity for the community and the citizen.

By virtue of this Constitution, Slovakia was a Republic. The center of gravity of the political power resided in the Parliament of eighty members elected for five years by universal suffrage, direct, equalitarian and by secret ballot. They enjoyed immunity from arrest. The Parliament elected the President, adopted the Constitution, had the power to vote or modify constitutional laws; it voted the budget, approved State expenses, ratified commercial agreements, declared war and signed the peace; it voted laws regarding money, public finances and taxes. Modifications of the extent and composition of national territory were likewise to be approved by Parliament. Laws were promulgated by the President and published in the official Collection of Laws. It was possible for every citizen, man or woman, of ethnical Slovak origin to participate in the life and constructive activity of the State through the intermediary of the National Unity party sprung from the resolution of Žilina of October 6, 1938.

The interests of the citizens of German nationality were represented by the German party and those of the citizens of Magyar nationality by the Magyar party. These two non-Slovak parties sent three deputies to Parliament.

At the head of the State there was a President elected for seven years and eligible for a second term. He appointed and suspended members of the government, as well as high officials, university professors, high-ranking officers and magistrates. He exercised the right of amnesty and grace, assumed the functions of Commander-in-Chief of the Army and possessed the right of suspensive veto against the legislative decisions of the Parliament. He could be condemned only for the crime of high treason by the Council of State after being accused by the Parliament.

This disposition alone bears sufficient proof that the Slovak Republic was not a dictatorship, since over the head of the chief of the State there was an organ of control, unheard of in a totalitarian regime. To be valid, the acts of the President had to be countersigned by the qualified minister.

The government was made up of nine members: the prime minister, the ministers of foreign affairs, interior, finance, national education, justice, economy, national defense, and communications. The government was dependent on the Parliament from the legislative point of view, but could make ordinances in order to complete certain laws; in case of urgency it could also issue decrees. The ordinances were to bear the signature of the head of the State and the majority of the members of the government.

The Council of State alone, besides qualifying as High Court of Justice, had the option of establishing the list of candidates for legislative elections or relieving a deputy from office. Like the deputies, its members enjoyed parliamentary immunity. They numbered twenty-seven: six were appointed by the President, and six were designated by the National Unity party; the German and Hungarian parties, as well as the various corporations, each had the right to appoint a member; finally, the head of the government and the Speaker of the Parliament were by law members of the Council of State.

The guilds of peasants, merchants and artisans, laborers in industry, employees of banks and insurance companies, members of liberal professions, and employees of public administrations were endowed, by virtue of a special law, with an organization conferring upon them the greatest autonomy.

The Constitution defined the fundamental rights and duties of citizens as protection of life, liberty, private property, the right of meeting, liberty of the press, liberty of opinion, protection of marriage, protection of work. It likewise specified the rights of ecclesiastical communities and non-Slovak nationalities, fixing rules determining nationality; in addition, the Constitution granted the citizens the right of association in political and intellectual matters.

The Slovak Constitution clearly set forth the fact that labor was protected and that the exploitation of socially weak classes was forbidden. Furthermore, the Slovak State, in principle, did not plan to interfere with private initiative nor with private capital, thus establishing a system of free economy. However, the task of the State in economic life was to exercise a regulative influence and watch over social balance. Social function was attributed to ownership in that the owner was "compelled to manage his property in conformity with general interest." The fundamental charter further stipulated that the class struggle and its violence were to give way to cooperation of all economic forces.

By reason of the fundamental principle of collaboration and harmony within the social body, the Constitution forbade strife between capital and labor and any trouble brought to the general organization of labor (Art. 87). In order to emphasize in a special way the ethical bases of economic life, it proclaimed the obligation to work (Art. 76).

To characterize this Constitution, it is fitting to add that it was founded on certain principles of the liberal State and on others of Christian democracy such as they had been defined by the encyclicals *Rerum novarum* (1890) and *Quadragesimo anno* (1931). It is from the latter that it borrowed the idea of syndical organization of workers.[50]

If one wishes to pronounce judgment on this Constitution, one can disregard neither the moment in which it was drawn up nor the principal currents of ideas that influenced its drafters. The time, through the political events then developing in Europe, foreshadowed the start of World War II. It was because of the atmosphere then prevailing that the political grouping born of the Žilina Agreement and known as the "National Unity party" could be sanctioned by the Constitution. It is obvious that, in this system which comprised three political parties (Slovak, Magyar and German), the Slovak party was to play a leading role. Although forming a coalition with respect to the German and Magyar minorities, it did not prevent its deputies from having complete voting liberty.

If according to the Constitution the power was vested in the Parliament, the war was soon going to modify this principle and establish a system in which the executive was clearly going to have the upper hand. It was incumbent on the Parliament to check the government and especially its head, in his inclination to exercise personal power.[51] One can affirm nonetheless that the regime of authority had become general in all the States drawn into the war. That was an evolution at once inevitable and regrettable that fate was not willing to spare Slovakia.

---

[50] See the article of Dr. Jan F. Gleiman: "The Spirit of the Slovak Constitution," *The Slovak Republic*, p. 120.

[51] "There was no opposition within the Parliament, but during the existence of the Slovak State there was a constant tension between the Parliament and the Executive Power." Konštantín Čulen: "The Parliament and the Government of the Slovak Republic," in *The Slovak Republic*, p. 120.

The Problem of Political Unity

The Jews—In the Hungarian regime, Slovakia had more than 4 per cent Jews, one of the highest percentages in Europe and surpassed only by Poland. This situation was explained by the favorable conditions that Slovakia offered the well-known business talents of the Jews.

The Jews profited by the liberal spirit of the Slovak people who before the war of 1914 had lived in the state of resignation. They took root in the cities and towns and became an important economic factor.

The rural districts were especially suitable to the activity of the small Jewish tradesmen who had come from Poland, Rumania, Lithuania, or the southern part of Hungary and rare were the towns that did not have their Israelite merchant. The innkeeper, butcher, grocer, and baker were most often Jews. They would open generous credits to the peasant and were able to make irresistibly attractive for him their *krčma*, worthy competitor of the pub. Eventually, the peasant perceived that he had "drunk" his property and had to sell it to pay his debts. Then the only road left open for him was that of emigration. Many of those who stayed in their village, with their material position and psychological resistance broken, remained at the mercy of the Magyar tribunals and tax collectors. Slovak literature found much inspiration in this dramatic theme and numerous celebrated novels and songs relate the progressive downfall of villagers too weak to resist the lure of the *krčma*.

The sons of Jewish families established in the country studied in the city and took up liberal professions. Whereas the Jewish tavernkeeper was powerful in the small town, the Jewish lawyer, doctor, banker, or wholesaler were influential in the city.

Under the Czecho-Slovak regime there was little change in their situation. Their attachment to the "reason of State" became still more narrow. Mr. Darras grasped the situation very well when he wrote:

> As to the Jews, very much attached up to 1918 to Budapest of which they were too often only informers in the Slovak rural areas, the anti-Semitism that developed in Hungary the day after the fall of Béla Kuhn contributed to making them very loyal citizens of the Republic.[52]

[52] M. Darras, "Onze ans de vie indépendante en Slovaquie." In the symposium, "La Tchécoslovaquie 1918-1930," p. 210, *Le Monde Slave* Paris, (May-June, 1930).

After helping the Magyars to realize their aims at domination in Slovakia, they did not hesitate to render the same service to the Czechs.[53]

Such was in a broad way the situation of the Jews at the end of the First Czecho-Slovak Republic. With a few exceptions they were privileged citizens in the country. Of 598 lawyers inscribed in the Bratislava Bar there were 291 Jews,[54] and of 2,000 students registered in the University of Bratislava, there were 600 Israelites.

In the 1930 census, out of 3,300,000 inhabitants, there were 136,737 belonging to the Hebrew religion in Slovakia. Following the territorial changes of 1938, this number fell to 87,487.[55]

From the beginning of the Slovak State, there was a tendency to limit to a certain degree the economic power of the Jews. Soon this moderate tendency, which aimed at opposing "any encouragement from the outside,"[56] was distorted by another one of Hitlerian inspiration. While the first was represented by Monsignor Tiso, the second found its protagonists in Tuka and Mach. In respect to the latter, Monsignor Tiso stated before the National Tribunal of Bratislava in 1947: "This current could be checked, it could be influenced, but it could not possibly be stopped."[57]

The first measure taken by the government on the Jewish question was decree No. 63 of April 20, 1939. It concerned the legal definition of the Israelites and the conditions for reviewing their nationality. According to the newspaper, Slovák, of March 13, 1940, Monsignor Tiso formulated the principle of the limitation of the role of the Jews in the life of Slovakia in the following manner:

> We give to the Jews the possibility of spreading their activity within the limits of the 4 per cent which they represent in our population. This is a very special method of procedure dictated by reason. It is not a question of

[53] It is interesting to note that many Jewish families modified their names to make them correspond with the political changes. For instance, under the Hungarian regime, a family bearing the name of Cohn adopted the Magyar spelling, Kuhn or Kunossy. After the fall of Austria-Hungary, the same family then chose the Slovak form, Kunosi. This name, still sounding foreign, was changed to Kunošík after the establishment of the "popular democracy" in 1945 in Bratislava.

[54] Fritz Rössler, Die Slowakei (Dresden: 1943), pp. 133-44.

[55] Census of December 31, 1938.

[56] Monsignor Tiso's statement to the Slovak Parliament, February 22, 1939. See: Dr. Jozef Tiso, Die Wahrheit über die Slovakei (Munich: 1948), p. 168.

[57] Ibid., p. 171.

imitation of foreign examples. . . . Within the limits of this 4 per cent, the Jews will be able to carry on their activity in the different professions, in the school system. . . .

The same principle was applied to Jewish property. It was not a question of thrusting the Jews from economic life, but of limiting quantitatively and qualitatively the property which they held. This limitation was to be realized by means of agreements between any Israelite owner of property or business and a Slovak who was going to become his co-owner. The former kept 49 per cent of his property and the new owner took 51 per cent. The Jew had the right to choose his associate, and the part that he lost had to be paid him.

New measures taken by the Tuka government unfortunately went further. It must be acknowledged that they were inspired by certain criteria from the Nuremberg laws on the Jews in Germany. It is nonetheless essential to note that the *Codex Judaicus* which resulted met such opposition in the Parliament of Bratislava that in order to enforce it the government had to have recourse to an executive measure. As a matter of fact, it was published on September 10, 1941, not in the form of a law whose vote had not yet been acquired, but as a decree-law.

For Monsignor Tiso the Jewish question naturally constituted a serious case of conscience. It did not, however, lead him to resign, for he knew that after his departure the Germans would impose on Slovakia a government which would be at their command. He therefore remained determined to attenuate the consequences of this decree as much as he could in practice. Indeed he made extensive use of a disposition of the *Codex Judaicus* which authorized the President to grant exceptions, and he applied it to 9,964 Jews carrying on economic activities, which, taking into account the members of their families, brought the number of those who benefited from it to 40,000 (about half of the Jews in Slovakia).

The policy of the Slovak government consisted at first only in limiting the disproportionate economic power of the Jews, while respecting their personal liberty. Afterward this policy was thrown out of gear by the Germans in a manner as ingenious as odious. In fact the Germans elaborated on the plan of a Jewish colony in eastern Europe, a sort of European "Birobidjan," a reconstituted Jewish fatherland somewhere on the frontier of Poland and Russia. At the order of Germany all the nations of Central Europe were to collaborate in the realization of this plan, according to

which they were made to believe that the Jews should work and
govern themselves on an autonomous territory. An agreement was
therefore concluded between the German government and that
of Bratislava, by which the former took the responsibility for the
personal security of the Jews who were going to be expatriated,
while the Slovak government paid to the German agency entrusted with the organization of the Jewish colony a sum of five
hundred Reichsmarks per person as transportation and establishment expenses. A total of a hundred million crowns was actually poured into Germany to this end.[58]

If these measures were revealed later as extremely deplorable
there is no doubt that even the extremist element of the government which was a party to the Jewish deal with Berlin was in
good faith and that no one at that time had the least idea of the
diabolical intentions of the Germans vis-à-vis the Jews thus assembled.

Concerning the most dramatic stage in the destiny of the
Israelites in Slovakia, we shall listen to the delegate of the International Committee of the Red Cross in Bratislava who observed
their life struggle in 1944 and 1945:

> Slovakia: Many thousands of Jews had been forced to
> leave the country and enlist in what was called "labour
> service," but which in fact seems to have led the greater
> number to the extermination camps. At the same time, a
> large proportion of the Jewish minority had permission to
> stay in the country, and at certain periods Slovakia was
> even looked upon as a comparative haven of refuge for
> Jews, especially those coming from Poland. Those who
> remained in Slovakia seem to have been in comparative
> safety until the end of August 1944, when a rising against
> the German forces took place. While it is true that the
> law of May 15, 1942, had brought about the internment
> of several thousand Jews, these people were held in camps
> where the conditions of food and lodging were tolerable,
> and where internees were allowed to do paid work on
> terms almost equal to those of the free labour market.[59]

[58] This figure was mentioned in the bill of indictment against Monsignor
Tiso by the prosecutor, A. Rašla. According to the statement of D.
Wisliceny, collaborator of A. Eichmann, made before the International
Tribunal in Nuremberg, the Slovak Government expatriated about
17,000 Jews in the spring 1942, and about 35,000 more in the summer
until September, 1942. See: *The Trial of the Major War Criminals*, III,
276-78, and XIII, 300. This makes a total of 52,000. The number of
60,000 mentioned by Eugen Kulischer in *The Displacement of Population in Europe* (Montreal: 1943), p. 114, seems to be exaggerated.
[59] *Report of the International Committee of the Red Cross on Its Activities*

The Catholic Episcopate in Slovakia as well as the Vatican were extremely preoccupied with the evolution of the Jewish question that Germany exerted itself in precipitating. A pastoral letter of protestation against the Jewish persecution, signed by seven bishops, was read from the pulpit in all the churches on March 22, 1943. The Vatican, for its part, through the intermediary of its diplomatic representative in Bratislava, Monsignor Giuseppe Burzio, as well as by the Minister Plenipotentiary of Slovakia to the Holy See, Karol Sidor, intervened with Monsignor Tiso with a view to moderating the extremists. The result was, according to the reporter of the International Committee of the Red Cross, that "in 1944, the Jewish community had managed to secure an almost complete suspension of forced emigration toward the territories under German control."

And the same reporter continues:

At the time of the rising, the interned Jews escaped from the camps; some returned home, and others took to the hills. The measures of repression which followed fell on the Jewish population as a whole. The German military authorities summoned the Slovak government to make wholesale arrests for the purpose of deporting the Jews to Germany. The order dated November 16, 1944, laid down that all Jews should be mustered in the camp of Sered, and to that end, that Jews living in the capital should previously be assembled, on November 20, in the Town Hall of Bratislava. On the same day, the delegate went to the Town Hall and noted that only about fifty Jews had obeyed the summons. The rest had gone into hiding, as the Slovak authorities had foreseen, either by fleeing to the country or concealing themselves in the town in the so-called "bunkers." In his concern over this situation, the President of the ICRC[60] wrote to the Head of the Slovak government asking him to put an end to the deportations. Monsignor Tiso received this letter on January 2, 1945, and answered at length on January 10. He recalled the fact that up to that time the Jews had been spared, adding, however, that in view of the rising, his government had been forced to yield to the pressure which had been brought to bear upon them. He concluded by saying: "To sum up, it remains wholly true that in the solution of the Jewish question, we have endeavoured to remain faithful to humane principles to the full extent of our powers." Official aid to the fugitives in the "bunkers" was out of the

During the Second World War (September 11, 1939-June 30, 1947) (Geneva: 1948), I, 645-46.
[60] Dr. Max Huber.

question; the delegation in Bratislava, however, with the
help of the Slovak Red Cross and, in the provinces with
that of the Catholic Church, succeeded in providing them
with funds,[61] which were handed to their spokesmen and
which allowed them to support life during the last months
of the war.[62]

The ICRC delegate further acknowledged that the national
governments of Central Europe spared the Jews as much as they
could. He wrote:

> [In Hungary], as in Slovakia, the Jews were relatively
> spared, in so far as the local government retained a cer-
> tain freedom of action. But when German pressure was
> reasserted, from March 1944 onward, the position of the
> Jews became critical.[63]

In Slovakia it was the uprising provoked by the Russian partisans which had the most disastrous repercussions on the Jews.
From the hands of the Slovak authorities, their fate passed into
the Gestapo's. Even at that time the dispossessed government
aided the Jews as best it could.

The same report went on, "Even in 1944, the ICRC representative in Slovakia was still able to buy foodstuffs, principally sugar,
that he had sent to his colleague in Vienna for the Jewish population."[64]

The report also acknowledged a little farther on: "The delegate to Bratislava contributed to this work by buying foodstuffs
in Bratislava, particularly sugar, which he sent to Hungary. These
supplies were deposited in warehouses and put at the disposal of
the *Judenbüro*."[65]

It is very obvious that the Slovak government knew of these
purchases as well as their destination. In authorizing these exportations, it contributed as it could to the relief of the Jews.

Before the national Tribunal of Bratislava, Monsignor Tiso
declared on the subject of the Jewish question:

> I am persuaded that the accusation has no piece in its
> hands to prove that I took the initiative in the events
> which have taken place or that I even approved or aided
> them in any manner. I am responsible, for my part, only
> for what it was strictly impossible for me to avoid.

[61] These sums came from the Joint American Distribution Committee.
[62] *Report of the International Committee of the Red Cross*, I, 646-47.
[63] *Ibid.*, I, 647.
[64] *Ibid.*, III, 409.
[65] *Ibid.*, III, 523.

Unfortunately, the fate of many Jews from Slovakia, in Hitler's concentration camps, was the same as that of millions of other Jews. All these sacrificed human beings make one more appeal to the world's conscience for a universal solution. Only world order solidly established will be able to prevent the recurrence of similar events which are a disgrace to all humanity.

Protestants—It is an undisputed fact that Catholicism was the predominant ideology of the Slovak State. The Protestants were in no wise shut out from public life, however. So it was that General Čatloš, a Lutheran, was a part of the government and that Parliament had five Protestants: Messrs. Peter Zaťko, Miloš Vančo, Emil B. Lukáč, M. Morháč and Ján Líška. In religious matters the State practiced a policy of equality. The Protestant clergy, schools, and institutions were treated in the same manner as their Catholic counterparts. Furthermore, the Protestants were able to keep all the privileged positions which by reason of their political intimacy with the government of Prague they had acquired in Slovak economy during the course of the First Czecho-Slovak Republic.

The Protestants' political loyalty to the Slovak State left no room for doubt at first. The Synod of the Slovak Lutheran Church which met on March 2, 1940 at Tatranská Lomnica to proclaim a new constitution for its religious community did not hesitate to make this act of loyalty in the introduction:

> Faithful to the tradition of our religious beliefs as well as to our country, we have taken into consideration the present needs of the Protestant Church, the nation and the Slovak Republic that we wish to serve even in the future in the spirit of our historical individuality, without moreover losing sight of our great final goal which is the building of the Kingdom of God on earth, in the hearts of men, in the family, in the Church and in Humanity.
>
> We therefore put our activity into the service of the glory of God, the strengthening of the Church, the happiness of the nation and the Slovak Republic, for which we implore a bountiful and supreme divine blessing.

Yet as the situation became more difficult and as the chances of the Slovak State were reduced, wedged as it was between Germany which was about to be conquered and Russia which was elated over a victory that was never nearer, the political particularism of the Protestants got the upper hand, and the old problem existing in the national body since the fifteenth century again made its appearance.

As a matter of fact, Protestantism, now representing 13.5 per cent of Slovakia's population, is a Czech, or in a lower degree, a German importation. It means also a distinct cultural pattern. It appeared in Slovakia for the first time in the fifteenth century during the Hussite wars. Later on, in the seventeenth century, after the famous defeat on White Mountain, a second wave of Czech Protestants settled in Slovakia. It is not without interest to quote what Bohuslav Tablic (1769-1832), a prominent Slovak Protestant, wrote about the Czech religious immigration in Slovakia:

> When in 1620, after that fatal battle on the White Mountain, there was a large emigration among the Czechs for religious reasons, more than thirty thousand of those emigrants, Czechs and Moravians, found refuge in Hungary and Poland. They settled in scattered farming groups among the Slovaks in Nitra county, so that they could take care of their abandoned belongings or visit their friends, or once the storm of persecution was over, simply return home with all their furnishings. However, when they lost hope of turning back into their fatherland, and having in the meantime bought settling places, land, pastures, and other grounds, they found security under the protection of big landowners on the settlements of Myjava, Vrbové, Lubina, Stará Turá, etc.[66]

And even though after a certain time those settlers adopted the Slovak language in every day life, they did not manage to get rid of their nostalgia for their origin and cultural background; they retained Czech as the language of their religious services. The Magyar historian, André de Hevesy, explains this in these terms:

> When the Hussites of Bohemia introduced Protestantism to the people of Upper Hungary, the Protestant Slovaks adopted Czech as the ecclesiastical language. Too, in these regions, the Protestants favored the study of Czech, while the clergy and Catholic aristocracy early encouraged the language of the people, Slovak.[67]

As long as Catholics and Protestants suffered together under Magyar domination no serious problem came up between them. There has never been religious friction or intolerance among them on the properly Slovak national level. It even seems that in

[66] Quoted in: *Opinions about the Necessity of a Common Literary Language for Czechs, Moravians, and Slovaks* (Prague: 1846), p. 102.
[67] André de Hevesy, *L'Agonie d'un Empire: l'Autriche-Hongrie* (Paris: 1923), p. 39.

the second half of the nineteenth century, national consciousness asserted itself equally among the Protestants as well as Catholics owing especially to the work of Protestants as eminent as L'udovít Štúr, Karol Kuzmány, and Štefan Marko Daxner, who were at that time the great interpreters of the Slovak national idea.

Then at the turn of the century a distinct easing up was shown in this respect within a group of Slovak Protestant intellectuals. Having studied in Prague, these latter came under the influence of Professor Masaryk's "realism." Instead of encouraging them in the struggle for national rights against Magyar imperialism, he suggested the idea of saving the Slovak people from Magyar absorption by drowning them in the Czech sea. In short, it was to serve the "progressist" idea that "hlasism"[68] cropped up in 1898, a Protestant opportunist tendency which flaunted discreetly as its program "Czechoslovak" cultural and political union, becoming by this fact what could be compared to a Czech fifth column in Slovakia. Far from constituting a serious literary or political movement, this tendency was in reality only a local manifestation of the spiritual decadence of its epoch, some sort of "fin de siècle" spirit.

As a matter of fact the eternal criterion of political ontology is defined in the terse sentence of Spinoza: *Unaquaeque res, quatenus in se est, in suo esse perseverare conatur.*[69] The Slovak Protestant circles were altogether weary of leading the painful existence that reigned in Slovakia, so that, according to the pragmatic rule which brands them in history, they preferred to throw the helve after the hatchet. Someone has said that "an intellectual is a man whose civic virtues are inversely proportionate to his schooling." Never was this definition truer than in the case of the "Hlasists." They called themselves realists, when they were only defeatists. Faced with the alternatives of the struggle against the Magyars or national suicide, they chose the latter.

From the standpoint of political ethics, such an act constitutes desertion. In abandoning the Slovak nation in its century-old effort to persevere in *suo esse*, in its will to live, and in adopting the idea of national and linguistic unity with the Czechs, they separated themselves from the ensemble of the nation morally; biologically the "Hlasists" became dead weight, a foreign body to the interior of the nation.

[68] See note 11 of the Introduction.
[69] Everything, as far as it exists in itself, strives to persevere in its being.

It is therefore that "hlasism" and its protagonists that Mr. Beneš strove to sell Slovakia his centralist conception of the "Czechoslovak" State:

> Slovakia received religious reform from the Czech countries: Lutheranism, which expanded greatly completely adopted Czech religious literature, the Bible, hymns, religious polemics and theological literature. . . . This evangelical tradition has lasted until today and must be considered one of the strongest elements that have preserved throughout the centuries the bond of national unity between the Czechs and Slovaks.[70]

The memory of the Kralice Bible (1579) and the Slovak Protestant minority constituted, according to Mr. Beneš, a political force sufficient to maintain in the twentieth century the unity of Protestant-minded Czechia and the deeply Catholic Slovaks. Mr. Beneš, a politician of the "realistic" school, thus claimed to effect "Czechoslovak" union in leading Slovakia against the will of the overwhelming majority of its population, that is by the ear and not by the hand.

The historical fault of the Slovak Protestants was to fall in spiritually with Mr. Beneš' futile and undemocratic policy. Can this attitude be explained?

It is obvious that, in a system which would have considered Slovakia as a member-State of a Czecho-Slovak federation, the influence of Slovak Protestants would have been reduced to its fair proportion by the democratic way of elections. It happens that they had ambitions that far surpassed their numerical percentage. Practicing more a policy of complaisance vis-à-vis the Czechs than a properly called Slovak policy, many Protestants desirous of gaining or preserving their predominant position in Slovakia as well as their participation in the Prague government, were always ready to compromise and finally abandon Slovakia to "Czechization"[71] and tolerate Prague's exploitation of its economy. For this reason the Protestants were for Prague a hotbed from which were recruited members of government as well as high Slovak officials in Czecho-Slovak administration and diplomacy. Messrs. Milan Hodža, M. Ivan Markovič, Ivan Dérer, Juraj Slávik, Jozef Kállay, Metód Bella, Štefan Osuský, Ján Papánek, Vladimír Hurban, and others, can be pointed out as examples.

---

[70] Beneš, *Discours aux Slovaques*, p. 8.
[71] For Milan Hodža it was just merely a "linguistic integration." See the introduction to his book: *The Czecho-Slovak Schism*, p. 15.

These politicians and diplomats did not cease being in the government and high administration, while the majority of the Slovak people, except for 1927-1929, remained in the opposition for twenty years. It is their collaboration with Prague, which formed the most serious obstacle to a real understanding between Prague and Bratislava. They encouraged Mr. Beneš in his centralist policy, for if Slovakia had made up an electoral unit with political parties not dependent upon Prague, with a national Diet and government, it would have chosen its own representatives to the central government and would not have left it up to Mr. Beneš. The Slovak Protestant minority, the "Czechoslovaks," thus allowed Mr. Beneš to disfigure democracy greatly in actual practice.

Thus it is in purely opportunist reasons that we must seek the explanation of the support brought by Slovak Protestants to the idea of a "Czechoslovak" State. It was in no wise the desire to see the principles of a "democracy à la Masaryk" applied but the desire to be in power which led them to Prague.

The serious threat which hovered over the Slovak State during the second half of the war reawakened among the Protestants the memories of the power and political positions they had enjoyed in the First Czecho-Slovak Republic. So it seemed natural for them to change their attitude and bank again on their benefactor, E. Beneš, a refugee in London, by adopting the prospect of a third Czecho-Slovakia.

Several Slovak Protestants of note who had emigrated to western Europe during World War II collaborated in the realization of this plan. Among them were Milan Hodža, Štefan Osuský, Ján Papánek, Jan Lichner, Juraj Slávik, and others.

Communists—In Slovakia more than anywhere else communism is a foreign ideology, an imported article. Contrary to the spiritualistic mentality of the Slovak people, materialism did not succeed in taking root among them. In spite of its Slav mask, in 1935 it had found adhesion only with 13 per cent of the electors, many of whom were not Slovaks.

To the Slovaks, who carried on a desperate contest in the name of the national idea, it is obvious that the ideology of the international proletariat was to appear incompatible with their political efforts. Monsignor Tiso knew very well that in pitting the working class against the middle class, communism categorically denies the very essence of the nation. That is why one of the first acts of the Slovak government after October 6, 1938,

was, by reason of its obvious dependence on Moscow, to forbid
the Communist party as dangerous and contrary to the very principles of the Christian and national community. This measure
is explained much more by principles than by tactics. Far from
constituting an act of "totalitarian policy," it was an act of defense. In order to justify it, Monsignor Tiso made the following
statement on October 8, 1938:

> Our policy will not be socialistic, but social. We are
> not going to stir the people up against one another. Our
> education will lead them to harmony and mutual under-
> standing. The basis of our policy is work for all: work paid
> according to personal merit.[72]

By this very fact the Communists fell into illegality. The
Slovak State did not pursue them; nevertheless some of them left
the country for foreign parts. Mr. Clementis, for instance, left
(a fact which is rather curious) for London where in 1939 he
spent a certain time in prison. Only Mr. Široký and a much inspired Israelite, Mr. Frisch, went to Moscow. The other Slovak
Communists remained in the country: Mr. Kopasz together with
such intellectuals as Messrs. Husák, Novomeský, Poničan, Okáli,
and others. Especially after the Germano-Russian Pact, they ran
no risk whatsoever there.

It was only in 1942, when Hitler attacked his partner, Stalin,
that the Slovak Communists' position became complicated. The
Minister of Interior, Mr. Mach, a personal friend of Novomeský,
advised them at that time to remain quiet and to be extremely
cautious. Later, at the behest of the Germans, the supposed communist leaders, Široký and Ďuriš (whom the Russians had
dropped by parachute), were imprisoned so that they would
not be able to participate in any political activity at all. Thus it
was from the prison of Bratislava that Mr. Široký organized the
first cell of resistance to Monsignor Tiso's "fascist" regime, and
that he gave orders to his friends who, as Mach's political pro-
tégés, could discreetly get to work.

The Communists boast that from this moment Široký played
the role of veritable leader of the resistance in Slovakia and
prophet of events to come. At the beginning of June, 1942, he
is supposed to have sent from prison to his political friends secret
instructions thus expressed:

[72] See: *The Slovak Republic*, p. 147.

In the practical realization of the forms and methods of
the struggle for liberation (sabotage and guérilla warfare)
which must lead to the organization of a single front, we
can not lose sight of the fact that, following a plan stated
with clarity and penetration, this movement and this struggle will have to end in an uprising of the Slovak people.
This uprising, in depending upon the Russian war of liberation, must bring, in close liaison with the Red Army and
the other insurgent nations of Central Europe, a mortal
blow to German imperialism.[73]

If one admits that that is not a question of *vaticinatio ex
eventu,* one is in the presence of a prophecy worthy of assuring
its author the halo of political wisdom. And if the clandestine
activity of the prisoner Široký is authentic, it proves that the
regime of the political prisoners of the Slovak State was far from
being as rigorous as the Communists described it.

During this time the Slovak laborer knew nothing of communism. The State assured him of an open work market with the
rigors of the Sunday shift unheard of. He organized one of the
most perfect systems of social insurance. Paid holidays, family
allowances, a month's double pay for Christmas, a satisfactory
health service relying upon a chain of the most modern sana-
toriums and hospitals, almost unlimited supplies, and a sound
currency, contributed to making him forget the advantages promised to the proletarians of the Soviet paradise.

The best proof of the efficiency of the social system of the
Slovak Republic was that until 1944 no act of sabotage was committed on its territory. It was only toward the close of the war
and before the prospect of a victorious advance of the Russians
that minds got worked up. And it was this psychosis of an inevitable change that the Communists were able to exploit exten-
sively for their political ends.

The Cultural Restoration

Can one imagine anything more revolting for a nation in the
twentieth century than being, in the field of education, at the
mercy of a foreign nation? Such a situation constitutes one of
the most execrable forms of international feudalism.

The cultural development of Slovakia, stifled first by Budapest,
then by Prague, succeeded in springing fully into life only in the

[73] Edo Frisch, "The Attitude of the Allies with Respect to the Insurrection,"
Pravda, Bratislava, (August 24, 1949).

Slovak State. Its first task consisted in giving the country all the
schools that the foreign regimes had up to that time refused it:
a polytechnic school, a school of natural sciences, and a school
of economics. Little Slovakia, mutilated by the arbitrament of
Vienna, did not hesitate, in order to complete its school system,
to make important investments in the construction and equipment of numerous schools.

To obtain a better organization of intellectual work and
facilitate the publication of scientific and artistic works, Monsignor Tiso founded at Bratislava the Slovak Academy of Arts
and Sciences which was immediately endowed with considerable
financial means. It published many works and reviews in Slovak
as well as in French and German.

Hand in hand with this Academy, the *Matica slovenská* pursued and broadened its work. According to its former statutes, this
institution was destined to popularize culture and also the works
of Slovak writers. In the course of the Slovak State, it was granted
a publishing house which printed hundreds of thousands of
volumes every year and published several dozen scientific and
popular magazines each month. The *Matica slovenská* likewise
owned one of the most modern presses available; it also operated
a chain of bookstores in all the most important cities.

In the primary schools a great effort was made with a view
to modernizing the buildings and increasing their number. The
period of obligatory primary education was raised to eight years.
The Slovak State also had the task of making the teaching personnel and textbooks Slovak. For the first time in the history of
the country the schools had only Slovak teachers.

In secondary education the publication of new manuals permitted the exclusive use of Slovak texts.

As regards the Slovakization of the personnel for secondary
education, the results were the following from 1938 to 1944:

	Ethnical Origin of the Teaching Personnel	
	Slovak	Czech
October 1, 1938	345	523
June 30, 1939	512	256
December 31, 1939	668	122
December 31, 1940	680	73
December 31, 1941	713	38
December 31, 1942	700	26
March 1, 1944	728	25

Whereas there were only 24 Slovak professors at the University in 1938, the number rose to 46 in 1944.

During the Slovak State, young people found it possible to have a taste of higher education, as one can note from the statistics indicating the number of students registered annually:

	University	Polytechnical School	School of Economics
1938-1939 ...	1,763	68	0
1939-1940 ...	2,246	570	0
1940-1941 ...	2,702	853	263
1941-1942 ...	2,748	1,371	401
1942-1943 ...	3,294	1,444	653

During the same years the total number of students registered, including those in the Catholic and Protestant Schools of Theology, was 2,034, 2,969, 3,859, 4,555, and 5,432.

These results are all the more remarkable in that Slovakia lost more than a million inhabitants in 1938 following Munich.

In spite of the war, Slovakia strove to maintain intellectual liberty. Thus the Communist Novomeský could direct the *Budovateľ*, a "capitalist" economic weekly; and Mr. Trachta, the editor-in-chief of the *Národná obroda*, Bratislava Communist paper after 1945, was in charge of a paper in Berlin for the Slovak laborers working in Germany. Likewise the Communist poets, Poničan and Kostra, published poems of socialistic tendency, and the novelist Tatarka had his short stories printed in complete freedom in the most widely read magazines. A school of pro-Communist surrealists (Fábry, Žáry, Procháska, Krno, Reissel, Bunčák in Bratislava drew attention by the publication of progressist poems. The literary critics of the same tendency (Chorvát for example) wrote their articles freely in the magazine *Elán*.

In the bookstores it was possible to see *Mein Kampf* along side of the anti-Nazi Encyclical of Pope Pius XII, *Mit Brennender Sorge,* the latter in perfect Slovak translation.

The statistics on the works published in Slovakia from 1939 to 1941 are as follows: in 1939, 466; in 1940, 785; in 1941, 865.[74]

[74] These statistics are taken from the following works:
> Dr. Jozef Tiso, *Die Wahrheit über die Slovakei*, pp. 183-84.
> K. Čulen, *Czechs and Slovaks in the Administration of the Czecho-Slovak Republic,* pp. 164-81; and
> Anton Štefánek, *Zur Soziographie der geistigen Kultur in der Slowakei* (Bratislava: 1944), p. 414.

If one considers that in the Protectorate of Bohemia-Moravia the German government closed 70 per cent of the institutions of higher learning for the whole duration of the war and exercised an unduly severe censure on all manifestation of political and cultural life, one is obliged to acknowledge that the Slovak State was able to assure educational possibilities to its youth, and in its cultural life, development worthy of praise.

Economic Development

Could independence assure Slovakia its economic equilibrium? Did not this country which had for many long years been exploited by Prague run the risk, once it was free, of being exploited by Germany?

Certain projects of Goering clearly betray the German intentions in this respect. Among the Nuremberg documents there is the record of a conference that he had with his staff on October 14, 1938, on the planning of the economy. He says this about Slovakia:

> I count upon the complete industrial assimilation of Slovakia. Bohemia, Moravia and Slovakia will become German dominions. Everything possible must be taken out. The Oder-Danube Canal is to be speeded up. Search for oil and ore are to be conducted in Slovakia.[75]

It is thus at the threat of German interference that Slovak economy had to be organized.

In order to strengthen its influence in Slovakia, the Reich exerted strong pressure on the government of Bratislava with a view to having the Jews dispossessed of their goods which would be given into the hands of citizens belonging to the German ethnical group. With this in mind, the latter received large subsidies from the Secretariat of German Affairs. From the beginning this covetousness had to be thwarted.

Another manner in which Germany went about imposing its influence in Slovakia consisted in absorbing the capital from certain enterprises. Thus the *Hermann Goering Werke* brought the only important ironworks of the country, that of Podbrezová. Too, the copper mines of Krompachy were put back in a state of exploitation by means of German capital and were the object of important investments destined to modernize the equipment and plant; at Turany the Germans financed the most modern and the

75 Mendelssohn, *The Nuremberg Documents,* p. 91.

best equipped sawmill in Slovakia. They had the existing factories adapted to war production, such as the metallurgical ones of Dubnica and Považská Bystrica.

This interference did not impede the development of the Slovak economy, and a considerable increase could be noted not only in the production of armaments but also of articles of everyday consumption without relation to war needs.

The ascending tendency of industrial production is shown by the statistics of the Institute of Economic Research that was created within the National Bank of Slovakia. The index of industrial production compared with that of some other European States was the following from 1939 to 1942:[76]

	1939	1940	1941	1942
Slovakia	100	106	113	120
Bulgaria	100	112	118	112
Sweden	100	91	84	88
Denmark	100	81	77	77
Finland	100	40	42	44

During the first years serious difficulties had to be surmounted arising from the shortage of equipment and certain raw materials. This was possible owing to as much foreign trade with the neutral States as with the Axis countries. Slovakia exported wood, cellulose, paper, barley, cattle, alcohol, sugar, chemical products, electric bulbs, cable, bakelite articles, glass and silver ware. The exchanges contributed to the creation of new capital which permitted new investments. From 1939 to 1942, 122 enterprises were founded in Slovakia. They were divided among the different branches of industry in the following manner: the chemical industry, 34; textile industry, 16; food, 33; metallurgical, 2; wood, 7; paper, 4; glass, 5; leather, 3; construction materials, 9; others, 9.[77]

This tendency continued even in 1943 and 1944. It was blocked only by the acts of war which took place on the territory of Slovakia during the autumn of 1944.

The English publicist William Diamond describes the progress made in Slovak industry during the war:

Slovak's brief experience as an independent State had a salutary effect on its industry, which expanded in an effort to replace products once obtained from the factories

---

[76] Dr. Vojtech Krajčovič, "Der Anfang der Slowakischen Industrie im Sebständigen Staate," *Slowakische Rundschau* No. 7, (Bratislava: 1943).
[77] *Ibid.*

of the Czech lands and, under German pressure, to increase the output of armaments. The establishment of new
enterprises and the increase in the number of industrial
workers raised the importance of Slovak industry in the
country as a whole. The industrial capacity of Slovakia increased, particularly in metal and woodworking, mining,
textiles, footwear, and food processing.

In the period 1934-37, 91.5 per cent of the total industrial employment of the country occurred in the Czech
lands. In 1946, the Czech proportion dropped to about 84
per cent. Similarly, before the war 93 per cent of the total
value of Czechoslovak industrial production derived from
Bohemia and Moravia. At the end of 1946, their share had
dropped to almost 85 per cent.[78]

As regards public finances, it must be noted that after October
6, 1938, the government of Bratislava had to have recourse to a
public loan of 300 million crowns, "loan for the economic reconstruction of Slovakia." Opened on February 23, 1939, it was covered at once.

In the fiscal year of 1939, the State budget was balanced.
Slovakia's budget, which rose in 1940 to two billion crowns,
reached three billion in 1944. Every year it admitted of a considerable surplus, totalling in millions of crowns the following:
in 1939, 436; in 1940, 130; in 1941, 550; in 1942, 316; in 1943, 185.
In 1944, as a result of the war, public finances reported a deficit
of 54 million crowns.

Such good management of finances facilitated the work of
reconstruction, the scope of which must be emphasized. Slovakia
made enormous efforts and accomplished much in the domain of
public works. In the midst of war it constructed 26 miles of railroad;[79] for 67 miles it put a double track where there had been
only one line from Bratislava to Košice; it renewed completely
89 miles of railroad. In 1943, 54 miles of new lines and 65.5 miles
of double tracks were got under way; 144 miles of automobile
roads and 699 miles of tarred roads were constructed.

The telegraph and telephone system was increased by 6,116
miles of lines and the cable system by 165 miles. Post offices were
opened in 600 villages. Many other villages, isolated until that
time, were equipped with telephone booths.

The country made much progress in electrification too. While
in 1939 the villages with electricity numbered 775 (28.4 per cent),

[78] Diamond, *Czechoslovakia between East and West,* p. 172.
[79] The total railway system then measured 2,700 kilometers.

as early as January 1, 1944, that number reached 1,130 (42 per cent).

The harnessing of the rivers was the object of comparable concern; 124 miles of works were effected on the Váh between the Hungarian border and Žilina. Two important dams were built and two others were begun in 1943. A dam 88.56 feet high, which was not to be completed until ten years later and which was to be one of the largest in Europe, was begun on the upper Orava at the Polish border. The submerged surface specified 13.12 square miles and the dam was calculated to retain 398,940,000 cubic yards of water. The works necessitated the evacuation of six villages and 7,000 people.

During the four years 1939-1942, the Slovak State assigned two billion, 488 million crowns to public works; 10 per cent of the national revenue, a proportion which had never been attained under the preceding regimes, Magyar or Czech, were allotted to the betterment of industry.

A comparison of the economic and commercial structure of Slovakia with that of Germany and Hungary at that time brings out the global efforts of Slovak economy. In the light of statistics, Slovakia appears to be a more advanced country, having a better balanced economy than Hungary, for example.[80]

Economic structure:

	Agriculture and forestry	Industry and mines	Commerce and communications	Public services and liberal professions
Germany ...	27%	42%	17%	14%
Hungary ...	58%	19%	9%	14%
Slovakia ...	57%	20%	10%	13%

Structure of foreign trade:

	Heads of cattle		Foodstuffs		Raw Materials and semi-manufactured products		Finished products	
	Imp.	Exp.	Imp.	Exp.	Imp.	Exp.	Imp.	Exp.
Germany	3%	0%	29%	1%	57%	16%	11%	83%
Hungary	0%	13%	7%	44%	53%	12%	40%	31%
Slovakia	1%	5%	9%	10%	23%	38%	67%	47%

80 See: Hermann Gross, *Die Slowakei in der Grossraumwirtschaft Europas* (Bratislava: 1943), p. 4.

Finally comes the question of the "economic collaboration" of Slovakia with Germany. The Slovak State benefited the German war machine but little from the economic point and it affected less harmfully the Allies' interests than did the Protectorate of Bohemia-Moravia. Statistics express better than any commentary the degree of political liberty Slovakia enjoyed during the war as opposed to the Czech countries. Mr. Bohdan Chudoba, a Czech deputy exiled in the United States, has acknowledged that under Monsignor Tiso's government "Slovakia was able to save much of its products from the hands of the Nazis, whereas the whole industrial and agricultural production of Bohemia and Moravia served the Nazi war machine."[81]

Mr. Kamil Krofta, former Minister of Foreign Affairs for Czecho-Slovakia and a Czech historian, indicates in his work, *Czechoslovak History,* that 600,000 Czechs worked in Germany during the war, and that in Bohemia-Moravia an equal number served the war aims of Germany directly and 2,000,000 indirectly. He evaluated in crowns the Czech contribution to the German war with these figures:

1. Spoliations caused by German administration
   of the banks ....65 billion
2. Losses in industry and commerce...............38 billion
3. Losses in agriculture ....45 billion
4. Losses on communications ....25 billion
5. Contributions called matriculation.............42 billion
6. Confiscation of Jewish possessions ....30 billion
7. Arbitrary conversion of currency ....135 billion

In addition to these sums which total 380 billion crowns, Mr. Krofta estimates at 106 billion, 5 million crowns the damages which the Reich caused the economy or public property of the Protectorate.[82]

In comparison with these figures, the Slovak contribution to German economy was trivial. Mr. Alois Matura, a Czech professor of public finances at the University of Bratislava and an expert in economics, completely confirmed this before the National Tribunal at the time of the proceedings that were instituted in 1946 in Bratislava against a deputy of the Slovak State, Peter Zaťko. Mr. Matura stated that under the item of deliveries made into Germany, Slovak industry suffered losses amounting to one

[81] Bohdan Chudoba, "Czechoslovakia, A Study in Disintegration," *Thought* XXV, (March, 1950), 90.
[82] Kamil Krofta, *Czechoslovak History* (Prague: 1946), p. 845.

billion crowns during the war years, while Czech industry suffered losses of 38 billion 443 million; that the losses of the National Bank of Slovakia were two billion, 555 million, whereas those of the National Bank of the Protectorate were 235 billion crowns; that the administration of the Finances of Slovakia suffered a loss of two billion, 727 million by virtue of the financing of the German debt in the clearinghouse, while that of the Czech countries for the same reason was 60 billion. The total of all the losses for Slovakia mounted to a little more than six billion crowns, whereas for Bohemia and Moravia it reached 429 billion.[83]

According to evidence given at the same trial and at Monsignor Tiso's by Mr. Imrich Karvaš, former governor of the National Bank of Bratislava, Slovakia was able to resist the economic demands of the Reich more efficiently than any other neighboring state. Germany had to pay in gold or foreign currency for all the products that Slovakia furnished. The Slovak Republic's credit with the other states constantly increased. Thus, Czecho-Slovakia inherited large sums in the foreign currency which had been deposited by Mr. Karvaš in Moscow, Sweden, and Switzerland.

In spite of the war, the Slovak State enjoyed visible prosperity until the end of its existence, and the Slovak crown was held in high esteem in Zurich. Before taking refuge in Austria, the government had all the stock of foodstuffs distributed to the population, especially in the poorest regions of Kysuca and Orava; according to Mr. Matura's evaluation, this stock was greater than that of 1938. Every Slovak was at that time able to supply himself with hundreds of kilograms of sugar. On March 31, 1944, the civil servants and workmen received a three months' advance in salary.

In 1945, at the time of its liquidation, the National Bank of Slovakia deposited in the National Bank of Prague three-quarters of a billion crowns in gold and currency. This sum constituted, at the beginning of the Third Czecho-Slovak Republic, the new crown's only cover.

The Slovak State was able to raise its standard of living considerably in spite of the war and without having to limit the freedom of work.

[83] Tiso, *Die Wahrheit über die Slowakei,* p. 180.

The Foreign Policy

Germany—The broad lines of Slovakia's foreign policy were determined by its relations with Germany. The Reich was able to lead the natural aspirations of the Slovaks to independence, but it did not hesitate to exploit the situation thus created.

After the collapse of the Western political system in Central Europe, everything pointed to the evolution which was going to take place. So it is not the fact of German influence itself,[84] but rather the methods and forms that it took which were going to surprise the world in general and more particularly the nations that were to be the victims. The agreements and treaties that Germany concluded with several of these nations to align their foreign policy as long as peace should last, and to secure their military co-operation for a possible war, did not at all resemble what the Romans called *foedera aequa*. They were *foedera iniquua* in both the literal and figurative sense. Imperialistic Germany, once more in history, fell like a crushing block on all the little nations in its orbit, and the treaties which sanctioned the modalities of its preponderance accentuated the humiliation of the nations abandoned to their misfortune.

On March 15, 1939, when it instituted the "Protectorate of Bohemia and Moravia" at the very center of the European continent, Germany gave only a brutal expression of its desire for colonial domination. Once again it witnessed the absolute lack of psychological sense which constitutes one of the historical constants of its policy. In such a situation, a Latin would probably have made of Czechia an "associate state." Hitler felt the need of humiliating the Czechs and making them sign for their humiliation.

At bottom it is the same desire to humiliate the weakest that inspired the "Schutzvertrag" which was concluded between Germany and Slovakia on March 18 and 23, 1939. To understand better the signing of such a "treaty" by Slovakia, the alternative which it confronted at that time must be considered: either it had to become a State dependent on Germany for the questions of

---

[84] Mr. Coulondre, French Ambassador to Berlin, sent to the Quai d'Orsay, on December 15, 1938, a report whose conclusion was thus expressed: "The vassalization of Czecho-Slovakia is unfortunately already almost an accomplished fact." *Le Livre Jaune Français* (Paris: 1939), p. 45. At the same time, Mr. Ripka said in London: "After Munich no alternative was left open to the mutilated and disrupted State but to become the vassal of the German Reich." *Munich: Before and After*, p. 272.

foreign policy, or else be occupied by Hungary with the Reich's consent, as was the case with Sub-Carpathian Ruthenia.[85]

Informed by Ribbentrop at the time of his visit to Berlin the evening of March 13, 1939, of a movement of Hungarian troops to the Slovak frontier, Monsignor Tiso clearly saw the danger. On October 6, 1938, he had sought in vain an international guarantee for his country,[86] and no other means remained to insure Slovakia's existence except to obtain the pledge of Germany's formal responsibility. So he sent a telegram to Hitler on March 15, 1939. Ribbentrop's information unfortunately was exact and Tiso's fears justified. In fact, after occupying Sub-Carpathian Ruthenia, the Magyar Army attacked eastern Slovakia. It profited by the fact that the Slovak Army, completely disorganized by the departure and sabotage of the Czechs, was scarcely beginning to be formed again. The Magyars occupied the Sobrance district, and their air force killed many people during the bombardment of Spišská Nová Ves. The peasants of the whole of Slovakia hastily rejoined their regiments, determined to defend their country. The government of Bratislava sent a telegram and a note of protestation to Berlin. It is obvious that Ribbentrop had planned to put Slovakia in a precarious position from the very beginning and oblige its government to appeal to Germany. According to this pre-established plan, the Slovak representatives were called together for March 18, in Vienna, where Ribbentrop presented them with the famous *Schutzvertrag*.[87] Monsignor Tiso and Ďurčanský stubbornly opposed Ribbentrop's propositions. They would have accepted a treaty "between equals," but Hitler, desirous of playing the role of "builder of a new order" in Europe, had no intention of being satisfied with equality. He wanted to crush the strong and "protect" the weak. There was no choice. Monsignor Tiso had no alternative but to resign. Coming out from this meeting crestfallen, upset, assailed with questions from the reporters, he thought he was doing right in explaining to them: "It is not a protectorate that Germany is imposing on us! It is a guarantee it is giving us."

When German political science wanted to classify the *Schutzvertrag* from the juridical point of view, the following analysis was given:

[85] See p. 76.
[86] See the *Manifesto of Žilina*, p. 68.
[87] See Appendix IV.

Unlike what is happening to Bohemia and Moravia, the relationship of the Reich with Slovakia, which has declared itself a separate and independent State by virtue of the first article of the law voted by the Slovak Diet on March 14, falls purely under international law. It would be out of order to speak here even of an "international protectorate." One could speak of it if Slovakia, in addition to its protection, had entrusted to the Reich the management of its foreign affairs.[88] Such is not the case. In conformity with article 4 of the Germano-Slovak agreement of March 23, 1939, Slovakia was to direct its foreign policy in accordance with the Reich. The relationship of Germany and Slovakia belongs to the fundamental form of international law of friendship, to the *amicitia*, in the Roman sense of the word (Triepel). In the particular case where "friendship" is linked with a relationship of protection, some authors speak of "protection." Perhaps it would be better to say *Schutzfreundschaft*, that is "protective friendship," a term that was at times used in German political literature.[89]

The protagonist of German "friendship" and the peddler of the word *Schutzfreundschaft* in Slovakia was Tuka. Thus he represented an extremist tendency bringing together, aside from the Minister of Interior Mach, only a few persons of the political "outskirts of society" (Mutňanský, Striežnec, Murgaš). Moved by personal reasons, they attempted to take advantage of the weaknesses of their leader.

As for Tuka's attitude, it can be explained by his past experiences. In fact, Tuka had been condemned by the Czechs in 1929 to fifteen years' imprisonment for high treason, and he had actually served a term of nine years. The old man that he was then had lost physical and moral equilibrium, and the hatred that he felt for the Czechs pushed him into the arms of Germany.

Monsignor Tiso and the other members of the government were far from having any illusions about the exact position of

---

[88] On the definition of the protectorate, the opinion of the authors of international law is generally unanimous. Let us quote only that of L. Oppenheim: "The protectorate agreement is not to be confused with the protection agreement by which one or several States promise to protect a weak State without, however, absorbing the international relations of the latter." Quoted in *International Law* (5th ed.; New York: 1937), I, 168.

Such was the case of Slovakia in relation to Germany. Therefore it is astonishing that a work like the *Dictionnaire Diplomatique*, published by the Académie Diplomatique Internationale, mentions the Slovak Republic (IV, 1062), in obvious contempt of the facts, as a protectorate. It would be difficult to find an explanation for such reasoning if Mr. Beneš did not figure among the principal collaborators of this work.

[89] W. G. Grewe, "Protektorat und Schutzfreundschaft," *Monatshefte für Auswärtige Politik*, Vol. VI, Berlin, No. 4, (April, 1939).

Slovakia in Germany's orbit. Nor were they blind to the scope of the *Schutzvertrag,* an agreement which did not express their wishes. In fact, it was a matter of an imposed act, escaping from a strictly juridical evaluation and serving only to emphasize the presence and material preponderance of Germany in the Carpathian area. It was a political act par excellence. Dictated by the Germans with a view to a future war with Poland[90] or a European war, the *Schutzvertrag* however corresponded in Central Europe neither to a change in the balance of power after Munich nor to anything materially new whatsoever. The mere presence of Germany at its frontiers would have been just as difficult for Slovakia with or without the *Schutzvertrag.*

It is in this realistic manner that Monsignor Tiso looked upon Slovakia's new position. He resigned himself to his country's geopolitical imperative, while at the same time feeling as little dishonored by Slovakia's relations with Germany as a Lilliputian facing Gulliver. The problem is a millenarian one: that of power politics. As long as there is not a genuine world juridical system, the little nations will always have to bow before the great neighboring imperialisms. Slovakia was controlled by a formidable neighbor who profited by the absence of any system of international balance, and it is certainly not the national-socialist ideology which bound it to the Reich.

From the beginning, Monsignor Tiso constituted a precious counterbalance to Tuka's extremism. As head of the government, he strove with the Minister of Foreign Affairs Durčanský to keep the country out of the cold war raging in Europe as long as it did not change into actual war. Once he was elected President on October 26, his influence became preponderant. Since Germany recognized Slovakia as a State, Tiso thought it natural to act as the head of the State with respect to Germany. On September 3, 1939, when hostilities were opened between Germany and the West, Slovakia did not budge. Even during the war, Tiso meant to all intents and purposes to remain neutral. The *Schutzvertrag* was a treaty for protection, not for an alliance.

Friction did not fail to arise between the two poles represented by Tiso and Tuka. The German Minister at Bratislava, Bernard, was obviously on the side of Tuka who was devoured by the desire to seize power. Discontented by the spirit in which Monsignor Tiso was conducting the State, Bernard began to exploit

[90] See: Dr. Anton Rašla, *Tiso and the Uprising* (Bratislava: 1947), p. 71.

the ambitions of the old Tuka the better to connive against him, and he submitted the case to Berlin. Seeing in Tuka a sure means of increasing German influence in Slovakia, Hitler consented to put his stakes on him.

Thus it was that President Tiso, Prime Minister Tuka, Minister of Defense Čatloš, and also Mach, demoted chief of Hlinka's guard,[91] were invited to go to Salzburg, July 28, 1940.[92] Ďurčanský, whose name had not been mentioned, also went to Salzburg. "Den Zigeuner, den will ich nicht mehr sehen!"[93] cried Hitler on seeing him, and he reproached Monsignor Tiso violently on his account.[94] As Mr. Martin Sokol, President of the Slovak Parliament, was to explain in 1947 in his testimony before the National Tribunal of Bratislava during the Tiso trial, Hitler's anger against Ďurčanský stemmed from the fact that the latter conducted himself "as Minister of a sovereign State."[95] Hitler immediately proceeded to a recasting of the Slovak government. He insisted that Tuka combine the Ministry of Foreign Affairs with the office of Prime Minister. Mach became Minister of the Interior. Tuka's aspirations were in the process of being realized. Backed by Hitler, on his return he gathered Bratislava's population in front of the National Theater and from the balcony announced that he was inaugurating "the new era of Slovak national-socialism."

Then plots began to be woven about the person of Monsignor Tiso. The Germans desired to thrust him from power and replace him by Tuka. Their man of confidence, Karol Murgaš, who became director of the Propaganda Office, stated on August 21, 1940, to Deputy Čarnogurský:

> Tiso can no longer remain in the presidency. He must resign from office toward the end of November, 1940. If we cannot gain our ends in any other way, we shall present him with a death warrant to sign. It will be an insur-

[91] Hlinka's was a national guard destined to keep order within the country.
[92] See: Tiso, *Die Wahrheit über die Slowakei,* p. 41.
[93] "I do not wish to see this gypsy again!" Hitler was alluding to Ďurčanský's black hair and eyes.
[94] Čulen, *Biography of Msgr. Tiso,* p. 263.
[95] Under the title "Ďurčanský Eliminated," the *Grenzboote,* Bratislava newspaper of the German minority of Slovakia, published on July 30, 1940, an editorial criticizing the policy of the Minister of Foreign Affairs and the Interior of the Slovak State. This article reproached Ďurčanský for leading a "clique" which claimed to abide by "its own ideas" and which wanted to make of Slovakia a turntable for Europe. "All these people must disappear immediately, for they are political Utopians."

mountable case of conscience for him, a priest, and Dr. Tuka will become president.[96]

Was Monsignor Tiso to surrender the State's destiny to Tuka or continue to struggle against him and those who were backing him? Parliament's most serious-minded men begged him to remain.[97] Realizing his heavy responsibility toward the whole nation, he remained at his post.

On November 24, 1940, in Berlin, Tuka signed Slovakia's adhesion to the Tripartite Pact. The old stickler for formalities, dazzled by the ostentatious ceremony at the Reichskanzlei, exclaimed: "This act is of great historical importance for Slovakia. We have been officially accepted by the great nations which make up the Tripartite Pact." The political consequences of such an adhesion did not concern him. Here as elsewhere it was "the acknowledgement to Slovakia of the same rights as the other members of the international community" that most impressed this professor of the philosophy of law.[98]

Counting on the Hlinka guard, and Bernard's successor, von Killinger, Tuka prepared a coup d' état for January 1941 that was destined to remove Monsignor Tiso from office.[99] Čatloš, having learned of the plans, saved the situation by resolutely putting himself with the Army on the President's side. The famous fourteen points that Tuka had proclaimed on January 21, 1941, at Trenčianske Teplice, on the necessity for instituting a national-socialist system in Slovakia, consequently came to naught. As spokesman for Germany, Tuka had not found any support for his arguments, neither within the government nor among the people.

After this fiasco, von Killinger was replaced by a man of the NSDAP, Hans Ludin, who lost no time in following the path marked by his predecessor. On March 29, 1942, he went to Kežmarok where, before the Carpathian Germans, who had gathered for this purpose, he made an address against the President:

> I cannot imagine that the Slovaks can build their State on the principles of parliamentary democracy and consequently on liberalism. . . . Furthermore, it seems to me equally impossible that they can set up a Führerstaat here with parish priests as protagonists. I must say this frankly

[96] Karol Sidor, *Six Years Minister Plenipotentiary to the Vatican* (Scranton, Pa.: 1947), p. 121.
[97] Čulen, *Biography of Msgr. Tiso*, p. 480.
[98] Karl Braunias, *Die Slowakei* (Stuttgart and Berlin: 1942), p. 84.
[99] Tiso, *Die Wahrheit über die Slowakei*, p. 50.

for, in case of a catastrophe, the responsibility would fall on one person alone.[100] I insist on emphasizing once again the fact that the Reich prefers not to have to meddle, not even to the slightest extent, in the internal affairs of Slovakia. The men, or preferably the names, which exert an influence here on the evolvement are indifferent to the Great Reich. The fate of the Reich does not depend upon Sir X or Sir Y who is the head of the State here: we are merely interested that it be a man whose friendship for Germany can in no wise be doubted.[101]

This discourse was an unheard of violation of custom and diplomatic tact. In spite of everything, the President never thought of surrendering.

On November 25, 1941, Tuka signed the "Antikomintern Pact" in Berlin. Again he made an exalted speech in which he expressed his joy in being among the other ministers of the satellite states and in seeing "Slovakia treated on a footing of equality." The Antikomintern Pact was actually the last collective manifestation of the powers of the Tripartite Pact and their allies. It was one more official reaffirmation of the *Pax Germanica* in Central Europe. On the internal level, it could entail a reinforcement of the repression against communism, but in the international scheme, it had only a Platonic importance. It was one of those cases of beating the empty air, a gesture ever recurrent in the Axis' policy.

Monsignor Tiso never did believe in the all-powerful might of Germany. Endowed with sound good sense, he understood perfectly that a small State like Slovakia could do nothing except wait for the end of the struggle of the big nations without drawing attention to herself. Free from all political doctrinairism, unlike Tuka, he remained always in expectation vis-à-vis Germany. He considered Germany's strength as a contingency of an historical moment. He conceived of Central Europe's organization after the war in the guise of a regional union. It was Sidor who became the propagator of this idea abroad. On July 16, 1943, the *National Zeitung* of Berne and on August 3, 1943, the *Schweizer Illustrierte Zeitung* wrote: "Sidor is the champion of the conservative coalition of Central Europe: Poland, Slovakia, Hungary, Croatia." Monsignor Tiso, too, on whom the war imposed great caution, had the courage on several occasions to express his adhesion to

---

[100] It obviously meant Monsignor Tiso.
[101] Quoted in Dr. Vladimír Clementis, *Messages from London* (Bratislava: 1947), p. 220.

this plan. Along these lines, a passage must be quoted from a discourse that he gave on August 15, 1943, at Nitra:

> Of course we Slovaks are realistic enough to understand that State sovereignty varies with different theories and circumstances. We are not slavish partisans of any and every outworn theory. If Europe some fine day demands a new political system founded upon independent states, we shall not oppose it, provided that the principle of equality be recognized for us as for the others.

He developed more precisely the same idea on September 5, 1943, in an address delivered at Prešov: "If there is a power desirous of defending the independence of the Slovak State better than the German Reich does it, each citizen of this State will pledge to it a greater loyalty and fidelity."[102] Through this statement, Monsignor Tiso uttered indirectly a grave reproach to the Western powers which for twenty years had abadoned the Slovaks to the mercy of the Czechs without interior statute or international guarantee.

Scarcely concerned over Hitler's *neue Ordnung*, Slovakia favorably welcomed the idea of a Danubian federation. Mr. Ďurčanský, former Minister of Foreign Affairs, published at Bratislava in German and at Geneva in French a study titled: *Central Europe, Past and Future*, in which he advocated a confederation grouping the States of this region.[103] Besides, the official organ of the National Unity party, *the Slovák*, published an editorial on August 20, 1944, signed by Mr. Joseph Kirschbaum, anticipating the establishment of a federation of Central Europe after the war. The provocative nature of that article was stressed by the fact that the diplomatic representative of Slovakia to Berne endorsed the plan of Mr. Milan Hodža, former Prime Minister of Czecho-Slovakia and at that time a political refugee in London.[104] The author did it under proviso that Slovakia form a distinct unit therein and be treated on an equal footing with the other members.[105]

---

[102] Dr. Jozef Tiso, "Ueber aktuelle Fragen," *Slowakische Rundschau* No. 9, Bratislava, (1943).

[103] See *La Revue de Droit International* No. 1, Geneva (1944); and Ferdinand Durčanský, *Mitteleuropa in Vergangheit und Zukunft* (Bratislava: 1944).

[104] Milan Hodža, *Federation in Central Europe* (London: 1943).

[105] These facts allow us to realize the difference between two imperialisms in Central Europe. In fact it is hardly imaginable that the head of present Slovakia would utter with respect to Soviet Russia sentences comparable to Monsignor Tiso's, or the *Rudé Právo* of Prague or the ambassador of

The fact that the idea of a federation of Central Europe was adopted by Slovak political personalities and that it was analyzed in the press could not fail to awaken German attention. Minister Ludin protested to Monsignor Tiso and asked him to dismiss from office the director of the *Slovák* and also Mr. Kirschbaum. Monsignor Tiso refused.

Hungary—A war marked the first relations between Slovakia and Hungary. During their campaign against Sub-Carpathian Ruthenia, March 18-23, 1939, the Magyars attacked Slovakia. In the course of violent combats supported by the artillery and the air force, the Magyars, several times more numerous than the Slovaks, occupied forty-two villages in spite of the heroic resistance of Colonel Malár's troops. The German General Engelbrecht offered to intervene, alongside of the government of Bratislava, against the Magyars. This action would have practically brought on the occupation of Slovakia by Germany, and would have also permitted Germany to take Hungary both from the north and the west, simultaneously.[106] The evening of March 24, Mr. Ďurčanský sent an emissary (Dr. Szilárd) to Budapest to put the Hungarian government on its guard against this snare. Budapest then stopped the advance of the Magyar Army and opened negotiations.[107]

A memorandum by the head of the political division of the Aussenamt dated March 27, 1939,[108] related the Magyar-Slovak incident on the eastern frontier of Slovakia in the following way:

> On the morning of March 18, certain Hungarian detachments, advancing from the south and east, entered eastern Slovakia from three directions: from Kapušany through Pavlovce in the direction of Michalovce, from Ungvár in the direction of Sobrance, and from Berezny in the direction of Ubla-Svina.
> From the outset the advance seems to have met with strong resistance from the Slovaks and came to a complete standstill in the evening of March 24. The line of demarcation occupied at the end of the encounters would probably be, apart from minor deviations, about 10 to 15 kilometres

Czecho-Slovakia to Washington or Paris commenting favorably on the European Union.

[106] Mr. Coulondre, French Ambassador to Berlin, points out in his report of March 19, 1939, a "German attempt to occupy militarily all of Slovakia and even Sub-Carpathian Russia." *Le Livre Jaune Français*, p. 105.

[107] This event proves that it was by foiling Germany's aims on their soil that the Slovaks succeeded in establishing their State.

[108] *Documents on German Foreign Policy, 1918-1945.* Series D, Vol. VI. Washington, D.C. Document No. 111, pp. 137-38.

inside Slovakia, to the west of the administrative boundary which, under the old regime, separated that country from Carpatho-Ukraine. About 100 to 150 persons were killed during the clashes and roughly twice that number wounded. It is to be regretted that as late as the afternoon of March 24, the Hungarian Air Force carried out a bombing attack on the airfield at the volksdeutsch settlement at Zipser Neudorf,[109] thereby causing the death of a number of civilians.

Following the outbreak of hostilities, Count Csáky had proposed negotiations to the Slovak government on the question of determining the eastern frontier between Slovakia and Carpatho-Ukraine. After some hesitation the proposal was accepted by the Slovak government. Delegates from both sides met in Budapest for initial talks on Monday, March 27, at 12 noon.

On April 8, an agreement was reached. Despite the service that Slovakia had rendered, Hungary retained the Sobrance district, thereby imposing a new frontier between the two countries.[110]

Not content with annexing land, the Magyars then began to molest the Slovaks who had had the misfortune of falling under their domination. They confiscated their lands and incessantly offended their national feelings in various ways. The head of the Slovak minority in Hungary. Mr. L'udovít Obtulovič, was forbidden to practice law and had to leave for Bratislava.

Of course the population of the Slovak cities (Bratislava and Nitra among others) organized demonstrations to demand the return of the territories that had been taken from them and to protest against the measures taken in respect to the Slovaks in Hungary. The press was filled with abuses, resulting in a state of angry agitation on both sides. Hungary missed no chance whatsoever to awaken German suspicion and point out that Slovakia did not merit the Reich's "confidence." Thus on April 30, 1940, Mr. Géza Szüllö denounced to the Parliament of Budapest the personal meetings that the diplomatic representative of Slovakia to Madrid was to have had with the former chargé d' affaires of Czecho-Slovakia in Spain. Mr. Szüllö even concluded his address with this patronizing statement: "A good government cannot get along without culture, and it takes time to acquire it.

109 The German name for Spišská Nová Ves. At that time a small German minority was living in that town, founded in the Middle Ages mostly by German settlers.
110 Ripka, *Munich: Before and After,* pp. 392-93.

It is too bad that those presently governing the Slovak people are so young; they have not yet had time to become civilized!"

Addressing Slovakia, the Minister of Foreign Affairs of Hungary, Mr. Stephen Csáky, stated that his country had attempted to carry on "brotherly relations" with Slovakia, but that his efforts had not been welcome. "The Magyar government," continued the minister, "has proved that it is disposed to manifest the greatest patience in the interest of peace and order. However it realizes perfectly well that there is a limit and that the camel's back could be broken by a straw."[111]

In answer to Mr. Szüllö's insult, a Slovak deputy, Mr. Konštantín Čulen, replied on May 7, 1940, to the Parliament of Bratislava:

> If we had not had to suffer for centuries under the yoke, if we had had Slovak schools, if they had not imprisoned us in the name of Szüllö's "high culture," if they had not confiscated our possessions, if we had been able in the past to live a free national life, if the renegades who Magyarized the name of their fathers had worked on the lands they had inherited, the deputy Mr. Szüllö would have seen what the little Slovak people had been capable of.[112]

If polemics were violent on both sides, they were undoubtedly less justifiable on Budapest's side. Whereas the Magyar minority in Slovakia had its schools and newspapers and its deputy in the Parliament of Bratislava (J. Eszterházy), the Slovaks, who were much more numerous in Hungary after Munich, enjoyed nothing like that. The Hungarian government allowed the Slovak minority only one newspaper, the *Slovenská sloboda* (*Slovak Liberty*).

Little by little, however, relations were bettered. Commercial relations, which were intensified between the two countries outside the political pale and to their mutual benefit, plus the hardships and suffering resulting from their participation in the German war in the east, worked toward a closer agreement between the two peoples. Although the Slovaks never ceased thinking of it, they abstained from demanding the return of the regions they had lost on November 2, 1938 by virtue of the arbitrament of Ribbentrop and Ciano. The Magyars too appeared more cautious

---

[111] Konštantín Čulen, *Zum slowakisch-unkarischen Verhältniss*, (Bratislava: 1940), p. 9.
[112] *Ibid.*, pp. 12-13.

than before, feeling that this thorny question would inevitably be put back onto the carpet at the close of the war.

The Vatican—The Holy See acknowledged the Slovak State immediately by approving Mr. Karold Sidor's appointment as Slovakia's Minister Plenipotentiary and by naming to Bratislava the former apostolic nuncio of Prague, Monsignor Saverio Ritter, who actually went there to assume the position. Now, a difference of opinion arose at once between him and Ďurčanský as to the origin of the Slovak State. Whereas the Vatican thought that Slovakia, after the German occupation of Czechia, was from the legal point of view the residue of the former Czecho-Slovak State, Minister Ďurčanský maintained that Slovakia represented an essentially new State and that there was no juridical bond between the two. In his opinion the Czecho-Slovak State completely disappeared after Slovakia's declaration of independence. According to Ďurčanský, Monsignor Ritter could therefore not "continue holding his office as apostolic nuncio" of Prague in Slovakia without a new accreditation. In this he disagreed with a note from the Secretariat of State of June 5, 1939, addressed to the Slovak Ministry of Foreign Affairs. Whereupon Monsignor Ritter returned to Rome and the Holy See sent Monsignor Giuseppe Burzio as chargé d' affaires to Bratislava.[113]

Another diplomatic difficulty arose between Slovakia and the Vatican à propos of Monsignor Tiso's candidacy to the office of President of the Republic. The Holy See, especially in trying times, does not wish ecclesiastics to hold political office. Too, when Monsignor Tiso appeared as the only candidate for the Presidency, the Vatican did not fail to express its reservations to Mr. Karol Sidor, Minister of Slovakia, as also to Monsignor Buzalka, the Auxiliary Bishop of Trnava, during his visit *ad limina* in the first half of the month of September, 1939.[114]

However, Monsignor Tiso was aware of the lack of political leaders capable of having real authority over the people and their chance, however slight, of being respected by the Germans. Therefore, he decided to take on this office and, if need be, "suffer martyrdom" as he expressed it on September 17, 1939, at Nitra, during the episcopal ordination of Monsignor Škrábik, bishop of Banská Bystrica.[115]

---

[113] See: Sidor, *Six Years Minister Plenipotentiary to the Vatican,* pp. 4-5.
[114] *Ibid.,* p. 61.
[115] *Ibid.,* p. 62.

Despite his previous reservations, Pope Pius XII took cognizance of the election when it was made, and cordially gave Monsignor Tiso his apostolic blessing.[116]

A third question drew the Vatican's attention to Slovakia: the Jewish problem. It was of great interest to the Germans that the Jewish question be dealt with in the same manner here as at home. They therefore insisted until Tuka was disposed to imitate them. This problem constitutes in fact the last point of his Trenčianske Teplice program.

After the publication of the Jewish Code in September, 1941, by the government of Bratislava, the Slovak bishops met in Nitra on October 7. Under the chairmanship of Monsignor Kmeťko, Bishop of that diocese, they drafted a memorandum to the government in which they criticized the provisions of this code and asked for its "revision in conformance with Catholic doctrine." They sent a copy of the document to the Holy See. The State Secretariat intervened three times in Bratislava to modify the code and soften its application. The Vatican energetically insisted that Monsignor Tiso and the government, while upholding the interests of Catholicism, respect the human condition of the Israelites.

Monsignor Tiso, put by Tuka's uncompromising attitude into an embarrassing position, was exposed to the complaints of two opposing tendencies. One reproached him for not protecting the Jews effectively enough; the other, for doing it much too well.

The Jewish question was therefore a bone of contention in the relations between Slovakia and the Vatican. For a long time it occupied the chanceries on both sides, and preoccupied the consciences of responsible persons still more.[117]

If from the Catholic point of view we can believe that Monsignor Tiso's policy was not always effective, at no time did the Holy See doubt the good will of the President. The Vatican showed its interest in the new State on May 18, 1944, by conferring upon Monsignor Kmeťko, Bishop of Nitra, the title of Archbishop *ad personam*. The ecclesiastical dignity of Saint Methodius which for a thousand years had waited for a titular, turned again to that historical city.

Poland—Since the High Middle Ages, within the bounds of the Kingdom of Hungary, the territories of Upper Spiš and Orava had been a part of Slovak territory. Yet the Polish delega-

[116] See Appendix V.
[117] See p. 99.

tion to the Peace Conference in 1919 claimed of Czecho-Slovakia
the Duchy of Tešín and the northern regions of the Orava and the
Spiš. After long deliberations the Supreme Council of the Allied
and Associated Powers decided on September 17, 1919, that a
plebiscite would be held in the territory which until April 1,
1914 had been the Duchy of Tešín. The same procedure would
take place in the communes of the districts of Námestovo and
Trstená in Orava, in the communes of the Spišská Stará Ves
district, as well as in the commune of Javorina of the Kežmarok
district, county of Spiš.

A lively propaganda campaign took place on both sides with
this plebiscite in view. On July 10, 1920, after a struggle of
eighteen months, the representatives of the interested parties—
Mr. Beneš for Czecho-Slovakia and Mr. Grabski for Poland—gave
up the plebiscite with one accord and agreed to accept whatever
solution should be proposed by the Allied and Associated Powers. In conformity with the decision of the Ambassadors' Conference, these communes were allotted to Poland on July 28,
1920, in compensation for Tešín's coal basin that Mr. Beneš
deemed indispensable to Czecho-Slovakia's economy and which
he wanted to recover at all costs. On February 11, 1924, the
Commission on Delimitation cut from Slovak territory twenty-
five communes (twelve in Orava and thirteen in Spiš), or an
area of 225.48 square miles with 24,700 inhabitants. After Munich, Poland "rectified" its frontier with Slovakia by occupying
a strip of land to the north of Čadca (Trenčín), Námestovo
(Orava) and the western part of Javorina (Spiš).

When in September, 1939, Germany had invaded Poland,
Slovakia reoccupied these lands in answer to the appeals of the
population. The Reich put the administration of the lands back
into the Slovaks' hands by a treaty signed on November 21, 1939.
By virtue of the same text, a little country of Skalité (district of
Čadca) that had been annexed by Poland after Munich, also
came back to Slovakia, which thus retrieved 298.76 square miles
of land and 35,000 inhabitants. In addition, Hitler offered Monsignor Tiso the Polish enclave of Zakopané in the Tatra. He not
only declined the offer, but he never claimed a single village
which ethnically and historically was not genuinely Slovak. "We
want only what is ours," he replied to the Germans.

During the occupation of Poland, Slovakia was for the Polish
refugees a passageway to Hungary and Yugoslavia. Obeying
orders from the Polish government of London, they could thus

join the free Polish forces. They found all the material support
necessary among the inhabitants, and the Slovak administration
for its part aided a number of fleeing Poles by granting them
identification papers without the knowledge of the Germans.
The diplomatic and consular representatives received instructions to the effect that in case of need these papers would be valid
for a longer period, and that aid and counsel would be given to
those wanting it.

Italy, Spain—Independence put Slovakia in contact with Italy
as well as with the Hispanic world which it had not known until
then except through books.

The favorable Italian attitude toward Magyar revisionism
after World War I and Ciano's responsibility for the highly
detrimental decision of the Vienna Arbitrament to Slovakia, were
to reflect heavily upon Slovak-Italian relations. The Mussolini
Government as well as the Italian press continued siding with
Hungary in all subsequent Slovak-Magyar disputes. Aware of
this situation, Prime Minister Tuka dreamed of a *rapprochement*
and planned a courtesy visit to Mussolini and Ciano to air this
question. But, symptomatic enough, because of lack of enthusiasm
and excess of red tape in Rome, he could not put his intention
through.

As to Spain, there were no reminiscences of the past which
would interfere with the establishment of heartful relations. At
the beginning of the armed conflict in Europe the Spanish government, having decided to remain neutral, sent the Slovak government a telegram in September, 1939 asking it to take the same
attitude. Obviously, Slovakia could not desire anything better
than to stay out of the war. Subsequently, good relations between the two countries were stressed mutually by a very profit-
able trade agreement and by student exchange. Moreover, the
Spanish press was always very attentive to Slovakia's aspiration
toward remaining on the map of Europe.

The U.S.S.R.—During the winter of 1939 when Mr. Pushkin,
who had just been appointed Minister of the U.S.S.R. in Slovakia,
handed his credentials over to Monsignor Tiso, he addressed a
sentence to him which was clearly far from being a formula of
customary propriety: "Because of the war raging in Europe, the
fact that our two States enter into diplomatic relations exceeds
the bounds of their mutual interests." The exact meaning of this
sentence was not to be understood until later. Russia established
an enormous legation in Bratislava, where she had never had any

consular representation before. Located on the Danube between Vienna and Budapest, this city forms an excellent observation post in Central Europe. In was this region, much more than Slovakia, that interested the Russians. They were now in a position to follow carefully all the reactions of the nazi hold on the peoples of the Danubian sector.

Minister Ďurčanský planned to lean on the Russians in order to defend Slovak interests against Germany, but his fall in Salzburg prevented him from carrying out his plans.

On June 12, 1942, when hostilities broke out between Germany and Russia, Slovakia found itself drawn into the conflict. Tuka, without consulting either the government or Parliament, merely drew up a declaration of war on the U.S.S.R. and sent it to the press and radio.[118]

This participation in the war against the U.S.S.R. provoked extremely violent reactions in governmental milieus as well as among the people. To cut all commentary short, Tuka declared that he alone was responsible for the foreign policy. Actually he had no right to declare war or sign the peace. The government was constrained moreover not to insist, for it knew that to act differently would automatically have brought on pure and simple occupation of Slovak territory by the Germans or else the formation of a new and more accommodating government.

As for Monsignor Tiso, he stated to his collaborators that the war against Russia "was in no wise made in the interest of Slovakia and that they had to limit themselves with giving to the Germans what they could not avoid giving."[119]

The United States, Great Britain, France—After Munich, Slovakia found itself within Germany's orbit by the very fact of its geographical location. However, it tried to interest Western democracies in its fate.

Having been recognized *de facto* by Great Britain and France, and having granted the *exequatur* to the consular representatives of these two countries, Slovakia prepared to send consuls to London and Paris. Mr. Harminc, who had been named to London,

[118] In an article by Colonel Jozef Marko, man of the regime established in 1945, these lines are found: "It is characteristic to note that, no more this time than previously, has the war been declared in conformance with the Constitution of the Slovak State. It is Tuka and Mach who declared it almost alone. The Slovaks who refused to go to the front leaned on this argument to plead innocent before the military courts." Information Commissariat, *The Military Aspect of the Uprising* (Turčiansky Sv. Martin: 1946).

[119] Čulen, *Biography of Msgr. Tiso,* p. 480.

was able to reach England effectively and take up his duties. France, on the contrary, gave no evidence of any eagerness to admit a consul from Slovakia into Paris. When the war broke out between the Reich and the Western Powers, Great Britain and France recalled their consular representatives from Bratislava.

Despite the commitments it had been constrained to enter into vis-à-vis Germany, Slovakia remained practically neutral with respect to the Western Powers until the end of the war. The President did not wish any more than did the Parliament to enter into conflict with the United States of America and Great Britain. In 1937, when he was a deputy and the vice-chairman of the Hlinka party, Monsignor Tiso had made a trip to the United States at the invitation of the Slovaks of America, where he was able to ascertain the excellent living conditions of his compatriots who had emigrated. Nothing could have persuaded him to commit an act of hostility, were it purely symbolic, vis-à-vis the power that together with Canada had most widely contributed to the democratic formation of the Slovak people in assuring them all the freedoms accorded to its own citizens.[120]

Nevertheless on December 12, 1941, a communiqué appearing in the Bratislava press announced that Slovakia was in a state of war with the United States and Great Britain. The country was dumfounded and in consternation about the news, for rare were the Slovak families from which one son or a close relative had not emigrated to America.

Commenting on this event in the presence of his collaborators, Monsignor Tiso contented himself with saying: "No competent constitutional organ has declared war. America knows very well that we shall not attack it either in the air or on the sea!"[121]

The French government of Vichy recognized the Slovak Republic on April 25, 1942. It was the French ambassador in Berne who communicated this decision to the Slovak chargé d' affaires, Mr. Radlinský. It was a question of an exchange of diplomatic representatives. This was never realized. However, there was no one in Slovakia to declare war on France!

---

[120] In America there are a million naturalized Slovaks who emigrated after 1880.

[121] The following days, the author of these lines was received in audience by the President; he did not hide how much revolt and indignation this unheard of news had caused. "The United States and Great Britain had not recognized the Slovak Republic *de jure,*" he added. "Therefore no war was possible between the Slovak State and these Powers." "It is another of Tuka's rages," was Monsignor Tiso's reply.

Diplomacy

Organization—The Slovak State, recognized by twenty-seven European and non-European States, immediately undertook to organize its representation abroad. Whereas until that time the Slovaks had always been represented in the world by Magyars and Czechs, now they were finally going to be able to make direct contact themselves. The possibilities thus offered to Slovak diplomacy, especially with regards to the future, did not escape the Minister of Foreign Affairs, Mr. Ďurčanský. Unfortunately, since he had fallen into disgrace among the Germans in 1940, it was not possible for him to realize his plans.

His successor, Tuka, who held the offices of Prime Minister and Minister of Foreign Affairs, was less dynamic. Both tired and narrow-minded, he saw only the present. He said that Slovakia was too small a country to be able to influence in any way the march of events in Europe. Therefore he was rather timorous and satisfied with a very modest budget that did not allow him to create diplomatic and consular representation except in states and cities presenting the most interest for Slovakia. Legations were opened in Budapest, Warsaw, Moscow, Berlin, Bucarest, Sofia, Rome (with both the Quirinal and the Holy See), Madrid, Bern, Helsinki, Belgrade, and later Zagreb. There were consul-generals in Vienna, Milan, Stockholm, Prague and London. In addition there were several honorary consulates in Europe and two commissions on repatriation, one in Paris and the other in Brussels. In certain cases a legation's jurisdiction extended to several states. Thus the Berlin legation was competent for Denmark and the Baltic states; the one in Madrid, for various states in Latin America. It assured at the same time the liaison between the Slovaks of North America and Bratislava.

Political Mission—A difficult task was incumbent upon Slovak diplomacy by reason of the dramatic conditions in which the Slovak State had entered the European political scene, and because of the hostility of a very great number of states to which it was exposed "up to its bitter end." Although the principle of nationalities that had served as a basis for the creation of a Slovak Republic is a modern idea and consistent with development, the Slovak State had to struggle incessantly against the prejudices which prevailed in certain states in western Europe. This was particularly true of the role that Germany had played at its birth and of its foreign relations with this dreaded neighbor, such as they had been formulated in the *Schutzvertrag* of March 23, 1938.

Yet it can be stated that, in spite of the realism which prevailed from the beginning among Slovak diplomats with regard to the end of the war and the political future of Bratislava, all, with two or three exceptions, were deeply convinced that the territory inhabited by the Slovak people would remain in the future an important factor of the Central European policy.

Diplomacy's immediate task consisted in consolidating as much as possible the international position of the State in relation to its neighbors and other European nations. Its principal activity, however, had as its goal to make Slovakia's role known as a political factor in the Danube basin. Opposed to the imperialistic tendencies of Budapest, Prague and even Berlin, it proposed to draw the world's attention to the fact that the Slovak problem was in effect a European problem independent of Magyar or Czech interests.

Slovak diplomacy raised its mission above considerations of the political regimes of the time, and it manifested this attitude even vis-à-vis the Germans. Slovak foreign representatives not only did not permit any German interference in their affairs, but they often conducted themselves with such independence that they gave reason for suspicion—and often well founded at that. Further, until the beginning of the conflict with the U.S.S.R., Slovak diplomacy kept in contact with certain powers already at war with Germany. For example, Mr. Sidor, Slovak Minister to the Holy See, was on friendly terms with Mr. Papée, Polish Ambassador to the Vatican, even after the breaking off of diplomatic relations between the two countries; the Slovak legation to the Quirinal carried on relations with the British and French embassies during the summer of 1940 in the midst of war. This latter case bears mentioning more in detail by reason of the serious political consequences that it was to have for Slovakia. In fact, Slovakia had to procure cotton from Brazil for some of its textile manufactures, especially for the Tiberghien Sons' firm of Trenčín, a business sustained with French capital. Since Britain at that time had control of the maritime traffic between Europe and the countries overseas, Slovakia had to ask the British embassy in Rome to help facilitate the obtaining of the necessary *navicert*. As might be expected, this request provoked fears among the English as to the point of final destination of this very important article of war. Mr. Nosworthy, the embassy's commercial counsellor, asked if this cotton would be used in Slovakia or if it were destined for Germany. In order for him to transmit the Slovak request to the Foreign Office, he had to have explanations regarding the political and economic relations then existing be· tween Slovakia and the Reich. The Slovak legation put into his hands two memoranda which, while admitting of the relations based on the *Schutzvertrag* of Slovakia with Germany, argued that the Slovaks were not at war with the Allies and that from the economic point of view they were independent and were maintaining practically a neutrality policy. The legation of Rome began these negotiations on Mr. Ďurčanský's initiative.

The betrayal of a member of the legation had the two memos fall into the hands of Ambassador von Mackensen, who did not lose any time in communicating them to Ribbentrop. This was one of the principal motives for which Hitler, on July 29, 1940, had Monsignor Tiso and certain members of his government come to Salzburg for a "protestation visit," during which Monsignor Tiso had to be subjected to violent reproaches on the anti-German plots of Slovak diplomacy.[122]

The cotton incident brought about Ďurčanský's downfall as well as the removal of Zvrškovec, Minister to Rome. Henceforth the Slovak diplomats had to guard against having any initiative of this sort.

When Tuka became Minister of Foreign Affairs, German "counselors" came to take up their abode in the principal services of the central administration, an act which corresponded to a reinforcement of German control over the country. This measure, however, spared the Ministry of Foreign Affairs. Consequently the diplomatic representatives in the majority of cases had to preserve their administrative independence vis-à-vis not only the Germans but Tuka also.

Slovak diplomacy was torn between the pro-German leanings of some of its members who overestimated Germany and the importance of its "protection," and the Czecho-Slovak leanings of certain others. It amounted to two opportunisms: one with respect to the present, the other with respect to the immediate future after the war. The Czecho-Slovak leaning numbered four or five names, among which were those of Messrs. Szathmáry,Ország, Gejza Krno, and Rakšányi. For these men, the existence of the Slovak State was only an episode. They attempted during the

[122] See p. 120.

war to get in touch with Mr. Beneš in London and offer him their services.

However, by a great majority, diplomacy remained faithful to the idea of a Slovak State. It included persons who refused to bow to the demands either of the Czechs or the Germans; consequently penalties were imposed upon some of them at the instigation of the latter. *La Gazette de Lausanne* of August 4, 1944,[123] reported how Mr. Karol Sidor, appointed Minister of the Interior in March, 1939, found himself, under German pressure, obliged to resign and be dismissed from political life. Next he was appointed Slovak Minister to the Holy See. The same newspaper also points out:

> Professor Ferdinand Ďurčanský, former Minister of Foreign Affairs, is being watched by the police. As early as 1940, he had been obliged to resign as minister—that at the personal request of Mr. von Ribbentrop. The former Minister to the Quirinal, Dr. Zvrškovec, likewise recalled in 1940, is also under the surveillance of the Gestapo. The Slovak Minister in Rumania. Dr. Milecz, was dismissed from his post, as also the chargé d' affaires in Madrid, Dr. Mikus. The press attaché at the Slovak legation in Berne, Dr. Grébert-Kubínsky, resigned from his office as a protest against the violation of liberty of his country.

Mr. Danihel, commercial attaché to the Stockholm consulate-general, had also resigned.

Economic Effort—Slovak diplomacy had also to exert serious effort on the economic plane. The new Republic had an interest in entering the European market on its own. The economic barriers set up between the countries at war did not facilitate its task. The Slovak State did not succeed any the less in intensifying considerably its commercial exchanges with other countries. It had a favorable trade balance and was able to pay its purchases in dollars, in merchandise, or through the clearing-house.

This all required an activity which was not customary in Slovakia, and the Slovaks often had to deal with partners much more experienced than they. Yet it is to be noted that the State's economic machinery as well as the competent service of the Ministry of Foreign Affairs, filled their role in a satisfactory manner. Slovak products found purchasers in all the European countries with which Slovakia could maintain trade relations.

Foreign trade, especially with such neutral countries as Switzerland, Turkey, Sweden, Spain, and Portugal, was principally

[123] "La Situation en Slovaquie,"*La Gazette de Lausanne*, August 4, 1944.

responsible for the strengthening of the Slovak crown, reputed in the countries of Central Europe for its solidity.[124]

Cultural Efforts—On the cultural plane, the Foreign Service was no less active. Outside the country, among the legations, attachés had as their mission the propagation of Slovak cultural values. Their relations with newspapers, magazines, universities, and the radio stations in the countries where they held office made their country known in Europe. At the universities of Rome, Vienna, and Leipzig, Slovak language courses were organized.

Certain representations abroad, the legations of Madrid and Berne and the consulate-general of Stockholm in particular, published information bulletins. Through the intermediary of diplomatic and consular representatives, Slovak books were published abroad. Thus in the domain of history, the only objective works from that period on Slovakia that it is possible to find today in the libraries of Paris, London, Rome, and in the Library of Congress in Washington are those that the "Society for Slovaks Abroad" published at that time.[125] Other books relating to Slovakia were published in foreign languages, either on the initiative of Slovak representations or else with their collaboration.

In addition, the legations and consulates facilitated studies and foreign student and artist exchange. Never had so many Slovak students been able to study in the universities of Vienna, Berlin, Leipzig and in Switzerland, Italy, and Spain. Unfortunately, after October, 1939, with the start of the war, it was no longer possible for young Slovaks to study in France or Great Britain.

Humanitarian Action—Toward the end of the war, Slovak diplomacy realized important works of a humanitarian nature which it is fitting to mention here. Mr. Jozef Mračna,[126] chief of the political section of the Ministry of Foreign Affairs at Bratislava, persistently defended the cause of the American, English and French war prisoners who had escaped from Germany and taken refuge in Slovakia. Regardless of protests from Berlin, he protected the Jews hunted down by the Germans, and also the Italian and Rumanian diplomats who, after the capitulation and break of Rome and Bucarest with Bratislava in 1943 and

---

[124] It was often called the Danubian dollar.
[125] Spoločnosť' pre zahraničných Slovákov, Bratislava.
[126] In recalling this fact, we pay homage to a deserving man who was to be shot by the Russians in April, 1945, in Bratislava.

1944, remained "confined" in the luxurious Pieštany spa until almost the end of the war.

In résumé, the fundamental role of Slovak diplomacy during the war was to make known to the world Slovakia and the problems which claimed attention in this small nation both on the European and international plane. In addition, especially from the economic and military point of view, it had to resist the exaggerated demands of the Germans. Thus the diplomacy of the young Slovak Republic preserved very estimable human and national values.

The Uprising of August, 1944

With the Russian advance into Poland the days of the Slovak Republic were numbered. The population, of which 90 per cent were partisans of an independent Slovak State, was extremely anxious about the future. The great powers had forgotten about the existence of the right of the self-determination of peoples as well as the principles of the Atlantic Charter. Without worrying about what the Slovak people might think of Mr. Beneš, they had assured him full powers in Slovakia, a fact of which he often boasted on the London radio.

The Slovak Communists (Husák and Schmidke), directed by Russian parachutists, were the first to organize behind the front a system of resistance against the "reactionary" government of Monsignor Tiso. With Russian aid they proposed to establish a communist government and make Slovakia a Soviet republic.

As for the Protestants, who remembered the time when their leaders (Hodža, Dérer, Slávik, Ivanka, Markovič, Bella, and others) were able to govern Slovakia by leaning not on the majority of the people in conformity with the democratic principle but on the Czech majority of the Prague Parliament, they declared themselves favorable to the ancient regime. From this milieu came Messrs. Lettrich, Ursíny, Josko, Tvarožek, and Styk. In the person of Colonel Golian of the Slovak Army, they found a technician and military collaborator.

Communists and Protestants had already met during the existence of the Slovak State. At Christmas, 1943, the two groups had secretly agreed to oppose a political resistance common to "the Germans and Monsignor Tiso's regime." Two weeks after the conclusion on December 12, 1943 of the Friendship and Mutual Aid Treaty between Stalin and Beneš, the aforementioned group declared themselves ready to lean on the U.S.S.R. "We wish to collaborate," they said in a secret document, "with all the nations and all the Slav States, and especially with the U.S.S.R., in which we see the guarantor of liberty and the full flowering of all the little nations, principally the Slav nations."

The bulk of the population was greatly perplexed. Fiercely resisting German domination, the Slovaks were equally opposed to communism and Beneš, who had since then become a mere plenipotentiary of Moscow. This undeniable majority was waiting for the moment when the military command, due to the constant retreat of the Germans, could put at the disposition of the Allies the two Slovak divisions that were guarding the Carpathian passes in the extreme eastern section of Slovakia. Monsignor Tiso knew that General Malár, who was commanding them, was already in touch with the Red Army and that he had received Russian assurances that they would not try to penetrate prematurely into Slovakia.[127] The Slovak military command figured that when the Russians reached Cracow in Poland and Miskolcz in Hungary, it would be the propitious time to pass over to the Allies. At that moment the two Slovak divisions were to attack and allow the Russian Army to enter Slovakia without difficulty. This plan facilitated the Russians' quick occupation of Slovakia—an empty enclave on the military chessboard—sparing the country any combat or destruction. General Čatloš, Minister of Defense, had sent two emissaries to the Russians about the middle of August, 1944. It was their mission to agree on the details of that plan. For this operation he had proposed to the Russians the date September 15, 1944. But an unforeseen event was to bring on the most disastrous consequences for Slovakia.

For a certain time a brigade of partisans had been formed in the forests of central Slovakia in the Turiec region. It was composed of French, Russians and Slovaks. There were two French companies there, prisoners of war who had been able to remain in Slovakia in spite of German protestations. Mr. Léon Chollet, professor of French at the University of Bratislava, had been the organizer; Captain de Lanurien was their leader. The Russians in this group of partisans were mostly parachutists from the staff of guerrillas of Ukraine at Kiev and had for their leader Commander Popov, the man whom Colonel Osmolov was later to succeed. The Slovaks were commanded by Captain Pagáč. The

[127] Čulen, *Biography of Msgr. Tiso*, p. 344.

guerrilla companies, heterogeneous in their composition as well
as in their political aims, were only awaiting the word which
would set them in action. The soldiers in the Slovak Army, quar-
tered in the barracks of the region, were also consumed by im-
patience.

The Russian partisans made the Slovak guerrillas' first contact
with the U.S.S.R. easier. On August 4, 1944, a Soviet plane took
into Russia Messrs. Schmidke and Ferjenčík, who were already engaged in the resistance. Captain Velichko, chief of the information services of the Russian sector of the guerrillas, asked weapons
of Colonel Golian, who was in command of the Banská Bystrica
garrison. "The latter," as it was reported by Colonel Jozef Marko,
one of the main organizers of the uprising in the Turiec region,
"granted them to him on condition that Velichko promise not to
engage in action without coming to an understanding with the
Slovak military authorities. Velichko agreed to bind himself only
until August 20. Then he became very active and put before
Colonel Golian accomplished facts."[128]

Ou August 24, Captain Velichko learned that a special German military train was traveling from Budapest toward Turčiansky Sv. Martin where he was stationed. He promptly sent thirty
men in Slovak military uniform to blow up the Strečno tunnel
located on the train's course. Around eight o'clock in the evening,
when the convoyed train arrived at Turčiansky Sv. Martin, the
stationmaster announced to the conductor that the tunnel had
been blown up by guerrillas. German General Otto then ordered
the train to return to Budapest. The stationmaster, by agreement
with the Russian guerrillas, opposed the request. General Otto
then demanded to be put in touch with the chief officer of the
garrison. He was then taken before the orderly officer who, in
league with the guerrillas, advised General Otto to spend the
night in the barracks "under Slovak military protection" and not
to go back to Budapest until the next day. He agreed to this plan
and was led with his men to the barracks by a guerrilla unit
dressed in Slovak uniform. He did not at all suspect the trap into
which he had fallen.

Lieutenant Colonel Perko, commanding officer of the garrison
of Turčiansky Sv. Martin, fearing German retaliation, tried to
prevent any violence to General Otto and his men. Two years

---

[128] Information Comissariat, *The Military Aspect of the Uprising* (Turčiansky Sv. Martin: 1946), p. 34.

after the incident he explained his grave apprehensions at that time:

> Any arbitrary local action of military units against the Germans could threaten the success of the uprising by provoking a premature, bloody occupation of Slovakia by the Germans and the surrounding of our divisions in east Slovakia. The government of Bratislava could pretend to the Germans to be breaking with guerrilla action. It could not do as much when the regular army was involved. This consideration motivated my efforts to keep our army out of these actions. I did not succeed . . . ![129]

Another of the Slovak military personnel who took part in the uprising, Commander Kuchta, explains how the Slovak Army was enveigled into the uprising by Russian guerrillas, contrary to the plan set forth:

> The military command of the resistance wanted at all cost to gain several days in order to carry their preparations into effect. Captain Velichko did not want to give in and insisted either on taking the Germans unarmed to the headquarters of the guerrillas at Sklabiňa or else executing them in the barracks.[130]

At dawn on August 25, when General Otto and his men were getting ready to return to Budapest, the orderly officer asked them to put their weapons down. On the Germans' refusal, rapid firing broke out during the course of which twenty-eight of them, including the general himself and a woman, were killed by submachineguns.[131] After this massacre six hundred Slovak soldiers taking out three tanks and three trucks loaded with ammunition left the barracks and joined the guerrillas. The morning of August 26, they occupied the cities of Nemecké Pravno and Prievidza.

The same day, the communist political and military leaders (Schmidke, Lietavec, Rob) and Protestants (Lettrich, Ursíny, Golian) met in the Žarnovica valley to take counsel together. They decided to start an uprising the next day. During the night

[129] *Ibid.*, pp. 9-10.
[130] *Ibid.*, p. 54.
[131] Of course, Colonel Rašla, who was the Public Prosecutor of Monsignor Tiso during his trial before the National Court of Justice in Bratislava, was careful not to breathe a word about these executions in his indictment, as well as in his book entitled *Tiso and the Uprising*. In fact, it was these executions which make the responsibility of this premature movement which cost the lives of several tens of thousands of Slovaks and Jews fall not on Monsignor Tiso, but on the organizers of the movement.

of August 28, the guerrillas occupied the radio broadcasting station of Banská Bystrica from which, on August 29, at 1:15 p.m. the news of the uprising was announced. Thus it is that Banská Bystrica was to go down in history as the center of the resistance. The insurgents then proclaimed the "communist" republic at Turčiansky Sv. Martin, the "Soviet-Slovak" republic at Nemecké Pravno and the Czecho-Slovak republic at Banská Bystrica.[132]

At Bratislava these precipitate events aroused general consternation and everyone expected a violent reaction from Berlin; for from March 1944 on, as H. Ludin was to testify before the National Tribunal at the Tiso trial in 1947, certain Reich milieus "flirted with the idea of occupying Slovakia."[133] Only two days before, German units had taken up their post as sentinels on the Moravian-Slovak border.[134] At the same moment, the Germans attacked Monsignor Tiso violently on the subject of his Minister Čatloš, "a person in whom they could place no confidence, who promised them all they asked him for: additional battalions, equipment, etc. . . ., but who never delivered the goods." They asked for his immediate dismissal. On August 25, Monsignor Tiso was in the position of being obliged to promise General Hubitzky, chief of the German military mission, that he would transfer command of the Army to General Turanec while keeping Čatloš as Minister of Defense.

The evening of August 26, Minister of the Interior Mach delivered an address on the Bratislava radio in which he clearly warned the guerrillas that their activities would surely result in the intervention of the German Army.[135] In fact, General Hubitzky, seeing that the units of central Slovakia were going into the resistance, told Monsignor Tiso that the situation required the presence of the Wehrmacht in Slovakia. Monsignor Tiso was powerless to oppose this decision. He could only give in, which he did, according to Ludin, "after serious struggles with himself."[136]

The following decision appears in paragraph 2 of the proceedings of the August 28 session of the government of Bratislava:

---

[132] According to a report of the Slovak Minister of Foreign Affairs which was sent to Mr. Karol Sidor in Rome and published by the latter in his book, *Six Years Minister Plenipotentiary to the Vatican*, p. 237.
[133] Rašla, *Tiso and the Uprising*, p. 39.
[134] *Ibid.*, p. 38.
[135] *Ibid.*, p. 39.
[136] *Ibid.*, p. 43.

The government affirms that in the interest of the security of lives, the public weal and the existence of the State, the severest measures, strengthened by all the means at hand, be used against the guerrillas. These measures will be taken by the security bodies as well as by the Slovak armed forces in collaboration with the German units, by virtue of a specific agreement between Germany and Slovakia.[137] The German units which in conformity with this agreement, will come to Slovakia, will be under the orders of the Commander-in-chief of the Slovak Army and will remain in the country as long as said country deems it necessary.[138]

The next day Čatloš announced on the radio the decision so made. Then at the order of the Germans who wanted to imprison him, he had to remain prisoner on parole, at the Presidential Palace.

The same day, the morning of August 29, General Turanec, who had just been appointed Commander-in-Chief of the Slovak Army, went by plane to Banská Bystrica to examine the situation there. Upon his landing at the aviation camp of Tri Duby, the guerrillas took him prisoner.

Meanwhile General Malár, who was commanding the two divisions on the east front, landed in Bratislava and in a radio plea begged the Slovak units in the rear not to let themselves be inveigled into "premature" actions. This word was to be fatal for him. At the height of desperation, the Germans then decided to disarm the Slovak Army. President Tiso received the order to announce the sad news to the population on August 30 and resigned himself to it, knowing that any resistance would result in the immediate extermination of the Slovak units. Upon General Malár's return by plane the next day, he was apprehended by the Germans and expedited to a concentration camp in Germany where he was soon to be executed. On August 31, his two divisions were surrounded and the soldiers who did not succeed in escaping were sent into Germany with their officers. In Bratislava as in other towns of western Slovakia, the Wehrmacht's tanks occupied the barracks during the night of September 1. General

---

[137] This agreement was still to be concluded.
[138] When Mr. A. Rašla states in his book, *Tiso and the Uprising,* p. 41, that this movement arose after the arrival of the Germans in Slovakia, it changed the course of events, for the Germans came for the express purpos of liquidating the uprising. Lieutenant Colonel Emil Perko speaks the truth when he writes: "Although I mobilized troops secretly from August 27 on, I saw then that nothing (sic!) could prevent the Germans from invading Slovakia." See *The Military Aspect of the Uprising,* p. 11.

Berger, in command of the German troops, demanded the effective imprisonment of Čatloš who, however, succeeded in escaping and joining the insurgents on September 3. His bravery was badly rewarded. When the Democrats tried to place him at the head of the revolt in place of the unpopular Colonel Golian, the Slovak Communists under Lietavec, urged on by the Russian guerrillas commanded by Chernogorov, imprisoned him. The Slovak Army tried to free him; they were not successful and Čatloš was transported to Moscow by plane.

After the disarming of the Bratislava garrison, the news that the members of the government and Monsignor Tiso had been executed by the Germans spread to Banská Bystrica. Many who had hesitated before, now joined the insurgents. But the President denied by radio the news of his death and condemned the insurrection; so the soldiers, faithful to the idea of the Slovak State, left the rebel units and went back home. The Democrats were very much disappointed with the Russians for abducting Čatloš. Finally only the Communists remained enthusiastic.

In the meantime, the insurgents formed at Banská Bystrica the National Slovak Council which was composed of thirty members, half Communists and half Democrats. Of these only two were Catholics. On the communist side the principal persons were Mr. Schmidke, a former cabinetmaker; Mr. Husák, director of a carrying company; Mr. Daxner, a magistrate; and Messrs. Takáč, and Lietavec, civil servants. Among the Democrats were Mr. Lettrich, a lawyer; Mr. Ursíny, former deputy of the Agrarian party; Mr. Šrobár, a former minister; Mr. Pauliny, director of the Tatra Bank of Banská Bystrica; Mr. Josko, director of the Ružomberok cellulose manufacture; Mr. Štefánik, a magistrate; Mr. Štefunko, a sculptor; Mr. Viest, the section chief in the Communications Ministry; Mr. Janšák, section chief in the Public Works Ministry, and Mr. Kvetko, a veterinarian.

The insurgents' principal task was the liquidation of their political adversaries. So it was that they assassinated a great number of people, two of whom were deputies in the Parliament, Slameň and Šalát; the director of the National Wheat Office, Klinovský; two Catholic priests, Šeda and Nemec. They took forty persons away to Liptovský Sv. Mikuláš; another two hundred were sent to Ružomberok where they were imprisoned in the château of Nemecká Lupča.

It is interesting to note the extent to which all these men, united in the same pro-Russian sentiments, deviated in their ultimate aim. The few Catholics who had participated in the insurrection desired to chase the Germans out, while preserving the Slovak State; the Protestants wished for the reestablishment of Czecho-Slovakia. As for the Communists, while pretending at times to be partisans of the Czecho-Slovak State, they desired the creation of a Slovak-Soviet Socialist Republic within the bounds of the U.S.S.R.

The events in Slovakia inspired in Beneš a new argument destined to support his policy in the Western world. In fact, he stated on the London radio that the Slovaks on their own had taken arms against the Slovak State because they preferred the reestablishment of Czecho-Slovakia. The facts were quite otherwise: whereas the great majority of the Slovaks were strongly anti-nazi, only a weak minority, because deprived of its former privileges, was hostile to the Slovak State. But this distinction completely escaped the Western nations, and the uprising presented in this manner could only strengthen Beneš' position with the Allies.

In order to keep in contact with the insurgents, Beneš sent Mr. Němec to Banská Bystrica. This political plenipotentiary had for his mission to force the National Slovak Council to subject itself entirely to the authority of the Czecho-Slovak government of London. Further, General Viest was sent to Slovakia as chief of military operations. The English and Americans for their part sent observers.

On September 29, at Banská Bystrica, despite the opposition of Beneš' plenipotentiary, the National Slovak Council voted for a resolution by which it made clear its point of view on Slovakia's position within the frame of the future Czecho-Slovak State. It asked for the establishment of a dual federation within which Slovaks and Czechs would have equal rights. Conscious of the strengthening of national feeling since the creation of the Slovak State, the leaders of the revolt understood that it was absolutely necessary for Slovakia to possess a legislative and executive organ of its own. Thus they adopted the autonomist program of the former Populist party against which the Protestants had struggled during the twenty years that the first Czecho-Slovak Republic lasted. Shortly afterward, a delegation composed of Messrs. Ursíny, Novomeský, and Lieutenant Colonel Vesel was sent to London to present these resolutions to Beneš. The latter, wishing to bind himself in no way, told them that "the question of the political structure would be resolved only in the country itself by the authorized and competent members who would be designated for this purpose."[139] Yet he proposed to them the following provisory political structure:

a) The existence of three principal central institutions: the Central Assembly, the Presidency of the Republic and the government of the Republic, whose powers would be determined.

b) The Republic would be composed of four provinces or regions: Bohemia, Moravia, Slovakia, and Sub-Carpathian Ruthenia, each possessing a provincial Diet and executive power.

c) It would be essential, in the State's new organization, to proceed to the decentralization of the Central Parliament; the legislative power would be decentralized toward the provincial Diets, then toward the assemblies of the districts and municipalities.

d) The State would be organized neither under "dualism" nor "federalism," but would be unitary.[140]

So, faithful to his policy of twenty-five years, Beneš preferred to ignore the national Slovak problem, reducing it to a mere question of regionalism, similar to the question of Moravia. This attitude disappointed the Slovak delegates. Convinced that Beneš had learned nothing, they had to return to Slovakia emptyhanded.

After this fruitless meeting, Mr. Beneš "sent the order to his friends from Bohemia and Moravia not to risk any gesture of solidarity with the insurrection in Slovakia, and this order was admirably obeyed."[141]

From both the military and political points of view, the uprising lacked cohesion. The command was split between tendencies that were Russian (Velichko, Osmolov), Slovak (Golian) and Czecho-Slovak (Viest). These divergencies served to undermine the efficacy of forces that were not very important. The insurrection had at its disposal forces equivalent to four regiments, plus several specialized units, about twenty armored cars, and a dozen planes. It controlled three aviation camps, two of which were essentially destined to keep in touch with the headquarters of the Russian guerrillas at Kiev. On the other hand, the geographical contour of the region considerably facilitated the insurgents' operations. The central Slovak region as a matter of fact is considered to be of first-rate strategic value. Besides the front

---

[139] Beneš, *Où vont Les Slaves?* p. 283.
[140] *Ibid.*, p. 284.
[141] Dvorský, "Le drame de l'insurrection slovaque en 1944," *La Nation Slovaque* Paris, (February 15, 1949).

located in a mountainous region until then unknown to the Germans, this part of Slovakia acted as a veritable turntable having access to the Hungarian plain, Vienna, and the industrial regions of Silesia.

In order to liquidate the revolt, the Germans sent a considerable number of detachments into Slovakia as early as the night of August 30, 1944. From the admission of Berger's successor, General Höffle, the units listed below were charged with this task:

a) Police units: 5 police commandoes, each numbering a company and 24 patrols;

b) SS units: the 14th Division from Galicia; the 18th *Horst Wessel;* the *Dirlewanger* brigade; the *Schill* combat group equivalent to a brigade, and a Musulman regiment of the Vlassov Army.

c) Army: the *Tatra* 178th Division and the 208th and 209th *Volksgrenadiers* Divisions.

Before this overwhelming superiority in men and materials, the insurrection was doomed to failure. The Germans believed they could become masters of the revolt in a few days, but the particularly difficult mountain terrain of Slovakia thwarted their plans. The irritated Himmler personally went to Bratislava on September 12, to control German operations and ask the aid of the reorganized Slovak government. He formulated his requests in a categorical tone that roused the new Prime Minister, Štefan Tiso, to indignation.

Determined to win out at all costs, the Germans vigorously attacked resistance centers, and the country was soon dotted with common graves. In two months they literally crushed the Banská Bystrica units. Politicians and the military had to withdraw into the mountains. Seeing that they had been led into an endless catastrophe, the disappointed soldiers blamed their chiefs. When Generals Viest and Golian wanted to abandon their troops and take a plane for London, their men burned the plane. Obliged to flee, they hid in the hay in a barn, where they were soon discovered by the Germans and made prisoners. Taken to Bratislava, they were interrogated without respite, then sent to Germany never to return.

From the Slovak point of view, the uprising was a frightful military tragedy.[142] Whereas in the course of the whole war 2,500

---

[142] Thus one of its organizers recognizes it, General Vesel (who escaped from Czecho-Slovakia in August, 1948), in a statement made on his arrival in Frankfurt. See "Le IVe" anniversaire du soulèvement slovaque," *Le Monde* Paris, 1948).

Slovaks had succumbed on the eastern front, 25,000 fell during the insurrection, which caused in addition material damage estimated at 144,461 million crowns.[143]

On October 28, the national holiday of the Czecho-Slovak Republic, General Höffle organized on the public square of Banská Bystrica a military parade to celebrate the "victory." It is a matter of regret that Monsignor Tiso did not believe that he should abstain from taking part in this gruesome manifestation which, stated the General, marked the reestablishment of the authority of the government of Bratislava over this rebellious city.

What is the profound meaning of the 1944 uprising in Slovakia? To answer this question we must throw a little light on the role of the U.S.S.R. in this veritable national drama. Most of the insurgents were undeniably Slovak, but their leaders were bolshevik agents. The Machiavellian idea, born in the headquarters of the Russian guerrillas at Kiev, was very simple. The Russian parachutist constituency was to inveigle the adversaries of the Tiso regime into a rebellion which would give Hitler the opportunity of intervening and crushing the participants, whether they were national Communists à la Husák, or Democrats à la Lettrich. Once the rebellion was liquidated by the Germans, the Red Army would descend from the Carpathians to take the "Fascists" in hand. Thus the Communists of bolshevik tendencies would have a green light to take over the power in Slovakia.

This plan was to be realized, with the exception of a few details, with surprising precision. Once the machine was set in motion, owing to the aid of blind and credulous Slovaks, the Soviet agents who had been dropped by parachute tried to bring about the decomposition of the guerrilla units and they freed the Slovak communist soldiers from their duty of obedience toward their democratic chiefs.[144] Convinced that the Communists of the country, not numerous in relation to the rest of the population, would be incapable of dominating the situation under normal conditions, they set about sowing disorder and disintegrating the country socially.

On the strategic plane, it could be stated that the advancing Red Army stopped at once on the Carpathian slopes. The Zhu-

---

[143] One realizes the importance of this sum if it is compared to the German debt resulting from Slovak commercial deliveries, a sum which reached, by the end of the war, six billion crowns.

[144] Dvorský, "Le drame de l'insurrection slovaque en 1944," *ibid.*

kov Army," wrote a Pole who participated in the insurrection, "stopped in front of the Dukla Pass and watched from a distance the insurgents suffer their crushing defeat. At the same time on the other side of the Wisla, the Rokossovsky Army looked on with the same sang-froid at the destruction of Warsaw."[145] Left entirely to themselves, more and more closely beset by the Germans, the insurgents dispatched an emissary by plane to solicit aid from the Russians. The Russian answer was his confinement.[146] In Slovakia as at Warsaw, the Russians left the uprising in a bath of blood. Once again Russia was Germany's accomplice. It "sacrificed unheard of strategic advances, preferring the temporary occupation of the country by the Germans to its liberation by the non-Communists."[147]

Mr. Beneš, knowing that the massacre of Katyn had led to the diplomatic break between Poland and Russia in March, 1944, was at no cost willing for the uprising in Slovakia to be a cause of discord between him and Moscow. He found it wiser to remain silent.

Seen from this angle, the personalities who were drawn into this bloody venture appeared only as mere figureheads destined to blind part of the Slovak population to the intrigues of the bolshevist policy. Such were, alas, the Protestants who, conforming to the secret and allegorical orders of pastor Šenšel of Liptovský Sv. Mikuláš, did not hesitate to hang onto the runaway horse of the knight of the Apocalypse coming from the East."[148]

So the Slovak insurrection constituted a remarkable political victory for Moscow.

The End of the Slovak State

After the uprising, Berlin thought of instituting a German military administration in Slovakia. However H. Raschhofer, professor of international law and an expert of the German government on Slovak questions, advised against such a measure. Therefore the Germans limited themselves to watching the Slovak administration a bit more closely. Although annoying, this system allowed the authorities of Bratislava to safeguard the national interests more effectively than under a regime of pure and simple occupation. At the intervention of Monsignor Tiso, many soldiers

[145] Zdzislav Marynowski, "The Slovak Revolt in 1944," *Orzel Bialy* Nos. 43, 44, 45, 46. London, (1949).
[146] Dvorsky, Le drame de l'insurrection slovaque en 1944," *ibid.*
[147] *Ibid.*
[148] Clementis, *Messages from London*, p. 488.

who had been disarmed and deported into Germany were able
to return to their country. The government of Bratislava likewise
succeeded in getting a rather large number of Slovaks from the
hands of the Gestapo and the Feldgendarmerie.

Also the government can be credited with stopping the
evacuation of the civilians of eastern Slovakia ordered by German military authorities. The whole Prešov region, threatened
by Russian pressure on the Carpathians, was to be evacuated.
This insane order was finally rescinded.

Obliged to retreat, the Germans undertook to disassemble
certain important armament factories with a view to transporting
them into Germany or Austria. Here again the intervention of
the Slovak authorities to counteract these plans was undeniably
effective.

This Slovak drama resulted in a veritable stampede of persons trying to save themselves and their belongings.

Thus Ladislav Kniha, chief of the administration of the department of the Tatras (Ružomberok) and more concerned with
Slovak interests than the military orders given him, was shot by
the Germans. This is only one example among many.

The police of the Slovak State, far from persecuting the anti-
German constituency, protected it. In many cases it rescued from
the Gestapo persons who had taken part in the revolt. Numerous
Slovaks owe their lives to the chief and assistant-chief of police
of Bratislava, Messrs. Beňuška and Jurčo. On the other hand,
there was no one at all to save the latter from the German concentration camps when their "lifesaving" policy was discovered
by the Germans.

The last months of the Slovak State's existence were marked
by a general wish to affirm Slovakia's right to independence,
even in face of the end which was coming closer and closer, as
well as the prospect of Beneš' return.

Thus on October 7, 1944, the Union of Slovak Writers
launched an appeal to the population; the principal passage was
worded as follows:

> We express a steadfast faith in the life and future of
> the Slovak nation, in defending its individuality and con-
> sequently its right to form a State of its own. No violent
> intervention can change this principle. Each nation has
> the right to form a separate State, and thus it is of the
> Slovak nation on the territory inhabited by its ethnical
> *substratum*."

On January 14, 1945, a great congress of young Slovaks took place at Piešťany. It had been called with a view to deciding on an unequivocal attitude toward present and future events. These young people came from all corners of the country, formed themselves into a sort of youth parliament and voted among other things the following important resolution:

> The Slovak Republic is the vital and supreme expression of the nation's sovereignty; it is the only and exclusive State formation in which we want to live and work, where we can best develop our faculties and our noble contribution to the work of European civilization. No one in all of humankind can ask us to betray the laws that all the nations of the world hold sacred. That is why we stand irrevocably behind the Slovak State and we can but combat all those who would wish to deprive us of our State, whether it be under the emblem of "Czecho-Slovakism," bolshevism, or the crown of Saint Stephen. . . .
>
> We know that the Slovak nation, even amid the great events of war, will have sufficient moral strength to resist the cruel fate which it would have if we became victims of a foreign domination. As a conscious European nation, we wish to participate in the defense of the European spirit in order to be able to benefit by its advantages even after the end of the struggle that is dividing the world. We bow before the blood shed by the best of our nation's sons. It urges us to continue the struggle for right, a struggle which can end only with the victory of the Slovak spirit and European civilization.[149]

The Slovak parliament, convening on January 23, made an assertion destined to have historical significance:

> The Slovak nation, calling to witness the natural right conferred by God, was, is and will be a nation separate and independent, having its own existence. Whoever disregards this fundamental principle of our national life is for us an enemy who wants us to be slaves, whatever the mask under which it appears. The right to decide its own fate falls upon the nation alone, that is, on the Slovak Parliament elected to this end in conformance with the laws in effect, by an overwhelming majority of 90 per cent of the population. No government, whether it be made up of emigrants or not, can legally decide the fate of the nation. It results from the very principle of national individuality which asserts that the Slovak people can not turn

---

[149] Quoted in: G. Husák, *Our Struggle for the Future* (Bratislava: 1948), pp. 81-82.

its interests to perfect account and develop its creative
force on an individual and national plane save in a State
of its own.

In February, 1945, the Swiss government, after having recognized the Czecho-Slovak government, announced to the chargé
d'affaires of Slovakia at Berne that it would consider him henceforth merely a consular representative. Thereupon the Minister
of Foreign Affairs of Bratislava sent to Berne an *aide mémoire*
in which, inspired by the aforesaid ideas, he put himself above
political conjecture, and reasserted his faith in the liberty of the
little nations—liberty founded on the same principle as the independence of Switzerland itself.

Inasmuch as eastern Slovakia was already occupied by the
Red Army, all these statements can be considered theoretical.
But for Monsignor Tiso any compromise with bolshevism was
inconceivable. When the Slovak State was nearing its end, a Soviet agent made contact with the President's entourage to propose
that he declare a Slovak Soviet Republic at the propitious moment. He cited Rumania as an example, where in spite of the
Russian occupation, King Michael had remained on the throne.
Monsignor Tiso categorically declined this offer.[150]

The end of the Slovak State aroused an intense uneasiness in
the people and in political circles. Inevitably this State was going
to be replaced by a Third Czecho-Slovak Republic. The Slovaks
experienced at that time a feeling of profound perplexity. They
witnessed the fall of the State which they were in the habit of
considering as the manifestation of a natural right and the consequence of a normal evolution. The declaration of independence
which had been unanimously pronounced by the Slovak Parliament March 14, 1939, appeared legitimate to them by virtue of
the right of peoples to self-determination. And so they did not
hide their grief. They all thought that when Hitler, on March 13,
1939, had given Slovakia the alternative either of a military occupation like that which later took place in Bohemia, or the
separation of Slovakia from the Czech countries, Parliament had
done the right thing in choosing the second solution.

The leaders themselves had to accept the new state of affairs.
If Mr. F. Ďurčanský believed up to the last minute that the
Western countries would make a separate peace with Germany
in the very interest of Europe, it was a false hope.

---

[150] Čulen, *Biography of Msgr. Tiso*, p. 281.

The more the reality of the Slovak State dimmed, the more ardent became the idea of it. And it is not so much the fear of the Red terror as the hope of being able to work at the resurrection of the State that prompted the Slovak leaders to emigrate. It is in this hope that at Easter, 1945, the government with ten thousand persons of all social conditions set out on the road of exile.

How will history judge the policy and comment on the existence of the Slovak State?

Having appeared during the cold war between Germany and the West and bound irremediably to the general fate of Central Europe by its geographical position, the Slovak Republic during World War II could only defend its own national interest after the example of the neutral as well as the fighting nations. The only policy possible in such a situation was that of the lesser evil.

Even a versatile man like Milan Hodža had to admit at the end of his life in 1942 in London the obvious success of the Slovak State:

> Some political writers in this country (i.e., England)[151] used to be rather skeptical about Slovakia and her position and even about her political efficiency. Now doubts obviously prove to have been unfounded. . . . Slovakia has reached if not passed the Central European civilization level.[152]

C. A. Macartney, a British expert on questions of Central Europe, acknowledged also in 1942 that in the Slovak State, despite a certain political dependency with respect to Germany, the Slovaks "had more opportunity than they had ever enjoyed before to pursue their national and social integration, and established a distinctive Slovak nationalism as a factor of the Danubian situation."[153]

La Gazette de Lausanne was also obliged to concede that in spite of a certain dependency on the Third Reich, Slovakia, "led by really clever statesmen, had succeeded in making a rather enviable, almost exceptional place for itself among the satellite States. Its military contribution was, to tell the truth, not very important, for the OKW distrusted the Slovaks' small amount of ardor in fighting against their Slav brothers.' "[154]

---

[151] He then lived in Great Britain.
[152] Hodža, *Federation in Central Europe*, p. 94.
[153] C. A. Macartney, *Problems of the Danube Basin* (Cambridge: 1942), p. 122.
[154] *La Gazette de Lausanne*, August 4, 1944.

The Czech historian, B. Chudoba, said the following about the Slovak State:

> Slovakia remained a semidependent state under the Presidency of Father Tiso. It must be said that this priest, who used to be one of the rare Slovak supporters of Beneš' foreign policy (1935-1938), did all that he could to protect Slovakia from immediate Nazi administration.[155]

For Mr. K. Krofta, the Slovak Republic was "a juridically independent State, although strongly bound by the German Reich's protection. . . ."[156]

The Slovak State, established without bloodshed, will find its justification in the eyes of history. Despite an undeniable German political influence which, moreover, manifested itself in all the countries of Central Europe, this State brought internal independence to the Slovaks and made it possible for them to manage their own affairs, after a wait of a thousand years.

[155] Chudoba, "Czechoslovakia, A Study in Disintegration," *ibid.*, pp. 88-90.
[156] Krofta, *Czechoslovak History*, p. 803.

PART III

THE THIRD CZECHO-SLOVAK REPUBLIC

THE NATIONAL FRONT REGIME (1945-1948)

The High Contracting Parties having regard to the interests of their mutual security, have agreed to maintain close and friendy cooperation after the re-establishment of peace and to regulate their actions according to the principles of mutual respect of their independence and sovereignty and non-interference in the internal affairs of the other signatory. They have agreed to develop their economic relations on the broadest possible scale and to grant one another all possible economic aid after the war.

(Article 4 of the Treaty of Friendship and Mutual Aid between Czecho-Slovakia and the U.S.S.R., dated December 12, 1943.)

Before broaching the historical account of the Third Czecho-Slovak Republic, a basic fact must be stressed: this State had its origin in Mr. Beneš' connections and not in the will of the Slovak people. An influence pedlar, he was recognized by the Allied governments as President of the future Czecho-Slovak Republic while he was a mere exile in London during the war. The State machinery was actually re-established thanks to the U.S.S.R.'s military backing of Beneš on the basis of the Treaty of Friendship and Mutual Aid signed in Moscow by V. Molotov and Z. Fierlinger on December 12, 1943.

When he returned to Košice from Moscow under the escort of the Red Army in April, 1945, Beneš assumed the direction of a government created in Moscow and approved by Stalin. Next he was acknowledged as President of the Republic by a Parliament from which he had, in agreement with Mr. Gottwald, eliminated in advance all the parties and political personalities likely to oppose the National Front regime as well as the exclusive alliance of Czecho-Slovakia with the U.S.S.R. Strong in his position with the Soviets, he began to liquidate, in the name of "democracy" and by means of "popular" courts, all whom he suspected of resisting his policy of Sovietizing the country. Free of all control, he issued numerous decrees to introduce "popular" administration and a socialistically planned economy.

After the elections of May, 1946, he put Mr. Gottwald in power and entrusted the principal government offices to Communists. Having run the Sudeten Germans and a good part of the Magyars out of the country, he organized a "national" State in which Slovakia was to be more and more absorbed by Prague's revived centralism. Once again serious friction was evidenced in the relations between Slovaks and Czechs. Excuses were found to brush aside the Slovak Democrats little by little from the National Front. The decisive blow was struck against them in the summer of 1947, with the approbation of the Czech "democratic" parties.

The chain reaction provoked by the Czechs and Communists in Slovakia at that time was to result in the shifting of the center of gravity of the political forces in Czecho-Slovakia even more toward the left. In February, 1948, the Communists did nothing except legally strengthen their actual position established since 1945 under the kindly patronage of Mr. Beneš.

The Establishment of the Regime

"Doroshenko" Arrives on the Danube—Carrying out the agreements made by the Holy Alliance, the Tsar's Army went into Hungary in 1848 to defend the legitimacy of the Hapsbourg dynasty against the Budapest rebellion. When it crossed the Carpathians, it sowed terror among the Slovak population; whole villages fled before it to take refuge in the forests.

A hundred years later, history was destined to repeat itself in much more dramatic circumstances.

In expectation of the "liberation" by the Russian Army, the Czecho-Slovak government exiled in London had as early as May 8, 1944, concluded an agreement with the Soviet government concerning the relationship between the Czecho-Slovak administration and the Soviet Commander-in-Chief on the entry of Soviet troops into Czecho-Slovak territory. The inspiration for this document, which was signed by H. Ripka and V. Lebedev, supposedly was found in the "traditional" friendship recalled in the Mutual Aid Agreement between the U.S.S.R. and the Czecho-Slovak Republic of May 16, 1935, and in the Mutual Aid Treaty of December 12, 1943. Article 7 contains the following provisions:

> All members of the Soviet (Allied) forces on Czecho-slovak territory will be amenable to the jurisdiction of the Soviet (Allied) Commander-in-Chief. All members of the

Czechoslovak armed forces will be amenable to Czecho-
slovak jurisdiction. Civilians on Czechoslovak territory will
likewise be subject to this latter jurisdiction even in cases
of penal offenses committed against the Soviet (Allied)
armed forces, unless such offenses were committed in the
zone of war operations. In the latter case they will come
under the jurisdiction of the Soviet (Allied) Commander-
in-Chief. Any doubts about jurisdiction which may arise
will be settled by mutual agreement between the Soviet
(Allied) Commander-in-Chief and the Czechoslovak government delegate.[1]

After the Germans liquidated the insurrection, the Red Army
deemed it an opportune moment to rush toward central Slovakia.
Like a flood it submerged the country. The Russians relegated
the aforementioned agreement to the archives. The Soviet soldiers did not know of it and acted as they pleased. Field Marshal
Malinovsky's famous army corps, composed of convicts and
criminals, scattered panic as they went. Theft and rape marked
the advance of this victorious army.

At that time overwhelming misfortune came down upon the
cities and towns. Periodic bursts of gun fire would shatter the
night and in the morning the victims' bodies were displayed for
all to see. At Bratislava, the central hospital examined four thousand raped women. Many others would not make themselves
known. No one dared carry a watch; it would have been making
a gift of it to a Russian soldier! *Davai chassi!* (your watch!) became the catchword of Russian "liberation" in Slovakia.

One day, at Levoča's municipal movie, the newsreel showed
episodes of the Big Three Conference at Yalta. A scene without
special significance appeared on the screen: Churchill glancing
at his watch, accompanied by an attentive look from Stalin.
Someone in the hall could not keep from exclaiming: "Davai
chassi!" Twenty-five persons were arrested on the spot by members of the Soviet Security Police.

Entering the two-room lodging of a workman, a Russian soldier shouted: "Why, you are a middle class man!" and took all
that he could carry away—covers, eiderdowns, sewing machine,
etc. Russian military carts, drawn by horses covered with Persian
rugs, carried considerable booty toward the Soviet Union's frontiers to furnish the "bolshevik paradise."

[1] Académie Diplomatique Internationale, *Dictionnaire Diplomatique,* IV
(Paris), 1066.

Everywhere the Russians gave proof of an astonishing un-
restraint. One day, a soldier with a submachinegun under his
arm and a cigarette in his mouth went into a church where a
divine service was taking place. Without taking off his hat, he
approached the altar. He was followed by the eyes of all the
faithful, who held their breath. The singing and the organ ceased.
Everybody waited anxiously. Realizing the effect produced by
his intrusion, the soldier shouted to the frightened priest: *"Nichevo, nichevo! Rabotai!* (It is nothing! Get back to your work!)"
And looking up toward the organist: *"A ty, davai muziku!* (And
you, music!)" Then, having relighted his cigarette at an altar
candle, he left the church.

Behind the Red Army came the NKVD units. In the smallest
villages, they imprisoned all those designated as having been
partisans of the Tiso regime. To the great joy of the informers,
thousands of people were piled into prisons where they were
subjected to interminable questioning. The NKVD guards and
commandoes ran freely about the prison cells looking for particularly dangerous enemies of communism.

Twenty thousand Slovaks, almost all intellectuals—doctors,
officers, priests—were subsequently deported to Russia. Among
them may be mentioned the case of Mr. Martin Mičura, President
of the Supreme Court of Bratislava. A broad-minded Catholic,
he could have played an important political role; therefore it
was thought a matter of urgency to get him out of Slovakia.

Of all those deported, scarcely half of them ever returned
home after two or three years of hard labor, their health broken
forever. Some 25 per cent of them died and the rest vanished in
the colossal melting pots of U.S.S.R. hard labor camps.

The Slav "brothers" and "liberators," in fact, brought terror
everywhere! The contemporary Soviet writer Boris Gorbatov published a book titled *Doroshenko Arrives on the Elbe*, in which he
gathered together the worst exaggerations on the heroism of the
Russian soldier. In reality Doroshenko was an invader.

Mr. Beneš' Return from Exile—Contrary to Mr. Churchill's
advice, Beneš left for Moscow in December, 1943 to sign a treaty
of mutual aid with Stalin. By the stroke of his pen, he broke
psychologically with the Western Allies. The Czecho-Slovak government of London was the only one of all those in exile to play
Russia's pawn. They spoke at that time of Polish rigidity and
once again of Mr. Beneš' flexibility. Unfortunately, where he
should have faced reality with a practical mind, Beneš gave him-

self up to gratuitous assumptions. Determined to remain in power, he set about finding a thousand reasons to justify his policy.

When Beneš arrived in Košice with his government during the first days of April, 1945, he was incapable of feeling the heavy, tense atmosphere reigning in Slovakia. Without applause, without expression in their faces, the curious onlookers received him and his men, including two persons especially attached to him: Mr. Zorin, the new Soviet Ambassador, and Mr. Gottwald, President of the Czech Communist party and Stalin's agent.

On April 3, a solemn reception was given in honor of President Beneš. The ceremony took place in the Košice theater. One noticed among the Russian women in the service of the Red Army several dressed in nightshirts. These clothes were actually much sought after by the Russian women soldiers who took them for ceremonial robes.

A young aggressive Communist, Mr. Husák, the new Commissioner of the Interior in Slovakia, presided over the gathering. "The first Czecho-Slovak Republic is dead," he began. "Dead is its centralism, dead also is its false democratic policy. The new Republic will be a socialistic federation of two nations equal under the law: the Slovak nation and the Czech nation."

It was a defiance hurled at Mr. Beneš, President of the First Republic. With Mr. Zorin in his theater box and Gottwald, Fierlinger, and others in his shadow, he was no more than a prisoner of a clan.

On April 5, 1945, Mr. Gottwald, then Vice-President of the government, proclaimed the famous governmental program known under the name of Košice Agreement, which he qualified as the "Magna Charta of the Slovaks and the working classes of the Republic."

The Government and Parliament of the National Front—As early as December, 1943, at the time of his Moscow visit, Mr. Beneš had concluded with Mr. Gottwald a general agreement on fundamentals relating to the future government of the National Front as it was to exist in the reconstructed Czecho-Slovakia.

He wrote in his *Memoirs*:

> During this discussion the question of the National Front was mentioned for the first time. It was declared to be necessary that the government parties should form a united national front after liberation, that they should jointly prepare a single post-revolution programme and

that they should jointly undertake to fulfill it. I also agreed to the plan for the National Front on this occasion.[2]

The main point in these plans concerned the composition of the future government. It was decided that all the right wing parties would be branded as Fascists and dismissed from power under the pretext of collaboration. "All of us without exception regarded the ruthless liquidation of all fascism as a matter of course," states Mr. Beneš.[3]

These plans remained cursory, however, and Beneš seems not to have realized that the exclusion of certain parties was likely to be generalized and later would allow the Communists to get rid of all opposition, as their tactics essentially anticipated.

Moreover, these tendencies would have been comprehensible under new circumstances if they had had as their aim to exclude from public life the politicians of the Protectorate of Bohemia-Moravia, as well as those of the Slovak Republic. But they aimed purely and simply at the suppression of the parties depending on the peasant class, in order to bring it more easily under control after liquidating its chiefs. Thus it is that Beneš and Gottwald determined the fate of the Czech Agrarian party and the Slovak National Unity party.

This decision, heavy in consequences, was going to be fatal to the regime of the Third Republic, which, out of balance on the plane of internal policy, could not avoid slipping toward the communist extremity.

During Mr. Beneš' visit in the Soviet capital in 1945, the question of the personalities to form the government of the National Front was brought up at once and quickly settled. In fact, on Mr. Beneš' arrival in Moscow, a group of people were waiting for him at the airport. After the usual handshaking, Mr. Gottwald struck up conversation with him. "Excuse me for the time being. We shall talk tomorrow after my visit to the Generalissimo," Beneš then said to him. "You will not be received by the Generalissimo," replied Mr. Gottwald, "until after you have approved this list."

It was the list of members of the future government; Mr. Gottwald had had reserved for himself the office of Vice-Premier. Mr. Beneš could do nothing but approve it.

Such was, in short, the origin of the National Front, a profoundly revolutionary institution which was going to be placed

---

[2] Beneš, *Memoirs*, p. 272.
[3] Beneš, *Ibid.*, p. 271.

above the government and Parliament. It consisted of a committee of six members (one for each political party, four in Czechia and two in Slovakia) deciding on all important measures to be taken within the government as well as all the bills to be submitted to the Parliament's vote. The role of the government and Parliament were therefore limited to the discussion of problems already approved by the National Front.

Later on, the Czech and Slovak Communist parties were frequently going to use this unconstitutional organ to veto any measure or bill that might happen to be disadvantageous to them.

The National Front government was, however, only a camouflage for the strategic position that the Communists were able to create, with the complicity of other parties, within its framework. On June 8, 1945, Gottwald signed an agreement with Fierlinger and Zenkl, by which the Communist, the Social Democrat, and the National Socialist parties in the Czech lands established a so-called "National Bloc of the Urban and Rural Working People."[4] This was a purposely confusing title for what was in fact a closeranked socialist bloc within the government. For all practical purposes, this document meant an unconditional surrender of the Beneš party to the Marxists. In engaging the National Socialists to pursue their own political goals, the Communists managed virtually to prevent from the very beginning the formation of any anti-Marxist coalition in the future.

But the properly operational base of their policy remained the Marxist bloc embracing the Czech and Sovak Communists and the Czech Social Democrats.

The three-ring structure allowed the Communists a subtle game of constantly changing tactical alliances and exclusions within the National Front. While spreading insecurity among the partners, it assured the Communist party the position of croupier in the whole game.

A similar agreement creating the "Slovak National Front" was adopted on June 26, 1945, between the Slovak Communist and the Slovak Democratic parties.[5] Tied up by its nature to the "National Bloc of the Urban and Rural Working People" in the Czech lands, the Slovak National Front had for its main end the neutralization of the Slovak Democratic party.

After having formed a National Front government, the political heads of the Third Czecho-Slovak Republic felt the neces-

[4] See Appendix VIII.
[5] See Appendix IX.

sity of relying upon a legislative body composed of personalities who were also born of the revolution.

Thus, during the summer of 1945 the three hundred seats in the central Parliament were divided between Czechia (two hundred) and Slovakia (one hundred). According to Mr. Beneš' agreement with the Communists, the political structure of the State was to be founded on the four parties of Czechia—Communist (Gottwald), Socialist (Fierlinger), National-Socialist (Beneš, Ripka) and Populist (Monsignori Šrámek and Hála)— and Slovakia's two parties—Communist (Široký, Schmidke, Husák) and Democrat (Lettrich, Ursíny). Each of these parties obtained fifty seats in the Prague Parliament. The deputies were appointed by the conventions of their respective parties. In Slovakia they were appointed by the delegates of the national committees during the extraordinary assembly of the National Slovak Council on August 29, 1945, in Banská Bystrica.

The two parties of the Slovak National Front also shared in the laurels of the "liberation" as recompense for having collaborated with the Russian partisans in the uprising, although they were clearly in the minority in relation to the whole of the country.

The Catholics, who had nearly all rallied to the idea of the Slovak State, were accused of collaboration and were thus kept out of any political representation.

The Sovietization of the Administration—Henceforth from December, 1943, at the time of Mr. Beneš visit to Moscow, the Sovietization of the administration in Czecho-Slovakia was determined. In his *Memoirs,* Mr. Beneš reports how Gottwald conceived of the preparation of this revolution: "He stressed the necessity of forming national committees which would have to be used not only for the organization of revolutionary cells for the insurrection itself but also as the basis for the whole revolutionary civil administration." And Beneš concluded: "I did not oppose this conception."[6]

After reaching an agreement with the Communists, Beneš had to prepare public opinion in the Czech countries with regard to this plan. To this end, he broadcast a message from London on February 3, 1944, urging the population to create national committees of the communes, districts, and lands destined to become the organs of anti-German resistance and be

[6] Beneš, *Memoirs,* p. 270.

transformed afterward into the wheels of public administration.

The government of London, in its declaration of April 16, 1944, established the aims and defined the principles of the organization of the national committees.

On December 4, 1944, Beneš signed a "constitutional decree" aimed at giving a juridical basis to the system of national committees; in this, he had recourse to the old Czecho-Slovak Constitution of 1920, according to which the people are the only source of political power. He did not take into account the facilities given the communist minority to seize the power by means of such committees.

In the Košice program, the new government only confirmed the institution of the national committees. It declared that they spelled progress in comparison with "the former machine of administrative bureaucracy," and they were empowered, in their territorial jurisdiction, to direct all public affairs and especially, side by side with the central organs, to watch over the national safety. In this respect as in many others the national committees became the instrument of the governmental policy.

Governmental decree No. 4 of May 5, 1945, confirmed by another (No. 44) of August 7, 1945, stated precisely, by virtue of the constitutional decree of December 4, 1944, the organization, the powers, and the method of election of the national committees.

The communal and district offices were abolished and the institutions of mayors and district heads rejected as being middle class. The Communists stood up against even the most modest of the bureaucratic elements of the administration, as for example the town hall secretaries, whose jurisdiction, especially in matters of supplies, had been fixed by the State. They declared that the people themselves were going to seize the reins of power. In reality it was quite different. As soon as the national committees of the communes and districts were formed, their chairmen became in fact all-powerful and no longer recognized any laws. Then there began a period of settling of accounts that had accumulated for years between rivalling men, jealous women, and political adversaries.

From the beginning, the formula of the National Front assured the minority Communist party a key position even on the municipal and district level. No decision of the other parties carried any weight. The famous veto right in the little Slovak communes—as at the present time in the Security Council of the

United Nations—became for the Communists a means of universal
sabotage against the democratic effort. This negative attitude is
undoubtedly one of the most injurious contributions of the communist system in the present political world. Bolshevik (pertaining to a majority) in name, the Communist party is actually only
a menshevik (pertaining to a minority) dictatorship.

In his message to the Provisional National Assembly, President Beneš summarized the development of the situation as
follows:

> In the first place it will be necessary to reconstitute the
> whole administration of the Republic in determining the
> powers of the new institution—the national committees.
> I have already expressed my approbation on this point
> abroad and I consider it quite natural that they be inte-
> grated in our Constitution.[7]

It is, in short, this evolution encouraged by Mr. Beneš that
this future Czecho-Slovak Constitution of June 9, 1949, was
going to sanction in its Chapter VI (articles 123-133).

> *Czecho-Slovakia emerged, step by step,*
> *from the postwar confusion, and became*
> *once again a well-ordered democratic*
> *state.*[8]   H. Seton Watson

The Situation After the May, 1946 Elections—After the elections of the Constituent Assembly, set for May 26, 1946, the National Front decided in conformity with the Beneš-Gottwald
Agreement of Moscow, to suspend all the parties which formed
the National Unity bloc during the Slovak State. This measure
was actually aimed at the Catholics who, finding it impossible to
form a political group of their own, were going to be obliged to
give their votes to the Communist or Democratic parties. Their
chiefs, Široký and Lettrich, made advances to the Catholics. The
chairman of the Communist party of Slovakia even went so far
as to visit one of the most influential of them, young deputy
Kempný, to whom he made the most enticing proposals. But he
stretched forth his hand in vain.

To the surprise of all, the Slovak electors learned on the eve
of the elections that Prague was offering four parties for their

---

[7] Dr. Paul Levit, *The National Committees and the New Constitution*,
Ministry of Information (Prague: January, 1947).
[8] H. Seton Watson, "Eastern Europe" in the *Yearbook of World Affairs*
(London: 1949), p. 10.

choosing: Democratic, Communist, the Liberty party and the Labor party. This diversity aimed at confusing the electors. In spite of this scheme and after laborious negotiations, an agreement was finally signed on March 30, 1946, between certain influential Protestants and the representatives of Catholic circles. According to this pact the Catholics were to support the Democratic party. This act had a great political importance because in reserving a place in the Democratic party for the mass of Catholics, it created a vast Christian assemblage in the country. The stipulations formulated by the Catholics in Articles 3, 4, and 5 of the agreement were thus expressed:

Art. 3:   Elaboration of the electoral lists.
The presidium of the party will delegate for each electoral district two members entrusted with drawing up the list of candidates, assuring a place to the most capable persons and seeing to it that the proportion of two to one is respected between Catholic and Protestant candidates.

Art. 4:   Representation in the autonomous organs of the party.
The party agrees to establish a proportion of the offices to be distributed among Catholics and Protestants within its different organisms. This proportion will be seven Catholics to three Protestants except in regions where either Catholicism or Protestantism clearly dominates.

Art. 5:   Application of the proportion seven to three.
The aforementioned proportion will be applied in all economic and financial organizations or trade unions as well as in the institutions or enterprises falling under the party's influence: in banks and cooperatives, in the various industrial, agricultural or crafts unions. It will likewise have to be respected as far as possible in the public administration services over which the Democratic party has control.[9]

The success carried by the Democrats in the elections was stirring, as the following figures prove:

	Votes	Percentage	Deputies
Democratic party	999,622	62	43
Communist party	489,596	30.37	21
Liberty party	60,195	3.73	3
Labor party	50,079	3.11	2
Blank ballots	12,724	.79	..

[9] The complete text of the agreement is found in the publication of the Ministery of the Interior, *Conspiracy Against the Republic*, (Prague: 1947).

The history of these last two parties tells a great deal about the schemes that were brought to a head against the unity of the Catholics. Whereas Mr. Beneš wanted to disintegrate said unity by means of the Liberty party, the Communists made use of the Labor party. When it had been decided that the Catholics would rally to the Democrats, Mr. Vavro Šrobár, then Minister of Finance, acting at the instigation of Mr. Beneš, obtained in Prague the authorization to create the Liberty party. Following his example, the Slovak Communists then quickly created the Labor party, a mere branch of their own. The Liberty party was financed by funds that Mr. Šrobár had obtained by the discretionary unclamping of the frozen assets of certain enterprises in the process of nationalization. Thus this party was the result of maneuvers on the part of Prague, destined to throw the political structure of Slovakia into confusion. This plan, however, was doomed to complete failure. The party obtained only three deputies, two of whom were Slovaks, Messrs. Hanzel and Šabo, and one Czech acclimatized to Slovakia, Mr. Bruha.

Despite the existence of four parties, the forces were polarized around two: Democratic and Communist. The overwhelming victory of the Democrats was undoubtedly due to the Catholics. Electoral statistics prove, as a matter of fact, that the predominantly Protestant districts, Liptovský Sv. Mikuláš, Myjava, and Senica, had for the most part voted for the Communists.

Therefore, unexpectedly beaten in the elections, the Communists were puzzled. They had to prepare to leave their positions. In fact, ever since 1945, the Interior—especially the police department—as well as certain economic positions, had been in their hands. If at that time the Democratic leaders had acted, the Communists would have had to withdraw; but they were saved because of their veto right within the National Front, and the Protestants' indecision. Having caught their breath, they counterattacked. On June 11, 1946, in the session of the National Front in Prague, the Slovak Communists put on the agenda the question of the "subversive" elements in the Democratic party, and this nonconstitutional organization then adopted the following general lines:

> The political parties are in agreement on the necessity of organizing, by all legal means, the unrelenting repression of the fascist and subversive reactionary elements that, heir to Populist separatism, attempt to hinder the increasing building of Slovakia and the Republic by pro-

moting internal quarrels and stirring up a culpable agitation both within and outside the State.[10]

Immediately several Catholics of consequence, who were regarded as the makers of the agreement with the Protestants and among whom was the lawyer Ľudovít Obtulovič, were arrested and taken to a political prison camp set up hastily in Ilava. The heads of the political police, Messrs. Viktorín and Ilčík, particularly blamed the editor of the weekly paper, *Katolícke noviny*, Mr. Čarnogurský, and questioned him night and day on the negotiations and "secret clauses" of the agreement of March 30, 1946. They made him sign a sixty-page report on the subject of "the political complicity of the Democratic party with the enemies of the Republic and the regime of the popular democracy."

A violent campaign was launched simultaneously in Prague and Bratislava against certain leaders of the Democratic party.

The young deputy Staško became the target of all these attacks. At the opening of the Constituent Assembly, Mr. Nosek, Communist Minister of the Interior, forbade him to come into the room where the recently elected deputies were going to take their oath. "You have no right to prevent me from taking up the duties of my office!" said Dr. Staško, who had succeeded in crushing the Communist party in his electoral district of Orava. "I have the President's authorization to do it and I have the power," replied the Minister, glancing at the policemen standing in the doorway. Whereupon he drew from his pocket a letter addressed to the deputy and containing the same written prohibition.

And so the parliamentary career of this Democrat elected by the Catholic wing was brutally shattered on the very threshold of the Parliament. He was struck down only because he had shown himself to be a good Slovak patriot and too openly an adversary of the Communists. Immediately a series of articles appeared in the press accusing him of military treason and collaboration, although there had never been any question of it before the elections. He tried in vain to face up to these attacks. He was put in prison and placed at the disposal of both the Military Tribunal and the "People's Court."[11]

---

[10] Gustav Husák, *Our Struggle for the Future* (Bratislava: 1948), p. 185.
[11] As the accusations brought against him were ill-founded, he was finally accused, within the framework of the "white conspiracy," of attempts on the State's security and, with numerous "accomplices," he was condemned, in May, 1948, to six years of imprisonment. He escaped from Czecho-Slovakia to Vienna in 1961 and now lives in the United States.

Unfortunately the strongest party of Slovakia could not defend its deputy against Beneš and the Communists. Despite the historic merit of Slovak Catholicism, which had arrived at the point of assuring the Democratic party of the strongest representation of all the satellite countries of Russia, its leaders could not turn this to advantage. The party itself was hybrid in its composition, with a Protestant head and a Catholic body. These two religious faiths had become associated more by reason of their anticommunist feelings than from their desire to develop a positive political program. In spite of the stipulations of the agreement of March 30, 1946, the Protestants continued to keep the most important offices in the government of Prague, in the Slovak National Council, and the Board of Commissioners of Bratislava. So, out of a dozen governmental posts that reverted to the party, two or three at most, for appearance sake, were reserved for Catholics. This disproportion provoked constant tension between these two opposite poles of the party. Besides, the Protestants evidenced regrettable shortsightedness and indifference when the Communists started eliminating and imprisoning the Catholic intelligentsia.

As for the Communists, once they were put into the minority in Slovakia, they changed overnight from partisans of a federative constitution for the Republic into fervent Centralists. Thus Mr. Husák sacrificed the principle of national equality for power —using the strong-arm method. Thereafter he leaned on Gottwald, who had been able to profit by the spiritual disorientation of the Czech people to attract them to communism. Indeed, very much worried about the consequences that the expulsion of nearly three million Sudeten Germans could have, the Czechs, seeking to protect themselves from Germany and free themselves from their own culpability, had thrown themselves into the arms of the Russians as no other nation of Central Europe had done. This explains why in these elections the Czech Communist party had been able to obtain 40.2 per cent of votes with 93 deputies and the procommunistic Social Democrats of Fierlinger 15.58 per cent with 37 deputies, totaling almost 56 per cent of the vote and 130 of 231 deputies in Czechia. Thus, the National Socialists with roughly 24 per cent and 55 deputies and the Czech Populists with 20 per cent and 46 deputies remained in the minority. This success together with the result they obtained in Slovakia assured the Communists, for the whole of the Republic, 39 per cent of the vote with 114 deputies elected. In that way, since the beginning, the Marxist bloc commanded the absolute majority in the Parliament, that is to say 153, and the Czech "Socialist bloc" 185 seats out of 300. This Marxist victory in the 1946 elections made it evident that they would control the further evolution in Czecho-Slovakia.

Mr. Gottwald in Power—Impressed by the results of the elections, Beneš entrusted the post of Prime Minister to Mr. Gottwald. Why did the President of Czecho-Slovakia, who should have been above parties, commission the head of the Communist party to form the new cabinet? This is the question that the real Democrats asked. As a matter of fact, the Communist party, although commanding the greatest number of deputies, actually represented only 39 per cent of the electors. It made up the extreme left tendency of the National Front, and consequently did not seem prescribed for furnishing the head of the government. It would have seemed normal to choose this leader from the National Front's center of gravity, so that he should represent the average tendency emerging from the elections. An example of such a middle policy occurred in France after the liberation at the time of "tripartism" when the majority belonged to the three parties—Communist, Socialist, and the Republican Popular Movement. The French prime minister at that time, however, was not chosen from the Communist party. In fact, although the number of its deputies was the highest in Parliament, owing to its political leanings, the Communist party under free conditions could never have aspired to lead the government and rally a majority to its program. It is obvious that new Czecho-Slovakia, bound as it was by international agreements with Russia and controlled by the Communist police, was no longer a free "parliamentary democracy." It was rather a "popular democracy," and the "bourgeois" solicitude for entrusting the governing of the country's affairs to a body representing the aspirations of the majority of the electors was considered by the new moving spirits as a contemptible survival of outmoded regimes.

Quite as erroneous and still more marked was the solution adopted in Slovakia. Although the Democratic party had obtained on the whole a majority of 62 per cent of the votes (in a democratic parliamentary system, it could have governed without the participation of the communist minority) the Presidency of the autonomous government there was put into the hands of the communist deputy Husák.

As a matter of fact, these dispositions were to be fatal to Mr. Beneš; while his star was paling, Mr. Gottwald was becoming all-powerful. Unknowingly, Mr. Beneš had chosen his successor in designating him as head of the government.

The Liquidation of the Political Opposition

Purges and Administrative Tyranny—One of the first decisions of the new regime was the discharge of all officials until their appearance before the special weeding out commissions created by Order No. 99 of 1945 of the Slovak National Council. According to their degree of culpability, they were classed in four categories: the first included those who could be blamed for nothing and were subsequently reinstated; those who were declared guilty of trivial faults and were transferred to another office; the third, acknowledged guilty of more serious mistakes, were demoted and changed to a different branch of the administration. As for those who were convicted of "fascist" opinions, they were just simply removed from public service.

To the repressive measures were added economic sanctions. Confiscation of lands aimed not only at the Germans and Magyars, but also at the Slovaks acknowledged to be "traitors and collaborators" in the terms of Decree No. 104 of 1945. These confiscations were not the result of judicial decisions, but of purely political rulings dependent on the jurisdiction of confiscation commissions created in each district by Decree No. 64 of 1946. The findings of these commissions could not be reviewed.[12]

Little by little, the ever more invading planning encumbered all the machinery of the administration with red tape to an extent that had never before been attained. The communist regime suspended in practice the application of all laws, even those that the "bourgeois" theory of law was accustomed to call "constitutional." The communist State inaugurated an epoch in which the decisions prevailed over the norms. If they legislated at all, it was only to limit individual liberty more and more. Henceforth the collection of laws and decrees were only good for adorning the desks of the section chiefs of the commissariats since all the important measures were taken by the Central Committee of the Communist party. No one any longer knew the

---

[12] See: Ministère de l'Agriculture, *Ce que prépare le Ministère de l'Agriculture pour les paysans slovaques* (Prague: 1947), p. 20.

condition or the juridical status of his property, his apartment, work, food supplies, nor what his civil obligations or duties were.

Any one whose father, mother, brother, or some relative was classed among the "collaborators," "reactionaries," "enemies of the people," or "the fifth column of the West," was himself considered as a suspect and was sooner or later lost. He could no longer aspire to any right in the State. If he had an enviable apartment, a "nice communist family" was sent to cohabit with him, use his furniture, dishes, and linens. If one day his wife, in a moment of exasperation, came to the point of breaking a few plates, the "guests" called the police, who reported her for infringement on the "social function of the property."

If the suspicions grew more vigorous against him—something which never failed to happen when he had a fine apartment or estate—someone came discreetly to see him and tell him that the authorities wanted to question him on this man or that among his friends or acquaintances. Before pursuing the intruder, he would do well to take a change of linen and his tooth brush, for that evening he would not return home. If the imprisonment lasted more than two weeks, the housing commission, notified by the police, would give his wife a *výmer* (decision) that obliged her to leave the apartment within 10 days, the time of respite sometimes being reduced to 24 hours, in case of urgency. Such a decision was without repeal.

If the unfortunate man succeeded in getting out of prison, he found his apartment occupied by someone more "progressive" than he. Furthermore, he had no need for it any more, for during his "holiday" he had lost his position. He became an uprooted element ripe for the hard labor camp of the Orava Dam or the swamps of Svätý Jur.

The situation of the citizen changed radically if he were a Communist, not "Titoist," but "Kominformist," that is to say, "conformist!" In this case, he could obtain his passport, have a villa, an American car, gas, fabrics, shoes. He could have chicken every Sunday and wine every day. If he held a grade school certificate or carpenter's apprenticeship, he was likely to become a deputy, national counsellor, section chief of a commissariat, director of a state-controlled branch of industry, administrator of a nationalized enterprise or at least an agent of the national security.

The Police Regime—Though appearing peaceful, the country then struggled in convulsions of internal resistance. People sought to save appearances, while remaining nonconformists at heart. In order to watch carefully all the manifestations of this revolt psychology of an oppressed people, the new regime set up an extremely effective police network. It organized a powerful central system which, through its ramifications and setting up of cells, penetrated into the most varied sectors of national life. At one time, a large building located on the banks of the Danube sufficed for Bratislava to house the executive office of the Prime Minister, the Ministry of the Interior and the Office of Propaganda. Henceforward, not only did the Interior occupy this building alone, but in addition took possession of the building of the former Teachers' College, on Lazaretská Street, and the vast building of the former police offices, which had become the seat of the famous "7th Division" of the political police. Although a short time before, its offices existed only in the two principal cities of the country, Bratislava and Košice, it had branches ever after in all the chief towns of the districts. Confidential agents such as the Jacobin agents of the Terror kept watch over the villages and smallest factories. Observers were placed in the student houses and in the barracks. Monitor services were organized in the churches. In the towns, all who visited suspect persons were put under discreet surveillance. Towns were divided into small observation sectors. A well-placed house served as an observatory from which all the movements on the street were watched. The housing commissioner of Bratislava had certain strategic apartments evacuated in order to lodge police observers. In addition, they gladly called for the services of the concièrges.

It is needless to say that the suspect persons were shadowed. Members of the consular representations were especially watched.

The activity shown by the organs of the National Security is seen by a few eloquent figures: for 1946 alone, 17,422 crimes and 28,582 offenses were examined, 6,389 people were arrested and 7,226 questioned. Further, 109,276 accusations were registered.[13]

Penal Justice—Political criteria prevailed even to penal justice. A great number of examples could be given but the following is most commonly known: In the spring of 1946, a man named Sečkár was brought before the regional court of Bratislava to answer for the death of the town hall's secretary in a village of western Slovakia, Báhoň. At the time of the Slovak State, the

[13] See: *Pro—Mémoire du Comité d'Action Slovaque: adressé au conseil Economique et Social de l'O.N.U.* (New York: 1948).

accused, who was engaged in the black market, had been fined
on the intervention of this secretary. Upon the arrival of the
Russians, Sečkár rallied to the Communist party. He then denounced the secretary to the NKVD as a criminal and Fascist
whereupon the latter was stood up against a wall and shot. A
year later, the Báhoň case was referred to justice and Sečkár was
imprisoned. When his guilt was proved, he was condemned to
twelve years of prison by two of the three judges who made up
the chamber. A violent campaign was then launched by the
communist press against these judges (Markovič and Pavliotti).
The Communists of Bratislava and the Partisans' Union organized demonstrations against these "reactionary" judges who had
dared condemn their comrade. The police then imprisoned the
judges and released the criminal.

Here is another example: A certain Bacušan, an officer of the
Slovak National Bank, was in a shelter installed in the basement of
the bank at the time of the "liberation" of Bratislava by the Russians. Three officers of the communist police—hastily created—
went there to look for "fascist" criminals. Bacušan was guarded
by one of them while the two others went to search his apartment. They found money, jewelry, and other objects worth 150,000
crowns. Bacušan was then taken to Petržalka, a suburb of Bratislava on the right bank of the Danube, and was assassinated in a
cowardly manner by the three policemen who buried his body in
a field and shared the booty. A year and a half later Captain
Kukliš, a member of the Slovak National Council for the Democratic party, questioned the Council on the Bacušan case and
asked the Commissioner of Justice for an examination of it. A preliminary investigation was ordered and the assassination proved.
The three policemen were arrested. Without delay the Communists took an effective measure against any proceedings against
their agents. Seconded by the Socialists, they voted in the Parliament a law on "the immunity of the revolutionary acts for which
the police organization and the services for maintaining order
could have been responsible during the liberation." Mr. Beneš
signed the law, and the criminal police agents came out of the
affair spotless.

The People's Courts[14]—In December, 1943, at the time of his
trip to Moscow, Mr. Beneš had had an agreement with Mr. Gottwald on the organization of post-war justice. Relative to the

[14] Commissariat of Information, *The People's Courts*. (Bratislava: 1945).

interview which they had had on this subject, Mr. Beneš stated
that both had considered as a natural thing total liquidation of
all fascist elements,[15] without distinction.

When Beneš went back to London, he published a decree
regarding postwar justice. By virtue of the provisions of this
decree, the Slovak National Council (the revolutionary organization resulting from the "Slovak uprising"), voted on May 15,
1945, to pass Order No. 33 on the repression of crimes committed: (1) by fascist occupants; (2) by citizen traitors; (3) by
collaborators; (4) by traitors in the uprising, and (5) by culp-
ables of the fascist regime.

The first category of persons aimed at by this Order were the
foreigners (Germans) who had participated in the oppression
of the Slovak nation; the second were the important persons of
the Slovak State; the third, the civil servants who had aided the
latter in carrying out their policy. In the fourth category were
put all who had shown any activity on the regional plane with
a view to paralyzing the insurrection. The last took in those who,
on the local plane, had been active under the regime of the
Slovak State.

For the criminals of the first, second, and fourth categories,
the decree provided for the death penalty; for the third category,
the penalties went up to thirty years in prison and in cases of
aggravating circumstances, even the death penalty. For the last
category, the decree provided for hard labor with a minimum of
two years.

For judging all these crimes, three kinds of tribunals were
created: the National Tribunal in Bratislava, qualified to judge
crimes of national importance committed by political personalities of the Slovak State; the popular tribunals of the districts; and
the popular local tribunals.

No objection on the accusation act was permitted. The defense before the National Tribunal and the district tribunals
could be entrusted only to certain lawyers inscribed on a special
list of the Commissariat of Justice. The defense before a popular
local tribunal could not be entrusted to a lawyer.

According to Article No. 6 of the executive regulation No. 55
of 1945 of the Board of Commissioners, it was possible for any
citizen, on mere denunciation, to set a suit in motion against a
political criminal. This provision opened up unlimited possi-

15 See: Beneš, Memoirs, p. 271.

bilities to all vengeances and settling of all accounts. The political character of such justice was emphasized by Article 42 of the same executive ruling. This latter specified actually that the members of the tribunals would be chosen from the members of the political parties on the parity basis.

The decisions of all these tribunals were without repeal.

The Tiso Case—Discovered by the U.S. Army in Bavaria where he had taken refuge, Monsignor Tiso was extradited upon request of the Czecho-Slovak authorities. In October, 1945, in handcuffs, he was taken back to Bratislava together with several members of the former Slovak Government: the former Prime Minister Štefan Tiso, Minister of Interior Mach, Minister of Public Education Kočiš, Minister of Finance Pružinský, Minister of National Economy Medrický, and the Chief of Information Services, Tido Gašpar.

This event caused a sharp reaction among Tiso's friends as well as his enemies. One night some display windows of the CIK, the information office where photographs of the handcuffed Tiso had been exhibited, were destroyed. Also, the first literature denouncing Beneš and Gottwald as "two foreigners in Slovakia" was distributed. This touched off a hunt for enemies of the regime. About twenty students were arrested, including a well-known member of the Bratislava soccer team, J. Bačkor.

The Tiso case created the deepest concern not only among the general public but in political circles as well. Mr. Lettrich, who was at that time Chairman both of the Slovak National Council and of the Democratic party, admitted privately that in the interest of national policy he would have preferred that Tiso remain in Austria. Tiso's return had only widened the gulf which already separated the majority of the people and the government. The question was particularly trying for the leaders of the Democratic party who were hoping at this time to gain widespread Catholic support by exploiting their feelings of aversion toward the Communists and Russian occupation. However, since the draconian laws covering collaboration had been voted for by the Democrats as well as by the Communists, Democratic leaders were not able to reverse their stand. Consequently, the following three attorneys were named to draw up the charges against Tiso: L. Rigan, general matters; J. Šujan, political; and Colonel A. Rašla, military aspects.

The role of President of the National Tribunal was entrusted to Mr. Igor Daxner, a Slovak Protestant Communist, and that of

Vice-President to Mr. Bedrna, a Czech Communist. Mr. Bedrna who had taken refuge from the Germans in Slovakia during the war, later became the man behind the throne of the Czech Communist political repression in Slovakia. Of the Tribunal's seven members, five were Communists. The action of a Protestant-led Democratic party, in thus abandoning the Tribunal to the Communists, was that of a Pontius Pilate washing his hands.

The inquiry lasted nearly a year. Hundreds of witnesses were called. From the very beginning of the trial, Bratislava took on the appearance of an occupied city. Armed police and soldiers were seen everywhere. Public buildings were guarded and access could be gained only by the showing of identity papers. In the beginning the radio carried the depositions of witnesses often interrupted by statements of Tiso. Every Slovak who had a radio listened in; people in the villages gathered around any available set. Monsignor Tiso answered each question with the brilliance and clarity worthy of a shrewd attorney. He could skillfully put back into place those who had been appointed to attack him.

On the streets, in cafes, everywhere people talked of nothing but the trial. But at this point the government abruptly cancelled the broadcasts when it became obvious that the majority of the population clearly favored the accused and that the mere sound of the voice of this man, who had once ably steered the ship of state through troubled waters of the war, stirred up a wave of popular sympathy. Thereafter the public obtained information on the trial's development only through the newspapers. Furthermore, even the newspapers had to be cautious in giving accounts of it because any journalist who proved too indulgent to the cause of the accused found himself barred from the courtroom; such was the fate of Mr. Pakan, editor of the *Times* *(Čas)*, official newspaper of the Democratic party.

On January 3, 1946, the Catholic bishops of Slovakia forwarded a petition to the National Slovak Council on behalf of Monsignor Tiso in which they pointed out that the "outcome of his trial would have a tremendous effect on the opinion and attitude that one part of the Slovak nation would formulate in relation to the reconstituted Czecho-Slovak Republic." In this document the bishops expressed the conviction that Tiso had "sought to work for the good of all." In conclusion they stated: "The majority of the nation shares our belief that Tiso's intentions in his public activities were good and pure."[16]

[16] See Appendix X.

Yet even while the village priests were preaching every Sunday for those who "were suffering unjustly," the communist press was printing threats aimed at Tiso's defenders and carrying illustrations of the gallows reserved for Tiso and his government. The Catholics had few illusions as to the probable results of such a campaign. Still there were some persons, even within groups opposed to the President, who advised prudence and moderation. The ten-year prison sentence accorded former Finnish President Rytti, who had also been accused of collaboration, could provide a precedent to be imitated. Unfortunately, the Tiso case resulted in deepening further still the chasm which already separated the Slovak people and their new leaders.

In reality the new regime was proposing, by this court case, to put on trial the Slovak State itself. The prosecution tried to prove that the internal regime of the Slovak State had been a dictatorship; that the Slovak State had not represented the majority of its people; that Monsignor Tiso had been only an agent of Germany; that, although a Catholic priest, Tiso had persecuted the Jews; and that the concept of the Slovak State had been inspired by Hitler.

Nevertheless, the prosecution did not succeed in proving any of these charges. Two of the most important witnesses paid tribute in their depositions to the principles which had guided the creation of the Slovak State and its internal policy. These witnesses, who also paid personal tribute to Monsignor Tiso, were Ján Ursíny, Vice-President of the Prague Government (representing the Democratic party), and Monsignor Kmeťko, Archbishop of Nitra.

In response to questioning by the Tribunal's President on the subject of the government of the Slovak Republic, Mr. Ján Ursíny declared:

> Tiso is not one of those who would have imprisoned his political opponents. It was considered advantageous to have him as President. But, if Tuka had been President, there would have been a dictatorship.[17]

The Attorney-General called as witness against Tiso Monsignor Kmeťko, once a member of the 1918 Czecho-Slovak Revolutionary Parliament. Upon entering the courtroom, Monsignor Kmeťko proceeded to shake hands with the accused, much to the consternation of the Tribunal. During the course of his in-

---

[17] Čulen, *Biography of Msgr. Tiso,* p. 407.

terrogation, Monsignor Kmet'ko admitted having gone to con-
gratulate Monsignor Tiso upon his election to the presidency of
the Slovak Republic.

Pursuant to this admission, the following exchange took place
among the Tribunal's President Daxner, Prosecutor Šujan, and
Monsignor Kmet'ko:

> *Dr. Daxner:* I want you to enlarge on your statement that
> you had greeted with much joy the election and installa-
> tion of Monsignor Tiso as President. Will you please ex-
> plain what, precisely, prompted this feeling of happiness?
> *Msgr. Kmet'ko:* When Slovakia proclaimed its independ-
> ence, I might state that the country and its people, as
> many as 90 per cent, gave their support. I believe that
> very few Slovaks would have dared to say, "This State, we
> do not like." In fact, we recovered then the independence
> which we had lost after Svätopluk.[18]
> *Dr. Šujan:* What did the Slovak State signify to the people,
> in the way of moral support? Did it mean progress?
> *Msgr. Kmet'ko:* In the first place, as has already been stated
> by Hlinka, this is a question of a principle universally ac-
> cepted. Can one even conceive of a nation which would
> not desire its own independence? Could we imagine a
> poor man who would not wish to have his own small home
> and who would prefer to be dependent upon another man?
> Certainly not!
> *Dr. Šujan:* But this independence was in reality a de-
> pendence.
> *Msgr. Kmet'ko:* But it was ten times more advantageous
> than the Protectorate.[19]

As to the personality of the accused and his attitude on Jews,
Archbishop Kmet'ko testified as follows:

> The choice of Tiso completely reassured and satisfied
> us. His very person offered us a complete guarantee. Un-
> der this man of forceful character, this worthy ecclesiastic,
> we knew that we would not have to fear the nazi peril.
> This is the second reason why the choice of Tiso was much
> more pleasing to us than any other.[20]
> *Dr. Daxner:* What can you tell us on the subject of a
> memorandum by the Jewish rabbis?
> *Msgr. Kmet'ko:* I know that the Jews said, even to me, that
> Tiso must remain President; and that if he did not, all of
> them, to the last man, would be liquidated.[21]

[18] *Ibid.*, p. 370.
[19] *Ibid.*, p. 376.
[20] *Ibid.*, p. 370.
[21] *Ibid.*, pp. 371-72.

The position which Monsignor Kmeťko then took in favor of independence for Slovakia is of historic importance.

Dr. Šujan: After Munich, why did you abandon your favorable attitude toward the Czechoslovak Republic?
Msgr. Kmeťko: If a practical possibility exists for the independence of Slovakia, we favor that solution. If independence proves impossible, we would then, all of us, favor a Czechoslovak Republic.[22]

The newspapers which published this deposition were confiscated. Such a statement, pronounced by a personage whose moral and political authority infinitely surpassed that of the new Slovak leaders,[23] brought Mr. Beneš face to face with a naked truth. He clearly saw that, to the Slovaks, Czecho-Slovakia was only a last resort. Shortly afterwards, he made use of the visit of Mr. Lettrich, chairman both of the Slovak National Council and of the Czechoslovak Society,[24], to criticize the Slovak Archbishop's "opportunist" concept of the State:

We must frankly admit to ourselves what the final goals of our national effort are, what the general political program is. We must tackle the problems of the Czechs and Slovaks with complete sincerity on both sides. Archbishop Kmeťko stated during the Tiso trial that the Slovaks would like to have their own State and that it is only because of the impossibility of obtaining such a solution that they adhere to the Czechoslovak Republic.

This means that tomorrow or the day after, if such a solution were possible, the Slovaks would declare themselves in favor of it. This is a viewpoint which I reject on principle, which I do not and could never accept. I seek not an equivocal but a definitive and clear-cut solution. We could never again endure a new crisis in Czech-Slovak relations because it would mean the end of Czechoslovakia. After such a crisis, Slovakia would never exist as an independent State but undoubtedly would fall into Russian hands.

I do not believe that such a solution would be healthy for the Czechs, the Slovaks, the Russians, or for the general climate of Europe. At times it is necessary to consider all of these questions. And it is because of the latter that I am planning, before anything else, the drawing up of a new Constitution. I can only add that *the Czechs could never accept, under any future circumstances whatsoever, an independent Slovakia.* The Czechs, being neighbors on

---

[22] *Ibid.*, pp. 377-78.
[23] Msgr. Kmeťko was soon to die (1948).
[24] This society was founded after 1945 for the purpose of fostering friendship between Czechs and Slovaks, and the idea of a common State.

one side with Germany, which comprises seventy million persons, have a vital interest in having Russia, in the future, as neighbors on the other side. Thus it is impossible to accept as neighbor an independent Slovakia. This is a problem vital to the Czechs as a nation and a State, and it also demonstrates a lesson learned from Munich.

And in rejoinder to those who had envisioned a solution for Slovakia under some plan of central European federation, Beneš added:

> The current situation marks the end of all projects proposing any federation whatsoever for Central Europe. At the moment when Russia is established on our side of the Carpathians, all these plans will be of no avail.[25]

This controversy caused the greatest reaction of public opinion in Slovakia. Evidences of resistance began to appear. Some university students undertook the publication of a clandestine mimeographed newspaper which they named *The Slovak,* the name of the publication of the former Populist party of Hlinka. New arrests took place. At Topolčany, a young lawyer named Štefan Chalmovský organized a resistance group and distributed antigovernment literature. He and his group were imprisoned.

Throughout the duration of the trial, the Slovaks in the United States, who have for several decades constituted a large emigrant group (currently comprising over a million persons), cabled to the Slovak National Council protesting Monsignor Tiso's trial as well as his possible eventual condemnation. With a certain realism, the group affirmed in these messages their belief that the very existence of the Czecho-Slovak State would rest on the outcome of this trial.

On March 19, 1947, which was the feast of St. Joseph and thus Tiso's feast day, the women of Piešťany organized a demonstration calling for his liberation. That morning several thousand women dressed in black arrived in Piešťany from all the neighboring villages. They went directly to the church for the eight o'clock Mass, following which they assembled on the public square and proceeded to the district office. There they delegated a group of five women to see the Chief of the District; the others continued to parade in the streets. At noon the police used fire engines to scatter the procession. Many people were arrested throughout the area, notably Rev. Žilinčan from Krakovany and

[25] Čulen, *Biography of Msgr. Tiso,* pp. 382-83. The same ideas are developed by Beneš in his book, *Où vont les Slaves?* pp. 305-7.

Jesuit Fathers Eiselle and Potocký. The latter were accused of having organized the demonstration. An official of the central post office in Bratislava was relieved of his duties because he had allowed the delivery to Monsignor Tiso of several thousand telegrams and letters of best wishes which had arrived from every corner of the nation for his feast day.

The people became more and more apprehensive as the day neared for passing sentence. On April 15, 1947, Tiso was condemned to death. Minister of the Interior Mach, on the other hand, was let off with thirty years of prison. This contrast in sentences shocked the public, all of whom regarded Mach, who had been forced on Tiso by Hitler at Salzburg in 1940, as a Germanophile.[26] Mach owed his life to the fact that he had shut his eyes, during the time of the Slovak State, to the clandestine activities of the Communists, particularly of Husák and Novomeský, who, after 1945, shared in the official leadership of the new regime.

On the day following the sentence, one illustrious visit after another occurred at the Hradčany Castle in Prague. Monsignor Beran, Archbishop of Prague; Monsignor Forni, Chargé d'Affaires of the Apostolic Nunciature; Mr. Lettrich, chairman of the Slovak National Council—all arrived begging Beneš to grant clemency to the condemned. Although this privilege was reserved, according to the old Constitution, to the Head of State alone, Mr. Beneš entrusted the decision to the Gottwald government. Predictably, their vote was a death sentence, by majority. Mr. Beneš did not intervene and at dawn on April 18, 1947, as the radiant spring morning burst into life along the banks of the Danube, Monsignor Tiso was hanged.

To the eye of a stranger, the execution had no unusual effect on the people. No revolt occurred. No procession in the streets nor overt protest followed the event.

To the keen observer, recognizing a people which had been forced for centuries to live under pressure, it was apparent that Tiso's death had produced the deepest anguish, a wound so bitter that time itself could never bring solace. A mass feeling of profound depression permeated the country. Churches were filled even more than usual. Masses for the dead were celebrated everywhere. Men bowed their heads and women wept. What

---

[26] One day during the war, Mach presented his resignation to Msgr. Tiso, who replied: "Present it to Ribbentrop, who named you to the ministry."

else could they do, knowing full well that at their first move their "Russian brothers" guarding the border would be called in immediately against them?

At this time, as if by mere coincidence, the military command in Moravia, fearing some revolt in spite of all the threats to which the people had been subjected, organized full scale maneuvers near Malacky, a region overlooking Bratislava. Furthermore, the garrison of the Slovak capital was disarmed and replaced by Czech units.

Tiso's death was a victory for both the Communists and the Czechs. In his last statement to the Slovak people, entrusted before his death to the Capuchin priest, Father Hilarius, Monsignor Tiso termed himself a victim of antireligious and anti-Slovak elements. His exact words read as follows:

> In the spirit of the sacrifice I am about to make, I send this message to the Slovak nation:
>
> In harmony and unison pursue always, everywhere and in every respect the great principle: FOR GOD AND FOR THE NATION.
>
> That is not only the unequivocal intent of Slovak history, but also the explicit command of God, Who has made it the law of nature and has inculcated it into the soul of the nation and every one of its members.
>
> That precept I have served all my life and, therefore, I consider myself first of all a martyr to God's law. Secondly I feel that I am a martyr of the defense of Christianity against bolshevism, against which our nation must defend itself in all possible ways, not only in the spirit of its Christian character, but also in the interests of its future.
>
> As I beg you to remember me in your prayers, so do I promise to pray to God Almighty for you and supplicate that He bless the Slovak nation in its vital struggle for God and for country, so that the Slovak nation will always remain a faithful and devoted son of the Church of Christ.
>
> Bratislava, April 18th, 1947, 3 a.m.—Dr. Jozef Tiso.

The body of Monsignor Tiso was carefully hidden and no one knew what happened to it. However, on the morning of April 19, a fresh grave was discovered in St. Martin's Cemetery. Immediately a multitude of people gathered there and covered the grave with flowers. Was it really the tomb of Tiso? People believe so without being certain. There are some who believe, on the other hand, that the corpse was burned and the ashes scattered in the Moldau in Prague.

The Protestant leaders of the Democratic party fully realized that President Beneš had committed an irreparable error. They endeavored, therefore, to excuse themselves to the majority of the public by openly criticizing the President and the government. An editorial of this nature was published in the party journal, *The Times (Čas)*, but the issue was immediately confiscated by order of Prague. It was not until June 10, 1947, that the same newspaper dared publish a discreet comment on the judgment rendered, of which the following statement was noteworthy: "The sense of justice of the great masses of people is in profound contradiction with the National Tribunal's sentence."

Even after his execution, Tiso continues to be a source of worry to those who have the last word on maintaining order in the country; Tiso is more dangerous to them dead than he was alive.

In the West, opinion is still divided on the question of Monsignor Tiso. But there is one thing certain: Politics, like nature, has its own laws. And when a flood succeeds in breaking through the dike, it carries along with it everything in its path. In such a way, after Munich, all the "dikes" burst which had served to keep Hitler's Germany within its borders. The "flood" then carried away the Slovaks with their statesmen, as it did the statesmen of several other nations. On the subject of Monsignor Tiso, the English writer Douglas Reed expressed himself as follows: "His (Tiso's) crime was to have signed an agreement with Hitler. But if this test were applied to all, the politicians of Europe would all be guilty."[27] Reed also reminds us that these agreements with the German dictator were signed not only by the statesmen of the Western Powers but by Russia itself, the Russian agreement permitting the later partitioning of Poland with Germany.

The war years were for Monsignor Tiso a constant struggle dominated by that "tragic sense of life" of which Unamuno speaks so eloquently.[28] Commenting on the political message which Tiso entrusted to his confessor the evening preceding his death, Mr. Reed sums up his own convictions as follows:

"This man never made pretense of a hypocritical loyalty. He was both a sincere Christian and a Slovak patriot who died for his own convictions."

---

[27] Miguel de Unamuno, *Tragic Sense of Life* (New York: 1954).
[28] Douglas Reed, *From Smoke to Smother* (London: 1948), p. 18.

History will be the final judge of the question. It is now certain, nevertheless, that the sentencing to the gallows of Monsignor Tiso was an act of revenge on the part of Beneš and Gottwald, perpetrated against the representative of a people who opposed both the Czech totalitarianism of Beneš and the communism of Gottwald. Maurice Descotes admitted this motivation when he wrote: "It was not a collaborator but rather a creed and a political attitude that was put on trial."[29] In reality, a Catholic leader and a defender of the concept of a Slovak State had passed under judgment.

The Balance Sheet of Political Justice—The schedule of justice which was imposed on the Slovaks by their "liberators" is perturbing. Monsignor Tiso was hanged just like the Germanophile Tuka, a politician of bad inspiration of the Slovak State. Among the members of the Slovak government who had escaped but were still condemned to death in absentia were Dr. Ferdinand Ďurčanský, former Minister of Foreign Affairs, and Mr. Štefan Haššík, former Minister of National Defense. As for the other members of the government, they were condemned to imprisonment extending over the following number of years: Ferdinand Čatloš, Minister of National Defense, five years; Gejza Fritz, Minister of Justice, two years; Tido Gašpar, propaganda head, twenty years; Aladár Kočiš, Minister of National Education, seven years; František Lednár, Minister of Communications, four years; Alexander Mach, Minister of the Interior, thirty years; Gejza Medrický, Minister of Economy, seven years; Mikuláš Pružinský, Minister of Finance, seven years; Jozef Sivák, Minister of Education, three years; Julius Stano, Minister of Communications, five years; Karol Sidor, Minister of the Interior, twenty years; Štefan Tiso, Prime Minister, twenty years.

Out of sixty-one members of the Slovak Parliament, two were assassinated during the insurrection, four were condemned to death and one to life imprisonment; the total number of years of privation of liberty to which thirty-seven others were condemned reached 348 years and four months; seventeen were finally acquitted.

Whereas all during the Slovak State no one had suffered the death penalty, the "popular" justice ordered thirty-three capital executions in "liberated" Slovakia. A total of 5,006 condemnations to various punishments were pronounced by the popular tribunals.

[29] Maurice Descotes, *L'aspect de la Tchécoslovaquie* (Paris: 1948), p. 174.

The unleashing of these tribunals was such that the Minister of Justice, Mr. Drtina, could not help passing the following judgment on them: "Before the tribunals of the people many persons have appeared not because they were guilty, but because someone wished to lay hold of their possessions or take vengeance on them for special political reasons."

As one knows, the German and Japanese war criminals could enjoy the privilege of being judged by an international tribunal. However, the Allies committed the grave mistake, outside of Germany and Japan, of giving over the judging of those generally termed "war criminals" to the political tribunals of the respective countries. In this way, the Western Powers left the Communists' hands entirely free in dealing with their bitterest adversaries, contrary to the Roman juridical maxim: *Nemo judex in rebus suis.*

In Bulgaria, for instance, after the Russians entered the country, 125 political personalities, 25 of whom were ministers and 65 former deputies, as well as Prince Cyril and two members of the Regency, were executed on February 2, 1945, after the most cursory trial. The Communists thus easily got rid of an opponent in power in Bulgaria, Rumania, Hungary, Slovakia, Croatia, and elsewhere.

If the Nuremberg Tribunal had been given the Tiso affair, he would be free today, more justly so than Mr. Hjalmar Schacht, for example. This tribunal would have realized that Monsignor Tiso had fought morally and spiritually against naziism and that he had suffered keenly from the barbarous crimes committed by this regime in Slovakia and elsewhere in Europe.

The Relations Between Czechs and Slovaks

Before the 1944 revolt the "Czechoslovak" government of London estimated that it would be necessary to organize a regional committee on Slovakia after the liberation, with a chairman and a military commander invested for several years with dictatorial power.[30] In the course of the insurrection, Mr. Beneš modified his plans for Slovakia with respect to the regime; he did not, however, revise his position regarding the unitary structure of the State.[31]

---

[30] Husák, *Our Struggle for the Future,* pp. 155, 254.
[31] See the further development on pp. 189-99.

In March, 1945, the delegates of the Slovak National Council (Husák, Novomeský, Styk, Šoltész, Šrobár, Ursíny) met in Moscow with the representatives of the four Czech political parties to discuss the future position of Slovakia within the compass of the Republic. The Slovak demands were summed up in three points:

1. Recognition of the Czech and Slovak national dualism;
2. Recognition of the Slovak National Council as the legislative, governmental, and executive instrument in Slovakia;
3. The pledge of the Czech political parties to include in the future constitution the two principles stated above.

The Czechs—especially the National-Socialists (Beneš, Ripka) —adopted the first and second points but categorically thrust aside the third.[32]

The Košice Agreement of April 5, 1945, contained the following points on the subject of Czecho-Slovak relations:

1. Approval of the principle of fraternal equality between the Slovak and Czech nations;
2. Recognition of the Slovak National Council (a legislative body) and the Board of Commissioners (an executive organ) as constitutionally representative institutions of the Slovak nation;
3. Creation of Slovak units within the Czecho-Slovak Army.

In other words, the agreement proclaimed that "the Slovaks are to be masters in their own Slovak homeland, just as the Czechs in their national homeland."[33]

The Slovaks, who had had a taste of independence, read with skepticism, however, the Košice Agreement. When Mr. Gottwald promised them that they would be treated according to a principle of absolute equality, they understood quite naturally that the State was going to be organized on a federative basis. They also presumed that Mr. Beneš was finally agreeable to making Czecho-Slovakia a kind of Switzerland, in conformity with the promise that he had made to the Allies at Versailles at the time of the Peace Conference in 1919.

In the beginning, the Slovak Communists themselves strove toward such a solution. Mr. Husák wrote in June, 1945:

[32] Husák, Our Struggle for the Future, p. 160.
[33] The Program of the National Front Government of the Czechs and the Slovaks (Bratislava: 1945), p. 10. See Appendix VII.

On the Slovak side, the desire was expressed that the evolution in the two parties of the Republic be equal and harmonious and that, in accordance with the principle of equality, there should be, unlike what is happening at the present time, a Slovak and a Czech government with a Czecho-Slovak central government and parliaments at the top. The internal structure of the Czecho-Slovak Republic and the division of the power and the work would be easier.[34]

The Slovaks, a realistic people, no longer let themselves be influenced by speeches. They waited for acts. "The Magna Charta of Košice" was actually nothing more than a basis for discussion which was to find its exact interpretation in the Constitution. It is precisely on the subject of this interpretation that difficulties arose. Logically the Democratic party, representing 62 per cent of the population, would have been able to prescribe the will of the nation from a political point of view in the Constituent Assembly. Now it happened that this party was divided on its internal opinions. Its Protestant leaders, Messrs. Lettrich, Ursíny, and Hodža, knew very well that they owed their role only to a rather temporary historical coincidence: to the fact that the Catholic majority of the country was banished from politics for rallying to the idea of the Slovak State. Because of strong anticommunism sentiment in Slovakia, it was also clear that in the struggle for power they would first have to depend on the electoral Catholic masses; but in the long run they would be able to keep their position only by depending on Prague, that is to say, on a centralist system that would never permit the Catholic electoral body to choose its own head.

From this fundamental contradiction resulted all the political impotency of the Democratic party. Its politicians, who pretended before the electors to be partisans of decentralization, were actually opposed to it. In fact, from the moment Slovakia would have formed a member-State of a Czecho-Slovak federation, it would have thrust them from power as representatives of a minority. Mr. Lettrich, President of the Slovak National Council, consequently was obliged to speak differently in Slovakia than in Prague. In Bratislava he declared himself to be a partisan of legislative and executive decentralization and posed as a defender of the organs resulting from the resistance: the Slovak National Council and the Board of Commissioners. But when he

[34] Husák, *Our Struggle for the Future*, p. 106.

spoke to Mr. Beneš as President of the Czecho-Slovak Society, he declared himself for the close unity of the State against federalization and all the Slovak "separatist" tendencies.

Under these conditions the Slovak problem once again became a chronic disease of the Republic. The Czechs themselves understood that it was a matter of "squaring the circle." Mr. F. Weyr, professor of constitutional law at the University of Prague, and a member of the Constitutional Commission of the Parliament, made this statement after innumerable fruitless discussions:

> I think that a form of State has not been yet invented that is capable of reconciling certain demands: either we shall have national dualism and not a unity State, or else we shall have a unitary State by renouncing national dualism.[35]

Of course the Czechs leaned toward the second solution. And when it was a question of establishing the limits of the powers of the Slovak institutions in relation to those which were central, Mr. Lettrich, overwhelmed by the Czech experts, gave in step by step to the ever increasing demands of Prague which took from Slovakia one after the other "the prerogatives gained in the national insurrection."

The "national sovereignty" was thus dispersed following a cascade of Prague agreements (June 2, 1945; April 11, 1946; June 28, 1946), and the power of the Slovak national institutions lessened bit by bit. The central Parliament assumed the power in affairs "of interest to the whole State." Of course, Foreign Affairs, Foreign Trade, Finance, and Defense came under the jurisdiction of the same Parliament. Then the Czech jurists protested likewise when the Slovak National Council hoped to set up the region of the Tatras as a new district, for in their opinion here was a problem "of interest to the whole State." Likewise the Slovak high administrative officials were appointed by the President of the Republic. Thus the Bratislava commissariats became, as it were, mere services of the Prague ministries and were under their control. For instance, persons in Slovakia who needed an importation permit had to get it in Prague. For the least details, the ordinary citizen as well as deputies or commissioners had to go to the capital. For most of the population, that was a disagreeable situation. In spite of appearances, Slovakia was entirely governed by Prague.

[35] Dr. František Weyr, "About the So-Called National Sovereignty," *Lidová demokracie*, Prague, (February 16, 1947).

Mr. Lettrich himself, alas, encouraged this tendency toward centralism when he asked Prague that the Slovak Democratic party be permitted to participate in the elections in the Czech lands. For reciprocity's sake, "The Democratic party," wrote its official organ, *Čas*, "would raise no objection against the extension of the Czech parties in Slovakia if its own campaign were allowed in Czechia."[36] But the Czechs fortunately rejected this preposterous proposal.

The Slovaks were exceedingly indignant at this reappearance of centralism. Instead of persevering on the establishment of a constitutionally symmetrical system for the two nations, Mr. Lettrich was satisfied with an arrangement which was according to him neither a federation nor an autonomy, but a solution *sui generis*. Walking on two legs of unequal length, the Republic could not help limping.[37]

In regard to Slovakia's position within the Republic, the Communists evolved considerably. After their defeat in the May, 1946 elections they stopped talking of federalism and sought support from the Communist party of Prague which had just obtained 40 per cent of the votes in Czechia. From then on, they became fervent protagonists of the Prague agreements by which the Košice Charter had been modified to the detriment of Slovakia. According to this charter the Slovaks were to perform their military service in Slovakia and the Czechs in Bohemia, Moravia, and Silesia. However, as soon as the elections were over, the Slovak communist deputy Holdoš himself demanded of the Parliament of Prague the sending of Czech military units to Slovakia. Was he afraid of an anticommunist coup d'état? Nevertheless, his wishes were quickly granted. Czech units arrived with the tacit consent of the leaders of the Democratic party. No politician breathed a word about it and no mere citizen could have allowed himself to broach so delicate a subject.

So it was that Slovakia's "autonomy" withered away by stages. Many straight-thinking Slovaks thought that for the transitional period, marked as it was by the presence of the Soviets in Central Europe, it was necessary to find a *modus vivendi* with the Czechs. They reasoned that in the face of Russian pressure it was better to cohabit with the Czechs. In essence, they felt they could keep their own apartment in a common house; the en-

[36] *Čas*, Bratislava (January 8, 1946).
[37] See the article: Dr. Pavol Mrázek, "Constitutional Anomalies in Czech-Slovak Relations," *Národná Obroda*, Bratislava, (February 10, 1948).

trance, staircase, and heating would be shared in common, but there would be two distinctly separate apartments.

Such hopes were completely frustrated. The Czechs began at once to consider the whole house theirs. They reverted to their former mistakes. Instead of conceiving of the Slovak problem as national, they lowered it by placing it on a regional plane. "By refusing the unwholesome dualism of two unities," said the Czech National-Socialist deputy, V. Kubeš, "we are going back to the former idea of three countries: Bohemia, Moravia-Silesia, and Slovakia."[38]

The Czechs had not yet understood the meaning of the federative principle which strives for unity while safeguarding diversity. Thus they definitively alienated Slovak public opinion.

"Ecclesia Militans" I[39]

History—After Germany, Slovakia was the first country in Danubian Europe to be converted to Christianity. There still exists at Nitra today a little church that was consecrated in the year 833. The evangelization of Bohemia on the other hand began in 845 and of Hungary about 1000 A.D. The Slovak people owe their faith to the apostolate of St. Cyril and St. Methodius. To St. Cyril they also owe their old alphabet and the translation of liturgical works. These apostles, although from Byzantium, made an act of submission to the Pope and thereby linked Slovakia to Western culture. Since that remote period, Roman Catholicism has represented for the Slovaks the essence of spiritual heritage. Whereas the Reformation marks the apex in the history of Germany and the Czech countries with Martin Luther and Jan Hus as an historical and spiritual parallel that cannot easily be disregarded, Slovakia has known neither reformers nor deviationists. As a nation the Slovaks have never succumbed to any form of messianism or religious particularism. Up to the present day, Catholicism has been kept as pure in Slovakia as it has in Poland and it has unswervingly played an important role in national life. Banished from the schools under the Hungarian regime, the

---

[38] Dr. V. Kubeš, *Toward a New Constitution* (Prague: 1948).

[39] Of a population of 3.5 million in 1950, there were in Slovakia 80 per cent Catholics, 13.5 per cent Protestants, 6 per cent Uniats and 0.5 per cent Israelites. There are six Catholic bishoprics (in Nitra, Trnava, Banská Bystrica, Spiš, Košice and Rožňava). These dioceses formed a distinct administrative unity whose hierarchy had direct contact with the Holy See without having to go through the Archbishop of Prague.

Slovak language took refuge in the churches, where the people sang and prayed in their language. Despite the fact that the hierarchy was mostly comprised of foreigners, the ordinary clergy on the contrary remained closely bound to the people from which they sprang. It was the clergy who connected the national and the religious ideas.

By its history and religion, Slovakia is a country of distinctly Western appurtenances. "Slavism," which constituted for certain Slovaks a sort of escape from the oppression of the Magyars in the nineteenth century, was nothing more than a romantic aspiration which did not cross the threshold of the twentieth.

When after 1918, sons of the lower classes became bishops in Slovakia, the prestige of the Catholic Church on the national level increased. Too, the schismatic tendencies which manifested themselves in Czechia after World War I in no wise touched Slovakia. These tendencies ended in the founding of the so-called "Czechoslovak" Church which, although enjoying the support of the government of Prague, never succeeded in taking root on Slovak soil. With nearly a million adherents in Czechia, the "Czechoslovak" Church can be considered in spite of its name as nothing more than a manifestation of that specifically refractory mentality that is the characteristic trait of Czech spirituality.

In the course of the First Czecho-Slovak Republic, Czech Catholicism and Slovak Catholicism found under these conditions no basis whatsoever for collaboration on the political plane. As a member of the government coalition, the Czech Catholic party of Monsignor Šrámek rallied entirely to the anti-Slovak policy of Beneš, and had inevitably to follow its manifestly anti-Roman trend; in contrast, Monsignor Hlinka's party, driven back in the opposition, was able to defend vigorously Slovak national individuality quite as well as the liberties of the Church.

It was under the pressure of Catholic Slovakia, after about ten years of domination by catchwords: "Away from Rome!" (Bechyně) and "Rome must be judged and condemned!" (Masaryk), that the government of Prague was obliged to make a ruling on its relations with the Church. For the solution of the most burning points, a *modus vivendi* was concluded with the Holy See in December, 1927, and recognized January 20, 1928, by the Czecho-Slovak government. This agreement contained the following provisions among others:

1. Adjustment by the Church of the limits of the dioceses in accordance with the State's borders;

2. Acknowledgment by the State of the temporary character of the civil administration of certain ecclesiastical possessions and respect for Church property;

3. Recognition by the Holy See of the autonomy of the provinces of religious orders on Czecho-Slovak territory;

4. Nomination of the bishops by the Holy See; and the possibility on the part of the government to present objections;

5. Bishops' oath of loyalty vis-à-vis the State.

Yet, on the internal plane, the strife continued between the Catholic religion and Czech Marxism, particularism, and atheism. The attitude that Czech Catholicism and Slovak Catholicism adopted in this battle proves that Slovakia and Czechia are two different bodies and souls. Whereas Czech Catholicism showed itself to be opportunist and "governmental," Slovak Catholicism was able to remain attached to principles. As far back as 1928, the Bishop of Spiš, Monsignor Ján Vojtaššák, instructed the clergy of his diocese not to administer the sacraments to Marxists.[40]

This difference in attitude was recognized by the Holy See. In 1933, when the Papal Nuncio, Monsignor Ciriaci, had left Prague for reasons of anti-Catholic manifestations which had been produced in Czechia, he wrote to Mr. Hlinka to emphasize the loyal conduct of the *generosa gens slovaca* vis-à-vis the Holy See.

The political divergences between Monsignors Šrámek and Hlinka persisted until the end of the First Czecho-Slovak Republic.

Limitation of Religious Liberties—Although the Catholicism of Slovakia welcomed with satisfaction the establishment of the Slovak Republic as a national State, yet it is impossible to prove that the Slovak Episcopate was in any way compromised on the occasion of Slovakia's political relations with Germany during the war. The fact that Monsignor Tiso had been the President of the Slovak Republic offered the new regime of Prague an excellent pretext to combat Catholicism by accusing it of collaboration, seeking in that way to undermine the main prop of Slovak independence. A sharply defined tendency sprang from the govern-

---

[40] This decision provoked violent attack by Marxist political parties against this prelate. It was approved after many years by the decree of the Congregation of the Holy Office against communism, published in the *Acta Apostolicae Sedis*, July 1, 1949.

ment's religious policy in this first phase: it consisted in ensuring the silence, if not the complacence of the Czech Catholics in their fight against Slovak Catholicism. Unfortunately it must be acknowledged that this goal was entirely reached. As before the war, it seemed natural to Monsignori Šrámek and Hála, Czech Nationalists, to sit for the Czech Catholic party in a government which nevertheless had proposed to break down Slovak Catholicism. With the tacit consent of the Catholics of Bohemia, the government of Prague was able to indulge in some acts and take legislative measures injurious to the Catholics in Slovakia, while accompanying them with violent press and radio campaigns.

While three priests had already been assassinated during the insurrection, the new leaders of the country, made up almost exclusively of Communists and Protestants, attacked the hierarchy itself. Monsignor Vojtaššák, the Bishop of Spiš; Monsignor Buzalka, the Auxiliary Bishop of Trnava; Monsignor Pöstényi, Secretary-General of the Association of Saint-Adalbert (the largest Catholic Slovak organization), several canons, 170 priests, and several thousand lay Catholics were thrown into prison accused of fascism. They next attacked the rights of Catholics. By Decree No. 34 of May 16, 1945, the National Council nationalized the whole of education. Decree No. 47 of May 26, 1945 then nationalized the buildings and equipment of the private schools, without any indemnity for the communes, religious communities, or other moral persons who up to that time had been the owners. A Communist of long standing, the Commissioner of Public Education, Novomeský, appointed Protestants or Communists as directors of the schools that until then had belonged to religious orders.

Religious instruction became an optional subject. Crucifixes were taken from the classrooms. The recitation of prayers at the beginning of the classes was forbidden. The order was given to remove the portrait of the Pope from the schools—"a foreigner who had nothing to do with Slovak classes." The Holy Father's portraits were immediately replaced by portraits of Stalin and Gottwald, each as much a "Slovak" as the other!

In July, 1945, Monsignor Kmeťko, the Archbishop of Nitra, aided by leading persons of Catholic Action, launched a plea throughout the whole country in favor of independent schools. Several hundreds of thousands of signatures were collected from all classes of people. Suddenly this action was declared illegal and gave rise to a wave of arrests of lay and clerical, among others the Jesuit Father Janda, director of the Central Catholic

Bureau of Slovakia. It was in addition the occasion for confiscating typewriters from numerous vicarages and convents.

At the University they systematically removed all the professors known to be Catholics.

The Slovak National Council, by Decree No. 80 of July 25,
1945, put under State control all student houses which were under the direction of religious institutions. This measure struck
among others the largest student house of Bratislava, known under the name of Svoradov.

Freedom of association was as completely cut off. By its
Decree No. 51 of May 25, 1945, the Slovak National Council
proceeded to the dissolution of all associations excepting a few
explicitly named ones. Naturally the Catholic youth associations,
student and even adult associations were prohibited and their
possessions confiscated. A certain number of fighters for the
Catholic Action movement were imprisoned on this occasion.
Simple administrative measures sufficed for confiscating Catholic
institutions of charity (Charitas among others), maternity homes,
children's convalescent homes, homes for the aged and the poor,
and orphanages.

Elimination of Catholicism from Political Life—Even at the
beginning of the twentieth century, under the Hungarian regime, Monsignor Hlinka had been able to give to Slovak Catholicism a certain political importance which it was going to
keep under the Czecho-Slovak regime. The fact was due in great
part to the material independence of the Church. As the State
(i.e., Budapest or Prague) was not favorable to the free development of the Slovak people, whom it would have preferred
to see just merely assimilated, the civil service officials of Slovak
origin were, within the bounds of the Hungarian State particularly, entirely lost to their people. It was altogether different with
the priests, who were not dependent upon the State. That is why
the Church gave Slovakia a certain number of first-rate political
figures.

The regime which assumed power in 1945 wanted to break
forever the political strength that Catholicism represented. That
is why it suppressed the old Populist party. In May, 1946, before
the elections in the Constituent Assembly, certain Catholic persons of note earnestly requested the authorization to found a
Christian Republican party. The request was declined.

Although reviled, Slovak Catholicism kept its vigor and resistance. Toward the end of 1947 again, General Ferjenčík, Com-

missioner of the Interior, a Protestant, set himself the task of disintegrating Catholicism by asking for the subordination of the Slovak dioceses to the Czech bishops, the dispersion of the Slovak clergy in Czechia, and the sending of Czech priests into Slovakia.[41]

Quite different was the position of Catholicism in Czechia. To ensure its silence on the policy in Slovakia, the government did not touch religious liberties and independent schools. One can affirm that between 1945 and 1948, Czech Catholicism conducted itself as if the situation in Slovakia did not concern it. It was distant and at times disdainful. The Czechs could not pardon the Slovaks for having been less persecuted during the war than they. A Czech Jesuit put it clearly:

> The Czechs then under the heel of the occupant, severely persecuted and implacably decimated by mass executions, conceived for the Slovak bitter resentments which reflected quite naturally upon Catholicism. How could it have been otherwise, since the Slovak regime . . . claimed to be inspired by Catholicism?[42]

One can see from the very first how this reproach inspired by a nationalist resentment is hard to reconcile with the principle of the universality of the Church.

Religious Sublimation of the Resistance—Judged and condemned by the government of Beneš and Gottwald and abandoned by the Czech Catholics, Slovak Catholicism retired within itself.

On May 11, 1947, four weeks after Monsignor Tiso's execution, the university students organized a pilgrimage to Notre-Dame of Marianka, fifteen kilometers from Bratislava. Thirty thousand took part in the march. University professors, priests, students, and ordinary laborers participated, carrying on their backs a large cross as a symbol of the nation's sufferings.

On July 2, 1947, the traditional Levoča pilgrimage brought 130,000 persons together. In vain the communist agents tried to diperse the crowd by spreading the rumor that Russian airplanes were going to bombard the church. The people remained impassible.

---

[41] See: Comité slovaque de Libération, *Demande adressée à l'assemblée générale de l'O.N.U. sur la persécution religieuse en Slovaquie* (Buenos-Aires: 1949), p. 11.

[42] R. P. Kajpr, S.J., "Pour mieux comprendre le catholicisme tchèque," *Les Cahiers du monde nouveau, Paris,* (November, 1946).

The days following, July 5 and 6, another pilgrimage, which took place at Staré Hory, attracted 70,000 persons.

This polarization of opposing forces only increased the tension between them. The explosion, however, was to take place only when the Communists had completely consolidated their political position.

The Economic System

Nationalizations—In one of his messages from London, transmitted on February 3, 1944 (immediately after his return from Moscow), Mr. Beneš stated on the subject of the reconstructed economy of Czecho-Slovakia: "Our State will likewise operate a series of changes in the economic and social domain and will adopt for its policy and its economy the system of planning."[43]

All these reforms were given in details in Section XII of the governmental program of Košice, according to which the monetary and banking system, the key industries, insurance companies, and natural and energetic resources were to be put under the exclusive control and direction of the State.[44]

Pursuing the realization of this program and desirous of emphasizing the importance of the national holiday, Mr. Beneš chose October 28 to sign Decrees Nos. 100/1945, 102/1945 and 103/1945, relating to State control of banks, mines, insurance companies, and certain specialized industries. In conformity with their provisions, the banks and insurance companies were entirely nationalized. At that stage, in the different branches relating to industry, the enterprises occupying less than a given number of workers (150-500) remained private. The proportion of each industry which, given this criterion, was nationalized was as follows: mines, 100 per cent; iron smelting, 100; sugar refineries, 80; electricity, 73; chemical industry, 72; metallurgy, 68.5; glass, 65; leather industry, 53.5; gas, 50; textiles, 47; ceramics, 46.5; paper industry, 45.5; distilleries, 31.5; breweries, 27.5; confection, 25; flour-milling, 14; food, 9; and wood, 8 per cent.

The manpower of the nationalized enterprises totalled for the whole Republic 570,000 workmen as against 430,000 in the non-nationalized sector.[45]

[43] Ministère de l'Information, *Le Plan économique biennal tchécoslovaque* (Prague: 1947), p. 3.
[44] *Ibid.*, p. 3.
[45] See: "Le syndicalisme ouvrier de la Tchéco-Slovaquie," *Cahiers du monde nouveau*, Paris, (November, 1946), p. 52.

This precipitate and dictatorial "legislation" of Mr. Beneš had a three-fold aim.

In the first place, these measures permitted the expulsion of foreign capital invested in industry, that is to say, Western capital: American, English, French, Swiss, Belgian, etc.

The second prompting was repression. Therefore the first nationalizations in Czecho-Slovakia were above all measures of political justice. By the decree of the President, No. 108/1945, the Czecho-Slovak State confiscated the property of the enemies of the Republic (Germans, Magyars, Slovak or Czech "Fascists and collaborators"). The expropriation of the property of the Germans, Magyars, "traitors" and "Fascists" in favor of the State was the object of Decrees Nos. 4/1945 of February 23, 1945; 50/1945 of June 5, 1945; 104/1945 of August 23, 1945; and No. 64/1946 of May 15, 1946, of the Slovak National Council. The Office of National Reconstruction was charged with the administration of all the wealth thus brought together.

Finally, nationalization aimed at reinforcing the political and economic position of all the *beati possidentes* of the regime which, after the return of the Beneš government from Moscow, did not fail to seize the key positions in administration, industry, police, etc. For reasons of propaganda, the crumbs were promised to workmen and peasants.

Thus, in a first stage—that is, until the beginning of the year 1948—63 per cent of Slovak industry was nationalized without consulting the people.

The Monetary Reform—A monetary reform was effected in November, 1945. The two decrees of the President, Nos. 91/1945 and 95/1945, formed the basis. They first suppressed the currency of the Protectorate of Bohemia-Moravia and the Slovak Republic to re-establish Czecho-Slovak currency; ordered the inventory of real and personal property, the freezing of bank deposits, and established the conditions of their liberation. The second had reference mainly to the control of bank deposits and checking accounts. Bank notes in circulation had to be turned in to credit establishments, each individual having the right to keep only a sum of five hundred crowns.

Union with the Czech countries which was again imposed upon Slovakia had disastrous consequences from the economic point of view. During the war, the economic development of the Slovak Republic on the one hand and the Protectorate of Bohemia-Moravia on the other had been different. Whereas the

Slovak Republic had safeguarded its economic individuality, that
of the Protectorate had been absorbed by the Reich. Since
Czechia's foreign trade was directed from Berlin, Prague could
only take cognizance of the operations done. It is understood that
this absorption had facilitated Germany's economic exploitation of Czech countries. As the Reichsmark lost its purchasing power, the Czech crown could but take the same course.
Although at the close of the war there were in the Protectorate 145 billion crowns in circulation, there were only 12 billion in Slovakia. Whereas in time of peace the national Czech
revenue per head had been slightly higher than the same national Slovak revenue, it is a well-known fact that the purchasing
value of the Slovak crown in the spring of 1945 corresponded
almost to the triple of the Czech crown.

Only the incapability and slackness of the directors of "liberated" Slovak economy enable one to explain the law on the unification of the currency, which established parity for the exchange of Czech for Slovak crowns. Still more than an insult to
economic good common sense, it was colossal premeditated theft.
In order to realize this operation, they had recourse to a sorry
figure in Slovak politics, who, as early as 1918, had rendered them
great service by his collaboration; Mr. Šrobár, this octogenarian,
a diletante in medicine as well as economics, was then appointed
Minister of Finance.

Thus 145 billions in fiduciary circulation for the Czech countries and 12 billions for Slovakia merged. Through the policy of
Prague, the Slovak crown, the "Danubian dollar," was merely
diluted in an inflationist wave.

Of the 157 billions thus brought together, the State by a radical act had 130 billions withdrawn from circulation. To prevent
inflation, the frozen mass guaranteed economically by the confiscated wealth that had belonged to the Sudeten Germans was
to be at the disposal of the Czecho-Slovak National Bank for the
time when industrial production and the wealth of the country
should have increased.[46]

The Office of National Reconstruction was charged with realizing the sale of this "cover" of the new currency. According to

[46] In 1950, the operation had only been realized in part as proved by the
following figures on the fiduciary circulation in Czecho-Slovakia:

1937 —	7,497,000,000	1947 —	60,962,000,000
1945 —	27,431,000,000	1948 —	74,821,000,000
1946 —	45,753,000,000	1949 —	66,897,000,000

the opinion of this office, the sale of the properties confiscated was to bring in the sum of 300 billion crowns to the State. Now in 1947, this office had realized only 20 billions, the remainder of the goods having been misappropriated by dishonest administrators. It was a scandal that caused much ink to flow in the democratic press. In the Prague magazine, *Dnešek*, a Czech journalist, Mr. Mareš, pitilessly stigmatized the collective theft of this national property by the regime's climbers and upstarts.

The Banking Reform—After the nationalization of the banks, a consolidation of financial establishments took place in Czecho-Slovakia. The *Živnostenská banka* in Czechia and the *Tatra banka* in Slovakia, establishments whose capital was the most important in the two respective countries, were entrusted with absorbing the other banks and their subsidiaries. Besides these two banks thus centralized, there remained only specialized financial establishments: the Czecho-Slovak National Bank, the Postal Savings, and the Investments Bank.

The two super-banks noted above became important financial factors of planned economy. They were entrusted with the financing of existing industry belonging to the State and to the communes, cooperatives, or private sector. They had an important role in internal distribution as well as in foreign trades. They controlled the corporations having the monopoly of a given sector in foreign trade relations.

The balance sheet of the *Tatra banka,* published after the consolidation, January 1, 1948, amounted to ten billion crowns.[47]

The banking reform of 1947 was, however, not to be definitive. On February 14, 1950, the Czecho-Slovak government approved a bill aimed at creating a single State bank replacing the Czecho-Slovak National Bank, the *Živnostenská banka, the Tatra banka* and also the Postal Savings. This concentration was going to constitute a stronger financial armature than all that had previously existed. Thus the State, after absorbing the private sector or bringing it under control, asserted itself in all commercial activity under the form of a single economic unit.

The Biennial Plan—State-controlled economy of the popular democracies means not only the nationalization of industry and important wealth of the country, but especially a permanently centralized management of the nationalized enterprises. This system makes the autonomy of each enterprise disappear into an

[47] See: "Slovenská Tatra Banka," *Pravda*, Bratislava, (December 25, 1948).

all-powerful State trust. Men and enterprises become mere wheels, technical accessories in an enormous economic machine.

After more than a year's careful study of the needs and financial possibilities, a law was passed on October 28, 1946, which set in motion the Biennial Economic Plan[48]—the apotheosis of controlled economy.

By the terms of Section I of this law, the following plan was proposed:

a) in industry, to exceed by 10 per cent by the end of the year 1948 the total level of the production of the year 1937;

b) in agriculture, to reach by the end of 1948 the level of pre-war production;

c) to effect a wide-scale construction program in matters of lodging, communications, hydraulic works, and agriculture;

d) to reach, in matters of transportation, the output of the year 1937;

e) to raise Slovak economy to the Czech economic level;

f) to ameliorate the Czech countries' regions that were in an unfair position economically.

Section III provided for investments for the territory of the Czecho-Slovak Republic amounting to 69,880 million crowns.

Section IV gave details on what was forecast for the economic development of Slovakia. Of the Biennial Plan's investments, a sum not to exceed 22,140 million crowns was destined to Slovakia and was to be distributed as follows:

a) for industrial and homecrafts production: 6,800 million;

b) for agriculture: 2,100 million;

c) for transportation: 4,710 million;

d) for the repair of residential units damaged by the war and for the construction of new residential units: 4,800 million;

e) for works of civil engineering, the harnessing of waterways, transportation and other public works: 3,730 million crowns.

Moreover, the government provided for the transfer of machines from Czech countries to Slovakia for industrial enterprises and homecrafts production; this would procure work for 26,000 persons.

This plan was too beautiful to be realized. The press commented a great deal on its development, but no statistics were given out at all. As regards the results, one has to be satisfied with

[48] See: Ministère de l'Information, *Le Plan economique biennal tchécoslovaque* (Prague: 1947), p. 3.

official statements, according to which the program as laid down was achieved only in industry. At the end of the Biennial Plan, the index of the products of current consumption reached only 79.7 per cent and the food industry 67.3 in comparison to the year 1937. For agriculture the figures were even less satisfactory:

> The Biennial Plan had been realized only to the amount of 72.8 per cent for plant production, 83.3 per cent for animal production, and 80.5 per cent for the whole of agricultural production. The importance of livestock remained lower by 8.2 per cent; and the pork meat supply, by 28.8 per cent to what they had been before the war.[49]

It is proper to note the criticism of the Biennial Plan made by Mr. Zápotocký, then President of the Council of Ministers, in his address to the National Assembly of Prague on October 7, 1948. After stating with satisfaction that the fundamental task of industrial production, namely, to reach the index 110 in comparison to 1937, had been realized, Mr. Zápotocký changed his tone:

> If our grain harvest in 1947, instead of the 275,000 trucks anticipated, had been only 185,000 trucks (of which 65,780 trucks of provisions of breadstuffs were bought instead of 105,920 the preceding year), it is understandable that the distributions anticipated by the plan could not be effected, and that the standard of living could not be maintained. If in spite of that we did not have to suffer from hunger, we owe it solely to the generous aid of our ally, the Union of Soviet Socialist Republics, and to our industrial production which, while accomplishing and in many cases exceeding the plan, allowed us to fill the gap of agricultural production by exporting more and by thus furnishing us with the possibility of importing foodstuffs.
>
> Still worse for us than the grain production were the consequences of the nonrealization of the plan from the point of view of animal production. Instead of 80,000 tons anticipated by the plan, only 46,327 tons of beef were produced in the first half of 1948, that is only 58 per cent of the total. Instead of 133,000 tons of pork, we obtained only 71,382, that is 54 per cent. Instead of 16 million hectoliters of milk, the production was only 10 million, or 62 per cent. The falling off which is indicated here could not be made up by the importation of meat and grease, no matter what proportions they might have taken.
>
> The loss suffered in agricultural production can be estimated at about 15 billion crowns. It is a matter of course

[49] Alfred Frisch, "La Tchécoslovaquie dans une impasse économique," *Témoignage Chrétien,* Paris, (May 13, 1949).

that such a deficiency could not fail to exert an unfavorable influence on rationing and the standard of living.

The building situation is the same. If the plan in 1947 was realized only up to the amount of 70 per cent and even for the construction of lodgings, 47 per cent; if, instead of the 61,000 lodgings planned, only 29,000 were built, one can understand that the housing crisis did not diminish but on the contrary increased. . . . But one could not hide the fact that the private capitalist elements which prevailed in these sectors share a great part of the responsibility for the nonaccomplishment of the plan.

It is an undisputed fact that our capitalist reaction, eager for disruption, counted on these gaps and serious troubles which resulted for our economy. There were those who exerted themselves greatly to aggravate the crisis already caused by a bad crop. These were interested in bringing about sabotage, black market, and the refusal of supplies. They supposed and hoped that the resulting poverty and hunger could be utilized for their seditiously criminal ends.[50]

. . . As long as we do not succeed in convincing and re-educating those who do not wish to understand, and as long as we do not force them to work and fulfill their duty, we shall run against obstacles and shall not be in a position to realize 100 per cent our plans for building a new society and definitely assuring all laborers a suitable standard of life.[51]

. . . We can not and will not allow individuals, whether in their work, their service, commerce, trade, business, or agriculture, to place their selfish and greedy interests above the interests of all; nor that for their personal advantage, they strike at the general advantage for all. We shall find means to defend our democratic and popular Republic against subversive elements, profiteers, panic-sowers and traitors. . . .[52]

The warmongers and speculators, who hoped to provoke a war psychosis and sow panic and trouble so that one cannot work and build in peace, will be taken back a peg.[53]

The Agrarian Reform—The agrarian reform of the Third Czecho-Slovak Republic finds its bases in the program so-called Hradec Králové, set forth by the Minister of Agriculture, Mr. Julius Ďuriš, in his address on April 4, 1947.

[50] See: Ministère de l'Information, *Le Plan économique quinquennal tchéco-slovaque* (Prague: December, 1948), pp. 13-15.
[51] *Ibid.*, p. 19.
[52] *Ibid.*, p. 21.
[53] *Ibid.*, p. 23.

It would be proper to emphasize and comment briefly on the essential points.

1. *The land will be reserved for those who cultivate it themselves.*

Mr. Ďuriš built this principle on the following fundamental ideas:

According to the 1930 statistics that he used, landed property was distributed as indicated below:

Percentage of owners	Extent of the property			Percentage
44 per cent peasants	From 0 to	2	hectares	4.5
27		2	5	10.0
24		5	20	30.5
4		20	50	12.0
1 large landowner	Above		50	32.0

In the light of these figures, the distribution of the great land property among little owners seemed justified, the average-size domain cultivated directly by the owner and his family having to be considered as the basic element of any reasonable agricultural policy.

It will be seen below that the expropriation of the large properties was actually the first stage in a communist agrarian policy which it was necessary to have accepted by the peasants. The last stage led to the State control of the average property, to end finally in *kolkhozes.*

The total confiscation of the properties of the Church (bishoprics, chapters, seminaries, parish churches), likewise promoted by the Communists, was much less inspired by the concern for ameliorating the peasants' situation than by the desire to subject the Church materially to the State in order to control its spiritual activities better.

2. *The rights of the purchasers of confiscated lands will be registered without delay in the land register.*

To rally the peasants to their policy, the Communists attempted to obtain the immediate application of this measure. They had not forgotten that in Czecho-Slovakia after World War I, at the time of the first agrarian reform, it was most often only after several years that the peasants succeeded in having the State record in the cadastral survey the properties thus acquired by them.

3. *The land holdings will be limited to 50 hectares.*

Although the agrarian reform realized by the First Czecho-Slovak Republic had limited the property to 250 hectares—admitting numerous exceptions—the communist reform was to go much further and post the limit at 50 hectares.

4. *The land will be reconstituted in order to increase its returns.*

In Czecho-Slovakia, where the agricultural holding was divided into 33 million parcels and distributed among 1,500,000 agriculturists, each cultivated therefore an average of 22 parcels.

5. *Cultivation will be mechanized.*

By obliging the peasants to buy expensive agricultural machines in common the State did not try so much to lighten their labor but wanted merely to clear the way for *kolkhozes.*

6. *The disparity between prices of industrial and agricultural products will be eliminated.*

Mr. Ďuriš here tackled a problem which, in the economic system of popular democracies, is without solution. Not only is the communist regime incapable of aiding the peasants in raising their living standard, but it is so arranged that the peasant class, politically inferior, becomes a tributary of the working class, a leading element of socialist progressism. In putting this measure into his program, it is obvious that Mr. Ďuriš acted only with a view to propaganda.

7. *The farmer will be integrated into the compass of the Biennial Plan.*

Peasantry—the last category of citizens still free—found itself thus introduced into the State's economic mechanism and through the unduly severe quota system of food deliveries, reduced to the role of servant to the working class.[54]

In this manner were the foundations laid for a State-controlled economy of distinctly Soviet inspiration in the Constitution itself. Put into the service of the policy of Moscow, Czecho-Slovakia's economy contributed considerably to the enslaving of the citizen and man.

[54] For details, see: Ministère de l'Agriculture: *Le Plan biennal dans "agriculture* (Prague: 1946).

The Errors of the Foreign Policy

Relations with the U.S.S.R.—Like a pylon, a State, in order to be solid, has to be anchored to the four corners of the world. Secured on only one side, it will inevitably fall in that same direction. A political axiom is at stake here.

In Section IV of the Governmental Program of Košice regarding the orientation of the foreign policy, the following passage is to be found:

> In expressing the unbounded gratitude of the Czech and Slovak nations to the Soviet Union, the government considers a closer alliance with the Great Victorious Slav Power of the East as the unshakable main principle of the Czechoslovak foreign policy. In the postwar period, the Czechoslovak-Soviet Treaty of Mutual Aid, Friendship and Collaboration—of December 12, 1943—will determine for our entire future the foreign policy of our State. The government will have to strive so that in the organization of the future peace, Czechoslovakia will be close beside the Soviet Union and on an equal footing with all the other democratic Slav States.

By this unconditional solidarity, Czecho-Slovakia, as a member of the international political community, gave up its liberty in favor of Russia. And so it was that Mr. Beneš and his government chose, serenely and without any outside pressure, that Czecho-Slovakia be a satellite of the Soviet Union. Thus they contributed to forming the Eastern bloc and so dividing the world at the very time when they should have availed themselves of everything to ensure its unity. All that happened afterward on the Czecho-Slovak internal plane is only a logical consequence of this lack of will and farsightedness on the part of the leaders responsible for the foreign policy.

Thus, a year and a half after the Russian "liberation," Jan Masaryk could ask himself the following question, but not without a certain oratorical affectation: "Will this State become the vassal of Soviet Russia, its present powerful neighbor; and will the new institutions that it is now creating not be a derivative of the Soviet regime?"

And with the charm that was his, he gave this reply:

> These are needless worries. The Czechoslovak nation, even after the postwar upheavals, will remain at heart what it was for centuries; it will simply enlarge its political and social foundations in comparison with the First Republic.[55]

[55] *Cahiers du monde nouveau,* Paris, (November, 1946), p. 25.

In 1947, Mr. Masaryk published a book, *Neither Iron Curtain nor Bridge,* in which he interpreted in a manner as ingenious as naive the position of Czecho-Slovakia.[56] For him this country was too stamped with liberty to be put behind the Iron Curtain, and its bonds of solidarity with the U.S.S.R. were too close for it to be considered a bridge between western Europe and the East.

This kind of theory could only serve to mask the reality of which Mr. Masaryk was himself going to become the victim some day.

The consequences of the unconditional alliance with the U.S.S.R. on the political plane did not fail to have their repercussions on the economic level. Mr. Hubert Ripka, in the capacity of Minister of Foreign Trade for Czecho-Slovakia, extolled a preferential system of exchange to be established in "the sphere of Soviet influence." He did it in the following way:

> The close friendly political ties which exist between Czechoslovakia and its great ally of the East, the Soviet Union, must find their counterpart in trade relations aiming at having our products sold on the Soviet market and assuring us the importation of merchandise, especially raw materials from Russia. We ought likewise to give our entire attention to the development of such relations—that only the progressive amelioration of communications can favor—with countries located in the sphere of Soviet influence.[57]

When later in his book, *Czechoslovakia Enslaved,*[58] Mr. Ripka proves astonished at the Soviet veto of Czecho-Slovakia's participation in the Marshall Plan, he lacks sincerity, for in large part, he himself had had a hand in creating the situation which could end only in the political and economic *diktát* of Russia. In December, 1947, he took another trip to Russia to sign a new trade treaty destined to compensate Czecho-Slovak economy for the government of Prague's forced relinquishment of the advantages of the Marshall Plan.

After Mr. Ripka's return, the communist press was profuse in praising Soviet comprehension, thanks to which Czecho-Slovakia was going to be able henceforth to buy Russian wheat below world-wide prices and have the assurance of finding outlets in Russia for its own products.

[56] Jan Masaryk, *Neither Iron Curtain nor Bridge* (Prague: 1947).
[57] Hubert Ripka, "La Tchécoslovaquie comme partenaire commercial," *Cahiers du monde nouveau,* Paris, (November, 1946), p. 57.
[58] Hubert Ripka, *Czechoslovakia Enslaved: The Story of the Communist Coup d'Etat* (London: 1950), p. 63.

What was actually the advantage brought to Czecho-Slovakia by this accord? While the Slovak peasants were delivering their wheat to the State for 580 crowns per hundredweight, Russian wheat cost 1,100. Despite this difference, Mr. Ripka was determined to keep his promises. Upon returning to Prague, he commented upon the agreement before the National Assembly: "Let us realize that we must pay the shipments of Soviet wheat." He then invited Czechoslovak industry and all authorities and organizations to spread their influence with a view to a complete and rapid development of the exportations in the U.S.S.R. At the same time, he expressed the hope that this appeal would be sufficient to make all those responsible for production be conscious of their duty; otherwise the Ministry of Foreign Trade would be obliged to have recourse to measures of constraint.[59]

Why, then, scarcely free from German tutelage, were the Czechs in a hurry to become Russian satellites?

The Germano-Czech Problem—It is known that at the insistence of Mr. Beneš, the Big Three (Atlee, Stalin, and Truman), by an agreement signed on August 2, 1945, in Potsdam, decided to rid the territories of Czecho-Slovakia, Poland, and Hungary of their German constituency by forcing them back into Ally-occupied Germany. This decision struck with one single blow 2,500,-000 Sudeten Germans who, by virtue of the same agreement, were distributed between the Soviet zone (750,000) and the American zone (1,750,000).

The brutal manner in which the government of Prague effected the expulsion of the Sudeten Germans terrified the Western world. Now far from solving a European problem, this ruling only served to poison German-Czech relations. The Czechs drove out the Germans but henceforth were full of apprehension for the future. A total lack of proportion and balance impelled the Czecho-Slovak delegation at the Paris Peace Conference of 1946 to ask that the historic boundary line be moved back by ten kilometers into German territory "to reinforce its strategic character."

It would be hard to imagine a request as unreasonable on the part of the Czechs. What they were doing, in effect, was renouncing the application of an historic principle which in 1918

---

[59] See *Zahraniční Obchod*, organ of the Ministry of Foreign Trade, (Prague), III, No. 4, 124. Quoted in the article of Paul Barton, "La mainmise russe sur l'économie tchéco-slovaque," *Rapports France-Etats-Unis,* (January, 1951).

had been to their distinct advantage in determining the frontier
of Bohemia and Moravia. Thus they weakened their own position and gave Germany another pretext to ask in the future for
the reconsideration, following the ethnological principle, of the
boundaries of this sector.

It was in trying to get out of this dilemma that the Czechs
determined, after the expulsion of the Sudetes, to lean unreservedly on the Soviet Union.

The Polish-Slovak Boundary—After the re-establishment in
Czecho-Slovakia of the territorial status quo which existed before
Munich, the Slovaks protested against the tying up of the Orava
and the Spiš of the north to Poland[60] which, after all, put into
practice at once in these regions a centralizing policy abolishing
the national privileges of the Slovak minority: Slovak schools,
sermons in Slovak in the churches, diffusion of the newspapers
of Slovakia, etc.

On May 15, 1946, the chairmen of the National Committees
of twelve communes of the Orava and thirteen communes of the
Spiš signed at Jablonka and Jurgov a protest against their being
joined again to Poland. The protest was then given to the Minister of Foreign Affairs of Czecho-Slovakia, Jan Masaryk, for him
to submit to the decision of the Peace Conference in Paris.

When the Russians learned of the demand, they advised Jan
Masaryk against presenting it to the Conference, and they let
him understand that they were prepared to arbitrate this dispute
opposing two Slav nations. Masaryk consented, and the Russians
pigeon-holed the dossier. Moscow, which had its own interests
to defend, suppressed the question of the Slovak minority in
Poland.

*The Exchange of Populations Between Czecho-Slovakia and
Hungary*—The program of Košice made provisions for the transformation of Czecho-Slovakia into a "national" State. Solemnly
approved by President Beneš in his Bratislava speech May 9,
1945, it determined the Czecho-Slovak policy with respect to Germany and Hungary. The government of Prague adopted the principle of collective responsibility toward the Magyars of Slovakia
who, just like the German minority at the time of the Munich
crisis, had in large part manifested their wish to be joined to their
country of origin. In this respect, Prague revealed itself as pitiless.
On April 11, 1946, the National Front adopted the decision regarding the political structure of the State, according to which

[60] See text p. 129.

only Czechs, Slovaks, and other Slavs would be citizens by right. This would exclude all nationals of non-Slav origin; these latter could neither elect nor be elected.

The arbitrary expulsion of the Magyars and the confiscation of their goods followed. The government of Budapest then protested before the Allied Control Commission by asking the Great Powers to conduct an inquest in Slovakia. Alone, the United States of America would have welcomed this request favorably.[61] The Hungarian government had no other means therefore than to try to discuss the question directly with Prague.

In the autumn of 1945, a delegation of the Hungarian Social-Democratic party went to Prague to study the possibility of a pacific ruling on the question. The Czech-Slovak government declared itself in principle ready to negotiate an exchange of populations. The official pourparlers were begun in December in Prague. According to Mr. Kertész, a Hungarian delegate, Mr. Clementis, then Under-Secretary of State in Foreign Affairs, made plans to "exchange the Slovaks from Hungary desirous of leaving the country, for an analogous number of Hungarians designated by Prague, all other Hungarians from Slovakia to be expelled later."[62]

As a result, about 150,000 Magyars from Slovakia had to be exchanged for the same number of Slovaks residing in Hungary. There would then remain in Slovakia 350,000 Magyars who would have to be forced out. The Hungarian delegation accepted the principle of an exchange freely consented to, but categorically refused the expulsion of the rest of the Magyar population that Prague had in mind. All negotiations failed without even giving rise to the publication of a final communiqué, and left the problem remaining in all its gravity, the Magyar minority having been practically outlawed.

On February 27, 1946, a covenant was finally signed at Tatránska Lomnica in Slovakia, on the exchange of populations between Czecho-Slovakia and Hungary. In accordance with this agreement, the Czecho-Slovak government could "expatriate as many Hungarians as there were Slovaks in Hungary naturally desirous of returning to establish themselves in Czecho-Slovakia."[63]

[61] See: Etienne Kertész, "Tout est calme sur les bords le Danube," *Courrier de l'Occident,* Paris, (October 15, 1949).
[62] *Ibid.*
[63] Association hongroise des Affaires Etrangères, *La déportation des Hongrois de Slovaquie* (Budapest: 1947), p. 5.

In the protocol attached to the Convention, the government of Prague pledged its word to suspend the expulsion of the Magyars from Slovakia, to stop their displacement and the confiscation of their goods; to pay a compensation to the officials of Magyar origin who had been removed from office, as well as to the retired, the orphans, and those who would be deprived of allowance because of their nationality, etc.[64]

The Peace Treaty of 1947 with Hungary imposed:

> . . . bilateral negotiations with Czecho-Slovakia in order to regulate the situation of the inhabitants of Magyar ethnic origin residing in Czecho-Slovakia and who will not be established in Hungary in the sense of the treaty of February 27, 1946, on the exchange of populations.

The treaty also decided the following:

> In case no arrangement would be concluded, reckoning from the present treaty's becoming operative, Czecho-Slovakia will have the right to bring the question before the Council of the Ministers of Foreign Affairs and ask the Council's aid in finding a definitive solution.[65]

Thus the question was put on an international plane. Already considering the exchange of populations in a bad light, the Hungarian government objected to any compromise concerning the 350,000 Magyars for whom provisions were not made in the agreement. Henceforth, all proposals from Prague ran up against a stubborn resistance from Budapest.

The irate Mr. Clementis had stated as early as October 31, 1946, in his report made before the Commission on Foreign Affairs of the National Assembly in Prague, on the evacuation of the Magyars from Slovakia: "As regards the definitive solution, if worse comes to worst, we shall be well able to find it by ourselves."[66]

No longer recognizing any minority, Czecho-Slovakia decided to disperse the Magyars in the Sudeten regions. The Office of Internal Colonization of Slovakia, presided over by a Communist, Mr. Čech, was entrusted with effecting "the regrouping of the Magyars of Slovakia" by transferring them to Bohemia. To justify this measure, the Czecho-Slovak government referred to the provisions of the presidential Decree No. 88/1945 on "the mobilization of manpower" which authorized the administration of the

[64] *Ibid.,* p. 5.
[65] *Ibid.,* p. 6.
[66] *Pravda* Bratislava, (November 1, 1946).

State, in case of urgent works of public interest, to subject to forced labor men from sixteen to fifty-five years of age and women from eighteen to forty-five for the maximum duration of one year.

Beginning November 17, 1947, this transfer was effected by cattle trains or trucks with an army escort, and sometimes during severely cold weather. Thus tens of thousands of Magyars had to abandon their homes. Many of them preferred to pass secretly into Hungary rather than go into Czechia.

Once again, Hungary protested energetically against these methods, at times throwing the responsibility on Slovakia. However, Budapest was wrong in accusing the Slovak people or "authorities" for this deportation. The fact that Mr. Vladimír Clementis, a Slovak and Under-Secretary of State in Foreign Affairs in Prague, had been entrusted with regulating the Magyar question, and the manner in which he had accomplished this task, did not in any way whatsoever commit the Slovak nation. A Communist, Mr. Clementis could lean only on his own party which did not amount to more than 30 per cent of the population.

To tell the truth, the policy of expulsion and transfer of populations was Messrs. Beneš' and Gottwald's invention. For the former, it was to strengthten the Czechs' position; for the latter, the Communists' position in Czecho-Slovakia. It was in the same spirit that, on Prague's decision, 250,000 Slovaks were also transplanted as agricultural workers in the Sudeten regions. Against this revolting procedure, the *Čas*, the Democratic party's organ, could only write with resignation: "The poor Slovak workman is incapable of freeing himself from this modern slavery."[67] Exposed to administrative pressure and mixed up with the Czech population, all these uprooted Slovaks and Magyars served to reinforce the number and position of the proletariat. The Slovaks of Hungary who were to return to Slovakia were recruited by a delegation of the Office of Internal Colonization among the workers that were not always Slovaks, whereas the Magyars who were pressed back into Hungary were almost all peasants. For the Magyars who suddenly discovered that they were of Slovak origin, ways had to be found to "re-slovakize" them, that is to say to provide them with the legal means to resume the nationality of their supposed ancestors whose language they often did not even know.

[67] *Čas*, Bratislava, (January 8, 1947). See also: *Appeal of the Slovak Action Committee to the Civilized World Concerning the Deportation of the Slovak Population in Sudeten by the Czechs* (Bridgeport, Conn.: February, 1947).

Authentic Slovakia did not forget that its territories in the south had been Magyarized by force in the eighteenth and nineteenth centuries, and that the Slovaks of these regions, practically outlawed after the Arbitrament of Vienna in 1938, had suffered considerably from the vexatious interferences of the Magyar authorities. In spite of everything, it had never envisioned regulating by violence the question of the Magyar minority. On the contrary, the Catholic bishops of Slovakia protested against the manner in which the government of Prague had carried on the deportations of the Magyars.

These deplorable events, like those of which the Slovak population was the victim in 1938, proved as much to the Slovaks as to the Magyars that the question of minorities and frontiers must be regulated on the international plane and not in a unilateral fashion.

Soviet Slavism—Desirous of fleeing Germanism, the Czechs fell into the Soviet neo-Slav trap. "It remains," said Mr. Beneš, "that Slavism is for us an indispensable point of departure and that any Czechoslovak policy must take it as such, especially after what will result from World War II."[68]

"Soviet Slavism"—which seeks its explanation in an opposition to Germanism—is really, in spite of Mr. Beneš' adherence, only a political scheme of Moscow, a matter of tactics.[69] It is a subtle game carried on by the U.S.S.R. that is speculating on the national feelings of the Slav peoples with a mind to integrating them the better in communism; it is a devious way to consolidate the forces of international communism in a specified geographical sector. And especially for the Slav nations, far from being a "point of departure," Soviet neo-Slavism is in political matters the end of all liberty.

Mr. Beneš' game was more than hazardous. *Incidit in Scyllam qui vult vitare Charybdim!*

The "White Conspiracy"

Like the other Russian satellite countries, Slovakia too was to have its conspiracy. However, while in Rumania, Hungary,

---

[68] Beneš, *Où vont les Slaves?* p. 257.
[69] This neo-slavism took the form of a vast political movement after World War II. Its directing organ was the Slav Committee in Moscow with General Gundurov at the head. Its annual manifestations were the Slav congresses which were always held in a different country. The first and fourth conferences took place July 5-6, 1945 and July 11, 1948 in Bratislava.

and Poland this supposed conspiracy was directed against the regime, in Slovakia it was set up against the Czecho-Slovak State. For a long time the Communists had been preparing a list of the persons who were supposedly enemies of the State. They were only waiting for the opportune moment to get rid of them.

The Communists had increased their vigilance at the time of the Ukrainian Resistance Army's (UPA) secret passage and flight toward the west through Slovakia. In the summer of 1947, the Ukrainian nationalist General Tarass Chuprenka's groups crossed the Tatra mountains and entered Slovakia. In April, 1947, a military pact had been concluded between the U.S.S.R., Poland, and Czecho-Slovakia with a view to pursuing them. In Slovakia, besides a few battalions of the regular army, three groups of former communist partisans had a share in this operation.[70]

A well-informed publicist stated:

> . . . The Czech troops were in violent combat against the UPA units, whereas the Slovak troops showed no zeal whatsoever. There were no serious encounters except near Turčiansky Sv. Martin and Ružomberok, where the students of a military school (Czech) were sent in pursuit of the UPA. The Slovak population fed and lodged the Ukrainian partisans and tried to guide them as best they could.[71]

The Ukrainians' defiance stirred up the spirit of resistance in Slovakia. It was then that the regime decided to combat this state of mind with a brutal preventive action.

The opportunity for engaging in such an action presented itself at the time of Mr. Beneš' trip to Slovakia, where each year he was in the habit of taking a rest at the Topolčianky Château. Since Monsignor Tiso's execution, the atmosphere in Slovakia was not at all favorable to him; nay, it was hostile. Thousands of anonymous threatening letters arrived daily at the Hradčany Castle. Mr. Lettrich, President of the Slovak National Council, had given Beneš to understand that it would not be opportune for him to spend his vacation at Topolčianky that year, but "reasons of State" demanded this trip. During the night of September 11, 1947, the presidential train, crowded with policemen, neared Bratislava. In Slovak territory the garrisons of the cities he had to go through had been alerted. All along the way, military patrols were guarding the railway track. Against whom?

[70] See: *Partizán*, Bratislava, (Otcober 28, 1947).
[71] Romain d'Or, *The Inclined Plane* (*Some Observations on Russian Expansion*) (Stockholm: 1948), p. 2.

The morning of September 12, it was learned from the newspaper that the police had discovered that a group of Slovaks were
prepared to take the President's life during his trip to Topolčianky
and that this group was in close liaison with a network of conspirators who were threatening the security of the State and the
regime. An organized search soon gave results. From the middle
of September to the end of October, more than two thousand
persons were imprisoned. Mr. Beneš was grateful to the police
for having thus saved his life. But this spectacular deed was to
have other implications which the aged man was not able to
realize.

Among those held prisoners, recruited from all social classes,
there were three deputies of the Catholic wing of the Democratic
party—Messrs. Kempný, Bugár, and Staško; a lawyer and organizer of the Catholic Front, Mr. Obtulovič; the editor of a
Catholic weekly, *Katolícke noviny,* Mr. Čarnogurský; the secretary of the Archbishop of Nitra, Abbé Beňuška; a professor of
theology at the seminary of Nitra, Abbé Murín; the editor-in-chief
of the Catholic review, *Verbum,* Mr. Jankovič; Mr. Obuch, the
private secretary of the Vice-President of the Council and Vice-
President of the Democratic party, Ursíny; the mayor of Bratislava, Mr. Kyselý; the chaplain of *Svoradov,* the former Catholic
students' house, Father Hutyra; the assistant director of Slovakia's
food industry, Mr. Jurčovič; a former university professor, Mr.
Rajec; the regional secretaries of the Democratic party of Žilina
and Námestovo, Messrs. Števík and Škorvaga; and also Messrs.
Tatarko, Vaško, and Fickuliak, respectively ex-colonel, commander, and captain of the Slovak Army. All these eminent people
and their friends formed the core of the "conspiracy."

A special commission of the Ministry of Interior of Prague,
headed by Dr. Mudra, a graduate of the NKVD of Moscow, was
sent to Bratislava to guide the investigation. Evidently Prague did
not trust the organs of the Slovak police although they were
communist.

The questioning took place according to a plan set up by the
Ministry of the Interior. The questions asked were mainly the
following:

> While you were studying, did you belong to any
> Catholic groups? What was your attitude toward the Slo-
> vak State? Have you been a member of the Populist party?
> Did you take part in the "national uprising"? What is your
> attitude with respect to the liberating work of the Red

Army? What impressions do you get from your contacts with this army? What did you do to favor the progressist forces in your country? What do you think of the Tiso trial, of the nationalization of industry, of the socialist revolution in Czecho-Slovakia? Are you for the autonomy of Slovakia or for the Czecho-Slovak federation? What do you think of the present regime? Do you believe in a third World War?

Mr. Mudra, who strangely resembled the French revolutionary Barnave, made remarks of this sort to the prisoners: "What do you still want, you Slovaks?" he cried out one day in exasperation to a "dangerous" conspirator. "You have autonomous organizations: the Slovak National Council, the Board of Commissioners. You live under the regime of dualism and you are still not happy."

"If Czecho-Slovakia were a dualistic State, only Slovak policemen would be competent for the investigation of my case!" was the reply.

Upon which Mr. Mudra ordered the director of the prison to throw this "reactionary element" into the dungeon at once.

Questioned one day on his attitude toward the regime, one who was being held in prison replied:

The regime? That interests me so little! What is a regime in relation to eternity? I have already seen a whole succession of them fall one after the other. They are so ephemeral! Look at your prison. Regimes and officials go away sooner or later. Only the lice remain!

This philosophical repartee struck the conscience of the examining magistrate and, beginning the next day, the cells were emptied one after the other. The floors were torn up, the repugnant walls were whitewashed and made ready to once again receive Slovak crosses[72] and patriotic verses.

The procedures of the investigation followed the Pavlovian pattern. The questionings often took place at night and sometimes lasted for forty-eight consecutive hours. Jakab, Bél and other brutes especially trained for this purpose, subjected the questioned prisoners to the most ingenious cruelties. Often at five o'clock in the morning the prison would ring out with the voices and groans of those being tortured. Following the maltreatments, one prisoner became deaf, a fact which was ascer-

[72] The Slovak cross is the double cross of Saints Cyril and Methodius, erected on the three symbolic hills: the Tatras, the Matra and the Fatra.

tained at the oto-rhino-laryngological clinic of the central hospital in Bratislava. Another conspirator had his teeth broken out and a third had his legs broken. A fourth was led in the middle of the night to a forest outside of Bratislava, where a summary execution was simulated. He was leaned against a tree and questioned before a group of policemen who stood ready to fire their submachineguns. A religious was beaten, slapped and held up to ridicule entire nights for three weeks for refusing to tell the "truth."

The news of these brutalities was not long in spreading about the city, and it gave rise to interpellations in the Slovak National Council and the Parliament of Prague. General Ferjenčík, a veterinary and Commissioner of the Interior (a mere instrument in the hands of the Communists), then went to the police prison to question those confined on the manner in which they had been treated. As he had been cautious enough to have himself escorted by the brutish men who were the authors of the tortures that had motivated this inquiry, his interlocutors were very reticent.

Thus General Ferjenčík was able at the end of his visit to make a statement about "the unfounded rumors which aimed at discrediting the police of Bratislava." This "expert" rendered a real service to the Communists at the decisive moment of their battle against democracy, and it was for good reasons that after the events of February, 1948, at the time when Mr. Husák relieved him of his duties as commissioner, Ferjenčík received Mr. Husák's most cordial thanks.[73]

Against all rules of penal procedure the investigation lasted three months, during which a good number of conspirators were kept in the police prison, permitted neither to receive visitors nor packages, nor write, nor take a walk. They were deprived of all sanitation, and slept on an empty sack or even on the floor. At times, to keep up appearances, the prisoners were taken to the prison of the Tribunal; but under the false pretext that there was no room, they were quickly returned to the police prison.

Finally the conspirators were classified in several categories, according to the gravity of their "crimes." The most harmless had engaged in the peddling of Monsignor Tiso's photographs bear-

---

[73] These facts do not prevent General Ferjenčík, now a refugee in the United States as a "victim" of communism, from playing the role of "defender of democracy."

ing the inscription "Slovak Martyr." Rumor has it that they had been developed in great numbers by several nuns detailed to the laboratory in the hospital of Bratislava.

The second group combined the elements who had been in contact with the chiefs of Slovak emigration abroad, especially with Mr. Karol Sidor, former Minister of the Slovak Republic to the Holy See, and with Mr. Ďurčanský, former Minister of Foreign Affairs of the Slovak State, in his absence sentenced to death by the National Tribunal of Bratislava at the same time as Monsignor Tiso. According to the police reports, Otto Obuch, the leader of the group, was in constant touch with these emigrants and furnished them with information on the conditions of the political and economic life in Czecho-Slovakia.

The third "skewer" included all the elements who, in case of conflict between the Soviet orbit and the Western world, were preparing to organize an armed resistance in the *hinterland* of the Red Army. These were mostly former officers of the Slovak Army. They were accused of keeping in contact with the exiles and with the information services of what remained of the Slovak Army in Austria.

The fourth and final group was directed by a university professor accused of having formulated a memorandum for Churchill asking for the independence of Slovakia.

There was no more question of an attempt on Mr. Beneš' life.

Before the Security Commission of the National Assembly in Prague, General Ferjenčík expressed himself on the subject of "the conspiracy in Slovakia" in the following terms:

> A tendency has existed and does still exist having as its aim to separate Slovakia from the Czechoslovak Republic. It is interesting to note that the conspiracy movements were never more active than at the time the Marshall Plan was proclaimed. The conspirators counted on the dissensions between the Great Powers, dissensions which, according to them, had to end in war. . . .
>
> This tendency has found and does find support in Populist spheres. . . . What proves it is the fact that since the liberation, thirty-six illegal groups have been found planning to destroy the Czechoslovak Republic. After the *Intermarium* Plan, seven to eight thousand emigrants maintain relations with relatives—counted by tens of thousands in Slovakia—and influence their ideology.[74]

[74] See: *Informations tchécoslovaques*, Paris, No. 158, (February 11, 1948).

All these events started a great crisis within the Democratic party. Three of its deputies and several of its most important persons were compromised by their resistance to communism, and the party itself was violently attacked. Mr. Ursíny, Vice-President of the Council of Ministers for the Democratic party, was the first sighted. He was obliged to resign at the beginning of November because of his secretary, Obuch. Mr. Hodža, Secretary-General of the Democratic party, was accused of burning the suspect correspondence of Obuch in Ursíny's offices in Prague, and was thereby considered an accomplice. The Communists asked that his parliamentary immunity be lifted. In addition, they organized manifestations against the "reactionaries" hidden within the Democratic party. Thus the Union of Slovak Partisans, dominated by the Communists, led an attack against the palace which housed the Slovak National Council. A group of demonstrators broke the doors down and got as far as the offices of Chairman Lettrich, who had just escaped through a hidden exit.

Following these events, on November 18, 1947, the Democratic party, under the concentrated pressure of Prague, lost two seats in the regional government of Slovakia and was reduced to a minority. It retained only seven out of fifteen seats, whereas the communist group occupied eight, distributed in the following manner: the Communist party received five; the Liberty party, one; the Labor party, one; the last went to General Ferjenčík, who, without being affiliated with any party, was practically playing the Communists' game. This was actually the "coup d'état" in Slovakia.

This whole evolution aimed purely and simply at the liquidation of the Democratic party. In the month of January, Mr. Kyselý, the Democratic mayor of Bratislava, was imprisoned and "worked on" by the police until he pledged himself to collaborate in the weeding out of the "reactionary" elements.

As soon as he was free, he launched a campaign against right-wing Democrats. Therefore, at the annual congress of the Democratic party, held on January 24, 1948, in Bratislava, he was stripped of his membership. But this measure in no way interfered with the evolution which continued its course implacably.

What was the Czech attitude when faced with these events in Slovakia? Instead of defending the Democratic party before the communist tide in the Parliament of Prague, the so-called Czech Democratic parties abandoned it to its enemies. Mr. Ripka, particularly anti-Slovak, could not deny the Czech responsibility in the political development in Slovakia.

Co-operation between non-Communist Czechs and Slovaks was made still more difficult because neither the National Socialists, the Populists, nor the Social Democrats were disposed to recognize the Czecho-Slovak dualism which had in fact existed since the liberation. All these parties were defending the traditional doctrine of national unity, and it was only grudgingly that they had to recognize the doctrine of two independent nations, with the hope that the experiment, both on the political and economic plane, would end in an attenuation or a progressive suppression of the dual system.[75]

The Czechs, satisfied at heart to see the Slovak "conspirators" liquidated, were far from foreseeing that these facts were only the prelude to what was soon going to happen in Bohemia. Faithful to the fiction of their mind, they preferred the totalitarianism of Moscow to the Czech-Slovak dualism.

February 1948

> *If you do not wish to take the bull by the horns, you will not be able to hold it by the tail.*   (Slovak proverb)

The Communists' seizure of power in February, 1948, could surprise only those who had no idea whatsoever of the political situation in Czecho-Slovakia. For the others, it was the logical end of a revolution begun as early as 1945. As a matter of fact, how could it have been otherwise in a State where the Communist party was the strongest (39 per cent); where the Prime Minister, the Under-Secretary of State in Foreign Affairs, the Ministers of the Interior, Finance, Agriculture, Public Education and Information were Communists; where the Minister of National Defense was a tool of Moscow; where the labor unions were entirely dominated by communist elements; where the police, carefully reorganized, was almost exclusively in the hands of the Communists? Since the 1946 elections it was obvious that the real power of the Communist party greatly exceeded in importance the number of its adherents and threatened to upset the internal equilibrium.

Furthermore, the Czecho-Slovak circles called "democratic" closed their eyes. Was Mr. Beneš himself not always preaching

[75] Ripka, *Czechoslovakia Enslaved,* p. 109.

"Slav fraternity," the glory of "the all-powerful Red Army," "loyalty to Soviet Russia," "popular democracy"? Was the Prague
government not the captive of Moscow from the summer of 1947
on, since it had not been in condition to adhere to the Marshall
Plan?

Its weak point in the first place was the Socialist party, the
Trojan horse in the ramparts of European democracy. The Ephialtes of this party was Mr. Fierlinger, who, as Vice-President of
the Council of Ministers, did not hesitate to betray his country
constantly and confide its secrets to the Soviet ambassador. On
his own responsibility, he came to an agreement with Mr. Zorin,
until 1947 the U.S.S.R. Ambassador to Prague, on the gift of the
Jachymov uranium mines to Soviet Russia. While the police pursued all individuals suspected of having relations not only with
the Western information services but with ordinary American,
English, or French citizens, Mr. Fierlinger was free to deliver
the Republic to the Russians, in the course of sumptuous banquets
given by the Soviet Embassy.

"There was no real coup d'état in Prague in February, 1948,"
acknowledges the Czech Populist deputy, Mr. Chudoba.[76] There
was only the exteriorization of a state of fact which had little by
little been established with the complicity of Beneš, the perfidy
of the Socialists, and the discord and impotency of the Democrats.
The unveiled truth flaunted itself in the light of day.

The stage setting for the "coup d'état" was very simple. On
February 12, 1948, the government discussed the case of seven
police officers, all Communists, whom Mr. Nosek, Minister of the
Interior, had appointed to Prague as a replacement of seven non-
Communists whom he had dispersed to the four corners of
Czechia. This measure, taken on his own initiative, particularly
displeased the Czech National-Socialists. With a majority of votes,
the Democratic ministers then begged Mr. Nosek to reconsider
his decision and defer until February 21 the final solution of
this contentious matter.

On February 18, Mr. Zorin, who had become Vice-Minister
of Foreign Affairs of the U.S.S.R., landed at the Ruzyň airport
under the same conditions which Mr. Vyshinsky found somewhat
earlier in Bucarest at the time of the Rumanian coup d'état. Certainly Mr. Zorin also had a specific mission to accomplish.

---

[76] Bohdan Chudoba, "Czechoslovakia, a Study in Disintegration," *Thought,*
(March, 1950), p. 97.

On February 21, when Mr. Nosek refused to bow before the majority, the Democratic ministers went to consult President Beneš, and in agreement with him, decided to offer their resignation.

With the assurance of a favorable reaction from General Svoboda, Minister of Defense, the Communists could cleverly take advantage of the opportunity. They brought workmen in trucks from all regions of Bohemia to Venceslas Square, and with the aid of the workmen's armed police, they organized one of those super-demonstrations characteristic of totalitarian movements. Mr. Gottwald spoke and launched a violent attack against the "reactionary elements" who had succeeded in working their way into the government. Then calling upon the freely expressed will of the mass of people shown by loud acclamations and noisy applause, he descended from the tribune to go speak to Mr. Beneš and ask him "in the name of the people" to chase the undesirable elements from the government.

On February 23, 1948, on the balcony of the National Theater in Bratislava (following Mr. Široký, Chairman of the Communist party of Slovakia), Mr. Zorich, Consul-General of the U.S.S.R. in the Slovak capital, said:

> In the U.S.S.R., two hundred million men are convinced that the reactionary forces will not succeed in destroying the regime of popular democracy in Czecho-Slovakia. Friends, we are with you and we believe that the blood shed by the Soviet soldiers on Czech and Slovak soil will not have been lost in vain and that, in the neighborhood of the U.S.S.R., the reaction cannot and will never triumph.[77]

These demonstrations lost no time in bearing fruit. On February 25, after receiving the investiture from Beneš, Mr. Gottwald formed a new cabinet composed of a few straw men and numerous Communists. His victory was complete. The Democratic ministers who had resigned became over night "enemies of the people," hunted beasts, and nothing else remained for them except to jump from a window, as did Jan Masaryk and the Minister of Justice, Mr. Drtina; or to flee secretly into the American Zone of Germany. Mr. Ripka was the first to flee.

Events in Slovakia happened in an analogous manner. Relying upon a crowd of workmen gathered together for this purpose in the streets of Bratislava, the Chairman of the Board of Com-

[77] *Pravda*, Bratislava, (February 27, 1949).

missioners, Mr. Husák, declared the Democratic commissioners removed from office. On February 26, a triple order of arrest was thrown at the leader of the Slovak Democrats, Mr. Lettrich, who had then to flee from the country. Messrs. Hodža, Fraštacký, Kvetko, Fillo, and others did likewise. Mr. Ursíny, Vice-Chairman of the Democratic party, was arrested on the charge of complicity with his secretary, Obuch.

Mr. Husák then formed a new Board of Commissioners composed of a majority of Communists. Two Catholic priests, professors Lukačovič and Horák, impelled by their personal ambition and favored in this sense by the Communists, became members of the new "autonomous" government. At the same time, Mr. Schmidke was named Chairman of the Slovak National Council.

The Democratic party, whose crest had fallen and who had been abandoned by the population for having failed in its promises, was transformed into the "Slovak Rebirth party." A few straw men rose up from its debris. A communist Democrat, Mr. Ševčík; an ambitious officer, Lt. Col. Milan Polák; and the former mayor of Bratislava, Mr. Kyselý, headed it up.

The events of February, 1948, proved that in a system of popular democracy, the executive prevails over the legislative. President Beneš never once thought of convoking the Parliament in a special session to solve the crisis.

On February 25 the day on which the Communist party organized a monstrous demonstration on Venceslas Square, an action committee of the National Front was formed, with an eye to cleansing the Parliament of reactionary elements. Messrs. Gregor, Janouš, Lindauer, Plojhar, Komzala and Ševčík (the latter two being Slovaks) were members.

Each deputy then had to attest in writing to his loyalty to the government. Several dozen were debarred and some took flight; others remained, neutralized by fear. Thus on March 11, 1948, when Mr. Gottwald presented himself before a "regenerated" Parliament, 230 deputies approved the events and adopted its program.[78]

The political consequences of February, 1948, were exceptionally serious for Slovakia. In further reference to the disastrous policy of Prague, for the second time this profoundly Catholic

---

[78] F. Komzala, "The Parliament in February, 1948," *Pravda*, Bratislava, (March 2, 1949).

and democratic people was given over to the mercy of a great totalitarian power. Already charged with collaborationism with Hitlerian Germany, it could at present be accused, by superficial and evil-thinking minds, of collaborationism with Moscow. Actually, however, it was quite different. The Slovak nation, in 1938 as in 1948, was the victim of Beneš' "political wisdom" and had to suffer the consequences.

The Betrayal of an Intellectual

> *History and its laws could not be per-*
> *turbed by the fancies and wishes of indi-*
> *viduals.*
> E. Beneš: *La politique extérieure de la*
> *République tchécoslovaque*
> (A statement of January 27, 1921, before
> the Parliament, Prague, 1921.)

Mr. Beneš was the symbol at one and the same time of the ambiguity and impotency of the Czecho-Slovak democracy. The end of the National Front regime, whose totalitarian character he had hidden from the foreigner's eyes since 1945, brought on his political downfall; and unlike what happens to true statesmen, in the case of Beneš, the politician did not outlive the man.

The manner in which Mr. Beneš abdicated during an interview with Mr. Gottwald on May 4, 1948, in Sezimovo Ustí, throws a glaring light on his real worth.

> When I put the question as to what I must do, I feel that it is my duty to leave and make it easier for you as well as for the president of the Council of Ministers and your party to replace me and choose a president who can sign the Constitution as a whole without any scruples. In the first place it is the Communist party's affair. It is not up to me to tell the Communists what to do, but I do not want to be a shackle for them. . . . I want to remain in contact with you. The situation can become difficult, a war can break out. . . . I know that you have your policy, that you do not need me. Yet I am always at your disposal. I do not want to do anything to oppose the Communists. . . . I do not know what the future holds in store, but I can assure you that I have never had, have not now, and shall never have designs against the State. I repeat it for you and your party.[79]

Desirous of not troubling the game played by the agents of the Kominform, the stake of which was the liberty of millions of

[79] *Čas,* publication of the Czech refugees in London, (January, 1949).

citizens, Mr. Beneš lowered himself to make humiliating statements to Gottwald. After being crowned with laurels by the
Communists for having effectively aided them to prefabricate
their victory of February, 1948, he disappeared in a manner unprecedented in history.

Mr. Beneš can be compared to a pilot who for thirty years had
navigated without helm on the agitated sea of European events.
His polestar was the interest of the State, "the reason of the
State." Ideas, principles, ethics did not count for him. He was an
opportunist who spent his life seeking an easy denouement to
difficult situations. Very often he came off without glory or honor.
Of an egocentric turn of mind, he judged every situation in the
light of the openings it presented his ambitions. His way of solving problems consisted of proposing synthetic solutions that threw
the adverse party off the track. He mixed substance and form,
the essential and the accessory. For him, a pear and an apple were
not always a pear and an apple, but at times a "pearapple." It
was in this way that Czechia and Slovakia became "Czechoslovakia." It was through this trickery, this artificial hybridization
of things that this mediocre man succeeded in becoming the
most important prestidigitator on the European political scene.
He invented recipes, compromises, and formulas that amazed the
world. Achieving his little commissions from both sides, this international broker made powerful friends for himself everywhere.
He had his biographers, panegyrists, sycophants, whether paid
or not, all over the world. The great world press published his
praises.

During the war he advised Roosevelt to put his faith in Stalin.
He was listened to. The sovietization of Central Europe and the
present chronic difficulties of the United States with Russia are
the result.

Between 1945 and 1948 he tried to marry two concepts as
different as democracy and socialism. On the democratic tree of
the Czech and Slovak peoples he grafted a branch imported from
Moscow. Thus, the "Slav linden-tree" put forth Red leaves.

Another of Mr. Beneš' dreams was to reconcile, as opposing
powers, the East and the West. His opinion on "the constant
progress of the U.S.S.R. toward democracy" is evidenced by what
he wrote on this subject:

> The struggle for harmony of feeling and reason in man
> has made the subject of some of the most beautiful works
> in Russian literature. And besides, the Soviet Union, by its

whole attitude, by its fight for a new social life and also for a new Slavism teaches its people and us in a striking way to seek that harmony. What the U.S.S.R. realized in twenty years before World War II in the political and military organization of the State, in the industrialization of the whole country, in the technique and application of science to the whole life of its people, and especially in the political realism that it cultivated during World War II, must not all this appear to us as a new, grandiose and fecund application of dry Western rationalism?

This false appreciation, at once esthetic and political, of Soviet Russia we find in Mr. Beneš' work, *Oū vont les Slaves?*[80] Yet certain people still see in him only one more victim of Stalin's "oriental ruse"!

Despite his agitations and all his ambitions, and with the legend that he had been able to create around himself, Mr. Beneš was not able to cross the Styx which separated him from eternity. All his life's undertakings completely failed during his lifetime. In the quality of a statesman, he collapsed before even approaching Charon's bark.

---

[80] Beneš, *Où vont les Slaves?* pp. 275-76.

PART IV

THE FOURTH CZECHO-SLOVAK REPUBLIC

THE COMMUNIST DICTATORSHIP (1948-1950)

> *Only the nations who have won by tears*
> *their right to existence are sure of living.*
> Gambetta

After gaining total victory over the other parties of the National Front, the Communists organized a dictatorship. They eliminated at will the political parties and politicians that they deemed refractory to their opinions. By the Constitution of May, 1948, they sanctioned the regime of people's democracy. The elections of late May, 1948, were a single list operation. After being assured of a constitutional majority in the Parliament, the Communists reserved several places for collaborators hand-picked from former democratic politicians, among whom were some apostate priests ready to facilitate the conversion of the country to communism.

In order to break those who were reticent, Prague reinforced the police system and established an unduly harsh justice. Spectacular trials, taking place in an accelerated tempo, were to discourage the recalcitrant. In addition, the schools, which had been reorganized from top to bottom in conformity with the Marxist-Leninist spirit, were to win youth over to the civilization of the socialist era.

By economic and administrative measures, the Church was bound and subjected to the State. The relations with the Vatican were practically broken, and the government spent its time in pushing Catholicism into the way of schism. In matters of economy, the Five-Year Plan, while strengthening the planning established in 1945, integrated Czecho-Slovakia into the vast economic zone of the Soviet orbit whose exchanges the U.S.S.R. controls.

In matters of foreign policy, Czecho-Slovakia had to accept the principle of solidarity by renouncing all quarrels with its neighbors—Hungary, Poland and eastern Germany. The year 1950 saw the weeding out of all Slovak communist personalities who did not follow perfectly the line drawn by the Cominform.

The policy thus inaugurated by the Communists resulted in the creation of a large resistance front against both Moscow and Prague; this front included "Titoists" and former members of the Hlinka party.

The Constitution of May 9, 1948[1]

The crisis of the Third Czecho-Slovak Republic of February, 1948 was unleashed by the problem of the new Constitution. The conceptions of the parties confronting one another on its fundamental principles were divergent to such a degree that normal political evolution had been practically paralyzed by the Communists' veto. The year 1947 had marked a tightening of position of two opposing tendencies in this respect. Owing to its tactics, the Communist party was to cut the Gordian knot to its own advantage.

Communist technicians needed only two and a half months to perfect all the details of the fundamental law. On May 9, 1948, the Constitution was unanimously voted upon by the 246 deputies present, the others having fled. At the solemn session of the National Assembly in the coronation room of the Hradčany Castle in Prague, Prime Minister Gottwald declared that, without the Soviet Union, the setting in motion of the Constitution would have been impossible. This was true.

The preamble defined the Czecho-Slovak State as a "people's democracy." In its authentic interpretation, this term designates a State "in which the laws are not only voted by the representatives of the people, but are also put into practice by them."[2] The traditional separation of powers set forth by Montesquieu was thereby rejected. The delegates of the people were to decide on matters of justice as well as on legislation and administration. The independence of the judge ceased to exist. This innovation, common to Nazism as well as to Communism, constitutes the most characteristic mark of any totalitarian system.

Rights and duties of citizens—In the first chapter of the Constitution, all the traditional liberties of the citizen were enumer-

---

[1] Ministère de l'Information, *Constitution de la République tchécoslovaque* (Prague: 1948).
Dr. Jan Hrázsky, *The Constitution of May 9, 1948* (in Czech) (Munich: 1949).
[2] Ministère de l'Information, *Constitution de la République tchécoslovaque, ibid.*, p. 11.

ated: equality before the law, liberty of person, liberty of domicile, secrets of correspondence and communications, liberty of place of abode, liberty of patrimony, protection of family and youth, right to an education, liberty of conscience and confession, liberty of expression and protection of cultural assets, right to petition, right of meeting and association, social rights. All these liberties could be limited or suppressed only by virtue of a law. However, certain discreet limitations were provided for:

> No one can be arrested if he is not caught in the act, except on a judge's warrant, written and justified. The warrant must be delivered at the time of the arrest and, if that is impossible, within the following forty-eight hours (Art. 3, par. 2).
> No one must be imprisoned outside of cases provided for by law; every person must be either released within the forty-eight hours following his imprisonment or else referred to the court or authority competent to carry on the proceedings (Art. 3, par. 3).

For a police agent who wished to effect a visit, a search or the confiscation of certain objects in the domicile of a citizen, it was sufficient to present a written and justified order delivered by a judge or a public authority within the forty-eight hours following (Art. 5, pars. 2, 3).

The Constitution put the citizen on his guard against any other than materialistic philosophy: "No conception of the world, no faith or conviction can bear prejudice to any one, nor can it constitute a sufficient reason to refuse to fulfill a duty imposed by the law" (Art. 15, par. 2).

Article 17 forbade using religious liberty "for other than religious ends," that is to say, political.

Article 21 introduced cultural planning. The law was to indicate the persons who were authorized to publish newspapers and magazines, and under what conditions, taking into account especially the fact that the profit must not be the goal of publication. The law was also to stipulate in what manner and according to what plan the publishing and diffusion of non-periodicals would be directed; this referred particularly to books, musical works and reproductions of plastic works of art while preserving freedom for science and art and taking into consideration the protection of works of value.

Films, broadcasting and television became the exclusive domain of the State (Art. 22).

According to Article 25, workmen were allowed to group themselves into the unified trade-union organization in order to defend their interests. Since this organization had been in the hands of Communists since 1945, the workman had therefore only to accept its preconstitutional character. Furthermore, in actual fact, it was not possible for workmen to remain outside of this organization. A variety of administrative pressure was exerted to persuade them to join it "freely."

Each citizen was endowed with the right to work; each citizen also had the duty to work in the interest of the community according to his capacity (Arts. 26 and 32).

All civic liberties were made illusory by the application of Article 38 which stipulated that limitations could be brought to the rights and liberties of citizens in time of war or in periods when the independence, integrity and unity of the State, its republican form, the Constitution and the popular and democratic regime, as well as public peace and order were seriously threatened. Feeling threatened in that phase of transition from people's democracy to socialism, the regime had thus created a "legal" basis to abolish personal liberties at any time.

The National Assembly, the President of the Republic, the government—The Fourth Czecho-Slovak Republic adopted the unicameral system. In a regime with the executive prevailing over the legislative, the bicameral system would have in fact been absurd. The National Assembly was to choose from its members its presidium which was composed of twenty-four deputies. This bureau was entrusted with examining the constitutional character of the laws, a charge which according to the former Constitution had been the lot of the Constitutional Court. In this manner, the Assembly became the judge of its own laws. The aforesaid presidium likewise fulfilled the role of the former permanent committee which had to expedite current business during the parliamentary vacation. It could in addition make urgent provisions, even if they required the promulgation of a law.

The Constitution also comprised an article which was favorable to Mr. Beneš. It stated exactly, in fact, that the election of the second President of the Czecho-Slovak Republic would not be subjected to the rule limiting the reelection of the head of the State to two terms.

Contrary to the former Constitution which provided for the collective responsibility of the government, the new one introduced individual responsibility. Thus, a vote of distrust with respect to a minister fallen in disgrace did not necessarily involve the fall of the Cabinet. Without provoking governmental crises, weeding out became possible.

National Slovak institutions—The First Article of the Constitution of the popular Republic of Yugoslavia recognized that the federation of the Yugoslav peoples was founded on the right of self-determination and included even the right of separation.[3] These dispositions of ultrademocratic character were lacking in the Czecho-Slovak Constitution, although the dualism of the Czech and Slovak nations was recognized.

Evoking the position of Slovakia within the Fourth Republic, the general rapporteur on the Constitution in the National Assembly, Professor Vladimír Procházka, avoided all juridical details. Was Czecho-Slovakia a federal State? No, said he. Had Slovakia an autonomous position? No, he replied. And he added that the solution given to Slovakia was entirely empirical and that it resulted from the "national Slovak uprising."

Chapter V contained clauses interesting regional Slovak organisms: the Slovak National Council, a legislative organ comprising one hundred members, and the Board of Commissioners, an executive organ with twelve members. The legislative jurisdiction was divided between the National Assembly of Prague and the National Council of Bratislava in the following fashion:

The National Assembly disposes of the legislative power in regard to: (1) the Constitution (boundaries, liberties of the citizens, citizenship, civil state, emigration, immigration, passports); (2) foreign policy (political treaties); (3) foreign trade (economic agreements); (4) national defense (military service, defense of the State); (5) internal order (police); (6) finance (currency, banks, insurance, budget, State debt, public loans, salaries of State employees, control of the State administration, customs, taxes and dues, State monopolies, patents, protection of samples, trade-marks, weights and measures, cartography; (7) health; (8) the social policy (social security and work protection); (9) technical building; (10) justice; (11) food supplies; (12) agriculture; (13) industry; (14) internal trade; (15) national education (information and culture); (16) transportation, mail, radio, postal check accounts; (17) the unification of laws and the judiciary organization.

[3] *Constitution of the Federative People's Republic of Yugoslavia* (Belgrade: 1946).

Article 95, paragraph 1, defined the competence of the Slovak National Council in recognizing its functions as follows:

1) The development of national culture, science, humanities; dramatic, musical and choreographic art; the plastic arts and the motion pictures; historical monuments, libraries, and museums; professional training in the domain of handcrafts and popular art; the activities and needs of the Slovak intellectual workers;

2) Primary, secondary, professional, and art schools within the compass of the law; nursery schools and infants' nurseries; popular education, physical culture, travel;

3) Public health and social welfare, except business that was or would be regulated in the future by single laws for the whole territory of the State;

4) The funds and donations insofar as their provisions concerned only Slovakia;

5) The connecting and dividing of communes and districts as well as adjustments and reapportionments of their boundaries and other topographical operations;

6) Technical questions regarding the building of communes and cities, and the provisions applicable to the construction, except the sections governed by a single economic plan; the construction and maintenance of roads, bypaths and bridges not financed by the State; matters of the local hydraulic supply circuit, except those dependent upon a single economic plan, in particular the harnessing of watercourses; construction of reservoirs and other hydraulic works as well as the building of ponds, water-mains and sewer systems;

7) Soil cultivation, except the affairs which would depend on the single economic plan; the protection of agriculture and forests against harmful animal and plant life and natural catastrophes; veterinary medicine and care relating to the raising of cattle; the care of fruit trees and pastures, hunting and fishing, the protection of rural and forest possessions;

8) Trades and business of small tradespeople where the personal return of the entrepreneur predominates; also matters relating to the local markets, with the exception of the cases where regulations of the right to work, organization and distribution, commerce and trades valid for the whole State territory are at stake;

9) Statistics and research on the special interests of Slovakia;

10) Matters of guardianship and the position of orphans.

In addition, the Slovak National Council was to exercise its legislative power in matters whose regulation was especially attributed to it by a law emanating from the National Assembly.

Government and ministerial decrees for the execution of the laws valid for the whole territory of the Republic were, of course, applicable in Slovakia.

The division of the executive power did not conform to that of the legislative powers. On the paper it appears to have favored Slovak institutions.

First came the matters reserved exclusively for the government of Prague (foreign policy, national defense, and foreign trade); then matters delegated by the government to the Board of Commissioners: (1) general internal administration; (2) administration of finances; (3) sanitation; (4) social administration and labor protection; (5) technical administration; (6) justice; (7) food supplies; (8) agriculture; (9) industry; (10) home trade; (11) national education, culture, and information; (12) transport and mail; and finally all those matters which on the legislative plane had come under the jurisdiction of the Slovak National Council and whose execution in Slovakia was incumbent on the Board of Commissioners.

Slovak national institutions did not depend upon the President of the Republic, as would have been logical, but on the government. It was the Prime Minister of Prague who was to convoke and adjourn the sessions of the Slovak National Council. It was he who could dissolve this Council and it was he who was to give his consent to the authentic interpretation of the laws voted by it. The government retained the right to appoint the commissioners in Slovakia, and they were individually responsible to it.

One can get an idea of the absolute dependence in which the Slovak national organizations were held with respect to Prague by reading Article 117:

> The Board of Commissioners and its members are bound to observe the directives and indications of the government. Each commissioner must also respect the directives and invitations emanating from the corresponding ministers. Moreover, each minister has the right to exercise his power directly in Slovakia while keeping the commissioner concerned informed.

As to the appointment of officials, the power of the Board of Commissioners was not considerable. It did not extend to the appointment of officers of the National Security, nor to those of the central departments whose jurisdiction related to the whole State (ministries, supreme courts, etc.).

For the officials whose nomination was reserved for the President of the Republic, the Board of Commissioners could not present its proposals directly to the head of the State. It had to have them pass through the intermediary of the government which could return them if they were in opposition with "the general policy." Here the government of Prague had at its disposal a powerful weapon against all the separatist and reactionary elements which could have escaped the watchful eye of the Board of Commissioners. In conclusion, in Slovakia no official or employee could be appointed without previous consent of the government.

According to Article 122, this is how Prague solved the conflicts in jurisdiction of the executive power:

> If a decree, a decision or a measure of the Board of Commissioners (a decree or measure of a commissioner) exceeds the limits of its power or is opposed to the Constitution, a law of the Slovak National Council, a governmental or ministerial decree, the government can annul it. It is the same if the decision or measure of the Board of Commissioners is in opposition with a governmental decision.

All these provisions tell a great deal about the real competence of the Slovak national institutions derived from the glorious "national uprising." After the administrative reform of 1948 had established the regional national committees accountable to the Ministry of the Interior in Prague, and the Five-Year Plan had extended its economic controls over the territory of the whole State, the political individuality of Slovakia almost disappeared. Its constitutional position in the Republic became that of a make-believe autonomy while practically all its vital interests were to be decided in Prague.

The national committees—The Constitution could do nothing but legalize the institution of national committees, organs of popular administration. Article 123 created national committees: local, district, and regional. The competence of the national committees was fixed by Articles 124 and 125 in these terms:

> The national committees are entrusted, for the territories under their jurisdiction, with the public administration in all its domains, especially with general internal ad-

ministration, cultural and school administration, labor protection, sanitary and social administration and, according
to certain special provisions, with the administration of
finances. Public administration is entrusted to other institutions only in exceptional cases and by virtue of a law
(Art. 124).

The national committees, as organs of a single popular
administration, have among others the following tasks to
fulfill: to protect and reinforce the popular and democratic
regime; to cooperate in the defense of the State; to watch
over national security; to contribute to the preservation
and prosperity of national possessions; to participate in the
elaboration and realization of the single economic plan; to
plan and direct, in the province of their jurisdiction and
within the single economic plan, constructive efforts of an
economic, cultural, and social order, ensure the conditions of a consistent agricultural and industrial production,
watch over the provisions and supplies of the population;
and look after public health (Art. 125).

They also had the right to pass judgments within the province
of their competence; among other things they were wielding was
a penal jurisdiction within the limits provided by law.

These committees thus became the typical organs of the totalitarian State.

Economic organization—The Constitution recognized three
forms of property and enterprise: those of the State, popular cooperatives, and the private sector.

Article 148 defined as national wealth: minerals and their extraction; the sources of energy and electric powerhouses and
gas-works; mines and forges; natural therapeutic sources; the
production of goods useful to the health of the people; enterprises
occupying at least fifty persons, unless it be a matter of popular
cooperatives; banks and insurance companies; transport by rail,
land, and air; public mail, telegraph and telephone; radio, television, and films.

The national assets which did not interest the whole State but
only the inhabitants of an administrative unit (community, district, region) could be entrusted to agencies of popular administration. The State was to administer the national wealth either
directly or through the intermediary of national enterprises constituting independent moral persons. Its administration was to
be direct in what related to the sector of exclusive national ownership (Art. 148), nationalized property and to those goods that

enter in the bounds of laws regulating home and foreign trade, as well as international transports.

According to Article 153, paragraph 2, the extent of the nationalizations already effected could not be reduced.

Next came the property of the popular cooperatives (labor or agriculture), made up of groups of workmen who had come together with a view to common activity and whose goal was to raise the standard of living for their members and other workmen, but in no case to glean the greatest possible profit from capital invested.

Lastly, private property was limited, in the domain of industrial production, to the enterprises occupying at the most fifty workers, and in the realm of agricultural production, to family properties of less than fifty hectares. The ownership of the land was guaranteed only to those who worked it directly.

The personal property of citizens (objects of personal usage, family houses, money acquired by work, inheritance) was declared inviolable (Art. 158, par. 2). Private groups with lucrative aims and monopoly in mind (cartels, trusts, unions) were forbidden (Art. 161).

Finally, the Constitution sanctioned socialist planning in economy. Individuals and corporations were obliged to adapt their economic activities to the State-wide economic plan (Art. 164, par. 2).

After only two years of experience, it was possible to say that the Constitution had been exceeded by events. The communist regime is by nature arbitrary. Therefore it can not endure a rigid juridical system capable of establishing certain limits to its omnipotence. Law constantly yields to decision. That is why the constitutions of popular democracies resemble skillfully arranged displays, but whose articles are not destined to be sold.

Slovakia's "autonomy" received the finishing stroke in the spring of 1950 when a Ministry of National Security was created in Prague for the entire Republic. The competence of the commissioner of the Interior of Bratislava was henceforth limited to the civil administration of the country. From that time on, it was the police regime of Prague that operated in Slovakia. So in spite of constitutional appearances, Czecho-Slovakia, like the U.S.S.R., became a strictly centralized State. From a binational structure it was transformed into a homogeneous socialist State.

The Elections of May 31, 1948

The events of February, 1948 were destined to have loud repercussions on the elections of the National Assembly. In fact, it was no longer the National Front that organized them, but the Communist party itself which, to save its face, was aided by what remained of the parties heretofore democratic.

Immediately after February, 1948, all the deputies of the National Assembly who had survived the weeding out that the action committee of Parliament had brought about (an organ completely lacking in any constitutional basis) were called upon to sign an act of loyalty toward the Gottwald government.

The Czech National-Socialist party fell into line.

After the imprisonment of Monsignori Šrámek and Hála, which followed their unsuccessful attempt at escaping in April, 1948, the Czech Populist party fell over night under the direction of Father Plojhar. It was the ambitious Rev. Plojhar who asserted German nationality at the time of the population census during the Bohemia-Moravia Protectorate and had afterward tried to please the Communists. Besides it mattered little to him that he had been interdicted by Monsignor Beran, Archbishop of Prague.

As for the Social-Democrat party—a communist Trojan horse— its chief, Mr. Fierlinger, had declared long before the elections that his party would merge with the Communists. This was soon realized.

The Slovak Democrats, completely cleansed of their "reactionary" elements, had only to accept their new situation.

All these various parties no longer offered any opposition to the Communists. Not only did they not represent an organized force, but they had no clear-cut political program. Furthermore, their newspapers had been suspended and their secretariats occupied by the Communists.

The old Democrats were quick to comprehend that their death knell had sounded. They were too weary, after the desertion of their chiefs, to continue the struggle. Too, when the State officials and the agents of nationalized industries were given the choice of signing a certificate of adhesion to the Communist party or of being dismissed and chased from their apartment, a great number of them chose the first solution. As for those who refused to sign—and they were numerous—they awoke to find themselves penniless and deprived of lodging. The result was an epidemic of suicides unprecedented in the history of the country.

On May 1, 1948, to celebrate the work holiday and the victory of February, the Communists organized gigantic festivities throughout the entire country. All laborers, intellectual or manual, under State control, including hospital doctors, school pupils and students, had to sign statements of "spontaneous" participation. It would have been "imprudent" for anyone to ignore the instructions. Thus it was that in the Slovak capital (with a population at that time of about two hundred thousand inhabitants) a monstrous gathering took place in which a hundred thousand paraded for several hours. In this way the communist torrent was able to engulf not only the parties but the electors themselves.

Once this atmosphere was created, it was easy to impose the new manner of election already widespread in the Balkans: a single list. The day before the elections Prime Minister Gottwald, in a speech delivered before the workers of the Walter factories in Prague, set forth in his manner the reasons justifying the adoption of the principle of the single list. He stated among other things: "Since the parties and organizations united in the National Front have only one single aim, it would have been illogical for them to separate to go to the elections."[4]

On this same occasion, he had the audacity to remember that the law did not forbid opposition lists. "If there are not any, the Communist party must not be made responsible, for then it would be the same as asking it to organize one itself," he stated without turning red.

> Indeed the opposition still exists (he admitted), but since it can no longer be hidden in the parties, it does not dare show itself. It has only blank ballot paper left for manifesting itself. Whereas before February, it was possible for this reaction to combat the Czecho-Slovak people from the inside, it now has no further hope except in help from abroad or in a new Munich. . . . But it is up to us to show that in this country, it is the will of the people that makes the law![5]

The electoral law, adapted meanwhile to the new needs, constituted an excellent instrument of pressure on the opposition.

[4] *Le Monde,* Paris, (May 30, 31, 1948).
[5] *Ibid.*

Previously, every elector had been obliged to pass through a polling booth, which henceforth was only tolerated. Under these conditions, only the boldest members of the opposition were tempted to use it. Nothing was easier then than to count them. In short, it was the pure and simple abolition of the secret ballot. Therefore an overwhelming communist victory was to be expected. The elections fully confirmed this expectation.

Of the total number of votes, the governmental list collected 89.28 per cent, while the spoiled papers plus the blank papers scarcely exceeded 10 per cent.

> In Slovakia only (writes *Le Monde* in its comment on the event), where the opposition to the Marxists of Prague has always manifested itself most keenly, 14 per cent blank papers were registered; this number is said to have risen to 25 per cent in certain rural sections and even— and this would be the record—to 39 per cent in certain sections near the Polish border.[6]

According to statistics, it was the districts of the Magyar border which showed themselves most favorable to the regime, those in which the Slovaks repatriated from Hungary had taken up their abode. Their vote for the regime was an act of loyalty to the country which had received them.

One might suppose that for these districts it would have been possible to determine the exact proportion of votes favorable or unfavorable to the government by relying on the results of the elections. But this is not the case, for in order to be sure of a favorable result, the regime deprived an average of 10 to 15 per cent of the citizens everywhere of the right to vote. Thus in the Parkan district only 8,000 electors out of 50,000 inhabitants were permitted to vote. To the percentage of blank ballots of Slovakia then must be added the votes of those who had not been admitted to the polls.[7]

In the 1948 elections as in those of 1946, it was Slovakia which, not only in Czecho-Slovakia but in the whole of Central Europe, gave evidence of the highest degree of nonconformity to the communist regime.

Out of 300 seats in the National Assembly, the Communists took 225, leaving only a few crumbs to the defeated democratic parties. "With a decreasing minority," stated *Le Monde*, "the

---

[6] *Le Monde*, Paris, (June 1, 1948).
[7] See: K. Čulen, "Ce que disent les dernières élections en Slovaquie," *La Nation slovaque*, Paris, (April 15, 1949).

Communists succeeded, by the elections game whose secret they have, in causing a powerful majority, if not a single party, to arise."[8] It was of capital importance that with 70 per cent of the seats they were assured of the constitutional majority of two-thirds.

In Slovakia the Rebirth party obtained only twelve seats, and the Liberty party just five; the Communists laid claim to the remaining fifty-four.

It was in this manner that the Communist party succeeded in realizing the second stage in its race for power. As a minority party, it had sabotaged the decisions of the democratic parties by its veto. Henceforward it held all the control levers in its own hands.

Justice

> *Any State government that renounces the moral principle of justice degenerates into a band of dictators.*
>
> G. Husák[9]

Communist Notion of Justice—Before February, 1948, justice had been a powerful political instrument against the enemies of the "National Front." After this event, the Communist party made of it a vigorous means of struggle, not only against the "reactionies," but also against the pseudodemocrats who, although having collaborated until then, refused to recognize its triumph.

From then on, the very concept of justice had to change. "Between law and discipline," said Mr. Vyshinsky, "the judge has to choose without hesitation the latter, for the law is only one form of the Party's discipline."

"The Party's discipline"—what a criterion that is! The citizen's private life, his ideas and actions become justiciable of the laws of a political group of which he is not a member. The communist regime in Slovakia made considerable effort to subject all individuals to its discipline; it perfected police organization, narrowed the control of persons, established a very severe repression of political "crimes."

Reorganization of National Security—Until 1948, National Security, a euphemism for the police, had comprised four dif-

---

[8] *Le Monde*, Paris, (June 1, 1948).
[9] Commissariat of Information, *The People's Courts*, (Bratislava: 1945), p. 11.

ferent sections: criminal, public order, State security, and information. At the end of 1948, all these services were combined and put under military regulations. The reorganized police was to have a single authority with planes and special units for boundary control at its disposal. In order to attain its ends, it had recourse to a network of spies recruited from civil volunteers.[10]

Administrative Measures—The regime assumed the right to control the life of its citizens closely. Administrative sanctions, until that time unknown, the slightest of which was the exclusion from public life, made provision for certain infractions on socialist discipline.

The action committee of the Czecho-Slovak Parliament published a regulation in four points at the beginning of April, 1948, which designated the citizens of the Republic who could be excluded from social and political life for their anti-popular activities. They were as follows:

1) Those condemned or pursued in justice in conformity with the Law on the Protection of the Republic;

2) Those guilty of infractions against the democratic order of the country; included in this category were those who publicly insulted the government, stirred up resistance against the governmental decrees and decisions, spread false news or diffused illegal publications, and organized the collective audition of foreign radio broadcasts hostile to the Republic;

3) Those responsible for economic disorder, those who encouraged workers not to come up to their normal output, who were involved in the black market, or those who dissuaded citizens from participating in voluntary brigades;

4) Those who profited by their public or political offices to become rich or who let themselves be bribed.[11]

A more serious administrative measure was the consignment of citizens to hard labor. The law of October 25, 1948 contained the following provisions on this point:

> The persons alluded to in Article 2 will be sent to labor camps to be educated in work in conformity with the provision of Article 32 of the Constitution according to which each citizen has the right to work within his capacities and contribute by his work to the profit of the community. The persons put in a labor camp will be employed in carrying out works undertaken by the State, mu-

[10] See: *Pravda*, Bratislava, (December 16, 1948).
[11] *Combat*, Paris, (April 4, 5, 1948).

nicipalities or the nationalized enterprises for the accomplishment of the economic plan (Art. 1).

Persons liable to be sent to labor camps are those aged eighteen to sixty, apt at the work from a physical or intellectual point of view, who wilfully shirk it or threaten the structure of the regime of popular democracy or the economic life of the country, especially the food control; persons condemned for administrative infractions to a penalty exceeding three months of prison (Art. 2).

The stay in the camps will be fixed for a duration of three months to two years by a commission of three members appointed by the national committee of the region (Art. 3).

The commission is authorized, if need be, to decide upon the interdiction of stay in a determined place for any person released from labor camps, on the confiscation of the dwelling and possessions of any prisoner, and on the withdrawal of his business license (Art. 4).

The commission is authorized to shorten the time of stay or, on the contrary, to prolong it beyond the two years if necessary (Art. 6).

Any person imprisoned in a labor camp is obliged to perform the work given him, whether within or outside the camp. He will be paid in accordance with his output. During his stay in the camp, he will not draw his salary from his former work (Art. 7).

Article 7 stipulated further that this remuneration could be given to the prisoner's family or to himself at the end of his stay.

The persons held in the labor camp will be reeducated from the moral, professional, and cultural point of view (Art. 8).[12]

Law on the Protection of the Republic[13]—Democratic states owe their existence to the spontaneous adhesion of their population. This general will is their best and most efficacious guarantee. Czecho-Slovakia lived between the two wars only because of its international alliances and the Law on the Protection of the Republic of 1923.

The reactivation of this law dates to 1945. However it was soon eclipsed by the law on the repression of political crimes committed during the war, which established popular tribunals. After the events of February, 1948 and the expiration of the laws of exceptional justice, the communist regime had to attempt to

[12] *Le Figaro,* Paris, (November 19, 20, 1949).
[13] Loi relative à la protection de la Republique populaire et démocratique tchécoslovaque, (mimeographed), (Paris: March, 1949).

confer a legal character to the acts of its arbitrary justice. Patterned on Law No. 50/1923, it had the National Assembly of Prague adopt the Law on the Protection of the Czecho-Slovak popular and democratic Republic dated October 6, 1948 and numbered 231/1948. This law, considerably perfecting the provisions of the preceding one, prolonged political justice in the country indefinitely.

This law proposed to protect the security of the State, the defense preparedness of the population, currency, the authority of public powers, public security and order. Its characteristic traits were the severe harshness of the penalties, an excessively wide margin of arbitrariness on the part of the judge and the identification of the regime with the State.

The crime of high treason, liable for from ten years to life imprisonment, could also be dealt with by capital punishment in particularly aggravating cases. Likewise, punishment by death was provided for by the law against espionage. Of course, the estimation of the degree of seriousness of a fault was left entirely to the decision of the judge. Any sabotage on the defense installations, any military treason, any attempt on the life of State officials as well as any act of violence against their persons were likewise liable to the death penalty.

The execution of persons responsible to the jurisdiction of the military tribunals was to be done by hanging.

A veritable innovation was introduced into criminal law by Article 32 on the colportage of news likely to disturb the public peace. In fact, this article considered not only false news, but also true news as a violation of the laws governing news-hawking.

In view of the interest that the Czecho-Slovak communist regime had in the activity of the political emigrants in Western countries, this law could not fail to include measures against the latter:

> Any Czechoslovak citizen who has left the territory illegally with a view to attacking the interests of the Republic or who, with the same intention, has refused to obey, within a reasonable time, the order given by the authorities to return to his country, will be liable to imprisonment for a period of from one to five years.

The day that the National Assembly of Prague voted the Law on the Protection of the Czecho-Slovak popular and democratic Republic, it also approved that statute which concerns the State Tribunal (No. 232/1948). The incarnation of political justice, this court was called on to judge the crimes liable to capital punishment or imprisonment of more than ten years, as well as any forfeit that the public prosecutor might have deemed opportune to submit to its jurisdiction. Each of the Chambers of the State Tribunal was made up of five members: a president, two magistrates, and two judges drawn from the lower-classes. The lawyer could be chosen only from a list drawn up by the Ministry of Justice in agreement with National Defense. After losing the traditional liberty of their profession, the lawyers in the socialistic order no longer had the role of defending the accused, but only if need be of drawing the attention of the tribunal to attenuating circumstances.

All this legislature had no other aim than to protect the power of the communist minority against an eventual rebellion of the democratic forces. It contributed to crush the individual who, through the economic setup, had already lost any semblance of liberty.

The Dance of Death of the Political Trials—After laying the foundations of the organization of the new judiciary system and codifying all imaginable political crimes in a popular democracy, the regime inaugurated the implementing of the new justice. New trials, fed by new victims, had to prove to the leaders the solidity of their power. They took place at an ever more accelerated scale.

A series of trials was geared to liquidate first of all the conspiracy of 1947. The first, in April, 1948, saw Mr. Ján Ursíny, still Vice-President of the Council in November, 1947, his secretary, Otto Obuch, and fifteen other Slovaks on the defendants' bench. All were accused of high treason and disclosure of State secrets. According to the president of the court, this judiciary action—as for those which were going to follow—had for its aim "to purge the Republic of the fifth column of imperialists and warmongers of the West." According to the act of accusation, Obuch had worked for the exiled enemies of the State. He was informed of the confidential deliberations of the government by his chief, Mr. Ursíny. He was condemned to thirty years' imprisonment, while Mr. Ursíny came off with seven.

On May 5, 1948, the State Tribunal of Bratislava judged a second group of conspirators. Of fourteen accused (among whom were three deputies of the Slovak Democrat party: Kempný, Staško, and Bugár), ten were condemned to punishment varying from one to eight years of prison.

On July 1, the same tribunal pronounced sentence against a third group composed of twenty-eight Slovaks. The leaders found themselves condemned to six or eight years of imprisonment, and the other "conspirators" incurred penalties of from five months to five years of imprisonment.

A fourth group composed of military headed by a former colonel, Mr. Tatarko, and a Slovak army captain, J. Fickuliak, was accused of dealings with the Slovak Liberation Committee of Buenos Aires. The condemnations went up to twelve years of imprisonment.

On October 20, 1948, the State Tribunal of Nitra pronounced sentence against "the resistance for the liberation of Slovakia," which included twenty-two persons accused of spreading anti-governmental tracts and performing acts of sabotage. Twenty-six of the accused were given a total of seventy-six years and two months of imprisonment.

Toward the end of December, 1949, at Žilina, the police seized the leader of a group of "white partisans," Commander Žingor. Organizer of an anti-German armed resistance in 1944, Žingor had led the Union of Slovak partisans in 1945. Having had scuffles with the Communists, he had taken to the maquis after February, 1948, living in the mountains of central Slovakia and finding aid among the population and even from certain national Communists, one of whom was Mr. Trojan, former director of the nationalized Baťa factories. Žingor and two of his principal accomplices were taken before the State Tribunal of Bratislava and condemned to death on October 21, 1950.

Since February, 1948, until the end of 1950, thousands of people were imprisoned and approximately twenty major political trials were held before the tribunals of Slovakia. Hundreds of accused had been condemned to prison and several dozens to capital punishment, while thousands were given over to a slow death in labor camps. The "padded" terror gave way to just plain terror. Whereas many men had fled the country, others, among whom were a number of soldiers of the regular army, had had to take to the maquis.

Culture in Terms of Politics

> *The cultural program of the Communists is the national Slovak program.*
> L. Novomeský[14]

Theoretical Tolerance of the Individualist Elements—According to the Marxist doctrine—life being an irradiation of matter—spiritual manifestations are only a suprastructure of fundamental economic ideas and social relations. The spirit is merely a term serving to designate a function of matter.

This doctrine is of capital importance for the understanding of the communist notion of culture. By principle this can be only materialistic. Now, since an important thesis of materialism is the historical continuity of spiritual phenomena, it follows that communism can not cut down with one fell swoop the bridges which link it to the past, from which it must depart by degrees. In the phase which marks the transition from capitalism to socialism, communism then admits certain manifestations or theses which, following its theory, are only survivals of a bourgeois epoch—among them the liberty of thought.

In the cultural program of the Czecho-Slovak Communist party, which was restated at its Eighth Congress in 1946, the Minister of Information, Mr. Kopecký, asserted that "the full liberty of artistic creation" would be assured.[15] Such liberties are, in fact, guaranteed by the constitutions of all the popular democracies. But the principal effort of communism consists in inculcating in the individual at the same time the idea of his spiritual inadequacy and the need to be a part of the collectivity. In this way it succeeds in making the liberty of the spirit entirely Platonic.

Communism does not attack religion directly any more than it does liberty of thought and artistic creation. It admits religion, not of course as an epistemological principle, but merely as a kind of museum piece or object locked up in the church and exposed for the veneration of a little handful of men who are still likely to be interested. In its conquest phase, communism even attempts to avoid direct conflicts with religion. It prefers to slip from the dogmatic terrain to the terrain of practical confrontations.

[14] L. Novomeský, *Communism and the Slovak National Idea* (Bratislava: 1946).
[15] See: Václav Kopecký, "National and Political Ideology of New Czecho-Slovakia," *Rudé Právo* Prague, (March 31, 1946).

As a good Communist, Mr. Novomeský, Commissioner of Public Education, was not in the least embarrassed to state:

Catholicism in Slovakia has a superb Cyril-Methodius Slav tradition and the social effort which is at the center of our noblest ambitions corresponds to the most beautiful and at the same time the most glorious tradition of Christianity."[16]

Another idea with which communism must take a position is the national one, a powerful cultural incentive. Mr. Novomeský did it in the following terms: "No concept facilitates the development of national Slovak life and the building of its superior culture in as wide a measure as ours."[17]

What are we to think of these statements emanating from the leaders of a planned culture? The Communists themselves acknowledge that they are nothing more than the expression of a tactical and transitory tolerance for "the resonance of modern individualism in the newly born culture."[18]

Actually the internationalist preoccupation of communist culture is manifest equally in education and in civic instruction, in the organization of culture as well as in the theory of art.

Education—In suppressing all the private schools, the State prepared the way in Slovakia for making education communistic as early as 1945. The reform of the school system which resulted in the "unified school" after September 1, 1948 emphasized its political character. Said an education specialist in Slovakia:

According to the new teaching the Czechoslovak school is a political school. That means that education and teaching will be directed in the spirit of the principles of popular democracy, resting on the theory of scientific socialism.[19]

And so the school became an instrument destined to serve the socialist concept of the world. Its aim was no longer to form men, but to produce members amenable to the orders of a socialist society.

The characteristic traits of the new school are: socialist emulation among the pupils, the introduction of Russian as an obligatory language in primary and secondary schools, the elimination

[16] L. Novomeský, *Communism and the Slovak National Idea*, p. 23.
[17] *Ibid.*, p. 31.
[18] Vincent Kramár, *Cultural Program of the Communist Party of Czechoslovakia and Art*, (Prague: 1946), p. 13.
[19] See: Ernest Otto, "Ideology and the New Nature of Education," *Pravda*, Bratislava, (December 9, 1948).

of instruction in the Western languages, the adding of the Soviet hymn to the national song of the Czecho-Slovak Republic.

However, Mr. Novomeský stated before the primary education inspectors gathered together on October 5, 1948 at Trenčianske Teplice, that the teaching of religion would be assured

> by virtue of the new school law and in accordance with the wishes of the ecclesiastical authorities. Religion will be taught by chaplains pursuant to a program established by the churches themselves. It is a regular subject, and those who teach it are regular members of our teaching staff, but they are nothing more. That means that they cannot assume an attitude contrary to our efforts at the scientific and socialist orientation of our school.[20]

The new law strengthened and narrowed the organization of the school system considerably. It raised the obligatory number of school years from eight to nine; that is, a child was required to attend school up to fifteen rather than fourteen. The first five of these nine years were reserved for primary education and the balance for lower secondary education. Although the number of *gymnasia* (secondary schools) in Slovakia was fifty-nine toward the end of 1948, the number of lower secondary schools was increased to 436 by November 1, 1948.

A great effort was made by the regime with a mind to integrating the universities and schools of higher learning in the Marxist political orbit. To achieve that goal, it abolished the autonomy of higher education in 1945 as a survival of the nineteenth century. This measure, under the pretext of collaboration or fascism, permitted the realization of the first purging among professors and students.

The position of communism vis-à-vis science is that of every totalitarianism which, far from letting itself be guided by the results of objective science, seeks on the contrary to enslave it. Besides, for communism there is no pure science, that is to say, neutral and universal. There is but the science that is "reactionary bourgeois penetrated by an ideology of hatred toward men" and the science that is "socialist progressist."[21]

The *Pravda* of Moscow of January 25, 1949, exposed the mission of the latter:

> In the socialistic State, scientific investigations are exploited in the interest of the people; they serve to develop

[20] See: *Pravda* (Bratislava, October 6, 1948).
[21] André Pierre, "Le secret scientifique en URSS," *Le Monde,* Paris, (February 17, 1950).

the productive forces of the country and ameliorate the material and cultural conditions of the worker. The imperialists, on the contrary, exploit the conquests of science in their struggle against the democratic forces of society, the people, and science itself. The scholars in capitalist countries are for the most part obliged to become the employees of all-powerful monopolies; by their discoveries they only contribute to the crushing of the workman and the unheard-of benefits of the capitalists.

And this newspaper did not neglect to conclude with this judgment: "In capitalist countries, science has become the instrument of imperialist aggression."[22]

Therefore it was natural that the regime should begin to transform the schools of higher learning into laboratories of Marxism-Leninism. At the beginning of a series of lectures on scientific socialism which were organized in December, 1948 for the teaching staff by the Action Committee of the Slovak institutions of higher learning of Bratislava, Mr. Novomeský told those professors still recoverable for socialist science: "Marxism-Leninism is an epistemological method, a method of scientific work that can and must be applied to all branches of science." He also indicated that the schools of higher education must be "the directing factor of the building and socialist reconstruction of our society."[23]

Once the principles were forwarded, nothing remained but to apply them. The professors who were not eager to embrace the ideology of the socialist university (about thirty of them between 1945 and 1948) were asked to resign.

The students followed their professors into the indoctrinating process. In order to eliminate the reactionary elements, the Commissariat of Public Education established a commission of verification which, under the pretext of idleness, excluded from the university many students who were not at all ready to renounce their democratic convictions. This measure provoked lively reactions at all levels of the population, so that Mr. Novomeský had to give an explanation of it in an article in the *Pravda* of Bratislava titled: :"Schools Are Made for Study!"[24]

At the same time the school administration instituted a close control on the political value of the students, a control which is ever active by means of a new university record which contains

22 *Ibid.*
23 See: *Pravda,* Bratislava, (December 16, 1948).
24 See: *Pravda,* Bratislava, (April 1, 1949).

their *curriculum vitae;* their entrance into the Communist party; their functions and activities as confirmed by a member of the central committee and approved by the seals of the party; the date of their joining the obligatory syndicate; the survey of the missions entrusted to them; the punishments which they incurred, the whole countersigned by the responsible men of the syndicate; their participation in the work shifts and, finally, the results of their examinations.

All students are required to take the course in Marxism-Leninism in the School of Philosophy, and a good grade in this subject is the requirement for admission to the examinations for the other schools.

Another requirement for the student is his participation in the work shifts. Following Yugoslavia's example, the regime organized youth shifts in Slovakia. For several weeks each student had to devote six hours a day to the program, with the rest of the time allotted to his own cultural development. The *Pravda* of Bratislava (October 10, 1948) provided a detailed explanation of the system:

> The *kultúrnik* (professor of political education) who gives these lectures explains what the difference is between socialism and capitalism, what planned economy is, the aim of this planning, the reason for the refusal to accede to the Marshall Plan. The members of the shifts take notes. Then a discussion is opened, beginning with the explanation of the terms: socialism, capitalism, bourgeoisie, planning in both the socialist and capitalist states. Next comes a comparison of the benefits to the people in a socialist and capitalist society. In this way the members of the shifts begin to know the world. They learn how socialism forges ahead.

Another new measure which finally aimed at "fascist" and "capitalist" students was the admission to the university, after a brief preparatory course, of a skeleton of workers chosen in the factories by the Communist party.[25] The registration of Stakhanovist workers was by principle provided for in the Schools of Law, Letters, Natural Sciences, and Pedagogy, as well as in certain branches of the Polytechnic School.

In addition, the regime decided to set right the penury of judges and attorneys, a good number of whom had previously been asked by communist justice to resign; this was effected by

[25] See: *Pravda,* Bratislava, (December 10, 1948).

organizing six-month courses for the better workmen. These new workmen-judges must serve as a link between bureaucracy and the working element of popular democracy.

Civic Education—The government realized that the idea of proletarian internationalism is foreign to the Slovak people, while the national idea always predominates in their sentiments and considerations. It therefore ranked the struggle against the petit-bourgeois nationalism as the prime task incumbent on the civic education of the people's democracy.[26] Among the working classes this struggle must first of all consist in the diffusion of the master-pieces of scientific socialism. The works of Marx, Engels, Lenin, Stalin, Gorki, Simonov, Fadeev, Ehrenburg, Gorbatov, Maka-renko, Tarle, Ostrowski, Sholokhov, Gladkov, Tynanov, Kraminov, Bazov, Nosov, Leonov, etc. were translated and printed in the hundreds of thousands. They replaced the Western authors in the libraries.

After a slow start in the nineteenth century, socialist litera-ture entered upon its golden age. A great number of specialists, or at least interpreters, of Marxism-Leninism worked themselves into all domains of public life to inculcate into the masses, in a more or less dilute form, this new conception of the world. In order to popularize science, the regime put the press, the radio, and the movies at the disposition of a small number of specialists and a host of dilettants. Morning or evening courses, community or district courses, clubs for workmen, writers, professors, or artists, constitute the principal means of this socialist illuminism —an illuminism which is as much concerned with the economic theories of Marx as the agrobiological theories of Michurin and Lysenko. If they were not successful in these courses, neither the railway employee nor the professor was considered qualified to practice his profession. As an article in *Le Monde* explains:

> Henceforth, persons desiring to exercise the functions of a judge, lawyer, or notary will have to take an examina-tion on Leninist principles. If they fail this test, they can-not present themselves for the law examination. Also, journalists are henceforth required to take evening courses bearing on Marxist teachings.[27]

Besides the reading of translations, the study of Russian is en-couraged, so that the workman or the peasant can drink directly

---

[26] Address by Mr. Pavlík, Commissioner of Information, before the activists in popular education, *Pravda*, Bratislava, (October 5, 1948).
[27] See: "Cours obligatoire de marxisme—léninisme," *Le Monde*, (January 15, 1949).

from the springs of socialist science. Many daily papers publish a course in Russian and in the introduction boast of the advantages that the knowledge of this language, the "first in the world," can present for each citizen. As in other satellite countries, Russian courses were organized even in the most remote villages in Slovakia. One is even tempted to wonder if it is the Great Russian eagle that uses socialist wings, or if, on the contrary, it is socialism which uses a language that, owing to the force of events, is in the process of becoming the diplomatic language of the Eastern world.

Cultural Institutions—All the cultural institutions of Slovakia were put in the service of progressive socialism by the new regime. *Matica slovenská* (the Slovak Institute of Arts and Sciences), was founded in 1863, and suffered the same fate. Although it had succeeded in resisting the ideological pressure of national-socialism during World War II, it was constrained to yield to Marxism. Its magazines (there were about a dozen) had to sing the praises of the socialist age. *Slovenské pohľady* (*Slovak Views,* a literary magazine founded by Jozef Miloslav Hurban in 1846 and which for a hundred years remained in the service of the national idea) likewise adopted the socialist ideology. The same is true of the historical, philosophical, linguistic, and other reviews published at that time by the various sections of this old national institution.

The *Academia scientiarum et artium slovaca* would also have deserved better than to become the principal center of the socialist interpretation of national life. Founded by Monsignor Tiso in 1942, this institution was destined to fill the scientific emptiness that the regime of Budapest (until 1918), and of Prague (until 1938), had created advisedly around the national Slovak individuality. The *Academia* had begun its activities by the publication of a series of monographs on Slovakia. The first five volumes dealt with geology (Professor Dimitri Andrusov), geography (Professor Jan Hromádka), ethnography (Dr. Rudolf Bednárik), national character (Professor Anton Jurovský), flora (Professor A. J. Novacký), fauna (Professor J. Babor), sociology (Professor Anton Štefánek), folklore (Dr. Andrej Melicharčík), anthropology (Dr. Ľudovít Franek), history (Dr. František Bokes), literature (Dr. Andrej Mráz).[28] In addition, it proposed pub-

---

[28] *Encyclopedia on Slovakia* (4 vols.; Bratislava).

lishing a dictionary of the Slovak language, a bibliography of Slovak literature, and an encyclopedia.

The communist regime seized upon this institution to make of it a center of scientific socialism in Slovakia. Instead of continuing to study the different aspects of Slovakia, it undertook the vulgarization of the Russian school system, Marxist philosophy, etc.[29]

Socialist Realism—For its theory of socialist art, communist orthodoxy found adequate expression in "socialist realism," a philosophy based on the thesis that "art takes its inspiration from the conscious belonging of the artist to the proletarian class."[30]

A congress of Czech and Slovak writers which was convened by the cultural division of the executive committee of the Czecho-Slovak Communist party defines the mission of the socialist writers in an extremely realistic manner:

> Writers must before everything else describe the great changes in our society, that is to say, either the colossal transformations of our nationalized production and enterprises, or the modifications remaining in our border zone (Sudeten zone), or the economic crises of the past, the unemployment of the preceding years or the events of February, 1948.[31]

This new esthetic school is proud therefore to consider art as a powerful spiritual tool serving the socialist building of the world and it stresses its political character which must oppose "Western formalism" judged anemic and lacking in ideological and political character.[32]

Unfortunately if a certain number of writers, true to themselves, preferred to give up writing rather than serve communism, others were found who tried to become, if not "engineers of souls" (Stalin), at least foremen of socialist cultural planning.

According to the Bratislava newspapers, by the end of 1949, eighteen Slovak writers had promised to write works in the socialist spirit. A poet had pledged to write an epic poem on the collectivization of the country; another, a satire on the lower bourgeoisie. One writer was to produce a novel centering on the

[29] Dr. J. Pavlík, *Evolution of the Soviet School and Education System* Bratislava: 1947); and Dr. Igor Hrušovský, *Theory of Science* (Bratislava: 1946), and *Engels' Philosophy* (Bratislava: 1947).
[30] See: Martin Dvorský, "Socialist Realism," *Slovensko*, Turčiansky Sv. Martin, (1950), No. 1.
[31] *Pravda*, Bratislava, (November 25, 1949).
[32] Martin Dvorský, "Social Realism," *ibid.*. . . . . . .

Stakhanovist hero; another, on the clandestine life of the party during the war. Two literary critics had promised to write works of socialist realism and the Marxist esthetics.

Further, a storm of enthusiasm was noted among the poets to sing of the superhuman qualities of Stalin, the "genius of the century."

"Ecclesia Militans" II

> As long as there are people who need faith in God and as long as this state of mind is part of their life, we shall have to take it into account.
> Čepička, Minister of Justice, June 25, 1949

SUBMISSION OF THE CHURCH TO THE STATE

Toward a Red Caesar-Papism—The balance between the Church and State was broken as early as 1945. After February, 1948, it became obvious that the State desired to subject the Church to its domination. To establish a Red Caesar-Papism, the communist leaders could take their inspiration largely from Tsarist and then Stalinian Russia; the supremacy of the State over the Church has been for many centuries an historical constant of that country.

In this respect, however, it is fitting to remember the fundamental attitude of communism toward the Church. Since it considers religion as the "peoples' opium," bishops and priests are only drug traffickers. Therefore the Church, in order to attain its ends, departs from communist legality. Its condemnation is decided upon in advance, but the method to be used to destroy it remains to be clarified. It is not a matter of attacking religion directly. In fact, communism is of the opinion that it is a superstructure of the economic-spiritual system founded on individualism and that it must collapse automatically when this base has disappeared. "You cannot blow the gas off," say the Communists, "you have to turn it off." Intelligent Communists therefore do not attack religion, dogma, and the cult head-on; they begin by slowly tying up the Church, then they make a docile servant of it; finally they deprive it of air, and it dies of asphyxiation.[33] Despite

---

[33] Mr. Husák clearly went beyond this communist discretion when he said: "Christianity is a legend of Emperor Augustus' times. . . ." or: "The voice of an insane bishop is not the voice of God, and it does not commit

all the communist subtleties with respect to the intermediary phases of evolution, and behind the skilful proportioning of the hot and cold shower bath practiced with regard to the Church, the final catastrophic event does not stand out any the less distinctly before our eyes.

After the events of February, 1948, the new Minister of Justice, Mr. Čepička, as secretary of the central action committee of the National Front, was entrusted with the problem of the relation of Church and State. On March 4, 1948, not without a certain precipitation, the bishops of Czecho-Slovakia gathered together to study the situation thus created. At the close of the meeting, a letter signed by Monsignor Beran, Archbishop of Prague, was addressed to Mr. Čepička. In the name of the bishops, he stated that the Catholic Church was bound to no form of government whatsoever and that it would continue to fulfill its mission faithfully to God and the State at the same time.

On the government's side, nothing yet indicated a precipitate evolution. Mr. Čepička, during a visit to Monsignor Beran, asserted to him that the Catholics of Czecho-Slovakia would have nothing to fear, that "the Church would be indemnified by annual endowments for what it lost through the confiscation of its goods" and that "the Czech Catholic schools would continue to exist under the new school regime."

The "Te Deum" of Monsignor Beran—If for Henry IV Paris was worth a mass, one wonders if all the promises of Mr. Čepička, Mr. Gottwald's son-in-law, were worth the *Te Deum* that Monsignor Beran, contrary to all tradition up to that time, was willing to celebrate June 14, 1948 in the cathedral of Saint-Guy in Prague, on the occasion of Mr. Gottwald's taking the office of President of the Republic. This attitude, by the excess of suppleness that it attested, provoked lively astonishment in the entire country and abroad and gave place to various suppositions and comments. It is certain that it was not without psychological pressure on this prelate that the new regime succeeded in making him act in such a way; but the result of his attitude was nil and the promises quickly went up in thin air. Monsignor Beran let himself get caught in a trap destined to compromise him in the eyes of the Catholic world.

us to anything. . . ." or again: "Even people clothed in a bishop's vestment can be mistaken." Dr. Gustav Husák, "People of Good Will," *Pravda,* (Christmas, 1949).

The day after the *Te Deum*, a delegation of bishops, still animated by the same spirit of conciliation, went to greet the new Chief of State. Mr. Gottwald had deigned to have a welcome in store for them which was termed pleasant and hearty. But while Mr. Gottwald gushed forth a volley of noble words, Mr. Čepička was already studying the measures which were going to be taken against the Church.

The Program of the Anti-Catholic Struggle—In fact, at the beginning of July, 1948, the central action committee of the National Front drew up its confidential program against the Catholic Church. The principal points were the following:

1) To undermine by all means possible, chiefly by compromising articles in the press, the confidence that the people evidenced for the Vatican;

2) To fight against the unity of the clergy by provoking dissension between the episcopate and the clergy, the clergy and the faithful;

3) To entrust the discussions with the religious authorities exclusively to Mr. Čepička, secretary of the central action committee of the National Front;

4) To sabotage the action of the mixed commissions established with regional and communal action committees concerned with ecclesiastical questions;

5) To collaborate closely with the "Czechoslovak" or "national" Church. To have the bishops of this Church take part in the official festivities and lavish respect and honor on them;

6) To accentuate the necessity of the unity of the people and the national Church. To consider the "Czechoslovak" Church as the first factor of unification, then in a more advanced phase, to envision collaboration with the Orthodox Church;

7) To employ the traditional weapons in the struggle against the Catholic clergy: the criticism of celibacy, the assimilation of the Church with capitalism, scandalous trials of "priests' immorality," etc.

The central committee of the Communist party formulated at that time certain demands regarding the Catholic Church:

a) Correspondence between the Vatican and the bishops will have to be made only through the intermediary of the government;

b) Pastoral letters can be made public only with the government's authorization; the clergy's sermons and addresses will be strictly controlled;

c) The "Czechoslovak" Church and the Evangelical Church
of the Moravian Brothers will be set up as the national Church;

d) Recalcitrant Catholic clergy will have to be compromised
notwithstanding the price or the means.

To prevent the clergy from being led on by political ambition, an episcopal conference of November, 1947 had again made
operative an article of the *Codex Juris Ecclesiastici* (Canon 139, 4)
according to which a priest could not be a candidate to the Parliament of Prague or the Diet of Bratislava without the consent
of his bishop. Yet the Communists succeeded in winning over to
their cause a Czech priest and two Slovak priests: Rev. Plojhar,
who became Minister of Public Health after February, 1948;
Rev. Lukačovič, who was appointed Commissioner for Technical Development in Slovakia; and Rev. Horák, who became
Post Office Commissioner in Bratislava. For refusing to obey the
orders they had received, they were inhibited by their bishops.

Of course the Communists were able to exploit skilfully the
presence of these ecclesiastics in the government. Their frequent
and naive declarations of the communist character of the first
Christians could not but contribute to the ideological confusion
among the Catholics.

In order to face up to this new policy which tended to drive
a wedge between the episcopate and the people, the bishops of
Czecho-Slovakia met in Nitra, Slovakia, on August 16, 1948 and
drew up a memorandum for the government in which they rose
up against the methods used. Among other things they declared:

> We are ready for any sacrifices and social burdens
> which they entail. We know that our faithful Catholic peo-
> ple know their bishops as well as the clergy know us. The
> people know perfectly well that their bishops will betray
> neither the country nor the nation.

This memorandum was read August 29 in all the churches.
Mr. Novomeský answered it in the *Pravda* of Bratislava Sep-
tember 12 and 19, 1948, with a violent article titled "On Winding
Roads." Hypocritically he accused the bishops of preparing, as
Cardinal Mindszenty had done in Hungary, a conspiracy against
the regime of popular democracy.

Another method that was employed to demoralize and disintegrate Catholicism consisted in using the political conformity
of some Protestant confessions and of the Orthodox Church. By
their attitude these confessions rendered considerable service to
the Communists. In Slovakia, as in Czechia, the electoral wards

with a Protestant majority voted for the Communist party in the elections of 1946 and 1948.[34] In May, 1948, the Patriarch Kovář, head of the so-called "Czechoslovak" Church, called together a synod which established for every believer the moral obligation "to aid the communist revolution and fight against American imperialism."[35]

In November, 1948, a congress of Christian Churches (non-Catholic) took place at the Hague. The Czech Protestants were represented by Mr. Hromádka, a professor in the Protestant School of Theology in Prague; he demonstrated his oratorical talents in persuading his colleagues that the system of popular democracy is at the same time nearer social justice and liberty of thought than the Western political system.[36] "In view of the total failure of the Western world," Mr. Hromádka stated, "performing a communist experiment is a necessity for us."

Another Czech Protestant notable of the first order, Professor Linhart, founded the Association of Christian Socialists in Prague. In its manifesto he stated that "only materialistic philosophy can explain the teaching of Jesus Christ which up to now has not been understood."[37]

From the beginning, the Communist party attempted to establish and strengthen the Orthodox Church on Czecho-Slovak territory. In order to provide a leader for this community comprising several thousand dispersed citizens, they imported a Russian from Moscow, Bishop Elevjferij, and they conferred on him the title of Metropolite of Prague. Enthroned in the presence of the Russian Ambassador and Czech communist leaders, he could benefit from the overt protection of the Soviet Embassy in all activities tending to develop this church imported from the East. His frequent trips across country aimed to win new faithful and to incite Catholics gradually to become a part of a Church which for communism was "less capitalistic than that of Rome."

To this propaganda favoring national and Orthodox churches, the Catholic episcopate replied in November, 1948 with a pastoral letter through which it put its faithful on their guard against the proselytism of the other churches.

---

[34] See: B. Chudoba," Czech Protestantism and Communism," *Slovák v Amerike*, New York, (January 22, 1949). In Slovakia, the three districts of Myjava, Senica and Liptovský Sv. Mikuláš are in question.
[35] *Ibid.*
[36] A thesis that Mr. Hromádka had developed at length in his book: *Between East and West*, (Prague: 1947).
[37] B. Chudoba, "Czech Protestantism and Communism," *ibid.*

According to an article appearing in the *Pravda* of Bratislava on December 3, 1948, this letter provoked the indignation of all the churches aimed at. In a common declaration, these latter accused the Catholic hierarchy of intolerance. It ran thus:

> Since religious freedom and the equality of denominations were sanctioned by the Constitution of May 9, 1948, no church here suffers from persecution. As Christians we see the necessity of transforming society now divided into classes, full of differences of opinion, wretchedness and wars into a family of children of God, equal and free.

In March, 1950, the same churches published a second common proclamation, this time directed against the Vatican, the gist of which follows: "Today the Vatican is an enemy of our people and of all peace-loving and progressive humanity."[38] On May 17, 1950, they approved the Stockholm Peace Manifesto inspired by the Communists. Thus, yielding on the international plane—as they had done on the internal plane—before the pressure of the regime, these churches became pawns on the chessboard of world communism.

The State's Psychological Break with the Church—On January 19, 1949, a delegation of bishops asked to be received by Mr. Gottwald with the idea of resuming negotiations. The episcopate also addressed to the government a memorandum making specific the *desiderata* of the Church. Yet by its repeated and ever more arbitrary interventions, the government clearly evidenced the fact that it was not envisioning any serious agreement.

The political pressure which was being applied day by day motivated another episcopal conference. Begun March 22, 1949 at Starý Smokovec in Slovakia, it was abruptly interrupted at the moment when Monsignor Lazík, Bishop of Trnava, discovered a microphone in the conference hall. This event marked the psychological rupture. The State had then crossed the Rubicon. In April, the Ministry of Public Education forbade the publication of the *Acta Curiae* by the dioceses; this led Monsignor Beran to exclaim: "In suppressing the diocesan bulletins, the Communists have done what the Germans themselves had not done during

---

[38] The following religious communities signed this document: the Czecho-Slovak Church, the Orthodox Church, the Protestant Church of the Czech Brothers, the Protestant Church of the Confession of Augsbourg of eastern Silesia, the Protestant-Methodist Church, the Unity of the Brothers, the Unity of the Czech Brothers, the Unity of the Baptist Brothers, the Protestant Church of the Adventists and the Religious Community of the Czechoslovak Unitarians. See: *Práce*, Prague (March 30, 1950).

the occupation." The Ministry of Public Education replaced them by the Bulletin of the Catholic Clergy whose drafting was entrusted to Communists and to apostate priests.

At the Ninth Congress of the Communist party attended by Mr. Malenkov, at that time chief of the cadres of world communism, Mr. Kopecký, the Minister of Information, warned the episcopate in an address delivered on May 28, 1949, that further negotiations between the Church and the State would be impossible. He stated among other things:

> We shall respect the activity of the Church and the freedom of religious life. It goes without saying that the educational and ideological interests of our State have nothing to do with faith and that, while recognizing religious freedom, we reserve to the State the right to govern and manage all teaching, without any exception, and the mission of directing all education, in and out of school, in the spirit of our scientific truth, in the spirit of the Marxist-Leninist doctrines.[39]

Governmental "Catholic Action"—On June 9, 1949, two emissaries presented themselves in Bratislava before Monsignor Šimalčík, Dean of the School of Catholic Theology, and said: "We are active members of the Catholic Action movement. Tomorrow it is going to hold an important meeting in Prague. Delegates from all the schools of theology will be there," they explained. "It would be regrettable if yours were not represented. We still have two plane spaces available for Prague and would be happy if you accompanied us." Monsignor Šimalčík accepted their offer.

On entering the meeting hall of Prague, the Dean signed an attendance list like everybody else. After an opening address and a few interventions, a member of the presidium began to read a proclamation addressed to all the Catholics of Czecho-Slovakia. First professing obedience to the Pope and bishops in matters of faith, morals, and discipline, the declaration then went on to describe the injustices of capitalism and finally to praise the work of the popular democracy, "the application of the principles of the Gospel of Christ." Recalling the famous sentence of St. Paul, *Nulla potestas nisi a Deo* (Rom. 13:2), the declaration was directed to the bishops and asked them to make an act of loyalty to the State. Its conclusion particularly threw detailed light on the meaning of this manifestation:

[39] *Lidové noviny*, Brno, (May 29, 1949).

> As faithful citizens of a popular democratic State, we
> decline all attempts coming from abroad that aim to im-
> pinge upon the sovereign rights of our people and State
> and sow unrest in our ranks. We cannot accept their giving
> us from the outside any order of a political character re-
> garding our internal affairs.

After hearing this passage, Monsignor Šimalčík together with
many other priests realized that they had been the victims of an
audacious practical joke. However, it was too late. In fact, on
June 11, 1949, all the communist newspapers announced the
founding of a Catholic Action movement with the names of all
the persons who had been present at the meeting in Prague. At
the same time couriers were sent into all the villages of the country to obtain members for the new movement and immediately
made their names public. Included among the signatures were
those of seven priests who had been dead for a long time, as well
as the names of the superiors of religious orders that had never
existed in Czecho-Slovakia. Thanks to these underhanded practices, several hundred priests and thousands of the faithful signed
the membership lists. The maneuver succeeded: to create a
false Catholic Action movement which would be in opposition
to the true one was undoubtedly a particularly fitting means of
troubling the believer.

The Communists' inauguration of the new Catholic Action
movement was the point of departure in Czecho-Slovakia for a
series of rapid and important events—"the 1949 storm." To prevent the bishops from reacting, the government detailed a commissioner to each consistory (episcopal office) on June 15. The
following day a conference of bishops meeting in Prague was
dispersed. On June 19, Monsignor Beran was interrupted by the
police during his allocution at the St. Guy Cathedral. On the
same day they placed him under house arrest.

On June 20, the Congregation of the Holy Office condemned
the schismatic Catholic Action movement by imposing excommunication *ipso facto,* reserved *speciali modo* to the Apostolic
See, upon all those who knowingly and willingly had joined or
would join in the future.

On June 26, a pastoral letter from the bishops of Czecho-
Slovakia dated June 15 was read in all the churches despite violent opposition from the police. In this henceforth historical document, the bishops enumerated the conditions of religious freedom:

1) The Christian conception of life should be respected in word and in act in public life and education.

2) The government should recognize the spiritual jurisdiction of the Pope of Rome as supreme head of the Church for religious and ecclesiastical questions, in accordance with the principles in operation, and declare that the exercising of this spiritual power does not impinge on the sovereignty of the State, but that it results naturally from the fundamental laws of man and especially from religious freedom.

3) Before the opening of the *pourparlers,* all the measures restraining and threatening religious freedom of the Catholics in Czecho-Slovakia, especially the freedom of education of youth, would be revoked.

Further, the episcopal letter asked:

That the Bulletin of Catholic Clergy published by the Ministry of National Education should be discontinued and replaced by the publication of ordinary bulletins;

That the decree of the Ministry of National Education on the vacancies of ecclesiastical charges and posts, the decree of the Ministry of the Interior concerning the restrictions on the freedom of meeting and association, and the decree addressed to the *gendarmerie* stations on the attitude to adopt against the Catholic Church be rescinded;

That all other decrees concerning spiritual exercises and all other religious acts be annulled.

The letter also asked the government to stop upholding the Catholic Action movement that it had just founded and stop covering it with State authority.[40]

The troubles that were being produced in Slovakia around this pastoral letter and the courageous manner in which the people defended their priests against the persecution of the police constitute a glorious chapter in spiritual resistance to communism behind the Iron Curtain.

On July 1, 1949, the Congregation of the Holy Office published its decree regarding the incompatibility of the Catholic faith with communist principles. It provided for the excommunication of Catholics who should persist in error. Mr. Čepička was not in the least embarrassed to return the ball. On July 15, he delivered a violent harangue against the Vatican, "sworn enemy

---

[40] See: Jean Čep, "La Lutte religieuse en Tchécoslovaquie," *Esprit,* Paris, (November, 1949), p. 674.

of the Republic." At the same time the government continued its struggle against the Church by organizing schismatic pilgrimages where apostate priests were delivering sermons arousing the population against the hierarchy and praising the government as the protector of religion.

The State Office for Ecclesiastical Affairs—After the events of June, 1949, which had evidenced the courage and independence of action of the bishops, priests, and faithful, the State decided to destroy the very foundation of this independence: the property of the Church. The provisions of the May, 1948 Constitution which limited land property to fifty hectares already applied to bishoprics, chapters, parishes, etc. Things did not stop there. First the State limited, by Law No. 46/1948 (Art. 1, par. 3), the property of the corporate bodies of the Church to thirty hectares. Next, it expropriated and made officials of the clergy. During the summer of 1949, the government had studied the measures to achieve this end. On October 14, 1949, the National Assembly of Prague passed two laws (Nos. 217 and 218) which had a particularly grave effect on relations between Church and State. The first created the State Office for Ecclesiastical Affairs, a veritable ministry whose titular was to be appointed by the President of the Republic. It specified the following responsibility for this office:

> to see that ecclesiastic and religious life be developed in compliance with the Constitution and with the principles of order of the popular democracy and so to ensure for each and every person the right to freedom of religion, a right guaranteed by the Constitution and founded on the principle of tolerance, religious peace, and the equality of all denominations.

The second law, closely aligned with the first, referred to the remuneration of persons active in the cult, and to the reimbursement of the real disbursements effected by the administration of the Church. It is advisable to quote its essential provisions:

> The State grants salaries to the ecclesiastics who carry on with its consent a pastoral activity or a duty in the ecclesiastic administration and in the institutions having charge of the formation of the ministers of the cult (Art. 1).
> The consent of the State can be given only to the ecclesiastics who are of Czechoslovak nationality, who are sure of the national point of view, who are morally irreproachable, and satisfy in general all the conditions required for the nomination of officials (Art. 2).

A religious activity in the churches and other religious groups can be carried on only by persons having received the consent of the State and sworn according to a formula which will be fixed by a governmental decree. All titularization (election, nomination) of these persons necessitates the previous consent of the State. Any vacant position must be filled within thirty days. If the Church does not satisfy this obligation, the State can take the necessary measures to ensure the proper functioning of the cult, the ecclesiastical administration and the formation of priests (Art. 3).

This legislation was completed by governmental decree No. 219/1949. By virtue of Article 18, paragraph 2 of this decree, if an ecclesiastic had ceased to fulfill the conditions required, the State Office for Ecclesiastical Affairs could bring the case to the attention of the competent authority of the Church. If this authority had not taken the necessary dispositions within fourteen days, the State Office then had the right to dismiss the priest and decide at the same time if his salary was to be suspended and his position declared vacant.

As for the remuneration of the clergy, the new legislation brought the following decisions: the priests, paid like other State officials, were to receive a basic salary to which was added a supplement proportionate to their rank and zeal. The annual basic salary of 36,000 crowns was to be increased by 3,600 crowns every three years.

In addition, members of the clergy were to receive a supplement of 48,000 crowns for the first category (bishops), 36,000 for the second (elderly priests), 24,000 for the third (middle-aged priests), and 12,000 for the fourth (young priests). Finally, the clergy was to profit by retirement pensions.

After setting off the advantages, it is fitting to see the obligations resulting from this legislation.

First, Article 20 of the governmental decree stated that all archbishops, bishops, and apostolic administrators must swear allegiance to the regime before the Prime Minister. The other categories of ecclesiastics must do the same before other high officials of the administration. This is the text of the oath:

I promise on my honor and my conscience to be faithful to the Czechoslovak Republic and to its popular democratic order, to do nothing which might go against its interests, security and integrity. As a citizen of the popular democratic State, I shall honestly fulfill the duties which are incumbent upon me owing to the position that I hold, and I shall try unreservedly to uphold the constructive efforts aiming at the good of the people.

Not content with having thus made priests officials, the regime put under the control of the State all that was left of the buildings or furnishings of the Church. Law No. 218/1949, by which it took in charge the material needs of the churches, contains the following articles in this connection:

> The State controls all the goods of the churches and other religious groups. Their representatives and the administrators of these goods will make a complete inventory of the furniture and buildings. Any change in the property of churches and religious groups is subject to the previous consent of the civil authorities (Art. 10).

By virtue of these measures, an inventory had to be made of sacred and votive objects. Government agents searched the churches and rectories to verify the inventories drawn up by the priests. Likewise, collections were forbidden in the churches because the regime feared that such money might be used against it.

After examining the content of the new laws the bishops found that they not only constituted a flagrant violation of the principle of supranational ruling on the affairs of the Church, but that they also were opposed to the religious freedom guaranteed by the Constitution. This position they made public in a statement addressed to the government which was dated October 21, 1949. Putting the government on its guard against the serious complications which could result in the life of the people, they asked for a reconsideration of this arbitrary legislation.

In a second letter bearing the same date, the episcopate gave the clergy certain rules of conduct to follow in the light of the situation thus created. Since it was impossible to oppose these new laws, the episcopate authorized the clergy to accept in principle the new regulations on salaries. Yet the priests were bound to send to their bishops a preliminary statement:

> I declare that I accept the new ruling on salaries because it arises from a measure that has taken the form of a law. In accepting this salary, I contract no obligation whatsoever contrary to my conscience as a priest and to the laws of the Church. I once more declare that I prefer the spiritual interests of the Church and the freedom of my priestly activity to the material guarantee of my existence.

After thus renewing the act of loyalty to their bishops, the priests could take the oath required by the civil authorities but only after adding, orally or in writing, the following passage: "Insofar as it is not in disagreement with the laws of God and the Church and with the natural rights of man."

On November 14, 1949, the Prime Minister, Mr. Zápotocký, replying to the collective letter of the bishops, spoke to them as delinquents. He accused them of refusing civic obedience, "of inventing fantasies on the threats of religious liberty," of "disturbing the peace."

In a memorandum to the government dated November 17, 1949, the episcopate raised its voice once again to shield itself against these accusations. It stated that the new laws and their application decrees put the Church outside the law; that they had given spiritual power to the State authorities; that, contrary to Article 17 of the Constitution, no religious activity could be carried on except with the State's consent; that the State, disregarding the canonical mission which had devolved upon priests, assumed the right to assign titulars to vacant posts and dismiss ecclesiastics. Asking for the suppression of governmental control exercised by the commissioners in the consistories, the episcopate solicited the reconsideration of all these unilateral dispositions. "We cannot give to Caesar what belongs to God," the bishops resolutely declared.

Henceforth no dialogue was possible. Despite the complaints and protestations, the State suppressed and, under pretext of economy, confiscated a great many rectories. It also laid hold of seminaries, chased the religious from their convents and monasteries which it then converted into offices or centers of Marxist education.

The False Capitular Vicars—The consequences of this policy were not long in coming.

On January 8, 1950, Monsignor Škrábik, Bishop of Banskà Bystrica, died suddenly. The day after his burial, the chapter proceeded among its members to the election of Canon Daniel Briedoň as capitulary vicar of the diocese. On January 14, he informed the State Office for Ecclesiastical Affairs of Bratislava of his nomination. This organism demanded that Monsignor Briedoň should formally ask consent in accordance with Law No. 218/1949. Since the reply was late in coming, the new capitular vicar was invited to go to Bratislava to make a verbal request for this consent and take the oath of fidelity. When he did neither, they obliged him to resign.

To get out of this position and "to ensure a normal course" to the dispatching of the business of the diocese interested, the State Office for Ecclesiastical Affairs in Slovakia appointed as administrator of the diocese Rev. Ján Dechet—one of the priests who had consented to collaborate with the Communists. With the aid of the civil authorities, he immediately occupied the episcopal palace and chased out the personnel who had been detailed there up to that time.

In an attempt to clarify the situation, the Slovak episcopate held a conference out of which came a letter dated February 17, 1950, addressed to each priest and presenting the detailed point of view of the ecclesiastical authorities. The bishops affirmed that the election of the capitular vicar had been effected in conformity with Canon 438 of the Code of Canon Law and that the *Modus Vivendi* did not require the consent of the government as it was a question of a capitular vicar whose office was only provisional.

Rome also let its voice be heard and declared Rev. Dechet *excommunicatus vitandus*. He, however, was neither impressed nor discouraged. On March 18 and 19, his enthronement took place with great pomp at Banská Bystrica. Two days before, the police had visited and searched the Catholic institutions and arrested the rector of the seminary, Rev. Jur Koza Matejov, as well as two professors. At the same time, government agents went through the villages of the diocese to invite the priests to participate in the solemn Mass. Thirty-five of them, only seven of whom were Slovak, were present at this sacrilegious service. It was assumed that the others had come from Czechia. A group of workmen from nationalized factories who were ordered to attend, served as public.

A similar evolution was soon produced in the other dioceses. Following the imprisonment of the Bishop of Spiš, Monsignor Vojtaššák, and his coadjutor, Monsignor Barnáš, in September, 1950, the Commissioner of Ecclesiastical Affairs in Slovakia, Mr. Holdoš, had a suspended priest, Andrej Schäffer, appointed capitular vicar by a group of patriotic priests. On November 5, 1950, this new "dignitary" took office in a ceremony attended by civil authorities and two hundred patriotic priests who had sworn obedience to the communist government.

By the end of 1950, the administration of the six Catholic dioceses of Slovakia was entrusted to capitular vicars of governmental obedience, the rightful bishops having been imprisoned or prevented from exercising their episcopal mission. The Uniat Church of eastern Slovakia was driven to Orthodoxy. In June, 1950, after Monsignor Gojdič's imprisonment—a Greek Catholic bishop of Prešov—eight hundred and fifty faithful of his diocese met at Michalovce and unanimously voted for their break with Rome and their subjection to the patriarch of Moscow. A priest chosen from the patriotic Uniat clergy was afterward consecrated bishop of this Neo-Orthodox Church. Thus chased from the cathedrals, the Roman Church had to take refuge in souls.

Political Pressure on Catholics—According to the new law, the religious marriage ceremony ceased to have legal value beginning January 1, 1950. Henceforth it had to be held after the registration of the civil marriage by the local national committees.

Catholics were then constantly urged by a powerful administrative machine to embrace, if not the party, at least communist ideology. Material sanctions hanging over their heads like the sword of Damocles caused a falling away.

Priests were obliged to humiliate themselves by acts of loyalty extorted from them. So it was that in December, 1949, the Catholic clergy of Slovakia were reported to have sent a collective congratulation to Generalissimo Stalin on the occasion of his seventieth birthday. It was luxuriously bound and contained a painting of Saints Cyril and Methodius, and read:

> We, the Catholic clergy, bless your efforts toward peace, for divine law commands us to do so. . . . To other congratulations we add ours, praying God Almighty to bless your work and give you the health and strength to lead the world to the triumph of truth, love, and beauty, in conformance with the divine plans.

The Deification of the State—In the Christmas number, 1948, the newspaper *Lidové noviny* published a drawing giving the communist conception of the Nativity: the Child in the manger represented the Five-Year Plan; Mr. Gottwald was St. Joseph, a woman of the people, the Blessed Virgin. Peasants in national costume and workmen carrying the products of their labors to the work of national reconstruction substituted for the Three Kings. In the foreground were the shepherds: a Yugoslav, a Magyar and—last but not least—a Russian.[41]

[41] See: *La Croix*, Paris, (January 21, 1949).

In a message addressed to the population at Christmas time, 1949, the governmental Catholic Action movement compared the red star to the one which had guided the three wise men to the manger in Bethlehem. "It is from the east," the message read, "that the light once came announcing the coming of the Messiah. Today the light which shines in the east brings peace and security."[42]

THE GOVERNMENT'S BLOW TO THE CHURCH

Suppression of Religious Liberties

Education—After 1948, religious instruction was reduced to a minimum. The priests, the religious, and the laymen who continued such instruction were subjected to an ideological control and had to take examinations on materialistic doctrines.

Spiritual retreats were forbidden to adults, as was any meeting of religious character organized outside the church.

And last, the State, having a monopoly on education both in school and out, took offense at interference from parents and Church.

The Press—After the events of February, 1948, the Ministry of Information simply suppressed the Catholic press. Thus it caused the disappearance of the review *Verbum,* whose editor-in-chief, Mr. V. Jankovič, had been put in prison; the review of the young *Plameň (The Flame);* the literary review, *Nová práca (The New Work);* the monthly magazine on spiritual life, *Smer (Direction);* and a quantity of weekly and monthly publications of popular interest, as *Posol Božského Srdca (The Messenger of the Divine Heart); Svätá Rodina (The Holy Family); Kráľovná mája (The May Queen); Katolícke missie (Catholic Missions); Duchovný pastier (The Good Shepherd),* etc.

By exception the regime allowed the publication of *Katolícke noviny (Catholic News),* a Bratislava weekly, but made life impossible for it. So this newspaper which had nearly 200,000 subscribers in 1947 was compelled, during the summer of 1948, to limit its circulation to 50,000 copies "because of the paper shortage." Then the November 14, 1948 number warned its readers that it would be impossible to take new subscriptions, "the present situation not permitting the taking of orders." Finally, in the spring of 1949, this weekly was infiltrated, then absorbed by the communist press.

[42] See: *Le Figaro,* Paris, (December 26, 1949).

Printing and publishing houses—According to the *Pravda* of Bratislava of November 19, 1948, the Ministry of Information nationalized the four main Catholic printing and publishing houses of the country by decree 1418/1948: (1) The *Lev* editions, founded by Monsignor Hlinka at Ružomberok; (2) the *Unia* editions, of the former Catholic Women's League, founded by Monsignor Filkorn in Bratislava; (3) the printing company of the diocese of Spiš; (4) the Association of St. Adalbert in Trnava, Slovakia's largest and oldest publishing house, founded in 1869 and raising two hundred thousand subscribers. Its management had been previously entrusted to Rev. Horák, who was suspended from his clerical duties.

Any work published on behalf of the Church, including prayer books, was henceforth subject to the preliminary censure of the Central Office of Information.

Slovakia's Central Catholic Bureau—At the beginning of February, 1949, the Ministry of the Interior in Prague forbade any activity in the Central Catholic Bureau of Bratislava. It was declared that the searches carried on in the homes of the employees of this Bureau had permitted the police to lay hold of "a vast amount of suspect material."

So it was that Catholicism was deprived of all means of defense of its interest in public life.

Pastoral letters—The only contact remaining between prelates, priests, and the faithful was the pastoral letter. It was not too much to expect, therefore, that the regime would attack this last link of communication. As a matter of fact, the police received the order to prevent the reading of a pastoral letter from the bishops of Czecho-Slovakia which was intended for June 26, 1949. On Saturday and Sunday morning they set about getting the letter in question from the priests, and they proceeded into the rectories to make searches that provoked violent reactions among the population. In several places the police were disarmed and insulted. Martial law was proclaimed in the region of Žilina and Turčiansky Sv. Martin. At Krupá two policemen were killed by an overly excited crowd and at Belá three persons died in a scuffle. Several hundred people were imprisoned. In Slovakia the incidents between communist and police formations and civilians rose to proportions hitherto unknown behind the Iron Curtain. Around Bratislava and in the capital itself, real combats took place and barricades were set up. The faithful had blocked the roads leading to the churches and from the rectories answered with fusillade the firing of the communist squads.

To cope with further developments, important Soviet detachments, ready for combat duty, were concentrated in Sub-Carpathian Ruthenia on the Slovak-Russian border.

Pilgrimages—Since the State had organized a Catholic Action independent of Rome, it likewise took the pilgrimages in charge. During the summer of 1949, the national committee of Levoča, a famous pilgrimage of northern Slovakia, wanted to go ahead of the town's priest.

The medieval town of Levoča, known under the name of Slovak Nuremberg, is located on a plateau rising curiously in the middle of a hollow surrounded by mountains. One of them, which is especially high, is topped by a beautiful church consecrated to the miraculous Virgin. To this place every July 2 came pilgrims from all over Slovakia.

A few days before that date, Rev. Vojtas, the parish priest of Levoča, was called in by the chairman of the national committee to discuss preparations for the pilgrimage. When he did not appear, policemen were sent to make up his mind for him. When the news spread in the city, the population hastened to the rectory to defend their priest should the occasion arise. The alarm bell began to ring, and as could be expected, a scuffle ensued. Ten "particularly dangerous agitators" were arrested and immediately referred to the itinerant court of Košice which condemned them to terms ranging from two to ten years. The regime thereby hoped to cool the ardor of the pilgrims.

The Slovak peasants, however, were not discouraged. Since June 30, groups had been arriving from all directions, although the Commissioner of Communications of Bratislava gave the order to block all means of transportation to Levoča. No train or bus was supposed to operate in that direction. Besides, the stores received an order to close along with the hotels and restaurants.

In spite of these precautions, a crowd of sixty thousand persons climbed the slopes of the "Mountain of the Virgin" (Marián-ska Hora) on July 2 at dawn, and the priests, who had come in civilian dress—thus evading the police—began to celebrate the traditional offices, followed by the faithful who were in a more recollected state than ever.

Faced with this calm, confident attitude, the fury of the authorities reached its height. It was impossible to disperse this fervent crowd. The police were powerless, and the soldiers themselves sympathized with the pilgrims. They then deprived the city of water, gas, and electricity; they also followed hot on the trail of the peddlers who had come to sell their wares. These coercive measures were known in the region with lightning speed. Help was immediately organized, and from all the surrounding villages people set forth for the besieged town to bring provisions.

Sunday, July 3, was an apotheosis. The number of people meeting together at that time was estimated at eighty thousand. The spirit of solidarity had triumphed over the vexatious interference of the regime. Unfortunately, this was to be the last spontaneous pilgrimage in Slovakia.

Seminaries—During the summer of 1950, all the seminaries under the control of the bishops were closed. On the other hand, at the beginning of the school year 1950-51, the State permitted the reopening of three schools of Catholic theology: Prague, Olomouc, and Bratislava. However, they had a carefully planned program in which some of the traditional subjects yielded to Marxism-Leninism. Interdicted priests were to carry on the teaching there.

Persecutions—After the events of June and July, 1949, the government clamped an iron hand on the Church. In Slovakia, the communist leaders of Prague decided to liquidate the religious communities first. The monasteries of the Jesuits, Franciscans, Redemptorists, and the Oblates of St. Francis de Sales were occupied by the police ever since the spring of 1950. To ensure operation in Bratislava, five thousand police organized a veritable hunting party against the regular clergy on the night of April 13, 1950. They carefully searched all the monasteries, then with all the religious collected, they transported them by truck to the eastern part of the country, where they crowded them into a few monasteries. Surrounded from the outside and kept under 24-hour surveillance inside, these traditional places of religious life were thus transformed into concentration camps.

The regime next attacked the three most prominent ecclesiastical dignitaries: Monsignor Ján Vojtaššák, Bishop of Špiš; Monsignor Michal Buzalka, Auxiliary Bishop of Trnava; and Monsignor Pavel Gojdič, Greek Catholic Bishop of Prešov. On January 11, 1951, the prosecutor accused them before the State Tribunal of Bratislava "of having, under pain of eternal damnation, kept the Slovak people in servitude, of having committed acts of high treason, military treason, and espionage." On January 15, Monsignori Buzalka and Gojdič were condemned to life imprisonment, and Monsignor Vojtaššák, an old man of 73 years, to 24 years of imprisonment.[43]

Relations With the Holy See

The Antecedents of a Rupture—During the war, the presence of a diplomatic representative to Bratislava from the Vatican frankly annoyed Mr. Beneš. Consequently, after consolidating the political situation of the Czecho-Slovak Provisory government of London by having it recognized by the Allies, he attempted to gain the sympathies of the Holy See. To this end, he sent to the State Secretariat two memos in which he did not fail to belittle the regime of Monsignor Tiso in Slovakia. One of them was sent to Rome by an intermediary of the apostolic delegate for Great Britain, Monsignor W. Godfrey, on January 7, 1941, and the other by the British government on July 15, 1943.[44]

All of Mr. Beneš' endeavors remained fruitless, although Monsignor Šrámek, leader of the Czech Catholic party, presided over his exile government.

It was not until 1945 that the Holy See renewed diplomatic relations with Czecho-Slovakia. Monsignor Saverio Ritter, the last apostolic nuncio to Prague before 1939, was sent there again. The government, while receiving him as a representative of the Vatican, formally opposed his automatic and traditional status as dean of the diplomatic corps. Monsignor Ritter then took the title of internuncio, although he had previously been accredited as apostolic nuncio to the Chief of State.

The measures of oppression that the regime did not cease to apply to the Church hindered the normal course of diplomatic relations with the Vatican. If the government of Prague did not ever go so far as to denounce the *Modus Vivendi* of 1927, it violated it between 1945 and 1947 numerous times, not only in spirit but in letter. In the domain of ecclesiastical goods especially, the State had recourse to acts of violence which justly provoked the protestations and reprobation of the Church. On several different occasions, the administrative authority assimilated landed property of the Church to private *latifundia* and divided it among the peasants. Monsignor Ritter's departure from Prague

---

[43] Ministry of Justice, *Trial Against Bishops Vojtaššák, Buzalka, and Gojdič Traitors to their Country* (Bratislava: 1951).
[44] See their text: Beneš, *Memoirs,* pp. 494-504.

in 1947 can perhaps be explained as a gesture of protestation against this arbitrary manner of acting. The direction of the nunciature then fell to the lot of Monsignor Forni—later appointed to Paris—who was replaced by Monsignor Senti, then by Monsignor Verolino. It was the latter who, in the course of a round of visits to the bishops of Slovakia at the time of the troubles unleashed by the schismatic Catholic Action in June, 1949, was obliged by the police to get out of his car and be submitted to a two hour interrogation. Having become a "persona non grata" and being accused of having become mixed up in the internal affairs of the Czecho-Slovak State, he had to leave Prague at once. However, he did not do it without obtaining in writing the assurance that the Ministry of Foreign Affairs would grant the visa of admission to his successor, Monsignor Paolo Bertoli, from the Berne nunciature—a visa that was never to be granted. In vain did the Holy See ask for the acceptance of two other diplomats. The only official remaining at the nunciature of Prague under these circumstances was Monsignor De Liva, whom the Prague government refused to recognize as an interim chargé d'affaires. His relations with the Ministry of Foreign Affairs were made more and more difficult until finally he was forbidden access.

At the beginning of March, 1950, Prague propaganda openly accused Monsignor De Liva of being the organizer of the so-called miracle of Cihošt[45] which, according to the communist papers, was only an "ingenious mechanical invention having as its aim the sowing of hatred and sedition against the Republic." Thus Monsignor De Liva—to quote from the *Civilta Cattolica*—"was represented by communist propaganda as a grotesque emissary from the Vatican who, within the shelter of his office, was charged with engaging in the most shameful mystifications and conspiring against the Republic."[46]

During March the police bore down upon Monsignor De Liva with increasing surveillance. Everyone who went to see him was photographed. In the end, on March 16, a press communiqué announced that the Ministry of Foreign Affairs had invited him to leave Czecho-Slovak territory within three days.[47] After this expulsion, the Czecho-Slovak chargé d'affaires, Mr. Ilja Ráth,

---

[45] On Sunday, December 11, 1949, the faithful of Cihošt parish, in Southern Bohemia, saw the massive cross of the main altar bow several times during the Mass to the right and to the left.

[46] F. Cavalli, S.J., Caratteristiche della lotta contro la Chiesa in Cecoslovacchia," *Civiltá Cattolica*, Rome, (April 15, 1950).

[47] See: *Osservatore Romano*, (March 29, 1950).

remained in Rome another month. At the end of April, the Czecho-Slovak legation to the Holy See also closed its doors, and its officials suddenly left Rome. This, in fact, was the breaking off of diplomatic relations between Czecho-Slovakia and the Holy See.

Fundamental Attitude toward the Vatican—The evolution just described was inevitable; Soviet Russia and its satellites considered the Vatican a powerful enemy.

To clarify the communist point of view with respect to the Holy See's role, it is necessary to give certain passages from the testimony of Mr. Antonín Hobza, former professor of canon law and international law at the University of Prague. Mr. Hobza's testimony was delivered in the case which took place in that city from March 31 to April 6, 1950, against ten religious. He stated, word for word:

> Apart from the fact that, in the terms of the agreements of 1929 with Italy, the Pope is the sovereign of a miniature State called the City of the Vatican, he is above all the spiritual leader of all Catholics. But more and more is this function giving way to another function which is political. In fact, ever since the Middle Ages the Pope has been intervening in world politics to purely secular ends which mock the doctrine of Christ. It is well known that the Pope is at present on the side of the American imperialists, spurring Humanity on to a third world war. But the Pope's absolute monarchy belongs irreparably to the past.

> Granted that the Vatican is an important international factor, various States continue to maintain diplomatic relations with it by means of nuncios and internuncios. According to an international custom generally recognized, they enjoy the same privileges as civil diplomatic representatives, and they have a similar mission, which consists in keeping in contact with the Pope and in following the many-sided evolution of the life in the States where they are accredited. Like all other diplomats, they are bound not to interfere in the internal affairs of the State.

> Now the relations of the nuncios and internuncios with the Pope are regulated not by international law, but by canon law, which for a modern State is totally lacking in juridical character. Numerous differences have come up during the past centuries between the Vatican and different countries because of this divergence between the law of the State on one hand, and the law of the Church as also the political aspirations of the Pope taking his stand on this law, on the other hand.

> The States which have adopted popular democracy and socialism refuse, on principle and in full consciousness,

the idea that a foreign official should be permitted to enforce, on State territory, any law whatsoever outside the will of the sovereign nation incarnate by the State. After a long, indecisive and confused historical evolution, the principle of the territoriality of law was finally realized to the utmost.

In the Czechoslovak Republic, the internuncio consequently has no right to impose on the bishops papal decrees which are in contradiction to the law, or to give instruction to the faithful on the manner in which they should conduct themselves with respect to a law or ordinance of civil authority. If he does, he violates international law, for he intervenes in internal affairs of the State. At the same time, he commits a crime against the Czechoslovak law for which—thanks to extraterritoriality—he can not be brought before a Czechoslovak tribunal. The Czechoslovak ecclesiastical official who, on the advice of the Pope's representative, encourages his subordinates to act in opposition to the laws in force likewise commits a crime.

As regards the concrete situation created by the committal of ten Church officials for trial, I express as an expert the following opinion: the accusation classifies in two categories the offenses of which these officials were guilty: first, offenses falling within the compass of high treason; second, offenses ascribable to espionage—both categories in compliance with Czechoslovak legislation. If the tribunal recognizes that it is proven that these crimes have been committed, we shall have to deal with crimes, even in the sense of international law. We all know that the enemies of the Czechoslovak Republic strive to disintegrate it, stir up acts of treason, and organize espionage. The Vatican works with them to the same end. But from the standpoint of espionage, the Vatican has a distinct advantage over the other States owing to the canonical obedience of the ecclesiastics that are subordinate to higher organs. For this reason the espionage of the Vatican exceeds all other systems of intelligence by its results. A State not recognizing canon law will not recognize, on principle, canonical obedience either.[48]

Mr. Hobza's logic would evidently be much more convincing if the Czecho-Slovak government were in a position to defend its sovereignty and the independence of the Republic as regards Moscow with as much vigor as it does with respect to the Vatican.

[48] Quoted in the newspaper, *Mladá fronta*, Prague, (April 4, 1950).

THE FIVE-YEAR PLAN[49]

Characteristic—If the Two-Year Plan marked a transition between individual and collective economy and still admitted forms belonging as much to one as to the other, the Five-Year Plan, on the contrary, constituted a homogeneous system founded on the principle of an exclusively socialist economy in which individual enterprise figured only as the exception confirming the rule and whose existence was generally condemned. Article I, paragraph 2 of the law dealing with the Five-Year Plan contained the following clause: "The existing capitalistic elements will all be progressively restricted and eliminated at the same time from all sectors of the national economy."

The Five-Year Plan then opened a new era and the text of the law which put it into force provided in the future for a succession of unending five-year plans.

The purpose of the plan was reconstruction, transformation of Czecho-Slovak economy, and the consolidation of the ties uniting workmen, agriculturists, intellectuals, and urban middle classes (Art. I). It was supposed to constitute an important step in the development of the popular democracy toward socialism through the strengthening of nationalized industry and the mechanization of agriculture. It proposed at the same time to augment the national income by 50 per cent (Art. 2).

Provisions Applicable to all Czecho-Slovakia—The Plan envisioned intensifying production for the entire Republic in the following proportions:

TABLE 1

INDUSTRY

	Gross Value of Production 1948 (billions of crowns)	Gross Value of Production 1953 (billions of crowns)	Percentage of Increase
Industry in General	288	454	57
Mines	13.2	17.8	35
Fuel and Power	9.3	14.1	52
Iron Smelting	31.2	46.4	49
Metallurgy	47.8	92.3	93
Chemicals	21.7	35.1	62
Glass	4.1	4.6	12

[49] Law No. 241 of October 27, 1948 concerning the first Five-year Economic Plan for the development of the Czechoslovak Republic, *Le Plan économique quinquennal tchécoslovaque* (Prague: December, 1948).

Building Materials and Ceramics	7.6	12.1	59
Paper	7.0	9.9	41
Wood	9.9	12.5	26
Textiles	46.0	77.4	68
Leather and Rubber	15.2	21.8	43
Graphic Arts	3.4	4.0	18
Phonographs	....	0.66	..
Films	0.37	0.57	56
Sugar Refining	8.7	10.2	17
Distillery	5.3	5.6	6
Brewing	5.7	9.6	68
Flour Milling	3.6	4.7	30
Food	34.5	61.8	79
Tobacco & Salt	....	12.8	..
Craft Activities	49.0	59.0	20

TABLE 2
AGRICULTURE AND FORESTRY

	1948	1953	Percentage of Increase
Agricultural Production in General	90.5	105.0	16
Plant Production	49.5	55.2	11
Animal Production	26.8	49.8	86
Lumbering	....	18.8	..

TABLE 3
TRANSPORTATION

	1948	1953	Percentage of Increase
Volume of Transportation	100%	140%	40%

TABLE 4
PRODUCTION OF CERTAIN BRANCHES OR ARTICLES IN FIGURES OF QUANTITY[50]

	1948 100%	1953 140%
Lignite	23,900,000 Tons	32,200,000 Tons
Coal	17,746,000 Tons	20,800,000 Tons
Electricity	7,400,000,000 Kwh.	11,200,000,000 Kwh.
Gas	420,000,000 M³	2,900,000,000 M³

[50] See: Ministère de l'Information et de l'Education populaire, *Du Plan biennal au Plan quinquennal* (Prague: 1949).

Crude Iron	1,460,000	Tons	2,700,000	Tons
Raw Steel	2,400,000	Tons	3,500,000	Tons
Locomotives	290	Units	480	Units
Tractors	9,000	Units	20,000	Units
Automobiles	14,000	Units	24,000	Units
Motorcycles	50,000	Units	75,000	Units
Farm Machines	1,100,000,000	Crowns	2,300,000,000	Crowns
Bicycles	220,000	Units	330,000	Units
Artificial Silk	6,800	Tons	11,000	Tons
Artificial Fibres	11,700	Tons	18,000	Tons
Radio Receivers	150,000	Units	300,000	Units
Electric Motors	220,000	Units	890,000	Units
Shoes	45,520,000	Prs.	72,500,000	Prs.
Tires	3,025,000	Units	7,400,000	Units
Cotton Thread	50,000	Tons	114,000	Tons
Wool Yarn	14,800	Tons	41,800	Tons
Linen Thread	9,500	Tons	12,800	Tons
Paper	197,000	Tons	320,000	Tons
Milk	32,359,000	Hectol.	47,000,000	Hectol.
Eggs	1,172,100,000	Units	2,000,000,000	Units
Beer	8,600,000	Hectol.	11,700,000	Hectol.
Bricks	835,650,000	Units	1,300,000,000	Units
Hollow Glass	126,420	Tons	137,100	Tons
Flat Glass	91,000	Tons	113,700	Tons
Rail Transports (Merchandise)	72,000,000	Tons	100,000,000	Tons
Road Transports (Persons)	140,000,000	Persons	307,000,000	Persons

TABLE 5
INCREASE IN LABOR PRODUCTIVITY

	1948	1953	Percentage of Increase
Industry	100%	132%	32%
Building	100%	153%	53%
Agriculture	100%	120%	20%
Transports	100%	130%	30%

TABLE 6
INCREASE IN NUMBER OF WORKMEN

	1948	1953	Percentage of Increase
National Economy	100%	105.6%	5.6%
Industry	100%	118.5%	18.5%
Building	100%	150.0%	50.0%

TABLE 7

FOREIGN TRADE

	1948	1953	Percentage of Increase
Volume	100%	140%	40%

TABLE 8

INVESTMENTS OF THE FIVE-YEAR PLAN

	Billions of Crowns 336.2
Industry	131.9
Agriculture	26.8
Building	4.6
Transports	52.9
Commerce and Touring	5.0
Construction of Dwellings	39.3
Social Welfare	8.1
Public Health and Social Security	10.3
Cultural Services	10.2
Bridges, Causeways, Hydraulic Construction and Investments of Public Administration	47.1

Provisions Applicable to Slovakia—With a view to "equalizing progressively the economic level of the regions," the Five-Year Plan devoted a specific effort to the economic recovery of Slovakia (Art. 29). Quoted below are the three principal passages (Arts. 30, 31, and 32) of the plan in this connection:

An accelerated economic development of Slovakia will be obtained by means of a gradual transformation of its economic and social structure. This will be accomplished first of all: by continuing the country's industrialization already begun; by increasing the productivity of work in agriculture; by raising in all enterprises the rank of qualified workers, especially those necessary for developing industrial production; and by intensifying the search for all sources of natural wealth, particularly mineral beds.

Production development as well as the raising of the material and cultural level during the period covered by the Five-Year Plan will be assured:

in industry: by increasing production in such a manner that its gross product value be 75 per cent higher in 1953 than in 1948; by creating approximately ninety thousand new jobs;

in agriculture: by increasing the total agricultural production in such wise that its gross product value reach 27.4 billion crowns in 1953, or 37 per cent more than in 1948; by increasing animal production so that its gross product value exceed that of 1948 by 98 per cent, and so that its share in the total agricultural production be 42 per cent; by rationalizing agricultural production (intensification of mechanization, amelioration of soil yield and the utilization of domestic animals, rational exploitation of areas designated for pastures, and the planting of forests on land not suitable for agriculture;

in building: by increasing production so that its gross product value in 1953 attain 15 billion crowns, and by augmenting the total manpower strength by thirty-five thousand persons;

in the building of lodgings and in the social services involving both health and culture: by increasing by 3.39 million square meters the land occupied by new construction and reconstruction; by creating homes for young people, thus providing lodging for 14,500 more persons; nurseries with 2,650 beds, seasonal recreation camps for 5,000 other children and school canteens for 70,000 children; by providing 3,400 more general hospital beds and 500 beds in specialized health establishments; by creating 420 additional beds in infant centers; by creating five Calmette (anti-tuberculosis) treatment centers with 250 additional beds; by building an infantile paralysis treatment center with 100 beds; by installing 13 health centers and 86 district establishments for national health; and finally by increasing the number of classrooms by 2,080; in the domain of higher education, by completing the technical schools of Bratislava and Košice; by building a medical school at Košice, new institutes at the Bratislava School of Medicine and a School of Music at Bratislava.

To ensure the accomplishment of tasks in the production and transformation of the economic and social structure, investments will be made for a total value of 96.2 billion crowns, or 28.6 per cent of the sum provided for the whole State.

From the sum of 96.2 billion crowns, there will revert: to industry 30.9 billion, or 23.4 per cent of the sum provided for the whole State; to agriculture 9.8 billion, or 36.5 per cent; to building 1.6 billion, or 34.8 per cent; to transportation 13.6 billion, or 26.3 per cent; to the construction of lodgings 13.7 billion, or 34.9 per cent; to commerce and travel, health and social welfare, social security as well as cultural services 10.9 billion, or 32.5 per cent; to bridges and street paving, hydraulic works, public land constructions and other investments of public administration 15.3 billion, or 32.4 per cent; and to other non-specified objectives 0.4 billion, or 0.11 per cent.

Aims and Results of the Five-Year Plan—During the first stage of implementing the nationalization program (1945-1948), 199 or 63 per cent of the largest industrial enterprises in the country became State property. An additional 291 or 32 per cent of the small-to-average size industries were nationalized during the second stage. By the end of 1948 the precarious economic condition of the remaining 5 per cent of Slovakia's businesses hardly served to make their private status an enviable one.[51]

Because of a lack of opposition in Czechia nationalizations were realized more rapidly. The first stage consumed 80 per cent of the enterprises and the second, 16 per cent. At the end of 1948 only 4 per cent of the private businesses remained.

The Five-Year Plan, therefore, with strong chains pitilessly attached each individual to the enormous machine of economic statism.

If Slovakia, after the discrimination of the past, had a justifiable desire to get industrialized, the communist regime profited greatly by it in order to proletarianize it. In March, 1946, there were 123,386 workers in Slovak industry. On July 1, 1948, there were already 208,213.[52]

According to the report presented by Mr. Zápotocký at the time of the eleventh Congress of the Czecho-Slovak trade unions, which was held December 11-15, 1949 in Prague, the number of union workers before February, 1948 was 274,416 in Slovakia and 2,249,976 in Czechia. After this event, the number jumped to 508,768 in Slovakia and to 3,072,956 in the Czech countries.[53]

Since work became an inescapable obligation for the socialist community, the individual is defenseless vis-à-vis the Leviathan State. Working conditions, while fixed by law, are the exclusive domain of the leaders. The workmen had been discontented with them. As early as fall, 1949, Mr. Zápotocký had recognized that fact:

> How can it be explained that, in a number of factories, one witnesses conflicts and misunderstandings on application of the new norms and working codes? That comes from the fact that the personnel of the businesses was informed on these points neither by responsible union

[51] See the article: Ing. Jan Bušniak, "The Second Stage in the Nationalization of Industry," *Pravda*, Bratislava, (September 2, 1948).
[52] See: *Pravda*, Bratislava, (September 15, 1948).
[53] See: *Pravda*, Bratislava, (December 12, 1948).

men, nor by the management of the business; that no meeting was called; that the question was not brought to light; that it was not explained to the workmen and discussed with them. Only when the conflict broke out was the question broached. Only then was our whole array of responsible persons alarmed, and, all out of breath, in all haste, one makes up for what ought to have been done before and had been forgotten.[54]

Consequently, absenteeism or tardiness in work had been labeled as sabotage or idleness and an entire, very efficacious system of re-education in labor camps was introduced to fight them. The arbitrary prolongation of working hours, the Stakanovist system of individual exploitation founded on progressive salaries could do nothing but slowly crush the average workman. Shock troops, display squads, Sunday brigades had taken the workman from his family. And the unions, entirely dominated by Communists, degenerated from a means of defense for the working class to the instruments of its oppression. The right to strike, the workmen's privilege in any democratic system, disappeared. After the events of February, 1948, salaries were reduced by 20.55 per cent in spite of the constant rise in prices. Granted that the purchasing power of an average monthly salary scarcely satisfied the needs of the workman, the government had to organize a second price scale applicable to practically the entire population except the working class. The lower prices anticipated for them was to be offset by the exorbitant prices to which the average peasant and the "bourgeois" element of the cities were subject. When the double sector was instituted, the Prime Minister stated that it was always preferable for the State itself to collect the appreciated surplus of the parallel market rather than to leave it to the speculators. In this way the State appropriated not only the profits of the black market but also the undignified role of the "black marketer" itself.

As regards the salaries, 60 per cent of the salaried people in 1949 were receiving less than 3,000 crowns a month.[55] The average civil servant graduate of a university earned between 2,500 and 3,500 crowns. The highest salaries in the administration did not exceed 5,000 crowns.

Here, for example, are the prices, in crowns, of several articles of ready consumption at the end of 1949:[56]

[54] See: *Pravda*, Bratislava, (December 12, 1949).
[55] A crown equalled 7 francs.
[56] See: *Pravda*, Bratislava (December 1, 1949).

beef (1 kg.) 240
pork (1 kg.) 300
veal (1 kg.) 320
bacon (1 kg.) 500
lard (1 kg.) 450
butter (1 kg.) 500
sausage (1 kg.) 250
sugar (1 kg.) 160
lemons (1 kg.) 250

oil (1 kg.) 272
chocolate (1 kg.) 500
rum (1 liter) 310
radio 8,900
toilet soap (1 kg.) 300
wool blanket 6,480
suit 5,000-8,000
a pair of shoes 2,000

Since 1948 the communist regime had been exerting great effort toward breaking the peasants' resistance against an ever-increasing State economic control. The plans for sowing, for cattle raising, the obligatory cooperatives for agricultural machines, and finally, the carefully fixed "contracts" for delivery of agricultural products for each commune had taken from the peasant the last vestiges of independence. His work was to be organized and controlled by the authorities, and he was obliged to sell the fruits of his labors to the State at fixed prices.

The norms assigned to the peasants were so high that it was impossible to accomplish them. In 1949, they fulfilled only 60 per cent of their obligations. Special police commissions in charge of searching their property succeeded in collecting 20 per cent more of the products required. According to the official statistics published on December 31, 1949, the following results were obtained for the principal articles: wheat, 82 per cent; rye, 84 per cent; barley, 69 per cent; hay, 58 per cent; oil seed, 77 per cent; milk, 54 per cent; and potatoes, 69 per cent.

As an idea of the way in which the delivery norms of agricultural products had been established, let us compare them with the grain output per hectare. Peasants cultivating from 15 to 20 hectares were to produce, according to the "contracts" of January, 1950, 22 quintals of wheat per hectare annually whereas the average output in Czecho-Slovakia was only 16 quintals; the owner of from 5 to 15 hectares was to deliver 19 quintals; the owner of from 2 to 5 hectares, 17 quintals per hectare; and the one who had less than 2 hectares had to furnish 14 quintals of wheat per hectare. A cultivated hectare of land further obliged the peasant to deliver to the administration 1,000 liters of milk, 100 kilos of meat, and 500 eggs per year.[57]

In order to satisfy the impositions set by the delivery contracts, the peasant, at times finding it impossible to obtain the

[57] See: *Derrière le rideau de fer,* Paris, (January, 1950), No. 2.

quantities required from his own crops, was obliged to pay dearly for such merchandise on the black market only to give it over to the State for a very low price. Those who were incapable of furnishing the specified quantities were fined, considered saboteurs, and finally ran the risk of being deprived of their property.[58]

All these measures aimed at harrassing private farming in such a manner that its sheer upkeep at length became impossible. Gradually realizing that he was incapable of meeting the overwhelming burdens imposed upon him, the peasant finally could not help accepting the idea of becoming a mere workman in the agricultural cooperative of his village, a cooperative whose establishment was greatly favored by the regime.

The properties confiscated from "traitors," "saboteurs," *kulaks*, and the Church, were organized into State farms *(sovkhozes)* which in 1950 accounted for 1,000,000 hectares. Besides, more than 700,000 hectares had been turned over to agricultural cooperatives *(kolkhozes)*, and the peasants who still refused to participate in either were finally forced to it. The final phase of the evolution of agriculture in Czecho-Slovakia was then not difficult to foretell. The land was to be made joint property, and the peasant, uprooted from his own domain, was to become a proletarian also.

The distribution of goods had not escaped State control any more than had production.

First of all, foreign trade was attacked. And because foreign trade was a spoke in the larger wheel of international relations, all suspect elements were immediately eliminated as were all the "fifth columns of the West" and all those suspected of secretly financing foreign resistance. According to a statement issued on November 17, 1949 at the National Assembly in Prague by Mr. Dolanský, president of the Office of State Planning, the government entrusted foreign trade to twenty-nine societies, each of which was to enjoy a monopoly in its area.[59]

Then, in turn, internal wholesale commerce was nationalized. Thereby the small businessman was put at the mercy of the State, and the government did not delay in organizing cooperatives for sale and consumption. As retail dealer, it became the absolute arbiter of the existence of the little businessman. De-

[58] *Le Figaro*, Paris, (February 6, 1950), makes comments on a decision of the Czecho-Slovak authorities made on this subject.
[59] See: *Pravda*, Bratislava, (November 18, 1949).

prived of the supplies which went to the cooperatives and over-burdened with taxes, the latter, after living through a period of uncertainty and worries, was finally satisfied to be able to sell his half empty shop to the State, even at a ridiculously low price.

The results of this wisely premeditated policy which was scaled at several levels, did not fail to make itself felt. In fact, whereas at the end of 1947 the figure for private retail business represented 77 per cent of the total, it went down to only 23 per cent for the first quarter of 1949. So then the roles were entirely reversed. Private business was henceforth on its way out.[60]

The New Foreign Policy

The Kominform—From 1945 on, Soviet policy tended to group the states of eastern Europe. The basis of this group was made up of twenty-one military alliances concluded between the satellite States and the U.S.S.R. as well as between the satellite states themselves. The bilateral character of these alliances, however, did not suffice to guarantee a real cohesion of the whole. In fact, a treaty concluded between Yugoslavia and Bulgaria brought to mind the idea of a Balkan union contrary to that of a single orbit directed by Moscow. To strengthen its hold on the satellite States, therefore, the U.S.S.R. created the *Kominform* in September, 1947. It was the Kominform which became the cynosure of the internal policy as well as the foreign policy of the satellite States. Guardian of communist dogma, it became its only authentic interpreter. Appealing to community of interests, it imposed unity of command.

In a statement which Mr. Clementis made to the Parliament of Prague on December 21, 1948, he gave the following explanation of this effort by Moscow:

> In foreign policy, the aims of the States which build up socialism can not be divergent. Our unity is deeply rooted in the identity of our interests. In our international relations, we have arrived at superior forms of cooperation which, while respecting the sovereignty and interests of the individual States, facilitate our having a widespread and profound collaboration in all domains.

Czecho-Slovakia and the Russian-German Game—At the Warsaw conference, June 24, 1948, the Soviet Union took a clear

---

[60] See: P. K., "L'élimination du commerce privé en Tchéco-Slovaquie," *Journal de Genève*, (September 8, 9, 1949).

stand on the German problem. Albania (Enver Hoxha), Bulgaria (Kolarov), Hungary (Molnár), Poland (Modzelewski), Czecho-Slovakia (Clementis), Rumania (Mrs. Pauker), Yugoslavia (Šimič), and the U.S.S.R. (Molotov) took part in this conference. By way of counter-stroke to the deliberations at London of Great Britain, France, and the United States on Germany, the Soviet Union rejected the plan alluding to the constitution of a West German federation.

When in July, 1949, the London plan was realized, the Russians bid higher by instituting the popular Republic of Eastern Germany. The immediate inclusion of the latter in the Soviet political orbit constituted an extremely delicate innovation. The German problem was becoming a sore spot in the U.S.S.R's relations with Czecho-Slovakia and Poland. In fact, any kind of rapprochement with Eastern Germany advocated by the Soviet leaders was to offend the Czechs and Poles. The closer the German-Russian relations became, the less convincing was the community of interests between the Czechs and Poles on the one hand, and the Russians on the other. The telegram that Stalin sent to Grotewohl on the occasion of his election to the Presidency of East Germany in October, 1949, in which he emphasized that Germany and Russia had been the two greatest victims of World War II, was just so much cold water thrown on the "Russophile" feeling of the Czechs and Poles. East Germany is very likely called upon to play an important role on the Russian political chessboard. And so the Russo-Czech and Russo-Polish relations may dramatically reflect the efforts of the Russo-Germanic relations, and it is likely at that spot that cracks may appear in the Soviet orbit.

Relations between Prague and Budapest—As long as a National Front government uniting Communists and Democrats was in power in Hungary as well as in Czecho-Slovakia, the Slovak Communists favored a brutal solution of the Magyar minority problem in Slovakia. After February, 1948, since the Budapest and Prague governments alike were subject to Moscow, their disagreements—which were proper among nationalist reactionaries—henceforth had to lose their raison d'être in "a socialist community of nations."

To justify the new conception, Mr. Husák stated at that time:

> Our State deems it its first interest to win all the workers
> over to its policy without distinction of nationality—in-
> cluding Magyars. Our party . . . must struggle on a class

plane and not on a nationality plane. . . . The more solid
the workers' union of the different nationalities, the stronger the Slovak people will be in its struggle against the
bourgeoisie and the remains of its own capitalist reaction.[61]

The executive committee of Slovakia's Communist party,
which met on September 28 and 29, 1948, decided on the rein-
tegration of the Magyars in political life. The program which
was created to achieve that end can be briefly outlined: restitu-
tion of Czecho-Slovak nationality to the Magyars; annulment of
the confiscation of peasants' goods; opening of Magyar primary
schools in 113 communes; creation of a cultural association of
Magyar workers; creation of the weekly *Uj Szó (The New Word)*
in Magyar; creation of radio broadcasts in Magyar; publication
of Magyar books and brochures; admission of Magyars in Slovak
syndical organizations; admission of Magyars in the Communist
party; choice of Magyar anti-Fascists as members of the party
organs and syndical organizations; foundation in Prague of a
society for intensifying the cultural and economic relations with
Hungary.[62]

Beginning in January, 1949 the conditions of the Magyars
deported into Sudetenland were eased up. Those who decided
to remain in Bohemia could ask for land allocation, and those
who preferred to return to Slovakia were so authorized—their
return having to be effected between January 1 and April 30,
1949. Finally, the State promised to restore their former property.

So it is that the citizens of Magyar nationality in Slovakia,
insofar as they had not been transferred into Hungary and were
not guilty of acts contrary to the interests of the State, could again
have Czecho-Slovak nationality and consequently all the civil
and political rights pertaining thereto.

The Hungarian government, by reciprocity, granted to the
Slovaks of Hungary rights derived from their nationality: the
use of their language, education in Slovak schools, free associations and newspapers, and freedom of economic activities. The
Minister of National Education of Hungary, Mr. Ortutay, defined
explicitly the concessions made to the Slovak minority in an address made at Békescsaba on November 12, 1948. According to
him, the Slovaks were to have their primary schools, their resi-

[61] *Pravda,* Bratislava, (September 30, 1948).
[62] For points 1-10, see *Pravda,* Bratislava, (March 24, 1949). For point 11,
see *Pravda,* Bratislava, (February 12, 1949). Mr. Duriš, communist minister of agriculture in Prague, was then named president of this Society.

dent teachers' college at Békescsaba, their scholarly textbooks, and a Slovak chair in the University of Budapest.[63]

The crowning point of the Czecho-Slovak-Magyar relations was the treaty of friendship and military aid which was concluded between these two States formerly torn by innumerable demands, pretensions, and reservations. Signed in Budapest on April 16, 1949, by Premier István Dóbi for Hungary and Antonín Zápotocký for Czecho-Slovakia, this treaty contains a preamble serving as a model for the relations of all popular democracies.

Considering that the disagreements previously existing between the two States had been "deliberately provoked and fed by the leading classes to conceal the identity of the interests of the two peoples," the signers agreed to adopt for the future a policy of friendly collaboration in all domains.

The Council for Mutual Economic Assistance—The application of the Marshall Plan in Western Europe and the Titoist desertion in Yugoslavia induced the U.S.S.R. to tighten the economic ties between the coalition States. In January, 1949, the Council for Mutual Economic Assistance was created in Moscow, having as members the U.S.S.R., Albania, Hungary, Rumania, Czecho-Slovakia, Poland, and Bulgaria.

Although known under the label of "Molotov Plan," the idea and realization of this Council are attributed to Karl Claudius, the former section chief of foreign trade to the Ministry of Foreign Affairs of the Third Reich. It is known that the latter elevated himself from the status of prisoner and war criminal, to become technical advisor to Mr. Mikoyan, the Minister of Foreign Trade of the U.S.S.R. During the war, Mr. Claudius had organized commercial exchanges between the countries of southeastern Europe and the Reich, as well as a *super-clearing*, with a central office in Berlin, between all the countries of the German orbit. Moscow adopted and perfected this system. Thus was created in the Soviet bloc a vast market whose controls were held by Moscow. Just like Hitler's Germany, the U.S.S.R. had found the means to control all the economic activities in its orbit and drain the wealth from the popular democracies.

An example from Slovak textile industry makes evident this uncontested truth:

> The nationalized enterprise *Slovenka* has been producing for exportation in the U.S.S.R. men's shirts of ar-

---

[63] See: *Pravda,* Bratislava, (November 13, 1948).

tificial silk. The Russians established the price of one of these shirts at 67 or 68 crowns, depending on the size. Now a kilogram of raw material costs 220 crowns; the corresponding dyes, 60 crowns; the total expenses for implementing it comes to 120, making a sum total of 400 crowns. The enterprise uses a kilogram of raw material to produce three shirts at 201 crowns. That means then a loss of 199 crowns, or 66.33 crowns per shirt. The sale price of the same article on the internal market is from 204 to 238 crowns. So on each shirt delivered to Soviet Russia, Czecho-Slovak economy loses the sum of from 137 to 170 crowns.[64]

This example is typical of the U.S.S.R.'s economic relations with the satellite countries. In this way Russia combines considerable funds, permitting it to play the role of capitalist, as for example toward China.[65]

The meddling of Russia in the economic affairs of the satellite countries has taken on such proportions that certain economists are tempted to speak rather of internal exchanges within the confines of a bloc than of international exchanges in the classical sense of the word.[66] For instance, in practice it is Russia that swaps Rumanian corn or Czecho-Slovak shoes. In the name of political solidarity, Russia has obliged its satellites to limit their commercial relations with the countries of the West. This has resulted in an intensification of the economic movements of the Soviet orbit.

Czecho-Slovakia's trade with the U.S.S.R. and its satellites nearly doubled after 1945. The statistics of this evolution are shown below in Table 9:[67]

TABLE 9
Czecho-Slovakia's Trade with the Soviet Orbit

Year	U.S.S.R. Alone	U.S.S.R. and Satellites
1937	0.9%	15.5%
1946	12.5%	23.5%
1947	5.8%	18.1%
1948	15.8%	31.5%
1949	23.6%	45.4%

[64] See: Alojz Macek, "Some Views of Czecho-Slovak Economy," *Slovenská republika*, Buenos-Aires, (November, 1949).
[65] According to the Sino-Soviet treaty signed February 16, 1950 in Moscow, the USSR granted a loan of 300 million dollars to the China of Mao-Tsé-Tung.
[66] See: Paul Barton, "La mainmise russe sur l'économie tchéco-slovaque," *Rapports France-Etats-Unis,* Paris, (January, 1951).
[67] *Ibid.*

The communications system itself is more and more centered on Moscow. In Slovakia, the only railway line making direct connections with the U.S.S.R., i.e., Žilina-Košice-Čop, was so overladen with the great traffic of merchandise trains (ten a day in each direction) that it proved urgent to build a second track. "Volunteer" brigades worked on it day and night. In the event of conflict with the West, it should play an important role within the Soviet system of logistics.

The effort demanded of Czecho-Slovakia by Russia obliged the Prague government to modify considerably the clauses of the Five-Year Plan. Some light manufactures had to adapt to the production of heavy industry, resulting in a shortage of articles of everyday use, the rationing of foodstuffs, and the weakening of the social and economic standard of the Republic's population.

Therefore it is not astonishing that toward the end of 1950, friction was evidenced in the relations between Moscow and Prague. The attack launched on December 8, 1950, by the organ of the Kominform against the *Rudé Právo* of Prague, because of the lack of ardor in its anti-Titoist line, unveiled a tension which ordinarily Moscow tries rather to conceal.

The goal of the new economic community is in no wise to raise the standard of living of the working class, but to set going a plan of economic preparations in view of an armed confrontation with the capitalist world. Since the creation of this community, the production of the satellite countries has become a direct factor in the planning and organization of Soviet military power. Henceforth the economy of these countries is understandable only as a coefficient of the Russian economic potential.

Thus the Council for Mutual Economic Assistance, which is also called *Comecon,* is in fact an ingenious pipeline through which the wealth of the countries ideologically dependent upon Moscow is discreetly siphoned into Russia to be put into stock, pending a definitive settling of accounts with the West.

The End of "National" Communism in Slovakia

> *A quite ephemeral glory suffices the in-*
> *numerable prophets of today. They are*
> *content to seduce part of the popular*
> *masses with an eye to ensuring for them-*
> *selves privileged political or economic*
> *positions.*
> G. Husák: *The Struggle for the Future*

On the political chessboard of the Kremlin, the role of each communist personality is determined and his mission fixed in advance by the chief of the cadres of world communism. Like plants in a botanical garden, all the communist leaders are classified, given an exact label mentioning the degree of their ideological maturity, their bourgeois tastes and their nationalist tendency. All their errors are carefully noted; these can serve eventually as a pretext for the superseding of persons who become undesirable—once their mission is accomplished.

In 1945 the Slovak Communists entered the Soviet orbit with their leaders showing different degrees of Marxist maturity. Lacking masters, Moscow had to be satisfied with apprentices whose ideological descriptions varied considerably. Moscow could not be ignorant of the difference in opinions of the principal ones. All, however, were acceptable, given the importance of the task to be performed.

The Slovak Communists had at that time three representatives in the government of Prague: Mr. V. Široký, Vice-Premier; Mr. Ďuriš, Minister of Agriculture; and Mr. Clementis, Under-Secretary of State in Foreign Affairs. At Britslava, they could obtain the vice-chairmanship, and after 1948, the chairmanship of the Slovak National Council (Schmidke), the premiership of the autonomous government (Husák), as well as the commissariats of Public Education (Novomeský), Economy (Pull), Interior (entrusted to a sympathizer), Communications (Bezek), and Social Welfare (Šoltész). It is interesting to place this team of communist leaders briefly in the national political framework.

An employee of a little bank in a county seat of central Slovakia, Mr. Široký, of Magyar origin very much emphasized by his accent, joined the Communist party when he was quite young. It was then a very small party. At the elections that took place between the two wars, they were accustomed to obtaining, in this Christian country where the people were recalcitrant to an imported ideology, from six to eight deputies representing from 10 to 14 per cent of the electors. The adherents of communism were recruited especially from among the Czech elements working in Slovakia and in a milieu of exalted progressist intellectuals: Slovaks, Czechs, Magyars, and Jews. But the party was totally lacking in trained leaders. Czech Communists in these conditions were to take charge of the Slovak cells. So Mr. Gottwald himself spent several years in Slovakia (from 1921 to 1925) as editor of a regional newspaper in Vrútky. In spite of the work of these veritable missionaries, the party's manpower remained meager in Slovakia.

In 1935, the Communist party sent six deputies to the Parliament of Prague, among whom were Mr. Clementis and Mr. Široký. A skilled lawyer, able linguist, and editor-in-chief of a communist literary and political review, *Dav (The Masses)*, Mr. Clementis rapidly became one of the lights of the international congresses of the party. Mr. Široký, however, was lacking in university training and spoke only Hungarian and Slovak. Thus he devoted himself to the work of internal organization. His role in Slovak communism was to awaken the inert mass of workmen. When Mr. Clementis was conceiving of the work of the communist parties of the different countries on an equal footing, Mr. Široký believed from the beginning in the world mission of Russian communism. This explains why Mr. Clementis went to London in 1939, after Germany had become the directing power of the Danubian space, while Mr. Široký, who had taken refuge in France after the Franco-German armistice of 1940, was passing into the Soviet Union. Soon, however, realizing the great possibilities that Slovakia offered to clandestine work, Široký had himself parachuted there by the Russians. However, he quickly drew the attention of the police and was arrested. The Minister of the Interior of the Slovak Republic had him imprisoned with some other Communists partly to get rid of potential elements of trouble, partly to take from Germany any pretext to meddle in Slovak internal affairs. So Mr. Široký and his comrade Ďuriš waited in the Bratislava prison for the day of their liberation by the Red Army. When they learned that the Russians were already in central Slovakia, they had themselves taken to the public prosecutor, Vagáč, with whom they reasoned as follows:

> Soviet Russia is going to be one of the victorious powers
> of this war. Without any doubt the Germans, in withdraw-
> ing, are going to try to take us along into Germany. If you

let them do it, you will have to answer for your conduct before the courts which will be organized by the Czecho-slovak government to judge collaborators. There is a way to save us while saving yourselves: you are going to plan our flight and flee with us.

Mr. Vagáč accepted this proposition. Late in February, 1945, he had Široký and Ďuriš taken by official car into the Russian military zone. In so doing, he was far from suspecting that he was getting some very important persons out of trouble: the future head of the Slovak Communist party and the future Minister of Agriculture.

Just after the "liberation," Mr. Široký was elected chairman of the Slovak Communist party which, by reason of the special political evolution of Slovakia during the war, kept its external independence. In this capacity he became one of the four vice-premiers in the Prague government.[68] From the beginning, Mr. Široký rallied unreservedly in the direction of Moscow. What was important for him was the unity of the working class of the world and not specific national State structures.

Mr. Clementis, on the other hand, of uncontested individuality, adapted badly to Moscow's austerity. A drinker of Russian tea, he smoked English tobacco. A proletarian by political ambition more than by conviction, he had married the daughter of a banker. In 1939, at the time of the conclusion of the German-Russian pact, he criticized Moscow severely and persevered in this attitude until the German attack on the Soviet Union. His sudden change, after Russia entered the war on the side of the Allies, did not succeed in bringing him back into the good graces of the leading men of the Komintern; and while Mr. Beneš was getting back to Czecho-Slovakia in April, 1945, by passing through Moscow, Mr. Clementis preferred to return directly in order to avoid any disagreeable encounter.

Undoubtedly, Mr. Clementis was quite well chosen for the office of Under-Secretary of State in Foreign Affairs beside Jan Masaryk in the first phase of the "National Front" (1945-1948). He had shown his worth in London in the government of the exiled Beneš, and the President was eager to reward him.[69]

Mr. Ďuriš was the editor of a communist provincial newspaper in 1938. His personal fanaticism and his friendship with

[68] See: J. A. Mikus, "Viliam Široký," *Le Monde*, Paris, (March 21, 1950).
[69] See: J. A. Mikus, "Le dilemme de M. Clementis," *Le Monde*, Paris, (November 9, 1949).

Široký, with whom he had been imprisoned and then made an escape, gained for him the office of Minister of Agriculture.

Beside the three persons just mentioned, Mr. Husák, Mr. Schmidke, and Mr. Novomeský clearly kept up the appearance of "grass root Communists."

Mr. Husák was a bespectacled intellectual. During the period of the Slovak State, he quietly managed a transportation business in Bratislava, but did not decline the offer of the Slovak Minister of National Defense, Čatloš, to go see with his own eyes the Russian paradise at the time the Germans were storming Stalingrad. During the uprising, Mr. Husák expressed the wish that Slovakia be directly integrated with the U.S.S.R. and considered as the seventeenth Soviet Republic. "It must be said openly," he stated in September, 1944 at Banská Bystrica, "that our people would welcome with enthusiasm the removal of frontiers and customs between us and the other Slav nations, especially between Slovaks and Russians."[70]

Without judging his capacity as a public official, it can be said that Mr. Husák was the best newspaperman of communist Slovakia. His official duties did not keep him from managing a review, *Nové Slovo (The New Word)*, in which he commented in grandiloquent dialectics on the events of the internal and foreign policy and tried to justify his points of view and personal actions.

Mr. Schmidke, a former cabinetmaker, was originally from German Silesia. Toward the end of the war, he began to prepare communist resistance in Slovakia. At the time of the uprising, he went to Moscow to take courses in communist political strategy and tactics. In 1945, he was the first head of the autonomous government in Bratislava, then became Vice-Chairman of the Slovak National Council in 1946. Vulgar and uneducated, he was the out and out enemy of all intellectuals, a group whom he deemed unsuited for defending the interests of the working class.

As Commissioner of Public Education, Mr. Novomeský became the apostle of Marxist culture in the country of old religious and peasant tradition that Slovakia is. Under Monsignor Tiso's regime, he directed an economic weekly, *Budovateľ,* and was

[70] See: Husák, *Our Struggle for the Future,* p. 5.
   Mr. Drtina, Mr. Beneš' observer in Banská Bystrica, wrote to London, October 11, 1944: "The political evolution of the uprising was such that at the beginning the radical and war-like tendency attempted to institute a Slovak Soviet Republic."

the best paid editor in Slovakia. In Mr. Mach, the Minister of the Interior, he had at once a friend and protector. It is an open secret that, owing to Novomeský's intervention, Mach, judged at the same time as Monsignor Tiso in 1947, was condemned by the National Tribunal of Bratislava to only thirty years of prison.

Mr. Holdoš, deputy of the Communist party, and a former member of the International Brigade during the civil war in Spain, was a specialist in purges. He it was who in the summer of 1947 launched a violent campaign against the former Slovak Democratic party. He counted on firm friendships in the Communist party in France and other Western countries.

Mr. Štefan Bašťovanský, Secretary-General of the Communist party of Slovakia, was likewise one day going to be called upon to play an important role after 1948. Before World War II, he was a railway employee and a member of the left wing of the Social-Democrat party. Široký's tool, he too was known as the conceiver and preacher of ideas that were violently hostile to capitalism and the Western World.

Mention must also be made here of the "gray eminence" of the Slovak Communist party, Mr. Edo Frisch. This highly sophisticated Israelite was the head of the press in Slovakia. Having spent the World War II years in Moscow, Mr. Frisch was certainly one of the most orthodox disciples of Marxism-Leninism. That is why he was also one of the most virulent agents of the Kominform in Slovakia.

These persons represented the elite of the proletariat of Slovakia. When, overnight, the communist administration of the country imprisoned "collaborators," "Fascists," "enemies of the people," "the fifth columnists of the West," and put their families out onto the street by taking their house or apartment without concern for their lot, they themselves obtained very fine, completely furnished residences that had been confiscated. Clementis, for instance, went to Prague to live in the former twenty-four room villa of the banker Petschek. His Bratislava comrades were not far behind him in luxury, of which one of the indispensable elements was the most modern of American cars.

Never had the capitalist regime concentrated a greater power in the hands of an oligarchy as limited. Real and personal property, security, liberty, and the fate of a nation depended henceforth on these arbiters. It was enough for one of them to indicate a wretched "pollice verso," and no law or action whatsoever could save him. The administrative Supreme Court itself, again an outworn institution in the regime of the popular democracy, could not but obey the least whim of these potentates.

All these leaders of the proletariat henceforth had their court. It is they who gave to society its new character. They made up a new nobility, having its customs, parties, and receptions. These new rich surrounded themselves with luxury which had no relation to what could be expected from "sons of the people" and rugged defenders of social equality. While the entire country was plunged in a poverty until then unknown, they had special food supplies as well as shoe and textile tickets.

The first task that Moscow and Prague entrusted to the Slovak Communists was the liquidation, under pretext of fascism, of a formidable political opposition.

Once this mission was accomplished, the Slovak Communist party, dreaming of an exclusive power in Slovakia, joined in the effort that Prague had been making since 1946; the hope was first to weaken and then liquidate the Slovak Democratic party, under the pretext of separatism. It was Mr. Holdoš who, as chairman of the Commission of Immunities at the National Assembly in Prague, effected in conjunction with the Czech democratic parties the lifting of the parliamentary immunity for the Vice-Premier, Mr. Ursíny, a Slovak democrat, as well as for three deputies from the Catholic wing of the same party, Messrs. Kempný, Staško, and Bugár. All four of them, under pretext of the discovery of a colossal conspiracy, were imprisoned between October and December, 1947, with 2,000 other Slovaks.

Supported as it was by all Czech parties, this maneuver of the Communists against the Slovak Democrats constituted a veritable coup d'état. Thus, although representing only 30 per cent of the electors, the Communists succeeded in destroying their adversaries who represented 62 per cent of the electoral votes of Slovakia. Broken by this blow, the Democratic party never got back on its feet.

Moscow had given the Slovak Communists two years to break the instinctive resistance which reigned in their country against communist theories and practices and to establish the order exacted by the Kominform. In spite of their efforts, the results were meager. The Communist party in Slovakia was able to win only 169,297 members and 67,135 candidates. Moscow compared these results with those obtained in the Czech countries, where the party numbered 2,064,000 members. Those responsible had to be sought out and punished.

Široký's role on this score was preponderant. The latter, devoid of all national background, initially represented the Stalinist tendency within the Slovak Communist party which, on his proposal, fused on September 28, 1948 with the Czech Communist party. Against the nationalist elements, Široký then defended centralism on the party plane as well as on the State plane. But he went further still: in international politics, he consistently preached obedience to Moscow. He became a member of all the important committees of the party from the broadest to the most limited. He it was who went off to Moscow to take Stalin, for his seventieth birthday, the gifts and best wishes of President Gottwald, the government, and "all the Czech and Slovak workers." So it was that he was the confidence man in Prague as in Moscow.

Quite different was Clementis' situation. Since the formula of the National Front had been replaced in 1948 by the dictatorship of the Communist party, this former collaborator of Beneš became undesirable. As early as February, 1949, when he was Minister of Foreign Affairs, he was surrounded by four Under-Secretaries of State (Hajdu, London-Gerhard, Geminder, and Mrs. Sekaninová), at least three of whom were of "Kominform leanings." At the same moment began a carefully gauged weeding out in the Ministry of Foreign Affairs. While Mr. Clementis was pronouncing violent tirades in New York against the policy of the Western powers, he was losing his own battle in Prague. Despite several warnings, he left Lake Success for Prague in the middle of December, 1949. At the station, his rival Široký, already victorious, was waiting for him. His political career was not to last but several months more. On March 14, 1950, he "asked" Prime Minister Zápotocký to release him from his duties as Minister of Foreign Affairs. From then on, he was a captive of the regime.

A month later, it was the turn of the communist leaders of Bratislava. It is fitting here to recall the succession of events which culminated in their fall.

On the night of April 13, 1950, Czech policemen surrounded the convents of the Slovak capital to deport the religious. The inhabitants of the neighboring villages became alerted and rushed to the besieged city to demonstrate their opposition to Prague's severe measures. Mr. Husák, the chairman of the autonomous government of the country and Commissioner for Ecclesiastical Affairs, was totally ignorant of the orders given by Prague. He called the Board of Commissioners together and did not hesitate to protest against the proceedings then in progress, so completely opposed to the psychology of the people and to Slovakia's particular conditions. He was immediately suspended from his duties, along with Mr. Novomeský, the Commissioner of Public Education.

On May 24, the Slovak section of the Communist party organized its Ninth Congress in Bratislava. This was Mr. Široký's opportunity to bring action against the "deviationists" and the "bourgeois nationalists."[71] Addressing 2,000 delegates, he asked:

> In what is bourgeois nationalism manifested in our party? In that it deems the national question essentially as a problem that is isolated, separated from class strife. . . . In the leadership of our party, the nationalists have a tendency to isolate Slovakia from the Czech working class, Czech progressive forces and the general current of socialist edification. In the Slovak section of the Communist party, the nationalists try to oppose, with bureaucratic machinery, the influence of the government of the Republic, and prevent the realization of its directives in Slovak political and economic life.

He then attacked Clementis violently:

> After the conclusion of the Russian-German pact in 1939—a pact which was of great importance for progressive humanity, since it detroyed the base, cowardly plans of the Anglo-American imperialists—Mr. Clementis took his position for the class enemies against the Soviet Union. He persevered in this attitude during the Soviet-Finnish conflict and the liberation of the western Ukraine and Byelorussia by the Soviet army. In London, Mr. Clementis was in the tow of the bourgeois emigration grouped around President Beneš, and his activities on the London radio, at the Slovak club and in the press, developed along the lines of bourgeois ideology, even after his return to Czechoslovakia at the time when he was Under-Secretary of State and later Minister of Foreign Affairs. His activities at the Ministry in Prague provoked just criticisms.

Next came Husák's turn. Mr. Široký declared that the latter was exaggerating the resistance to "Prague's centralism," that it was a "reactionary and counter-revolutionary" struggle . . . a struggle against the Czechoslovak working class, against its effort toward the setting up of socialism. . . . Mr. Široký continued:

> As regards the building up of socialism, a strong planned economy directed from a single center is the con-

[71] See: *Pravda,* Bratislava, (May 25, 1950).

dition of the success of the industrialization program of Slovakia. This essential difference between two aspects of centralism (that is to say constitutional and economic) can escape only those who get caught in the ideology of bourgeois nationalism and try to confuse reality by raising juridical questions of competence which, in a socialist regime, lost their raison d'être.

At Novomeský's address, Mr. Široký said among other things:

> School administration is concerned with the increase in the number of schools and pupils, but not with putting the school in the service of socialist edification and the Marxist-Leninist theory. In the setting up of the school system, a liberalism is manifest which leaves the door open to different ideological tendencies as well as to the enemy influences of our popular democracy.

As for Mr. Schmidke, the chairman of the Slovak National Council, Široký declared that he was not up to his job and that his deviation was the more serious because it was a question of a workman's having taken specialized courses in communist training in Moscow.

After Mr. Široký's indictment, there followed spectacular self-criticisms by those accused. Clementis recognized his failure at a time of hard testing for the international labor movement; at a time when Anglo-American imperialism was striving to turn the aggressive force of fascist Germany against Soviet Russia. But this statement was destined for the public at large; the real cause of Clementis' disgrace was elsewhere. In fact, leaning on Mr. Beneš' radicalism vis-à-vis the Germans and Magyars, Clementis, after 1945, had been too rigid in the solution of the problem of the Magyar minority in Slovakia. His fall marked the triumph of Mr. Rákósi, the Vice-Premier of Hungary, in a duel which went back to 1946.

Husák acknowledged having sided with the Slovak bourgeoisie and reaction elements against Prague between 1945 and 1948, and having thus contributed to the weakening of the unity and single direction of the State. He said:

> The Gottwald government has not been able to intervene efficaciously against the Slovak reaction because I defended the jurisdiction of the national organs. The exaggerated importance which I attributed to the national question, the struggles for vested rights, and my attitude toward the Constitution awakened doubts, caused uncertainty to be born in the Slovak workmen, and provoked

distrust with respect to the Czech nation and its working class.[72]

Husák acknowledged further that his "equalitarian" attitude with respect to Prague had been an error. As Premier of Slovakia's autonomous government he had attempted unduly to defend the prerogatives of the national executive against any encroachment of Prague, forgetting the preponderous importance of the working class, in the Republic and outside. Further, Husák's attitude in the very course of the "coup d'état" of February, 1948 in Prague could not escape Gottwald. In fact, his temptation to turn at that time to Moscow and not to Prague was such that he had the telephone communications between Prague and Bratislava interrupted for six hours. If the Gottwald plan had not succeeded so rapidly, Husák would have proclaimed Slovakia a Soviet Republic. By such a decision he would have won the sympathies of Moscow and affirmed his position in Slovakia; but the opportunity for that was now lost forever.

As to Mr. Novomeský, he acknowledged during his self-criticism having strayed from the logic of Marxism-Leninism:

> I thought that our importance as Slovak Communists would grow in terms of the energy with which we should be able to fight for the executive power in Slovakia. I did not understand that in so acting we were going to contribute to the strengthening of the anti-communist positions of our non-communist partners. In this way we took our stand on the ideological platform of the bourgeoisie, and in actual fact we permitted the bourgeoisie to carry on clandestine intrigues, then to fight openly against us.[73]

Novomeský's tragedy is very special. In fact, in the preface that he wrote for *Our Struggle for the Future,* a book that Mr. Husák published in 1948, he stated word for word:

> It is superficially said that revolutions devour their children. It is not true! The truth is at the very most that revolutions, having decided to remain faithful to their program, get rid of those of their children who would like to distort their meaning, their program, their goal.

Did Novomeský then betray the communist revolution in Slovakia? No. But he was mistaken about its meaning. As regards the uprising of 1944, the political aims of Moscow were very different from those of the local Communists. Novomeský

[72] See: *Pravda,* Bratislava, (May 27, 1950).
[73] *Ibid.*

had had the naïeveté to believe that the Russian parachutists of Kiev had come to help the Slovak Communists in their struggle against the "reaction." In reality, however, the Slovak Communists served no other purpose in the uprising than the extension of Moscow's designs.

The party's Congress accepted the self-criticism of Husák and Novomeský, but rejected those of Clementis and Schmidke. The premiership of Slovakia's autonomous government was then entrusted by Gottwald to a Czech Communist, Mr. Bacílek, a mechanic. Mr. Holdoš was put in charge of the Commissariat for Ecclesiastical Affairs.

For the Slovak Communists, this event was the beginning of their end—a destiny which was inexorably approaching. In December, 1950, Prague was to answer before Moscow for the irregularities in the delivery of industrial products to the U.S.S.R. To save his situation, Gottwald deemed it necessary to appease the Kominform by sacrificing the Slovak Communists, a fact which explains the arrest, in February, 1951 of Clementis, Husák, Novomeský, and Schmidke; as well as Okáli, Commissioner of the Interior; Šoltész, Commissioner of Internal Trade; Holdoš, Commissioner of the Office for Ecclesiastical Affairs; Horváth, Minister Plenipotentiary of Czecho-Slovakia in Budapest, and others. Such a sacrifice could but please Moscow. Were the Slovak Communists not defending with undue severity the acquired rights of Slovakia, its political individuality, the competence of its autonomous organs? Were they not living too much in the memory of the Slovak State? If they desired to maintain this State in the frame of the Republic, was it not that they had lost faith in a victory of the U.S.S.R. in an eventual conflict with the West, and was not their conduct in this respect a tacit conspiracy with the Slovaks in exile and with the capitalist world in general? The trial against Commander Žingor (October 18 to October 21, 1950) before the State Tribunal in Bratislava, could not but considerably strengthen the suspicions of Stalin in regard to all Slovak Communists. This former Communist, when interrogated in the courtroom on the subject of the political aims of his group, openly stated: "I also thought that in the future, Slovakia would have an independent position within a federation of Central Europe." Before these realities and doubts, Moscow could but give its consent to the measures taken by Prague.

In liquidating the Slovak Communists, Prague in reality liquidated the idea of the Czecho-Slovak State. Between 1945 and

1947, Mr. Beneš had destroyed the leaders of Catholicism, the foremost political force in Slovakia. In the course of the 1948 crisis, the Slovak Communists, with the support of the Czech Communists and Democrats, crushed the Slovak Protestants like Lettrich and Ursíny. Prague had finally suppressed the last political prop of the Czecho-Slovak State in Slovakia: the Communists.[74] The Fourth Czecho-Slovak Republic died therefore as the national State of the Czechs and Slovaks. A socialist Soviet State emerged.

The events in Slovakia of April and May, 1950, as well as of February, 1951, had on the internal plane a consequence of capital meaning: they consolidated the resistance of the Slovak people against Moscow imperialism and Czech patronage. In this two-fold attitude, the former partisans of the Slovak State were in agreement with the Communists à la Husák. "Alone the presence of important forces, charged with maintaining order, forbade the Slovaks an armed resistance against the policy of the central government," Roger de Craon-Poussy affirmed in *Etudes*.[75]

This evolution proves that in popular democracies the communist leaders are not the representatives of their electors, even when they think they are, but mere puppets whose strings are pulled by Moscow. After Gomulka, Rajk, Kostov, and many others, the Slovak protagonists on the world communist chessboard became "lewd vipers."

The great dupe of all these maneuvers is the hard-working people of the popular democracies. When they think they are electing their deputies and ministers, Moscow takes their place. As for the Communists in the countries that are still free, they have no assurance that their lot will be different from that of Rajk, Kostov, or Clementis. And if the macabre career of some gladiators of Stalin and his successors *(Ave Caesar, morituri te salutant!)* can be considered as a purely internal affair of world communism, the fate of peoples led on by naïve leaders must attract the attention of the still free world. To be sure, the communist leaders can not be prevented from throwing themselves over the precipice if they so desire, but their activity becomes a crime against humanity as soon as they impel the peoples to drown in the Soviet sea. To enlighten the masses on this point is a *must* of democracy in a free world.

---

[74] See Appendix XI.
[75] "L'Eglise catholique et l'Etat communiste en Tchéco-Slovaquie," *Etudes*, Paris, (December, 1949).

CONCLUSION

FOR A FREE SLOVAKIA IN A
FEDERATED EUROPE

A Hundred Years of Federalism Fails in
Central Europe

The land mass encompassed by the North Sea and the Mediterranean and stretching between Germany and Russia contains numerous political elements which differ ethnically, religiously, and psychologically. Such a differentiation has always considerably weakened the political value of that region. This alone explains why the Turks could dominate the Balkans as well as the Danube Valley for a century and a half. It also explains why the later Central Europe could be looked upon as "vital space" by Germanic, then by Russian imperialism.

If, during the nineteenth century, the absence of any broader policy concerning Central Europe's and the Balkans' problems was disturbing, the lack of political wisdom of the greatest state-formation of that area, Austria-Hungary, was disastrous. On several occasions, clear-sighted souls tried in vain in each of the nations of Central Europe to put political leaders on their guard. In this respect one may name for the Czechs such men as Palacký, Rieger, and Masaryk; for the Magyars, Széchenyi and Eötvös; for the Slovaks, Ľudovít Štúr, Štefan Marko Daxner and Milan Hodža; for the Serbs, Svetozár Miletič; and for the Rumanians, Aurel C. Popovici, famed for his book, *Die Vereinigten Staaten von Gross-Österreich*, which contained a penetrating analysis of the problems of the Austro-Hungarian Empire. In summarizing the situation, one can say that the history of Austria-Hungary after 1848 was but a succession of missed opportunities for giving a federal structure to the Monarchy.

In politics, the art of organizing consists in knowing how to combine several forces with an eye to working for a common interest. The Austro-Hungarian statesmen, however, did not succeed in distinguishing local from general interests. To be sure, the Austro-Hungarian dualism of 1867 had caused the antagonism between Vienna and Budapest to be forgotten. Nevertheless, the opposition of the Czechs and Poles to Vienna on one

hand, of the Croats, Rumanians as well as the Slovaks to Budapest on the other, had lost nothing of its violence. The political
forces engaged in this multilateral struggle considerably weakened the very idea of the Austro-Hungarian State, and at the first
opportunity, they reduced its power to nothing.

Central Europe, after experiencing an overextended centralization following 1848, was to fall into political and economic disintegration after 1918. Austria-Hungary was then replaced by
six successor States. Far from working for a common political and
economic consolidation, these States had disputes as interminable
as they were sterile, ranging from territorial questions to psychological complexes. These political differences caused the failure of those plans which aimed at the creation in Central Europe
of a vaster economic space based on preferential tariffs (the
Hantos plan—the Tardieu plan—the plan for agrarian union advocated later by Mr. Hodža).

The vital forces of the Danubian States, mutually paralyzing
each other by violent struggles, thus let themselves be eliminated
as European political factors. As for Mr. Beneš' Little Entente—
with its anti-Magyar, anti-Austrian and anti-Polish tendency—
it perhaps succeeded for a time in counterbalancing the inferior-
ity complex of its creator, but it constituted a serious obstacle to
the political consolidation of Central Europe.

From 1918 to 1938, the new States of East-Central Europe
were like the proverbial closed basketful of crabs. Each one of
them was dreaming up liberty, security, and even justice in its
own fashion, and it must be acknowledged that the discord and
lack of collaboration between the Danubian States and Poland
greatly encouraged Hitler to lay hold of them, whether by pure
and simple annexation as was the case with Austria, whether by
the establishment of a protectorate as he did with Bohemia and
Moravia, whether by military defeat as was his technique in
Poland, or whether by the political and military alignment of
which Hungary, Rumania and Slovakia were the victims.

The history of Central Europe after World War I proves the
danger of an exaggerated political independence and complete
scorn for questions of security. All the States located in this part
of the world wanted to remain independent one from the other,
and they did not see, in their political near-sightedness, that this
attitude would inevitably lead them one after the other into becoming German satellites.

During his exile in London, Mr. Beneš agreed for the first time with the Polish government regarding the creation of a Polono-Czecho-Slovak federation. But always the opportunist, turning later toward the U.S.S.R., he himself destroyed this project by concluding at Moscow on December 12, 1943, a treaty of friendship, aid, and collaboration with Stalin.

After the defeat of Germany, the political status of the States of East-Central Europe did not change. Moscow was merely substituted for Berlin, and the Slav nations remained as before the satellites of a country more powerful than themselves.

The lesson of this sad experience is clear. The mutual struggles of all the nations of East-Central Europe paralyzed the best of their spiritual and material forces that should have been used for the realization of higher goals. These struggles, with all the divisions and antagonism that they engendered, facilitated the coming of nazism, then communism, their brutal invasion in the Danubian basin and the complete subjection of the same. It is obvious that the disunion of these nations and their individualistic stubbornness could not logically end in anything save their enslavement.

This is the political reality that must be faced in looking at the future. This it is, too, that makes it necessary to seek remedies and study the reforms necessary.

The Criterion for Future Organization

If one wonders what criterion could serve as the basis for the organization of Central Europe, one must first of all examine those that dispute the ground: State-power criterion and the ethnical criterion.

Statism is a mechanical system, imposed by force and from above, which seeks its supreme justification in the status quo, in the continuity of the established power. It is a system which claims to justify itself by prescription. In a word, it is legitimism in time and space.

In the theory of law, it relies upon juridical positivism. Its fundamental error consists in wanting to apply to political—and thereby dynamic—phenomena, old patrimonial rules of inherited or vested rights.

Statism on the practical plane, and juridical positivism on the doctrinal plane have separated themselves from morals, a fact which makes it possible for them to carry on vast Machiavellian maneuvers on their respective terrains. For example, statism has no scruple in sacrificing to the "reason of State" important internal or international minorities. Often, not being able to lean upon the spontaneous will of an important part of the population, it strives to maintain itself by expedients such as a law on the protection of the state which annuls in practice all the constitutional liberties of a minority. It also happens that it had to strive to dissimulate by a Messianism in space its tendencies to domination.

It is not necessary to expand further on this phenomenon to be able to state that such an antidemocratic and reactionary criterion cannot lead to any stable solution whatsoever. It substitutes form for substance. Since the state is only an historically determined form of the life of a nation, it would not be reasonable in the hierarchy of values, to place this form above substance. The bottle is made for wine and not the wine for the bottle, and a stock of empty bottles does not constitute a wine cellar. Applied to society, this idea has been admirably expressed by the Reverend Father Riquet. Speaking of world organization in a sermon which he delivered March 27, 1949 at Notre Dame in Paris, he stated virtually: "A heap of dead cells does not make a living body."

The international community must not be a museum of inert political formulas resembling the Grevin Museum in Paris or Mrs. Tussaud's in London, but a society of living collective individualities.

History teaches us that states that followed one another in the course of centuries in the space of Central Europe were never stable constructions. The cause for this is clear: the political convulsions which shake this sector periodically are due precisely to a struggle between national individualities and states. In this space, any nation having succeeded in building itself into a state has always used power to impose its national—that is to say ethnical—hegemony on other nations. The political history of East-Central Europe is actually but a constant struggle between oppressed national individualities—rightly wanting to become states —and composite states which, through police power, keep minorities or whole nations in their dependency. Yet this struggle of statism has proved to be vain. History has in fact proved that a nation of Central Europe, however small it be, never abdicates its individuality in favor of another neighboring nation, whatever be the assimilatory efforts of the latter and whatever be the reason evoked to justify this effort in the eyes of the world.

At the same time that nations are proven historical constants, so are they the most authentic elements of political ontology. They constitute a pure functional essence which, in the course of two thousand years of European history, has proven itself to be one of the most solid pillars of a determined political and juridical organization. This essence provides therefore materials capable of permitting the building of an unshakable construction in the political order. It is in the coordination of nations in a federative frame, and not in their superposition and subordination in state-power structures, that resides the only chance of consolidating East-Central Europe. It is likewise the federative solution which will be the most efficacious for the defense of the rights of man. Jean Buchmann, in an article entitled "Doctrine politique de la démocratie sociale-chrétienne,"[1] rightly states that the nineteenth century has proclaimed the freedom of the individual, but has destroyed the freedom of the communities. And he continues: "The danger for personal freedom does not come from many strong groups, but from the predominance of one of them: what is to be feared is not the strong group but the single group."

Thus the problem of human liberty and the rights of man can be solved only hand in hand with a just regulation of the relationship between groups, and one notes that the twentieth century is dominated by a struggle for collective freedoms, whether national or only pertaining to minorities, by a struggle for the universalization of liberty.

The solution for all the nations of Central Europe will not be in statism, which has already failed so many times, but in federalism. Mr. Buchmann phrased the problem in these words:

> The real solution consists in the recognition of this pluralism of communities, in their reality and in their very finality, incarnating positive freedoms generative of autonomous and hierarchized juridical orders, and in the recognition of this autonomy as high as possible on the institutional plane. This means a decentralization and an organic representation.[2]

Some political personalities admit the national criterion with certain reservations. They believe that the strict application of

---

[1] Published in the report from "La semaine d'études" of Luxembourg, (July 24-31, 1948).
[2] *Ibid.*

the ethnical criterion would bring another weakening of Central Europe.

This opinion is false. Evolution can not permit itself to be blocked in mid-stream. Every nation aspires to justice, that is, to a proper political status, controllable from an international point of view. Such is the exact meaning of the law of self-determination of peoples. Its application, it is true, will bring a certain regrouping of the political structure not only of Europe but also of other continents. It will entail splits in the existing structures and the downfall of certain colonial empires and historical statisms. This evolution, however, is very natural and it would be erroneous to consider it as the origin of all the ills of humanity.

Against Masaryk the politician, who left the right road after 1918, it is fitting to quote here the ideas expressed by Masaryk the philosopher in his book, *The New Europe*:

> The problem of small nations and states is the same as the problem of the so-called small man; what matters is that the value of the man, the individuality of the man, is recognized without regard to his material means. This is the proper sense and kernel of the great humanitarian movement which characterizes modern times. . . . Modern humanitism recognizes the right of the weak; that is the meaning of all efforts for progress and for the recognition of human dignity; the strong will always help himself; the protection of the weaker and the weak, the protection of the small, of the individual, of corporations and classes, of nations and states—that is the task of modern times. Everywhere the weak, oppressed and exploited unite themselves; association is the watchword of our era: federation, the free federation of small nations and states will be the consummation of this principle securing the final organization of the whole of mankind.[3]

The uneasiness of our time resides in the absence of a world juridical order. The fundamental need of humanity consists in suppressing the jungle and no longer limiting the number of wolves. It is not the number of states in the world which is unfortunate; it is their anarchical relationships. Little does it matter that there be seventy or a hundred and twenty states if there is no world authority that can settle their differences according to the needs of the general interest. On a smaller scale the same applies to Central Europe. Little does it matter that two or three more national units are called upon to participate in its organization,

[3] Masaryk, *The New Europe*, pp. 25-26.

provided that this finally becomes a reality. But, whatever the circumstances, it will necessarily be based on the equality of the rights and obligations of all the participating nations. The celebrated Czech historian of the nineteenth century, František Palacký, expressed this idea in the following manner:

> For a union to be solid and lasting that groups several different nations into one political whole, not any one nation must have any reason to fear that this union will deprive it of any of its dearest possessions, but on the contrary each one must have the hope of finding in the central power defense and protection against possible infringements of its neighbors beyond the equality line; at that time each one will exert itself to endow this central power with a force such that it can assume the aforesaid protection with success.[4]

The principle of equality must inspire not only the organization of the legislative power of the member states of the federation, but also the general meaning of its policy. Further, it is rather the principle of proportional equality, slightly modified in favor of the little nations, that will have to be applied, for no nation however powerful could, for the stability of the whole, raise itself to where the interests of all the federated nations must converge. The faults committed in this respect in the old Austria-Hungary must warn against such attempts.

There is no doubt that a federation founded on the system of the plurality of nations can oppose effectively any attempt to upset its equilibrium from within or without, and that the principle of equality and mutual control will be the means of establishing an international democratic order in Central Europe.

_____

The preceding theoretical considerations permit the setting up of a practical table for the future federation of Central Europe. To avoid any superposition of nationalisms, it will be necessary to include the following countries: Albania, Austria, Bulgaria, Croatia, Czechia, Esthonia, Hungary, Latvia, Lithuania, Poland, Rumania, Serbia, Slovakia, Slovenia. Further, this federation will have to take in the Ukraine and Byelorussia which, although not geographically belonging to Central Europe in the strict sense of the word, have for a long time been making efforts

[4] Letter to the *Vorparlament* of Frankfurt in 1848, in Beneš, *Où vont les Slaves?* p. 266.

to rid themselves of the Soviet Union's hold on them; and if the Constitution of Stalin—which assures the nations of the U.S.S.R. of the right of self-determination, going as far as complete separation—were not a document of pure form, these two nations would already be free of the Russian regime, secret police and concentration camps.

Outside of the foreign totalitarian danger, another consideration pleads in favor of the federalization of Central Europe: the necessity of an interior consolidation of this region. Certain territories that have been coveted for centuries by several neighbors have made impossible the establishment of a stable political order in Central and Balkan Europe. Such was the case of Macedonia that the Serbs, Bulgarians, Greeks and Albanians disputed; Transylvania, whose territory, peopled sporadically with Rumanians and Hungarians, could not be divided between Hungary and Rumania in accord with the ethnical principle. Sub-Carpathian Ruthenia, claimed by the Ukrainians, the Magyars and, curiously enough, the Czechs, was in a similar position. Likewise, the carboniferous basin of Upper Silesia was a bone of contention between Germany and Poland; and the coal region of Těšín, between the Czechs and Poles.

All these territories ought to be built into particular political units or be endowed with a certain autonomy and international individuality, a solution which would eliminate differences and permit an efficacious European control of these sore points.

If its structure were thus reshaped on a regional plane, it would be much easier to integrate Central Europe in the European federation, considered the "categorical must" of the old continent.

The Slovak National Individuality and Its Federative Value[5]

In spite of having been tossed about for a long time from one domination to another, Slovakia presents today to the objective observer a well-defined personality.

From the geographical point of view, it is a Danubian country. Consequently, it does not form a unity with Bohemia, whose principal river, the Elbe, empties into the North Sea.[6] Even in

---

[5] See: J. A. Mikus, "Les Slovaques, un peuple et une nation," in *L'Age Nouveau*, Paris, (January, 1951).

[6] It is therefore impossible to speak of "the geographical bases of Czecho-Slovak unity" as does Mr. Jacques Ancel, who wants to save his thesis

the valley of the Danube, it has a specific character. Slovakia, unlike Hungary, is an especially mountainous territory, a fact which gives it a distinctive economic value. Its industry is much more advanced than that of the Magyar plain. Its mines, forests, waters—water power reserves—open up broad perspectives for development.

From the historical point of view, the Slovaks have had a different evolution from that of the Czechs. Their relations in the past, although frequent, have been none other than neighborly ones between Slav nations.

From the spiritual standpoint, the Slovaks possess a mentality all their own. Since the Slovaks are located at the center, so to speak, of the Slav world, they are with regard to the Czechs (a psychologically Nordic nation) a southern people.[7] Whereas the Czechs drink beer, a fact which makes them closer to the Germans, the Slovaks drink wine. With the latter, the exterior manifestations, the gestures are easy, spontaneous, lacking the heaviness and excess of braininess which characterize the Czechs. More than anything else, the psychology, the manner of thinking and acting constitute the principal criteria of their individuality.

The language only emphasizes the national Slovak personality among the Slav peoples. Codified by the work of Anton Bernolák and Ľudovít Štúr at the end of the eighteenth and during the first half of the nineteenth centuries, Slovakia has produced in the course of the last two centuries a literature that has affirmed its individuality with respect to Czech literature as well as to other Slav literatures. Slovak writers have produced works of value which can bear comparison with those of the other peoples of Central Europe.[8]

In cultural matters the Slovak nation relies now on a coherent and complete school system which includes, besides elementary and secondary schools, two universities, several teachers' colleges, a school of agronomy, a polytechnic school, a school of economic sciences, a conservatory of music, an academy of arts and sciences (*Academia scientiarum et artium slovaca*) which fulfills in Bratislava a mission of first-rate research, while the *Matica slovenská* continues to accomplish its henceforth histori-

ingeniously by saying that it is "variety which makes the unity" of Czecho-Slovakia. See Mr. Ancel's introduction to B. Mirkine-Guetzevitch's book, *La Tchécoslovaquie*, pp. 6-7.
[7] See: Mikus, "Les Slovaques un peuple et une nation," *ibid.*
[8] Milo Urban's novel, *Živý bič*, (The Living Whip), has been translated into five European languages.

cal, even though somewhat diminished, task. Thanks to this system, Slovakia is now in a position to assimilate all the modern manifestations of European culture.

Slovakia can effectively contribute to the formation of the federation of Central Europe, or just Europe, through its contribution of values which characterize its genius beyond all question. Among others, two can be given on the spiritual plane: religious feeling and the national idea.

In the course of the history of the Slovaks, religious feeling has constituted an extraordinary force of internal stability. The Slovaks, in fact, have never aspired to a particularist, national, more or less "orthodox," more or less Slav religion. Still less have they been atheists, for atheism after all is but a form of moral subjectivism. Their Catholicism has remained intact in spite of Czech Hussism, the German Reformation, Magyar Calvinism or Russian orthodoxy. All these heterodox tendencies have always run up against the unshakable faith of the Slovaks, who are persuaded that religion and morals are above both individuals and nations. They are persuaded likewise that the universal moral is the most efficacious protection of the weak—individual or nation—against any excess of strength.

The second element of stability of the Slovak people is the national idea. The Slovaks have, as a matter of fact, a deep feeling of patriotism completely devoid of any sort of chauvinism or intolerance vis-à-vis the neighboring nations. Even in the epoch when romanticism was leading the Magyar poet Petöfi and the German philosopher Hegel to aberrations of subjectivist exaltation, the Slovak genius remained perfectly well balanced. "He who is worthy of liberty knows how to appreciate the liberty of others," said the great Slovak romantic poet, Ján Kollár. The Slovak national idea, therefore, respects all other national ideas. The Slovak people, however, has always distrusted the various messianisms that have successively sprung up all around: the historical Hungarian messianism, the Czech anthropocentric humanism that served especially to conceal Mr. Beneš' maneuvers, German national-socialism, and lastly, the socialistic lie of communism. The Slovak has remained inflexible in the principles which historically make up his spiritual grandeur.

On the political plane, the Slovak people distinguishes itself by its sense of realities. Mountain dwellers accustomed to the changing forms of the terrain and to the caprices of the climate, the Slovaks follow attentively the curve of the evolution of events and are far from subscribing to fictions or "Don Quixotisms." When the ground is stony, when it is full of holes, it is regrettable for the cultivator, but he knows that all this must be taken into account. The Slovaks envision all problems in the same realistic manner, a fact that keeps them from being the victims of their own illusions and ensures good foundations to their construction.

Religious sentiment and realist patriotism indubitably have an international importance. In effect, it is in the conciliation at the same time of the general and the particular that there subsists the possibility of reconstructing the liberty, not only of Slovakia, but also the other enslaved peoples of East-Central Europe, and reestablishing the political equilibrium of all Europe.

From all these general affirmations, one conclusion is drawn: it is out of place to wish to minimize the Slovak problem by comparing it to the Alsatian, Basque, Breton, or Walloon problems that have sprung up around three great civilizations—French, Spanish, and German—or in contact with two of them. Slovakia is a marginal phenomenon neither of Hungarian statism nor of Czech culture. Nor is it any the more a formula of transition between two different civilizations. Only ignorance or bad faith could lead to such an interpretation. The Slovak nation is a reality, an historical constant which not only has survived since the ninth century all the political transformations of Central Europe, but which, according to C. A. Macartney, has been able to declare itself recently "as a new factor of the Danubian situation."[9]

After experiencing Magyar and Czech domination and German and Soviet totalitarianisms, the Slovaks want at last to be themselves and become not a dark corner of Budapest or Prague policy, but a valid link in a European federative system.

The Slovaks in the Free World

Faced with the evolution which ended in the Marshall Plan on the economic plane, in the Council of Europe on the political, and in the Atlantic Pact on the military plane, the Slovaks realize that the little states of Central Europe (Hungary, Yugoslavia, Austria, Rumania, Czecho-Slovakia, and even Poland) can no longer aspire to exist in the outworn form of "sovereign states." This pretension only resulted in political anarchy and wars. The death knell sounds for them. In Central Europe, Paul Reynaud's formula for Europe, "Unite or Perish," is particularly cogent.

9 Macartney, *Problems of the Danube Basin*, p. 122.

Under these conditions, federalism has become not only a political philosophy, but also a positive program for all Slovaks. As they are at present the victims of a two-fold oppression, that of Moscow and Prague, it is Slovak emigration in the Western world that is now the color-bearer of the idea of a free Slovakia in a federated Europe. This emigration, be it past (1900-1945) or relatively recent (1945-1950), calls for a federative reconstruction of the Europe of which Slovakia would be a constitutive unit.

The Slovak League of America—Since World War I, the old emigration, having found a new home in the United States, showed a keen interest in the fate of the Slovaks who had remained in their native country. In the Cleveland and Pittsburgh Agreements,[10] which the Slovak League of America concluded with the Czech delegates, it is stipulated that the Czecho-Slovakia to be created should have a federative structure. Even though disappointed by the policy of denationalization which was practiced vis-à-vis Slovakia by the government of Prague, the League continued to be concerned with the political vicissitudes of the little nation living in the region of the Tatras. Since 1907 the supreme organ of the old emigration to the United States, the Slovak League, at its Twenty-Ninth Congress in Cleveland on October 21, 1947, approved a resolution concerning the political situation of the Slovak nation after 1945, from which the following points are taken:

> The Slovaks constitute a distinct ethnical, ethical, cultural, and social unit with all the qualities of a national individuality which considers itself as such and wishes to live as such in order to be able to develop freely and preserve integrally its national character.
> Only a Slovak State, whose territory and independence will be recognized and guaranteed on the international plane, can assure the Slovaks of the lasting conditions of a peaceful evolution, the joy of living and a happy future.
> The Slovak League of America in the name of the Americans of Slovak origin as well as in the name of the Slovak nation, salute the idea of a federative union of European peoples, for it sees in this initiative a serious effort in sight of an equitable ruling of the international relations susceptible of ensuring a lasting peace and the conditions of a new life in a broken-down Europe. Pending this solution, even a federative union of the states of Central Europe would offer to the nations of this region better

[10] See pp. 2-3, 331-32.

conditions for a common peaceful life, a fruitful collaboration and an effective safeguard for their individual and collective interests.

The Slovak League of America is convinced that such a federation can be built only on the foundation of equal rights; all the nations belonging to this area of Europe, without distinction of territorial size or number of inhabitants, have to enter as states into this federative union.

The Slovak nation can adhere as a member in a federative union of the peoples of Central Europe only through its own State, for it is only thus that it will see all its rights assured and that it can fulfill all the obligations incumbent upon it in the framework of a reorganized Europe.

The Slovak League of Canada adopted the same program at its Congress, July 25 and 27, 1949. Since that time, both of the aforementioned organizations have in a series of declarations reiterated and confirmed this attitude.

Slovak Political Emigration—During World War II, the Slovak journalist, Peter Prídavok, formed the Slovak National Council in London. The proposed aim of the Council was to fight against German domination in Central Europe and the concept of the Czecho-Slovak State as set forth by Beneš and his government. At the close of the war, this Council was reorganized on a larger scale. Mr. Karol Sidor,[11] former deputy to the Czecho-Slovak Parliament (1935-1939), former Minister of State in the Prague government (1938-1939), and former Minister Plenipotentiary of the Slovak Republic to the Holy See (1939-1945), became its Chairman; while Mr. Prídavok assumed the duties of Secretary-General, and Mr. Joseph Kirschbaum became Chairman of the Foreign Affairs Committee. Matúš Černák,[12] a member of the autonomous Slovak government (1938-1939); František Hrušovský, a well-known historian;[13] Joseph Cíger-Hronský, a prominent writer and until 1945 director of *Matica slovenská;*[14] Joseph Cieker, Minister Plenipotentiary of the Slovak Republic in Spain (1944-1945); František Tiso, Minister Plenipotentiary of Slovakia in Moscow (1940-1941); Konštantín Čulen, writer; and Joseph Paučo, a newspaperman, were to become leading personalities of the Council. Later on, Mr. Emanuel Böhm and Mr. Štefan Blaško, exiled deputies of the Slovak Democratic party, as well as Prof. František Šubík, rallied to the cause.

[11] Died in 1954, in Montreal, Canada.
[12] Was killed by a parcel bomb July, 1955, in Munich, Germany.
[13] Died in October, 1956, in Cleveland, Ohio.
[14] Died in July, 1960, in Argentina.

In its program, the Slovak National Council Abroad asks that the self-determination of peoples, the famous Wilsonian principle which found its way even into the Charter of the United Nations, be applied to the Slovak nation. It does not call formally upon the Slovak Republic, but it declares that even if a Slovak State had never existed, it would be necessary at the present time to create one. It deems that the creation of a free Slovakia is in the interest:

1) Of the Slovak nation itself, for which it is the only way of liberating itself from neighboring imperialisms, large or small (Magyar, Czech, German, Russian, etc.);

2) Of the neighboring countries, for whom Slovakia has always been a sort of firebrand at the source of the quarrels between Czechs and Hungarians, Czechs and Poles. It is not doubtful that the existence of an independent Slovakia would neutralize the divergent interests of its neighbors;

3) Of Europe, which twice in the course of thirty years found itself drawn into war because of the political disorders of Central Europe.

So that Slovakia, a nation of four million inhabitants, may be able to leave its status as a satellite of great neighboring powers, the Slovak National Council desires that it be integrated into a European Union, or at least into a Central European Federation.[15] It is only in this enlarged compass that the Council sees the possibility of a reconciliation with the Czech people whose leaders, through their policy, made Slovaks fall under the influence first of Hitler, then of Stalin.

In Slovakia, the Slovak National Council relies upon the big majority of the noncommunist population, while abroad it brings together numerous Slovak refugees, no matter when they emigrated nor what might have been their former party affiliation.

Besides the Slovak National Council Abroad, there exists the Slovak Liberation Committee, founded in 1946 by Mr. Ferdinand Ďurčanský, former Minister of Foreign Affairs of the Slovak Republic (1939-1940). Since its inception, the Committee has presented to the United Nations and foreign governments some twenty memoranda dealing with the Slovak problem and claiming Slovakia's independence. Ďurčanský's group is generally con-

---

[15] See Chapter III, "La nation slovaque réclame son propre État dans une fédération européenne" of the memorandum concerning the political aims of the so-called Council of Free Czechoslovakia, published in Paris, October 1, 1949 by the Slovak National Council Abroad.

sidered a right wing of the Slovak emigration. As a professor of international law, Ďurčanský adopted the theory of the legal continuity of the Slovak Republic after its occupation in 1945 by the Soviet army. In 1946, during the Paris Peace Conference, he distributed among the delegates of free nations a statement urging the Allies to sign a peace treaty with Slovakia.

To better serve Slovakia's cause in the free world, the Slovak National Council and the Slovak Liberation Committee, after several unsuccessful attempts at amalgamation, formed on September 27, 1958, a joint Slovak Liberation Council, thus overcoming their previous tactical differences.

The smallest Slovak exile group is that of Joseph Lettrich. Because of its connections between 1945 and 1948 with the Beneš and Gottwald regime, it is usually characterized as the left wing of the Slovak emigration spectrum. In contradistinction to the two aforementioned organizations, inspired by the ideal of a free Slovakia, the latter still holds to the frame of a common Czecho-Slovak State, even though in the present Czech Communist-dominated Slovakia such a concept could hardly find any following.

The Lettrich group, composed mostly of Slovak Protestants, adhered to the Council of Free Czechoslovakia created in 1948 by Czech political exiles in the United States. This split of the Slovak new emigration along the religious line has been considered regretful by Slovak Catholics as well as some Slovak Protestants.

Mr. L'udovit Kandra, now living in Canada, has become the protagonist of reconciliation. Under the title "An Imperative of the Present" he published in *Slovenská Obrana* this appeal to the Slovak Protestants in the free world urging them to rally to the national cause:[16]

> The Protestants (of the so-called "Czechoslovak tendency") who claim to speak today in the name of the Slovak nation must know that very few nationalists are behind them. Among the Catholics, there is no one. Among the Protestants, a greater and greater number rally each day to the national leaning. We, the Slovak Protestants, no longer want to be strangers in the midst of our own people. God created us Slovaks, and gave to us, as to the Catholics, a common country whose defense must be for us a question of honor and duty.[17]

[16] *Slovak Defence* (Scranton, Pa.: June 17, 1949).
[17] Allusion to the opportunist attitude of several Protestant personalities

Given the unrelaxing grip of the Soviet Union on its European satellites and equal oppression of all religious denominations under communism in Czecho-Slovakia, that appeal has never lost any of its actuality.

Thus, together with their enslaved nation, and with the political emigrations of the other neighboring peoples and friends of Central Europe, the Slovak exiles still believe in a world organized on justice which one day will bring liberation for their native country from communism.

who adhered to the Council of Free Czechoslovakia created by certain Czech emigrants in Washington.

EPILOGUE TO THE ENGLISH EDITION

This book, which appeared in 1955 in French in Paris, is now being published in a completed and revised English edition. This seems to be justified for two reasons:

First, it is a book of political history as systematic as possible, covering the period from 1918 to 1950; other books on Slovakia which have in the meantime appeared are dealing with this subject either within a larger historical context or are written from another point of view.

Second, its main line, its basic philosophy as reflected in the interpretation of events, has been confirmed by subsequent developments. In all the periods analyzed in the book there can be found the same indomitable aspiration of the Slovak nation toward freedom and independence.

If from 1918 to 1938 Slovakia fought for equality within the Czecho-Slovak Republic, her effort between 1938 and 1945 can be characterized as one directed toward consolidation and survival on the map of Europe. Both of them ended in failure and deception.

The last period, since 1945, has been the most exacting because it is the most oppressive. Since then Slovak national life has been reduced to its biological subsistence. Several later developments had been anticipated in the book, for instance, a complete elimination of Slovak Communists. Clementis was hanged in Prague on December 3, 1952. Husák, Novomeský, Holdoš, Okáli, and Horváth were sentenced by the State Court of Bratislava on April 24, 1954, to penalties from ten years to life imprisonment. (See Appendix XI).

The liquidation first of Slovak Democrats, then of Communists, who had made possible, at least in appearance, the restoration of Czecho-Slovakia in 1945, has inaugurated a status of political lawlessness in Slovakia. For nobody who knows of the conditions prevailing there, do Viliam Široký, a Communist of Magyar descent, now Prime Minister of Czecho-Slovakia, and Karel Bacílek, the pro-consul of Prague in Bratislava, represent Slovakia in the Prague Government or in the Politbureau of the Communist party. More than ever the country is longing for a change. No wonder, therefore, that in 1956 the Hungarian uprising could not but considerably stir up the mind of the Slovak population against the Prague communist regime. Demonstrations took place in the most important Slovak cities at that time, a fact which was amply commented upon by the world press. The Prague government had to send six divisions to western and central Slovakia to pacify those unrests, while the Soviet army, securing communications between the Carpathian Ukraine and Budapest, subjected the eastern part of the country to its own control.

This political unreliability of Slovakia explains why the new *Czechoslovak Socialist Republic Constitution* of July 11, 1960 abolished even the remnants of her autonomy, thus bringing the country under a closer surveillance of the central government. At the present time its political status in respect to the Czech lands is that of a subvassal, while Prague retains the dubious honor of being one of the most loyal vassals of the Soviet Empire.

Nothing in this situation can possibly change the prevailing anachronistic mood between Prague and Moscow. For Khrushchev who claims the merit of de-Stalinization, the services of two old Stalinists like Antonín Novotný and Viliam Široký are still of greatest importance. Aware of their weakness in this respect, they are all the more subservient to Khrushchev. And in this way the fiction of the Czecho-Slovak State has a good chance to last as long as Moscow is able to secure its controlling position in the affairs of the satellites.

But even if this dark period should persist a long time, the Slovak nation, faithful to its longer past and to its traditional values, firmly hopes to rise some day as an ever victorious Phoenix from the ashes of the Soviet Empire.

October 25, 1962
Washington, D.C.   Prof. Joseph A. Mikus, J.D.

APPENDIX I

MEMORANDUM OF THE SLOVAKS TO THE PARLIAMENT OF HUNGARY OF 1861

Memorandum of the Slovak nation to the High Parliament of Hungary, containing its demands with the aim of a just enactment and guarantee by State law of national equality in Hungary, as expressed by the National Slovak Convention at Turčiansky Svätý Martin, June 6-7, 1861.

When we, as Slovaks, present our demands in the name of national equality before the law, we do not do it as if we perhaps

wished to gain recognition for the principle which today is stirring in the world and, in its true meaning, is being taken up by
our foremost and very ardent patriots. But we do it because form
gives essence to things, and we Slovaks are very much concerned that this form, in which our national equality is to be
realized, respond to the very nature of things as well as to the
needs of our political life.

And in this regard, it is our patriotic and also national duty to
make this known to the legislative assembly of our country, to
which we express a genuine trust.

Our history and national traditions tell us that we are the
oldest inhabitants of this land which is encircled by the Carpathian Mountains. Long before the advent of the Magyars our
fathers called this land their homeland; long before that time our
forefathers fought long and bloody battles for their national
independence against the oppressors from the West;[1] and long
before then they also had here, besides a flourishing agriculture
and commerce, besides fortified towns and castles, a state system,
individual institutions of which have been maintained to this time
in the Constitution of Hungary.

With the advent of the Magyars, during the first stage of
their development, the confederation of Slavic tribes found on
this territory disappeared and made way for a new confederation
which, during the course of one century, took an honorable place
among the other European states as the Hungarian State under
the crown of St. Stephen, and despite the catastrophies of nine
centuries, has maintained itself to the present time.

Common material and spiritual interests united the various
races of this land, like sons of a common mother, into one family
with a common task: to defend Western civilization against the
barbarian nations of the East, and together to defend and preserve their independence for further posterity against the ra-
pacious influence of the West. This task always found them ready
to serve mankind both with weapons in hand on the field of
battle, and with wise counsel in State assemblies.

Both in military array and also in common counsels, the men
of these races understood each other very well, despite all disparity of tongues. Love for their common homeland and mutual
fraternal trust were their best interpreters. Not one of them
thought of scorning the language of another race, nor hating it;

[1] The Germanic kings.

no one thought of increasing his own race by the ruin and eradication of another and of setting up his own racial individuality in the place where only sacred and patriotic interests common to all races can always and permanently maintain themselves.

Having its vital forces in the brotherly love and harmony of all the races, our country has successfully lived through the terror of Tartar devastation; she has successfully weathered the times when Islam on the one side, and Western absolutism on the other, threatened to swallow her. Religious wars hung over her like a thunderstorm, after which nature became only more beautifully green. Although not completely, nevertheless she has in a large measure freed herself from the bonds of medieval feudalism, granting her children personal equality. Nay, even the oppression of eleven years[2] could not stifle the breath of freedom in her bosom. What kind of result, sorrowful or happy, will come to be her lot, now when the nationality question stirring with the spirit of the time is awaiting its resolution?

We wish that this question might not become an incurable wound of our common mother, but that it would become for her an impenetrable shield warding off the darts of the enemy.

Our consciousness says that we Slovaks are as much a nation as are the Magyars or any other nation of this country; if national equality and civil liberty are not to be only a chimera, then it follows in a natural manner that as a nation we cannot have fewer rights than possessed by any other nation of our common homeland.

And yet, when we turn our attention to the legal status of 1848, we find that not only the previous Diets from 1791, 1792, and 1805, but even later laws, especially those of 1832-36 to 1848, recognize only the Magyar nation as a nation, speak only about the Magyar language as a national language or the tongue of the country, concern themselves only with the welfare of the Magyar nation and the Magyar language, making no mention about us, as if we, who are nevertheless the oldest heirs of this common country, did not exist at all in our homeland.

Refusal to recognize this is an injustice aimed against our national and civic rights, which we feel deeply and painfully; it is an injustice about which the spirit of the time has already rendered its verdict—an injustice that should be unanimously condemned in the country's assembly of true patriots.

[2] Meaning the absolutism that reigned from 1848 to 1859.

We, therefore, with regard to removing this injustice, demand:

I. That the individuality of the Slovak nation and the patriotism of the Slovak language be recognized by positive law and by inaugural diplomas,[3] and thereby the harmony of the nations be secured against the malicious attacks of their enemies.

We consider nations as moral personalities of mankind; through nations, even though they may vary in form, mankind advances to its own destiny, that is, to perfection.

It is a natural thing that we hold firmly to this definition with regard to ourselves and in our relation to the nations with which we have a common homeland.

Just as the recognition of an individual's personality is the first guarantee of freedom and civic equality, so among nations the recognition of national individuality is the first requirement of national equality; nay, the latter would be nonsense where there are no national persons to whom it related, or where these persons do not have legal recognition.

The centralization of the past eleven years did not recognize national personalities; therefore, instead of promised equality, it gave equal injustice to the nations.

We do not believe that the men whom the citizens of this country sent as legislators to the State Diet wished to attain the rebirth of any such centralization, even though in constitutional form. Therefore, once again in patriotic confidence we repeat that the recognition of national individuality is the first requirement of national equality, the cornerstone of the constitutional structure, which can be built solidly and permanently only on a natural, Divine Providence-given basis for the welfare and benefit of our entire country.

Since everything existing in the material world can exist only in time and space, therefore it is necessary:

II. To recognize the individuality of our nation in the area which it actually occupies as a coherent, undivided mass, under the name of the Slovak Region of Upper Hungary, with the apportionment of counties according to nationality.

The very substance of national equality makes this request irresistible, because a nation exists not only in the world of imagination, but also in the actual one.

It is, therefore, not enough to recognize its personality in a purely general way, but it is necessary to recognize every nation

---

[3] Patent letters by which kings, on their coronation day, assured the country of political freedom.

as it actually exists in the area which it occupies and which Divine Providence has marked out for it. A man would be guilty of contradiction and inconsistency, if he should recognize the individuality of a nation, but deny the borders within which this individuality is contained and within which it becomes an actuality.

If throughout many centuries there could exist, within constitutional Hungary, without the least difficulty for the country, districts of the Cumanians and the Jazygs, towns of border guards, ten communities of lancers, sixteen Spiš towns and forty-four counties—despite all topographical difficulties—as corporations endowed with individual municipal or territorial management; and if, before 1848, our homeland in its internal organization, without the least danger to its integrity and unity, could be subdivided into four districts, we see no reason why one coherent unit embracing the Slovak nation, in the area which nature itself has marked out for it and which it occupies in fact, could not find a place in our country as a Slovak Region of Upper Hungary at the forthcoming reorganization of regions and counties, which we expect from the Diet now in session.

And this is all the more to be expected, because real equality unmistakably presupposes such recognition; and the advantages of one language in a single region, both for the political and judicial administration, and the civil liberties emanating from a successful development, strongly recommend it.

The Slovak parts of the counties of Bratislava, Tekov, Hont, Gemer, Torňa, Abauj and Zemplín—marked by an ethnographical line—could be organized without significant difficulties either as new counties or, wherever possible, incorporated into neighboring Slovak counties.

The creation of one Slovak Region in Upper Hungary, according to the manner mentioned above, would make no changes in the present political division of Hungary except that in place of the dead boundaries upon which thus far the four districts of our country have rested, new borders would be instituted which would be inviolably determined not by human arbitrariness but by language and nationality and thus by the will of God and nature itself.

On this occasion we must take exception beforehand against the objection which our brother Magyars generally make to us, that in the Slovak counties of Trenčín, Orava, Turiec, Zvolen, Liptov, Spiš, and Šariš, there is a significant number of Magyars, most of them belonging to the gentry, so that in Upper Hungary the Magyar and Slovak nationalities are so intermingled that it becomes actually impossible to recognize the personality of the Slovak nation in one integrated region.

Yes, it is true that there are many denationalized sons in our nation; these, however, are not Magyars but sons of our race. Even the Magyar nation before the appearance of the great Széchenyi, numbered many such sons who claimed to be anything but Magyars; but the mighty spirit of time led them to know themselves so that they again fused with the nation from which they were descended. We too believe that this same spirit of time will arouse our renegade sons to realize their error and lead them back into the bosom of the nation and the people from which they originated.

Just as on the one hand, we cannot presume about the heroic Magyar nation that it would want to enrich itself with our renegades, or embellish itself with our national shame; so similarly on the other hand, in regard to the patriotism of our legislative body, we cannot believe that it could find an impediment to the realization of national equality in the above-mentioned apostasy of ours.

If, however, individuals of other nationalities should be found in the Slovak countries, they cannot claim chartered rights for themselves at the expense of the general population, just as individual Slovaks living in non-Slovak countries could not.

St. Stephen, in the testament to his son Emerich, said: "A kingdom of one language is absurd and fragile" *(Regnum unius linguae imbecille et fragile est)*. He also counseled his son to respect the customs, morals and habits of the various races living in the country; already under him there was established a unity and integrity of this country on the basis of the equality of races. The fact that the races grew into nations having a consciousness of their own individuality, and that consequently the unity and integrity of our homeland must no longer seek its foundations in racial but in national equality, is no fault or merit of ours, but the necessary result of progress which has its origin in Divine Law and cannot be halted or deflected in its course by barriers placed by human laws.

Not to recognize this progress would mean not to recognize Divine guidance in the life of individual nations and in the clearly marked development of individual states.

Just recently in the history of Italy, we saw that positive law and historical rights were unable to resist the events which had their origin in a higher law and right. The example of North America teaches us that sin, enmeshed in a state constitution, sooner or later will avenge itself against that very constitution, and that by the power of positive legality alone there cannot be created and maintained a unit which otherwise is not in agreement with natural and moral laws.[4]

We, therefore, do want our homeland saved from a similar sin when we demand to continue building on the foundations laid by St. Stephen and to form a union of our country that is in line with the spirit of the times and the necessities of life. We are not satisfied with having only *"regnum, indivisible et propriam habens constitutionem"* (a kingdom indivisible and having its own constitution) in legislative articles; we want more. We want this union to rest on a moral, natural foundation which in the course of time has grown out of life itself.

As we have already stated above, the moral character of this unity depends on genuine national equality actually and not artificially set up, with recognition of persons of the nations which actually exist. Only in this manner can our country incorporate the most sacred interests of the nations living within it; only in this manner will it provide for those nations everything they cannot find elsewhere; only thus will it become a mother loved equally by them—a mother who, just because she will give none of her equal sons priority before the others, will be able to look for equal support in time of danger and demand the same measure of help and sacrifice.

We who in the common past of these nations see the finger of God pointing to their common future, we feel and are conscious of the fact that the geographical character of Upper Hungary settled by us; that daily, intermittent, material and spiritual interests and mutual trade; even family and blood ties with our brother Magyars unite us in one strong union. Consequently we cannot be opponents of the integrity and unity of our country. Therefore in our Slovak region, impersonating the Slovak nation, let no one seek anything else but what really exists, that is, an infallible premise of national equality which, in turn, is the cornerstone of the unity of our country.

---

[4] Allusion to the slavery implied in the American Constitution.

III. If equality is that measure by which freedom and the rights of millions of citizens become an actuality in civic life and unite all members of the community into one harmonious whole, into one free community, how much greater then is the urgency of one country, which is supposed to be a harmonious unit of several nations living in it, to measure national and lingual rights by this scale. In accordance with this principle, we demand that in the region personifying our nation:

1) The Slovak language, alone and exclusively, shall be the channel whereby the stream of public, civic, ecclesiastical, and scholastic life shall flow; as an image by which the nation depicts itself in the spiritual realm, as the only means of raising the level of national culture, the Slovak language must not be restricted within the area of its own nation, in its own household, to a marginal role, to the role of a housemaid, but must legally occupy a plane of equality just like that of the nation itself within its confines.

We demand, therefore, that with regard to us Slovaks, in the coming reorganization of the country and counties, there be created in the Slovak region a court of appeals, also at least one business court in which the official language would be Slovak; that in the State Supreme Court, as well as in the highest administrative departments there be placed men, recognized by Slovak public opinion as Slovak patriots, consequently also perfectly expert in the Slovak language, as administrative heads for Slovak affairs, the number of whom, with the required personnel, would be in proportion to the population. They would perform not only official duties, but also, in time of need, would defend the interests of the Slovak nation.

The same holds good for the organization of the Commission for the Management of Scholastic Affairs.

2) Concerning the line which is supposed to be drawn in the country between the diplomatic language and our national tongue, we must first resolve the question as to what diplomatic language really is: In our opinion, among the various nations it is the "means of common understanding."

In this definition its limits are indicated automatically, namely, it is indicated that where it is not the proper language of a nation, it must not assume the right of a national language; that it must not take unto itself even a span of the field which belongs to another national language; that its limitations and rights begin where the exclusive limitations and rights of the national language end. Therefore, speaking with regard to us Slovaks, its borders commence beyond the borders of our Slovak region, in correspondence with non-Slovak and non-Slavic counties; in internal affairs and in the mutual official business of the highest administrative and judicial authorities of the State, whose tasks relate to the entire country (but not, it is understood, including here the affairs of parties, which always should be conducted in the proper national language); finally in the joint State Diet, here not excluding the use of other languages of the State.

We Slovaks, to whom the harmony of the nations of Hungary means far more than our own vain pride, are ready to recognize the diplomacity of the Magyar language in our country up to proper limits, not however because we would thereby be recognizing the supremacy of the Magyar nationality and language. As a nation we cannot fall so deeply, and it can never be our intention to renounce our national dignity. We do this, however, so that we might give our brother Magyars undeniable proof that for the sake of harmony among the nations of Hungary we are prepared to deny ourselves even the most sacred, God-given and inherent rights as much as is possible without committing gross suicide.

In accordance with the principle mentioned above we demand, and demand we must:

3) That the articles of the Diet which are not in accord with the principle of equality and freedom of nations, namely, articles 16:1791, 7:1792, 4:1805, 3:1836, 6:1840, 2:1844, 5. par. 3:1848, and 16-e:1848 be abrogated by positive law.

There is no nation which surpasses our brother Magyars in their love and jealous adherence to their language and nationality. But did the Creator of the world form our hearts and minds according to other rules than the hearts and minds of the Magyars? What hurts them, hurts us too; what they consider a treasure, so do we, just as dear and priceless. Also our language is to us the most beautiful and the most euphonic; to us it is the only means of national culture; to us, too, it is an image of our spiritual world, and we feel, just as do the Magyars, that the spirit of freedom and patriotic fervor, revealing itself to us in a magical way in our language, penetrates and nourishes our inner being; whereas against this, the same spirit, the same fervor in a language not our own, coming to us in foreign dress, seems to us to be strange, alien. Our language is so firmly joined together with our civic freedom and our patriotism that, within its natural confines and rights, it can be suppressed or recognized only together with these.

We further demand:

4) An authentic translation of the laws prepared by the Diet itself into our language.

We demand:

5) That for the proper political and legal training and education of Slovak youth, there be founded for us at the expense of the State, in a suitable Slovak city, a School of Law and in addition, a Chair of Slovak Languages and Literature at the University of Pest—all the more because this university holds significant estates in the upper parts of Hungary which are settled by the Slovaks. We ask also that our literary institutions be supported proportionately from State revenues.

6) That we always be allowed to establish national literary and civic-educational societies with the right of free assembly and the right to solicit the necessary funds for this purpose.

7) That Slovak communities within a national element not their own, as well as communities of other nationalities which are isolated in Slovak counties and cannot be marked out, have the right as a result of the principle of civic autonomy to use in civic life their own language and to foster freely and cultivate their own nationality.

Let no one accuse us of fanaticism because we want to have secured our language as a means of edifying our public civic life in our homeland, in the land of our birth and in the area in which it is native. We shall not force our language on anyone; we demand only that our language not be deprived of its natural right.

8) We demand that in the forthcoming reorganization of the House of Magnates, the highest interests of this multinational country, particularly the interests of our Slovak nationality be taken into consideration and proportionately represented.

IV. Finally, we declare that the interests of the Slovak nation in regard to civic liberty are the same as and identical with the interests of all the nations of Hungary, but that with regard to national freedom they are identical with the interests of all the nations hitherto oppressed by the laws, namely, the Ruthenians, Rumanians, Serbs, and Croatians. Thus, in the area which it inhabits, the Slovak nation demands for itself (that is, with regard to nationality and freedom) the very same rights which the Magyars already actually enjoy, and for this it wants to stand up and fight as one for all and all for one.

This solidarity, with which we identify ourselves for the interests of freedom and nationality before the eyes of the nations of Hungary, is compelled by the oppression of the non-Magyar nations.

These, then, are our demands which we present to the Diet of Hungary with regard to the enactment of equality.

Without the recognition of our national individuality, without marking out the region within which this individuality is contained, without equal rights for languages and nationalities in their separate ethnographic borders, there is no genuine equality for us.

We repeat again that the equality of nations is the cornerstone of the integrity and unity of our common homeland brought by the sense of universal history. Once it is awakened it will no longer slumber, but will only become strengthened in the consciousness of nations; nothing, therefore, can be withdrawn or subtracted from its worth, just as nothing could be subtracted from the worth of the prophetic books of Sibylla. History, however, teaches us that in fatal periods of nations or states a missed opportunity never returns again.

Our motto is: A single, free constitutional country, with liberty, equality and fraternity of nations.

At Turčiansky Svätý Martin, June 7, 1861.

As a result of the resolution of the Slovak National Convention in Turčiansky Sv. Martin:

(Signed) Ján Francisci, Chairman of the Slovak National Convention; Viliam Paulíny-Tóth, Recording Secretary; Ján Gottschár, Abbot and School Advisor; Štefan Závodník, Parish Priest and Dean; Alexander Pongrác, Parish Priest and Dean; Dr. Miloslav Hurban, Lutheran Pastor; Štefan Daxner, Landowner and Lawyer; Ondrej Michal Mudroň, Doctor of Laws; Štefan Hýroš, Parish Priest; Samuel Novák, Ján Moravčík, L'udevít Turzo-Nosický; Ondrej Hodža, Lutheran Pastor; Ján Jesenský; Ďord' Matúška; Ján Palárik, Priest and Writer.

APPENDIX II

For Peace in Central Europe

MEMORANDUM OF THE SLOVAKS TO THE PEACE CONFERENCE OF 1919

Slovakia to the Slovaks:
We are neither Czechs nor Czechoslovaks;
we are just simply Slovaks.
It is in the name of justice and lasting
peace that we demand the autonomy of Slovakia.

THE WORLD WAR AND THE HOPES OF THE SLOVAKS

The tyranny which the Austro-Hungarian Empire brought down upon the Slovak nation was well known to the entire world (Scotus Viator, *Racial Problems in Hungary*). And when, during the World War, the former empires began to vacillate, the Slovaks hoped that political liberty could be born for them out of the ruins of the old world. When with the downfall of the Central Powers, the former monarchy was broken up, the Slovaks joyfully greeted the idea of a new Slav State composed of the sister nations: Czechs, Moravians, Slovaks, and Ruthenians.[5] Each Slovak was persuaded that the Slovak nation would enjoy autonomy in this State, could preserve its national character and work at increasing its own culture. This hope was confirmed by promises of people in authority and particularly by the famous agreement made in America between the Czechs and Slovaks, signed in Pittsburgh, May 30, 1918, by the representatives of the two nations—among others, Professor Thomas Masaryk and Mr. Vojta Beneš.

The Text of the Czech and Slovak Agreement
Drafted in Pittsburgh, Pennsylvania, May 30, 1918

The representatives of the Slovak and Czech organizations in the United States, the Slovak League, the Czech National Alliance, and the Union of Czech Catholics, have deliberated, in the presence of the chairman of the Czech-Slovak National Council, Professor Masaryk, on the Czech-Slovak question and on our previous program manifestations, and have resolved as follows:

[5] The population of the Czecho-Slovak Republic is made up of 5,500,000 Czechs, 3,500,000 Slovaks, 3,000,000 Germans, 1,000,000 Magyars a n d 800,000 Ruthenians.

We approve a political program aiming to unite the Czechs and Slovaks into an independent State comprising the Czech lands and Slovakia.

Slovakia shall have its own administration, its own parliament, and its own courts.

The Slovak language shall be the official language in the schools, in governmental offices, and in public life generally.

The Czecho-Slovak State shall be a republic; its Constitution shall be democratic.

The organization of the cooperation of the Czechs and Slovaks in the United States shall be intensified and regulated by mutual consent as necessity and changing conditions shall require.

Detailed provisions concerning the establishment of the Czecho-Slovak State are left to the liberated Czechs and Slovaks and their legal representatives.

(Signed) Thomas G. Masaryk, Vojta Beneš, Albert Mamatey, Ján Janček, Jr., Milan Getting, Ján Pankuch, Reverend Joseph Murgaš, Reverend Ján Kubášek, Andrej Schustek, Reverend Pavel J. Šiška, Karel Pergler, Hynek Dostál, D. Fischer, B. Šimek, J. Zmrhal, Reverend Innocent Restl and Ján Straka.

The same agreement was concluded also in Russia.

How Deceived the Slovaks Were!

Never has a nation been as cruelly deluded in its hopes as the Slovak nation. In America, as the text above shows, it had been agreed that a Czecho-Slovak State would be founded in which the Slovaks would have autonomy, their own administration, a national Parliament, their magistrature, and Slovak as official language. The creation of a Czecho-Slovak State had been decided upon, but in this State two nations were to live, the Czechs and the Slovaks, both in all things free and equal. Now this agreement was not put into practice because those who seized the political power no longer want to hear about Slovak autonomy. They are working to create not only a Czecho-Slovak State, but also a single Czecho-Slovak nation, which is an ethnographical monstrosity. In this way, instead of having the liberty promised us, we have become the victims of a new servitude. Instead of obtaining Slovak autonomy, we have fallen under Czech domination. Czech hegemony has substituted for Magyar hegemony. We have merely changed yokes: instead of the Magyar yoke, the Czech yoke has been imposed upon us, all the more bitter and heavy because imposed by those who call themselves our "brothers."

The Peace Conference and Slovak Autonomy

The source of all our misfortunes comes from the fact that on September 4, 1919, when they approved at Versailles the idea of a Czecho-Slovak Republic, they did not stipulate and guarantee to the Slovaks the political autonomy which they had been promised. We hoped that in the subsequent course of the work of the Peace Conference, Messrs. Masaryk, Beneš, and Kramář would try to keep their promise and have inserted into the Peace Treaty what justice, the natural law, and the written agreement demand for the Slovak nation.

But while they speak in the "Peace Treaty between the Allied and Associated Powers and Austria" (Sec. III, Art. 53) of an autonomous territory for the Ruthenians to the south of the Carpathians, there is no mention made of the Slovak nation nor its autonomy.

It is why we came to Paris to demand what was solemnly promised us. We are also forced to take this step because of the sad state to which our nation has been reduced by Czech imperialism and self-seeking.

The Slovaks under the Czech Yoke

Slovakia became a colony of Bohemia and is treated as such:

Firstly, we are exploited materially. The Slovak peasants, judging with good sense, said that we were going to be united with a poor and little country which would continue exploiting us as much as possible. Alas, they prophesied only too well. The Czechs buy everything at a low price from the Slovaks, leaving only the rejects whose price naturally goes up. Under the Czech regime in Slovakia, requisitions of all sorts are so frequent and so rigorous that there had never been the like even during the war. The Czech government founded in Slovakia supply centers for wheat, beets, sugar, coal, leather, etc., whose traffic permits Czech civil servants to get rich, whereas the Slovak country becomes exceedingly poor. In many places famine rages, for instance at Trenčín. The Czechs put their hands on all the exploitations of mines, petroleum, watering resorts of Slovakia to the extent that the minister, Dr. V. Šrobár, a defender of the Czechs, was forced to make this admission in his report of August 4, 1919, at Turčiansky Sv. Martin: "Most of the Czechs come into Slovakia as into a conquered country and want to draw the greatest possible material profit from it at the expense of the Slovaks."

The best paid positions are held by the Czechs. Czech employees and teachers receive in addition to their salary a supplement of thirty or forty crowns a day while the Slovaks are only very slightly rewarded for the same work. The Slovak intellectual class is in a desperate way; it is never sure of its material position; the Czechs often remove Slovak civil servants and employees from office on the pretext that they are "Magyarons," that is Magyarized Slovaks. The Czech soldiers sent into Slovakia are paid six crowns a day and given excellent food, with meat for dinner and supper; on the other hand, the Slovaks who are obliged to do their military service in Bohemia get only three crowns a day, are badly nourished and clothed, and further are humiliated in all sorts of ways.

The Czechs therefore envision the Slovaks as their property: "our Slovakia," they say.

Secondly, the Slovaks are oppressed in their language. Above all material goods we put the love of our native tongue and our national individuality. Already our name "Slovak" shows that we are a separate nation, although related to the Czechs. We have our own language, more beautiful and more sonorous than the Czech language; we have our own literature and our history, evidenced by the fact that we lived a thousand years in Hungary under the Magyar yoke without becoming Magyarized.

The Slovaks have always loved and defended their country. For the Slovak language, the nation's best sons suffered all things in the Magyar prisons, and we preserved our nationality in spite of a thousand years of oppression. We entered into the Czecho-Slovak State with the fond hope that we would have nothing to fear for our nationality, but this hope was wretchedly dashed. It is already obvious that the Czechs tend to denationalize, de-Slovakize us, and make Czechs of us. What the Hungarians could not destroy in a thousand years, our "brothers" the Czechs intend to take from us at once. They wish to tear from us our Slovak soul and in its place plant a Czech one. This tendency appears clearly in many instances; for instance in the Slovak schools, where the Czech language was introduced as obligatory, while in Bohemia the Slovak language is not required. We were promised the use of Slovak as the official State language in Slovakia, but in reality Czech is used mainly. In our schools Czech professors who do not even know the Slovak language well, teach it nonetheless. When we asked for a Slovak university for Bratislava (Pressburg), the National Assembly of Prague voted for a national Czecho-Slovak university, and incomplete at that, for we were granted only two courses in the medical school (the third and fourth years). Only Czech professors were appointed to these chairs, with Czech as the language of instruction. There will not be a school of philosophy nor a law school, and Slovak youth will have to study at Prague and Brno—in Czech spirit. Thus we are deprived of the possibility of forming a Slovak intellectual class. The school of theology has been excluded from the university; that has been made a separate institution, but with Czecho-Slovak features, with Slovak and Czech professors. Anton Štefánek was put at the head of public education in Slovakia, and he is avowedly pro-Czech. The thirty inspectors of Slovak schools resigned August 4, 1919, because they had been made responsible to the Czechs; the *župans* (county heads) followed their example to protest against the Czechization of the Slovak schools.

Thirdly, the Slovaks are oppressed in their religious practices. One thing greatly irritates the Slovaks against the Czechs: religious intolerance. The heresy of Hus, unknown in Slovakia until now, is strongly propagated by the Czechs in our unfortunate country. On July 6, 1919, commemorative bonfires were lighted in the villages throughout Slovakia. Speeches were made against the religion of the Slovak people. Czech soldiers, Sokols, and employees make fun of the Slovaks' piety. Many statues of the saints have been mutilated, numerous churches profaned. Dr. Francis Jehlička, a deputy, interpellated the National Assembly on this subject, asking for the punishment of wild iconoclasts; but the Minister of National Defense, Mr. Klofáč, ordered an inquest under the direction of those accused. Naturally nothing came of this. As the anger of the people grew from day to day as a result of this vandalism, Dr. Šrobár, Minister for Slovakia, was forced to reprimand the Czechs in his report of August 4, 1919: "We entreat our Czech brothers to take into account the Slovaks' great piety and no longer offend their religious feelings." The Czech professors and teachers who were sent into the Slovak schools try to destroy the religious spirit of our youth to the point where the Slovak students organized a big meeting, August 3, 1919, at Ružomberok, to protest violently against the Czech professors.

Furthermore, they trample under foot the rights of Catholics, who make up 85 per cent of the Slovak nation. The Church's possessions are administered by government-appointed committees. It happened that Dr. Halaša, a Lutheran lawyer, was appointed administrator of a Catholic ecclesiastical property. The Czech State confiscated some of the Slovak Catholic high schools, for instance the episcopal gymnasium of Trnava. Whereas under the administration of Hungary, only our nationality was in danger; now under the Bohemian yoke, we are neither sure of our daily bread nor free to practice our religion.

Those Who Were to Protect Us
Against All These Abuses Do Not Do It

The first to protest against all these injustices, this Czech imperialism, should be the Slovak government. But such a government does not exist. To elude public opinion, a member of the central government was sent into Slovakia, Dr. V. Šrobár, a servile Slovak with the title "Minister with Full Powers for Slovakia." But this minister is only a caricature of a real minister. His "full powers" with respect to Prague and Czech imperialism are nil; he exercises full power only against conscious Slovaks and as we shall see, profits greatly thereby. The Minister for Slovakia is a minister against Slovakia; he works with his subordinates "to Czechicize and persecute the true Slovaks." There is an Official Gazette put out in Bratislava where laws, orders, and employees' nominations appear. In the first numbers of this paper, Minister Šrobár would sign the nominations, but then his name disappeared and he became the executor of Prague's will.

The second factor which ought to insist on Slovak rights is the Slovak representation in the National Assembly in Prague. Of the three hundred deputies, there are fifty-four who form the "Slovak Club." But what is their worth as representatives? They are not elected by the people, but appointed by the government, who chose them in part from Czechs (for example, Messrs. Pilát, Pfeffermann, Kolísek, Cholek, Rothnágel, and Miss Alice Masaryk, daughter of the president); in part from the bad Slovaks, pro-Czechs, centralists, unionists, enemies of Slovak autonomy. From the Autonomist party—although the entire Slovak nation is with them—only four have been admitted (Messrs. Andrej Hlinka, Karol Kmeťko, Jozef Sivák, and Ferdinand Juriga). From a "Slovak Club" made up in this wise there is no hope for the Slovaks.

The Autonomist Party is Persecuted

In this sad situation, the Slovak nation puts its hope in the Autonomist party *(Slovenská ľudová strana),* whose leader is Mr. Andrej Hlinka, a Slovak martyr, well known through Scotus Viator's book, *Racial Problems in Hungary.* Under the Magyar regime, this was already our largest political party. As early as 1906, it sent seven deputies to the Budapest Parliament to defend "our sweet Slovak language." Today this political party is stronger still, having the whole Slovak nation behind it, or at least 90 per cent of it. The essence of this party's program is "Slovakia to the Slovaks," that is, political autonomy at least as great as was promised us in the Pittsburgh Agreement. But the government hates this party and persecutes it.

Czech soldiers, Sokols, employees, and police persecute the Slovak party; even the postal service, which ought never enter into politics, sends our newspapers and letters only irregularly—they are kept and torn up. We have many proofs of this, but in vain do we make our claims to the post administration.

For the autonomists the right to meet is limited: either meetings are prohibited or they are dispersed, as for example the famous assembly of Žilina (August 17, 1919), where the Czech militia which was to assure order during the meeting dispersed the crowd and wanted to kill the speakers. It is only by these devices that the Czech regime can maintain itself in Slovakia.

This regime as we see it wants to establish itself by dint of bayonets—a practice which is impossible in a democracy.

The Slovak party, although persecuted, is growing daily. This terrifies the government, which fears the elections and does all it can to prevent or falsify them. Minister Šrobár does not admit elections before three or five years. Besides, the government prepares an electoral "gerrymander" so that the Czechs and the centralist clique have a majority. While the city of Prague alone must have forty deputies, entire Slovakia will have only seventy. In Bohemia the voting will be secret, but in Slovakia it must be verbal, a device which serves to influence and terrorize the Slovaks. In Bohemia women will have the right to vote, but not in Slovakia, thanks to the centralists. In Slovakia, in order that the number of electors be lessened, the government, in its electoral plan presented by Minister Švehla to the National Assembly, annexes to Bohemia the Slovak districts of Bánovce, Ilava, Púchov, Trenčín, Skalica, Nové Mesto, and Myjava. Thus even the historical boundaries of Slovakia are not respected. They do not fear tearing the beautiful body of our native land.

But while preparing future elections in this way, the elections are feared nonetheless. That is why they want to enact definitively on the Constitution of the Republic, on the rights of the minorities, before the elections, in the present revolutionary Parliament (not elected), which is completely opposed to the Slovaks. Therefore the Czechs wish to dispose of us without us and against us.

Appeal to the Peace Conference

Not being able to attain our goal by a parliamentary fight, we appeal to the Peace Conference where illustrious people are united, friends of justice and liberty. We address them with confidence that the Peace Conference may guarantee what was promised us. What we have on paper we wish to have in reality, being persuaded that it belongs to us also by natural law. We ask for a political autonomy, a national Slovak parliament, a Slovak government responsible to this parliament, our own administration and magistrature, and finally a complete liberty of conscience.

In the Treaty of Peace between the Allied and Associated Powers and Austria, signed at Saint-Germain-en-Laye, September 10, 1919 (Sec. III, Art. 57), we read: "The Czecho-Slovak State accepts and agrees to embody in a Treaty with the Principal Allied and Associated Powers such provision as may be deemed necessary by these Powers to protect the interests of inhabitants of that State who differ from the majority of the population in race, language, or religion." Well, we ask the Allied and Associated Powers to envision us as a minority different from the Czechs and to protect our interests by guaranteeing us the greatest possible political autonomy.

Our Arguments

We have the honor to support our humble request with the following arguments:

1) Slovakia, forming nearly half of the Czech and Slovak Republic, cannot be well administered by the central government of Prague, not only because Prague is quite far from Slovakia and not easily accessible, but also because the special character of the Slovak country demands a government other than that of the Czechs. Further, the Czechs and Slovaks are "brothers" who have never seen one another and rubbed shoulders with one another. The mentality and character of these two nations are entirely distinct. The Czechs are an industrial nation, the Slovaks are agriculturists. The Czechs are in great part Hussites, the Slovaks Catholic. The Czechs have lived with the Germans, the Slovaks with the Magyars. The Czechs are more materialistic, the Slovaks idealistic. There is not a Czecho-Slovak nation, but there is a Czech nation and a Slovak nation. We are not Czechs, nor Czecho-Slovaks, but Slovaks, and we wish to remain Slovaks forever. A glance at Slovak history shows that the Czechs and Slovaks are different nations. To former Great Moravia belonged the Morav-

ians, Slovaks, southern Poles, and the Trans-Danubian Slavs. The Czechs kept their own kingdom, but they recognized Great Moravia's superiority. At the end of the ninth century, the Magyars conquered Great Moravia and the southern Slavs. The Slovaks fell under the Magyar yoke, from which they were freed by the collapse of the Central Powers.

Therefore the Slovaks had nothing in common with the Czechs before the ninth century, and since then they have still better developed their individual character.

No one identifies the Yugo-Slavs with the Czechs; likewise the Slovaks differ from the Czechs. Geographic position alone has caused some likeness in the language, although there are Slovak philologists who identify the Slovak language with the Yugo-Slav language; for instance, Professor Czambel in *Slovenská reč*. The identification of the Slovaks with the Czechs is a mystification tending to subject the Slovaks to the Czech yoke.

2) The inhabitants of the Czech and Slovak Republic will not be able to work peacefully to increase production, and they will not be able to pay their war debts if there is not peace in the country. Czech imperialism, which we have just characterized, causes discord between Slovaks and Czechs, and prevents peaceful and fruitful work. *Concordia parvae res crescunt, discordia maximae dilabuntur.*

3) To counterbalance German imperialism on the Continent, they wanted to found a powerful Slav (Czecho-Slovak) Republic. But this republic will be weak if it is divided by discord caused by Czech imperialism. This republic will become strong if the Slovaks obtain satisfaction and if they are not subjected to Czech hegemony. It is in the interest of the peace of Europe that Slovakia be liberated from Czech hegemony, for otherwise there will be no lasting peace in this country. The Slovaks would already revolt against Czech oppressors if the country were not occupied by Czech militia which is ruining Slovakia materially. But the state of occupation cannot last forever.

4) The Magyar and German minorities that live in the territory of the Czecho-Slovak Republic are also discontented with Czech hegemony. They would gladly live with the Slovaks, but Czech hegemony irritates them and makes them unhappy.

5) The victorious Entente granted political autonomy to the Ruthenian nation which is in the Czecho-Slovak Republic, although it is smaller than the Slovak nation. The more then do we deserve the same favor.

6) Every convenant must be faithfully kept, but especially when sprinkled with human blood; that is true of the Pittsburgh one that we have already mentioned. The Slovak legionnaires who shed their blood for the victory of the Entente fought also for the freedom of the Slovak nation and not at all for Czech imperialism. According to Captain Vozka (a Czech), in the American legions there were 87 per cent Czecho-Slovaks, 68 per cent of whom were Slovaks.

7) Since the Czechs constitute only a third of the population of the Czecho-Slovak Republic, it cannot become a center of order and peace in Central Europe except on condition of giving satisfaction to the legitimate aspirations of all the nations which compose it.

To show to the Peace Conference that all we have just said is pure truth, we dare ask for Slovakia a plebiscite which will disclose the real feelings of the Slovak nation. This plebiscite must not take place under Czech terror, but under the protection of the Entente's army.

We entrust our fate into the hands of the Peace Conference. The right to existence was accorded us by the Creator; we hope that the glorious Peace Conference will guarantee it against the injustice of men.

Paris, September 20, 1919.

Andrej Hlinka,
Slovak Member
of the National Assembly of Prague.
Dr. František Jehlička,
Slovak Member
of the National Assembly of Prague.

Joseph Kubala,   Štefan Mnokel',   Dr. Joseph Rudinský,
Businessman   Journalist   Professor

APPENDIX III

THE BENEŠ PLAN FOR THE SOLUTION OF THE SLOVAK QUESTION IN 1938

[Mr. E. Beneš' Plan for the Solution of the Slovak Question in Czecho-Slovakia, September 22, 1938; Accepted by the Executive

*Committee of the Slovak Populist Party as a Basis for Negoti-
ations.]*[6]

In order that fraternal relations between Czechs and Slovaks
be planned definitively, and all future differences be eliminated
which until the present troubled wholesome Czecho-Slovak relations and harmed harmonious Czecho-Slovak collaboration in the
internal life of the State, the following agreement was concluded
with the full consent of the President of the Republic:

1) All political, economic and cultural differences appearing
within the Czecho-Slovak majority of the State shall in the future
be resolved in a spirit of fraternity between the Czechs and Slovaks as members of the national Czecho-Slovak family.

2) In this way the opinion of both sides, Slovaks and Czechs,
shall be henceforth respected at all times on the question of
Slovak ethnical individuality. Mutual tolerance shall be observed
at all times, whether they consider themselves Czechs, Slovaks,
or Czechoslovaks. Inasmuch as in political discussions it will not
be possible to avoid these questions, they shall be treated in the
spirit of tolerance and mutual respect. The same shall be true of
controversies over languages. The starting point shall always be
the principle of the absolute legal equality of Slovak, the literary
language of the Slovaks, with the Czech language.

3) It is agreed that in official State documents a terminology
will not be used which, by its character of exclusivity, would
oblige one or the other to give up a position of principle. In the
case where it will not be possible to avoid a term having meaning
in only one of the two languages, the equivalent text in the other
language shall always be equally reliable so that both ways of
looking at it be equally represented.

4) On the subject of public services, it is agreed that the
Slovaks, without religious distinction and political convictions,
shall receive in the services of the State (as civil servants, employees, or workmen), the number of positions, in all categories
without distinction, that fall to them in accordance with the
population of Slovakia (the count not kept for Germans, Magyars, Ruthenians, and Jews). If in certain categories this number
could not be reached for any reason whatsoever, compensation
shall be made in the proportion desired in another category. They
shall see to it besides that above everything else the Slovaks be
placed in Slovakia while necessarily and unreservedly recogniz-

---

[6] Beneš, *Où vont les Slaves?* p. 277.

ing the principle of state right for transferring civil servants and employees. They shall watch so that the number of Czech civil servants and employees in Slovak regions not exceed 30 per cent of the total number of employees. The positions occupied by Czechs in Slovakia shall be compensated for by the nomination of Slovaks in the same proportion in the other regions of the Republic so that Czechs may not take the place of Slovaks.

5) Close to the government there shall be created a commission of public services whose members shall be named by the government over which a Slovak minister shall preside according to a rotation agreement. This commission shall watch out for the above clauses with regard to the nomination of Slovak civil servants. All ministerial departments and other central services of the State shall have to furnish this commission with all necessary information so that it can function properly. Its reports shall also be sent to the chancellery of the President of the Republic.

6) Since for several reasons it has not been possible up to now to appoint the desired number of Slovak civil servants and employees in all branches of the State's service, everything shall be done so that in the coming years nominations shall be made in exact accordance with the percentage above established. Besides, the number of Slovak State civil servants and employees lacking today shall be filled to the extent of the desired proportion by appointing every year to come a certain number of Slovak civil servants and employees over and above their quota.[7] In so doing, account will be taken of the event where in certain categories there would be a temporary lack of Slovak candidates. The principles set forth in point 5 will have to be fully applied in seven years.

7) It is agreed that a parity commission of Czechs and Slovaks be created within the Prime Minister's office which will be directed alternately by a Czech and Slovak chairman. Its duty shall be to study the various economic questions regarding Slovakia and which have been contested up until now as to the respective role of Czechs and Slovaks. It shall first examine concrete matters: State orders, the question of economic and financial contribution to Slovakia from the historical provinces (Bohemia and Moravia-Silesia), the just establishing of tax bases, etc. The Supreme Office of Control (Audit Office) and competent min-

---

[7] "As Minister of Foreign Affairs, I gave the order at the end of 1934 to admit henceforth into the services of the Ministry one Slovak for every two Czechs."

isterial departments shall have to put at this commission's disposition the documentation and aid necessary to the successful accomplishment of its task. The commission shall prepare a report so that it will be possible to establish definitive directives on all economic and financial questions concerning Slovakia, and so that Slovakia receive in all things the share which belongs to it as derived from the population figure.

In matters of economics, the following dispositions shall be taken:

a) In the establishment of the budget, the credit necessary to Slovakia shall be ensured at least to a degree corresponding to the portion of State receipts collected in Slovakia, plus the share of customs duties and other receipts from the other regions relating to the economic life of Slovakia;

b) as to credits for national equipment, Slovakia shall be progressively endowed with credits which, according to the estimates of the said commission, shall be necessary to bring it progressively up to the economic level of the historical provinces;

c) in all the government appropriations consecrated to hydrographic economics, the betterment of the soil, etc., Slovakia shall likewise have a share according to the principles set forth above.

d) in all public economic institutions with State participation (including banking and other institutions, as for instance, joint-stock companies), the direction shall include Slovak participation prorated according to the population figure;

e) Slovakia shall be duly represented in all institutions of social policy.

8) A definitive formula shall be agreed upon for a new law on languages and the use of Czech and Slovak as official languages on the basis of absolute equality in fact and law for all the territory of the Republic.

It shall be necessary to guarantee by strong administrative measures that the Slovak language be used in Slovakia in all services and schools, which is already the case with a few slight exceptions.

9) It is agreed that the future administrative reform, if it is done on the basis of the system of the *župy* (counties), shall preserve the unity of Slovakia as a province and that the union of the *župy* would be realized within the Slovak provincial Diet.

The provincial Diet shall have legislative, administrative, economic, and consultative competence to be regulated and coordinated within the legislative activity of the whole of the State. In the domain of this jurisdiction, the provincial Diet shall put forth laws as, for instance, on questions of welfare, hygiene, social security, economics, and education as well as on all matters where it is a question of the execution of laws voted by the National Assembly, particularly insofar as they shall relate to the territory of the province of Slovakia. The administrative, legislative, economic, and consultative competence of the provincial Diet shall be regulated by a special law.

The common laws for the whole Republic shall be authentic in their Czech and Slovak text.

The supplementary details of competence shall be settled in common conferences of the political parties with all qualified Slovak representatives by reason of their necessary coordination with the competence of the provincial Diets of Bohemia and Moravia.

APPENDIX IV

THE GERMANO-SLOVAK AGREEMENT OF MARCH 23, 1939

The German and Slovak governments have agreed, since the Slovak State placed itself under the protection of the German Reich, to regulate by means of a treaty the situation resulting therefrom. For this purpose the undersigned plenipotentiaries of the two governments have agreed on the following provisions:

The German Reich assumes the protection of the political independence of the Slovak State and the integrity of its territory (Art. 1).

In order to carry out the protection assumed by the German Reich, the German Armed Forces shall at all times have the right to set up military installations in a zone bounded on the west by the frontier of the Slovak State and on the east by the general line of the eastern edge of the Little Carpathians, the eastern edge of the White Carpathians, and the eastern edge of the Javorniky Mountains, and to man these installations with such forces as the German Armed Forces deem necessary. The Slovak government shall arrange for the requisite land for these installations to be placed at the disposal of the German units. Furthermore, the Slovak government shall agree to an arrangement necessary for supplying German troops and servicing duty free the military installations from the Reich.

Military sovereign rights shall be exercised by the German Army in the zone specified in the foregoing paragraph 1.

Persons of German nationality who are engaged by virtue of a private contract in the setting up of military installations in the zone thus designated are to that extent subject to German jurisdiction (Art. 2).

The Slovak government shall organize its own military forces in close consultation with the German Wehrmacht (Art. 3).

In accordance with the agreed relations of protection, the Slovak government shall always conduct its foreign policy in close understanding with the German government (Art. 4).

This Treaty enters into force immediately upon signature and is valid for a period of twenty-five years. The two governments shall consult about an extension of the Treaty in good time before the expiration of this period (Art. 5).

In witness whereof the plenipotentiaries on both sides have signed two copies of this Treaty.

Vienna, March 18, 1939
Berlin, March 23, 1939

For the German government: For the Slovak government:
   von RIBBENTROP   DR. JOZEF TISO
                             VOJTECH TUKA
                         DR. F. ĎURČANSKY

Appendix V

LETTER OF PIUS XII TO MONSIGNOR J. TISO, PRESIDENT OF THE SLOVAK REPUBLIC

To the President of the Slovak Republic, from Pius XII.
Beloved Son, Illustrious and Honorable Man,
Greetings and Apostolic blessing.

By an official letter of last month, We learned that you were elected President of the Slovak Republic and that you have already assumed duties. We thank you for this news in praying God in His goodness to deign to grant to your nation, which is very dear to Us, true prosperity and felicity.

We approve your praiseworthy intentions, expressed in your letter, to want to strive, in the accomplishment of your task, to maintain and strengthen the relations which exist between us. We promise to support you in all your efforts to realize this plan.

Meanwhile, as a pledge of heavenly gifts, We gladly grant you Our apostolic blessing in the Lord, to you, Beloved Son, Illustrious and Honorable Man, as well as to the whole Slovak nation.

Written in Rome, at Saint Peter, December 5, 1939, the first year of Our Pontificate.

(Translated from the Latin)   Pius XII

APPENDIX VI

THE 1943 "CHRISTMAS AGREEMENT"

The ideological groupings in Slovakia—which even after October 6, 1938, have remained faithful to the principles of anti-Fascist democracy, and to the present day have actively opposed the political, economic and cultural coercion of the Slovak people, and which today represent the actual thinking of all strata of the Slovak nation—have decided to create a common political leadership, the Slovak National Council, as the only representative of the political will of the Slovak nation at home.

I. The Role and Aims of the Slovak National Council are:

1. Unitedly and centrally to wage the fight of the Slovak nation for the removal of the Nazi-German dictatorship, which is being enforced by the domestic usurpers of political power.

2. At the first opportune moment to seize all political, legislative, military, or administrative power in Slovakia and exercise it according to the will of the people until such time as freely elected representatives of the people are able to take over all power.

3. As soon as possible after the seizure of power, the Slovak National Council will make it possible for the Slovak people to elect freely its own representatives to whom the Slovak National Council shall surrender all power.

4. In its activity the Slovak National Council shall proceed in understanding with the Czecho-Slovak government and the entire resistance movement abroad, whose work in international and military domains it recognizes and supports.

II. The associated groupings and components of the Council have agreed on these principles:

1. It is our desire that the Slovak nation and the Czech nation, as the most related Slav nations, work out their future destiny in the Czecho-Slovak Republic, that is, in a joint State of the Slovaks and Czechs, and on a basis of equality.

2. We desire close collaboration with all Slav States and nations, especially with the Soviet Union in which we see the guarantee of a free life and universal progress of small nations generally and of the Slav nations particularly.

3. The future Czecho-Slovak Republic shall conduct its foreign policy in the spirit of these principles; therefore, in the international and military fields shall rely on the U.S.S.R.

4. The internal order of the future Czecho-Slovak Republic shall be democratic; but all fascist, racial, totalitarian tendencies, and such as shall be in conflict with these principles shall be eradicated. In this spirit the internal political regime shall be firm, but democratic. It is necessary to avoid the mistakes and errors of the past.

5. The concept of democracy must be carried over and intensified also in the economic and social fields, so that the distribution of the national income among all the inhabitants be as equal as possible and the life of every citizen be humanly dignified.

6. Culture, education, and learning are to be governed by these principles. Freedom of religious beliefs shall be preserved, but the influence of the churches on policies and leadership of the State shall be excluded.

7. The definitive regulation of these questions—and especially the legal, constitutional adjustment of the relationship of the Slovak nation to the Czech nation—shall be decided, on the Slovak side, exclusively by freely designated representatives of the Slovak nation.

Bratislava
Christmas, 1943

APPENDIX VII

THE KOŠICE AGREEMENT OF APRIL 5, 1945*

As the first homeland government of the Republic, the (Czecho-Slovak) government shall regard itself as the embodiment of the Czecho-Slovak State union founded on new principles. Putting an end to all old controversies, and proceeding on the basis of recognizing the Slovaks as a nationally independent nation, the government shall from the very beginning consistently strive to realize the principle of "equal among equals" in Czecho-Slovak relationship in order to establish a real brotherhood of the two nations.

Recognizing that the Slovaks are to be the masters in their own Slovak homeland, just as the Czechs in their national homeland, and that the Republic will be re-established as a joint State of equal nations—the Czechs and Slovaks—the government shall express this recognition in important acts of State policy.

It will see in the Slovak National Council, which bases itself on the National Committees of the towns and counties, not only the authorized spokesmen of the Slovak nation, but also the bearer of State power in the territory of Slovakia, State power being legislative, administrative, and executive, in accordance with the special agreement of the Slovak National Council with the President of the Republic and the Czecho-Slovak government in London.

The common State task shall be conducted by the government as the central organ, in the closest collaboration with the Slovak National Council and also with the Board of Commissioners, the executive organ of the Slovak National Council.

Within the framework of the newly established united Czecho-Slovak armed forces, and on the basis of united service regulations, Slovak national military formations shall be established—regiments, divisions, etc.—composed in most part of men, noncommissioned officers and officers of Slovak nationality, and using Slovak as the commanding and service language. The commissioned and warrant officers of the former Slovak Army who did not violate the national honor of the Slovaks and who are not under criminal prosecution because of their activity during the former traitorous regime, shall be taken into the Czecho-Slovak

* Portion dealing with the status of Slovakia.

Army in their present ranks—in so doing, recommendations and opinions of the Slovak National Council shall be abided by.

When the constitutional establishment of the relations of the Slovak and Czech nations is made, the new government of the Republic shall strive to have the Slovak legislative, administrative, and executive organs constituted in the same manner as the Slovak nation has them at present in the Slovak National Council.

The future division of jurisdiction between the central organs and the Slovak organs shall be determined by the authorized representatives of the Czech and Slovak nations. In the central State offices and economic organs of an all-State significance, the Slovaks shall be assured proportional representation in regard to number as well as importance of posts.

Appendix VIII

AGREEMENT FOR COOPERATION AMONG THE NATIONAL BLOC PARTIES OF THE URBAN AND RURAL WORKING PEOPLE

Prague, June, 1945, No. 2 in Small Current Events Library
Svoboda (Knihovnička Aktualít), Editor Gustav Bareš.

In joint consultations, the representatives of the Communist, Social Democratic, and National Socialist parties have agreed on the following principles and directives which shall determine their common policy:

1) While safeguarding their political and organizational independence, the National Bloc parties (Communist party, Social Democratic party, and National Socialist party) shall collaborate closely and take joint measures in all questions concerning the public life of the liberated Republic. They consider the Governmental Program agreed upon unanimously during the consultations in Moscow and adopted unanimously by the government on 5 April 1945 in Košice to be the political platform of the National Bloc. The thorough implementation of this program shall be the common task of the National Bloc parties.

2) In each locality of the Czech lands where the parties of the National Bloc exist, local coordinating committees of the National Bloc shall be founded. Likewise, coordinating committees shall be organized for districts, counties, and provinces. The su-

preme organ will be the Central Coordinating Committee of the National Bloc. In each coordinating committee on all levels, each participating party shall be represented by an equal number of delegates.

3) Within the coordinating committees, the parties of the National Bloc shall agree on common policies to be pursued on the municipal, district, county, and province level and, finally, in the government. The coordinating committees shall also establish the common political line for the parties of the Bloc in all other public questions which arise in the fields of politics, economics, social welfare, and culture.

4) The National Bloc parties agree that in the liberated Republic the trade unions, cooperatives, professional, cultural, and athletic associations as well as youth organizations shall be organized on a nation wide scale. These organizations shall be independent of political parties, membership shall be voluntary, and leadership elected through democratic procedure. The National Bloc parties consider it their duty to promote the formation of such organizations and to resist adamantly any attempt to split them. The aforementioned national organizations shall be permitted to criticize the government and the public administration.

5) Centrally directed trade-unions shall be organized to include, on the basis of voluntary membership, all categories of wage earners (workers, persons performing services, officials, technicians, engineers, and other intellectuals), whether employed by public or private enterprise. We recommend that the trade-unions be grouped into specialized sections for the various branches of industry and labor under a central body representing all trade-unions (Central Council of Trade-Unions). The permanent organizational structure of the trade-unions shall be adopted by the Congress of All Trade-Unions. In forming the general organization as well as the Central Council of Trade-Unions, maximum consideration should be given to proportional representation of trade-unions which existed before September 29, 1938.

6) A central occupational union of peasants shall be created, in which all peasants, particularly holders of small and medium farms, shall be associated on the principle of voluntary membership. The central occupational union of peasants (Central Union of Czech Peasants) shall be nonpartisan and independent of political parties, and shall be open to party and nonparty members. The directing organs of the Central Union of Peasants on all

levels shall be elected by the members according to democratic rules. The National Bloc parties shall follow a coordinated policy with respect to the Central Union of Peasants.

7) Cooperative movements of all kinds (consumer, producer, agricultural, and financial cooperatives, etc.) shall be purged from leadership imposed by occupants and traitors, and the members shall be permitted to elect new leadership. Henceforth, all branches of the cooperative movement shall be promoted through a common nonpartisan effort and developed according to the principle of unity and independence. Every effort by political parties and pressure groups to abuse this movement should be prevented. All citizens without regard to political party shall be free to associate in cooperatives which at all levels shall be governed by organs elected by the members of the cooperative in question. The National Bloc parties shall assist the development of a unified cooperative movement and coordinate their policies to this end.

8) The National Bloc parties pledge that instead of forming separate party youth organizations they will join in building a Central Czech Youth Union. This body shall avoid partisan discrimination and shall integrate on a nation wide basis the youth of the cities and rural areas, particularly working youth with an industrial or agricultural background, as well as students. In accordance with their respective programs, the parties shall be responsible for the ideological education of their young members. The Central Union of Czech Youth shall be a specialized independent organization. It shall enjoy democratic self-rule and the assistance, without interference, of all National Bloc parties.

9) The National Bloc parties agree on the need to build up the physical culture and sport movement on an integrated nation wide basis, on the principles of noninterference from the parties coupled with organizational unity. This new unified national physical culture organization shall be based on the Sokol. All loyal patriots, without distinction of political party, shall have equal rights in it.

10) In all fields of public life, the National Bloc shall promote its policy in cordial agreement and collaboration with the Populist party and all other components of the National Front such as the trade-unions and the central occupational and cultural organizations. The National Bloc considers that its mission is to be the leading and acting force in concentrating all sound components of the nation aiming at reconstruction of the liberated

Republic and its transformation into a really democratic and popular state.

11) The National Bloc parties of the urban and rural working people declare that their future actions shall be bound by the principles of the present agreement. They recommend:

a) that the political parties elect to the National Committees only those citizens, men or women, who are nationally and morally reliable and who so demonstrated under the German occupation;

b) that the National Committees of communities, districts, and provinces be everywhere formed by understanding among the governmental parties. So far as possible, the Committees should consist of equal numbers of delegates from the four parties, plus a convenient number of delegates representing the trade-unions as well as nonpartisan experts agreed upon by the parties, and loyal toward nation and State. In communities where some of the present governmental parties have only a thin representation, the local National Committee shall be appointed by agreement between the trustees of the respective governmental parties. Until the general and secret elections are held, community National Committees should be confirmed by a public meeting of voters, and district National Committees by conventions of delegates of the local committees of the district;

c) that the coordinating committees of the National Bloc parties see to the application of these principles;

d) that where agreement is impossible, appeal be taken to the coordinating committee of counties or provinces, or finally to the Central Coordinating Committee of the National Bloc.

12) The National Bloc parties further proclaim that they will seek the establishment of a Provisional National Assembly as soon as possible. Such a step will make possible the reconstruction of the government contemplated by the Governmental Program of April 5, 1945, in which due representation should be given to all successful leaders of the resistance at home and abroad. As soon as political, administrative, and social conditions become sufficiently stabilized, normal municipal elections shall be held in every community as early as possible. Being firmly decided to put these principles and directives loyally into practice, the National Bloc parties appeal to all their members to respect them and adopt them as common rules of conduct. Only a close collaboration among the National Bloc parties and their coopera-

tion with the Populist party can assure national reconstruction and the building of a Democratic People's Republic.

Done at Prague, June 8, 1945
For the Central Coordinating Committee of the National
Bloc of the Urban and Rural Working People:

> Zd. Fierlinger (Social Democratic party)
> Kl. Gottwald (Communist party)
> P. Zenkl (National Socialist party)

Appendix IX

THE AGREEMENT OF JUNE 26, 1945 BETWEEN THE SLOVAK DEMOCRATIC PARTY AND THE COMMUNIST PARTY OF SLOVAKIA

1) Neither party of the National Front has any other aim than the united, indivisible, democratic Czecho-Slovak Republic, built on the legally equal union of the Slovak and Czech nations and, in its foreign, Slovak and economic policies, depending on the Soviet Union, keeping brotherly contacts with all Slav states and nations, preserving the traditional friendly contacts with the Western allies.

2) Both parties of the National Front—the Democratic party and the Communist party of Slovakia—are aware of the fact that to perform successfully the tasks of one class or one political party is not sufficient, but that it is necessary to have harmonious cooperation of all working groups of the nation and of both our political parties which represent the will of the nation.

3) It is our unshakable will to preserve and consolidate the National Front, which is built first of all on the collaboration of the Democratic party with the Communist party of Slovakia, so that it can fulfill its great task of consolidation and reconstruction.

In the spirit of fraternal friendship of the Czech and Slovak nations, we want to maintain the most friendly cooperation of the Communist party of Slovakia and the Democratic party, federated in the Slovak National Front, with the political parties in the Czech lands, especially with the National Bloc of the Urban and Rural Working People which forms the core of political representation of the Czech nation.

4) Just as we fought together during the national uprising against the German invaders and their Magyar helpers, so together we want to cleanse Slovakia of nazi Germans, fascist Magyars, to achieve the exchange of the remaining Magyar population for the Slovaks in Hungary and abroad and thus contribute to the fulfillment of the governmental program to build the Czechoslovak Republic as a State of the Czechs and Slovaks.

5) By mutual collaboration we want to continue inexorably and uncompromisingly to expose and disarm all fascist, collaborationist and exploitationary elements.

Just as we value highly respectable, conscientious, and qualified citizens, even if they are not adherents of political parties, we shall just as certainly disarm characterless conjuncturalists, chameleons, and opportunists, as well as the prejudiced, even if they should cloak themselves with adherence to some of our parties.

7) Between the Communist party of Slovakia and the Democratic party there is complete agreement on the matter that local and district National Committees, just like economic, industrial, social, health, cultural, and other institutions of a national character, shall not become the domain of one of our political parties, but shall be so composed that they adequately represent all democratic and working groups of our citizenry.

8) The Democratic party and the Communist party of Slovakia are completely united not only in respecting and defending the right of religious confession, but also in the matter that Slovak citizens of whatever faith are equal citizens of our State. On the other hand, they expect that the churches shall not afford asylum to fascist culprits and shall not become tools of any sort of political agitation.

9 The Democratic party, just like the Communist party of Slovakia, is striving for extensive social reforms to raise the living and cultural standard of the working people and, on the other hand, the Communist party of Slovakia, just like the Democratic party, unshakably respects private ownership by peasants, tradesmen, businessmen, small and medium entrepreneurs, and officials.

10) Since there is agreement on all vital questions between the Democratic party and the Communist party of Slovakia, both parties shall strive for the end that, in the spirit of the collaboration of the underground and the uprising, the methods of honorable, open, sincere, and loyal collaboration become domesticated in all organizations and groups of the party.

June 26, 1945.

For the Communist party of Slovakia:

Karol Schmidke, Dr. Gustav Husák, Laco Novomeský, Dr. E. Frisch, Karol Bacílek.

For the Democratic party:

Dr. Jozef Lettrich, Dr. Fedor Hodža, Dr. Matej Josko, Dr. Jozef Kyselý ,Milan Polák.

Appendix X

PLEA OF THE CONFERENCE OF SLOVAK BISHOPS ON TISO'S BEHALF

To the Presidium of the Slovak National Council in Bratislava:

The Catholic Episcopal Conference of Slovakia, in past years, has more frequently turned to appropriate governmental offices in the interest of those who were suffering, imprisoned, or persecuted—without regard as to whether Catholics or non-Catholics were concerned. The example of the Divine Samaritan and His positive command prompted and encouraged us to raise our protective voice in the interests of the people who were suffering on account of political or racial reasons and we did that at a time when we could expect various humiliations in return.

This noblest Model in all history and His commandment, expressed in the Gospel, we bear in mind even now when we respectfully commend to Your Graciousness the fate of the former President, Dr. Joseph Tiso. We do this not only because a Catholic priest is concerned, but also because the solution of his personal problem will have a far-reaching influence on the thinking and behavior of a part of the Slovak nation in respect to the renovated Czecho-Slovak Republic and its representatives.

Furthermore, we are prompted to take this step also by the generally known actuality, which is conceded by all objective critics, that Dr. Joseph Tiso always was a zealous priest of virtuous life. In his extensive activity he tried to work for the good of the whole and did not enrich himself personally.

The administration of justice belongs among the most difficult tasks of state power. Experience proves that this delicate task is aggravated when the judgment of political transgressions is concerned. History tells us how many fatal mistakes were made dur-

ing political trials; and this results from the delicate task of im-
partially judging the activities of a political opponent. So it is no
rarity that after rendering severe verdicts in political trials, sooner
or later a call for their revision was made.

In judging the activity especially of a political leader, his in-
tentions also should be given consideration. The majority of the
Slovak nation is convinced with us that the intentions of Dr.
Joseph Tiso while performing public functions were the best.

Certainly some mistakes were made and the Catholic Bishops
of Slovakia did not fail to bring these to his attention. However,
here we must mention the generally known reality that even the
most clever political leaders frequently made serious mistakes.
Nevertheless an unbiased observer—whether a contemporary or
historian—can deduce an over-all judgment only when he evalu-
ates also the good and positive things they did. And this thesis
often outweighs the mistakes which they made in their weakness.

It will be pertinent to the matter at hand to shed some light
also from another viewpoint on the mistakes which are ascribed
to Dr. Joseph Tiso. We respectfully point out at least some of the
circumstances.

After the most recent announcements of the present governmental personalities, even the Žilina events of October, 1938, appear in a different light than that shed by the one-sided propaganda; nay, even in the press it was demonstrated that in those
political changes practically all Slovak political parties had participated.

Here it is necessary to recall also the very important document which has just now been made public during the Nuremberg trials; we mean the letter of the ruler of Hungary sent to
Berlin on March 13, 1939. This weighty circumstance gives an
altogether different significance to the March 14, 1939 decision
of Dr. Joseph Tiso and the other political leaders of that time.
One should think about what would have happened with the
Slovak nation if the plan of Horthy had succeeded.

We also know that after the issuance of anti-Jewish regulations, Dr. Joseph Tiso did want to resign from the presidency.
That he did not do so happened because he tried to hamper and
ameliorate the effects of those provisions, as well as to prevent
a greater evil. It is worthy of consideration that what the ruler
of the larger and more independent Hungary could not prevent
in his country, Dr. Joseph Tiso could not prevent in Slovakia.

After considering all the circumstances after the passage of time, even other pilloried political mistakes—such as the war in the East, the events of August 29, 1944—can be judged otherwise than the manner in which it is done by a one-sided propaganda.

The entire Slovak public is following with attention the developments of events around Dr. Joseph Tiso and in its majority is taking a negative stand toward those efforts which would incite hatred against his person. Thereby the unfortunate splintering of the nation is increased when unity of all forces is so greatly desired for the important work of construction. It will be to the credit of the farsightedness of the State and will serve the peace of the nation, if the case of Dr. Joseph Tiso is solved in a cautious way and not with merciless hardness. The above thoughts have prompted us to submit respectfully our plea for your gracious consideration and favorable decision.

With an expression of profound respect:

(Signatures):

Dr. Karol Kmeťko, Archbishop-Bishop of Nitra; Jozef Čársky, Bishop-Apostolic Administrator of Košice; Dr. Andrej Škrábik, Bishop of Banská Bystrica; Dr. Jozef Tomanóczy, Vicar General of Spiš; Dr. Pavol Jantausch, Apostolic Administrator of Trnava; Dr. Eduard Nécsey, Ordaining Bishop of Nitra.

Bratislava, January 8, 1946.

APPENDIX XI

TRIAL AGAINST "BOURGEOIS NATIONALISTS" IN THE COMMUNIST PARTY OF SLOVAKIA

(*Pravda*, Bratislava, April 25, 1954)

Main points of the act of indictment

The trial of a group of "bourgeois nationalists" in Slovakia, headed by Dr. Gustav Husák, former Chairman of the Board of Commissioners for Slovakia, and consisting of Ladislav Novomeský, former Commissioner of Education, Dr. Daniel Okáli, former Commissioner of the Interior, Dr. Ivan Horváth, former Minister Plenipotentiary of Czecho-Slovakia in Budapest, and Ladislav Holdoš, former Chief of the Office for Church Affairs in Slovakia, took place between April 21 and 24, 1954 before the criminal senate of the State Court in Bratislava. The act of indictment as read by the public prosecutor contains the following points:

While the Czech and Slovak people, after a common struggle for national liberation and after a long struggle for the elimination of the exploiters, were starting to build a new Czechoslovak State, the defendants committed criminal acts, damaging the national and State interests of the Slovak people and directed against the security and unity of the common Czechoslovak State.

The preconditions for liberation of Czechoslovakia were created by the Soviet victory in World War II. The Czech and Slovak people took power in their State and embarked on the road of a people's democracy and of building socialism, thus creating the possibilities of a new relationship between Czechs and Slovaks in the spirit of equality. Czechoslovakia was renewed as the common State of two equal nations. The Slovaks became masters in their country to the same degree as the Czechs in theirs.

The establishment of the principle of equality between the two nations put an end to the old frictions. The Košice program of April, 1945 and the Constitution of 1948 recognized the Slovak national organs, the Slovak National Council and the Board of Commissioners, as the organs of State power on Slovak territory. Slovak representatives participated in the work of Parliament and the central government, while the Slovak national organs tried, with the help of the Czech working class, to overcome as soon as possible the backwardness of Slovakia with respect to culture, economy, and so forth.

Supported and directed by the Western imperialists, the Czech and Slovak bourgeoisie stood against this policy inaugurated by the Czech and Slovak working class, trying to break the unity of the two nations. The defendants, who were renegades from the Slovak working class, assisted the reactionary bourgeoisie in their endeavors.

The ideological background of their treachery consisted in their attempts to solve the national question of the Slovak nation, not in collaboration with the Czech working class, but mainly in cooperation with the Slovak bourgeoisie. Eventually they accepted not only the leadership of that class, but also the Slovak fascist puppet State. Later on, they successfully penetrated the leadership of the Slovak national uprising and assumed important positions in the new People's Democratic State. They misused their positions in the Slovak National Council and in the Board of Commissioners in a criminal way in order to isolate Slovakia from the Czech working people and from the construction of socialism, thus strengthening in Slovakia the remnants of capitalism and jeopardizing the achievements of the Slovak working class. Their aim was to break up the common Czechoslovak State and hand Slovakia over to the reactionary bourgeoisie and the mercy of foreign imperialists.

In this activity, the defendants were directed by Vladimír Clementis, the proven enemy of the Slovak nation and agent of the Western imperialists who, in the trial of the anti-State conspiratorial center led by Rudolph Slánsky, was unmasked as a member of the leadership of this center. It became apparent from the confession made by Clementis that the defendants formed a group of bourgeois nationalists acting in common understanding.

In the case of Husák, Novomeský, Okáli, and Horváth, this development started long ago in the pre-Munich Republic, when the Slovak left wing intellectuals gathered under the leadership of Clementis around the periodical DAV. This group, originating in bourgeois society, posed as an ally of the Communist party, and some of their members even joined the party; in reality, however, DAV remained an exclusive group outside the party, following its own policy and educating young Slovak intellectuals in the spirit of Slovak bourgeois nationalism.

Clementis, Husák, and Novomeský managed to isolate the young Slovak intelligentsia from the working class and the Communist party. Slovak youth was thus isolated from the idea of class struggle and from unity with the Czech working class. This became evident as long ago as 1932, when Clementis, Novomeský, and others took part in the Trenčianske Teplice Congress of bourgeois nationalistic youth, agrarian and other youth groups, and accepted the separatist and autonomist platform of Hlinka's fascism.

Eventually the members of DAV became admirers of the imperialist agent Beneš and his conception, binding Czechoslovakia to the Western imperialists. They were not deterred by the fact that Beneš refused to recognize the existence of a separate and equal Slovak nation within the Czechoslovak Republic.

After Munich, Clementis quite openly joined the camp of Western imperialists. In the beginning of the war in Europe in 1939 and mainly during the Soviet-Finnish war, he openly expressed an antidemocratic and anti-Soviet point of view. Husák, Novomeský, Horváth, and Okáli at that time became collaborators of the Slovak fascist State, concentrating their endeavors mainly on securing a comfortable life.

Novomeský was a well-paid editor of the periodical *Budovateľ*, published by the fascist "Slovak Grain Co.," and thus became a propagator of fascist ideas in the economic world. The other three collaborated with the fascist regime in their capacity as lawyers. Novomeský was in close personal and friendly relations with Mach, Karvaš, Zaťko and others; Husák, mainly with Karvaš. (A. Mach and I. Karvaš were members of the Slovak government during World War II.)

When, after June 22, 1941, a warrant for arrest was issued against Novomeský, Husák, and others—as they had been members of the Communist party—Novomeský in a cowardly fashion visited Alexander Mach, then Minister of Interior, promising him in an abject manner that he intended to work for the Slovak fascist regime. After the warrant for arrest issued against Novomeský was revoked, his collaboration with Mach became even closer. He himself has confessed that this fact disoriented the ranks of the Slovak fighters against fascism. The other accused behaved in a similar way.

The treacherous activity of the defendants, Husák and Novomeský, against the Slovak national uprising was evident from the selection of officers for military leadership and from the hostile attitude of the leadership of the uprising toward the partisan units. Husák and Novomeský supported the endeavors to hand over the military leadership to the reactionary Beneš agents Viest, Golian, and others. They put the Slovak revolutionary forces directly to the service of Beneš, the agent of Western imperialists.

Their purpose was to create the preconditions for preserving the capitalistic order in Slovakia. Horváth has confessed that he agreed with Novomeský to leave all preparations and all decisions regarding the starting signal for the uprising of the Slovak revolutionary forces to Golian, Ferjenčík, and others, in the knowledge that such a decision was directly opposed to the interests of the U.S.S.R. When the uprising began, they tried to help the counter-revolutionary forces around the imperialist agents Ursíny, Lettrich, Viest, Golian, and others in order to neutralize the revolutionary forces of the workers.

These traitors entered the People's Democratic State under an obligation to officials of the former fascist Slovak State and to representatives of the reactionary Slovak bourgeoisie, Lettrich, Ursíny, etc.; and, through Clementis, also to Beneš.

Crimes Directed Against the Foundations of the Republic

As early as 1944, the accused cooperated with Clementis on their subversive activities. The accused Novomeský, Ursíny, and Lt. Col. Vesel, at that time representatives of the Slovak National Council, flew to London where Novomeský concluded with Clementis a treacherous agreement to the effect that they would try to make impossible the creation of a united State of Czechs and Slovaks and that they would not admit the authority of the central government in Slovakia. In 1945 Clementis returned to liberated Czechoslovakia as an agent of the French secret service and as a close collaborator of Beneš. Immediately after his return, Clementis renewed his contacts with Husák, Novomeský, and Okáli. The demoralized former member of the Spanish Brigade, Holdoš, commenting on his connections with the bourgeois nationalist group, said: "Owing to my Trotskyist views, I came gradually under the influence of Husák, Novomeský, and their accomplices and began fully to cooperate in the anti-State activities of this group."

The accused Okáli gave the following evidence about the formation and development of the bourgeois nationalist group: "I was present and took part in many conversations with Husák, in which we discussed not only problems concerning the Commissariat of the Interior, which at the time was also in charge of security, but also problems concerning the whole State. In those talks, Husák advocated the view that we must under no circumstances allow the Prague government to interfere in Slovak affairs. He emphasized that we must solve all our problems alone with Slovak authorities, disregarding the attitude of the Prague government. I promised that I would support this."

The final aims of the bourgeois nationalist group were described in the evidence of all the accused. The defendant Okáli stated: "The final goal of our hostile endeavors was the creation of such conditions as would enable the bourgeoisie again to assume power in Slovakia and resurrect the independent Slovak State."

Holdoš, too, gave evidence in this matter: "We endeavored to make Slovakia once again the fifth column of the imperialists so that the Slovak bourgeoisie could regain its lost positions and power in order to contribute to the disintegration of democratic Czechoslovakia."

In the negotiations concerning the relations between the central government and the Slovak National Council, the bourgeois nationalist group tried to enforce such an authority for the Slovak National Council and the Board of Commissioners as would strengthen the position of Slovak bourgeoisie inside the Slovak executive organs and hamper Slovakia's advance toward socialism.

As to the struggle concerning the Constitution, the accused Holdoš stated: "Up to February, 1948, we demanded such authority for the Slovak national organs that the implementation of our requests would have been exclusively to the advantage of the reactionaries. After February, we concentrated on obtaining such authority as would make possible an independent policy for Slovakia, disregarding the government. We were fully aware that we were damaging the interests of the State as a whole."

The bourgeois nationalists were well aware of the importance of the State machinery in the fight of the bourgeoisie against the workers. Hence, they tried to preserve as long as possible the machinery established by the fascist Slovak State, particularly the institution of municipal and district notaries, who were the backbone of the bureaucratic machinery of the so-called Slovak State.

Aid for Fascist and Treasonable Elements

The accused, who had obligations toward representatives of Tiso's fascist State, did everything in their power after the war to aid outstanding representatives of the fascist State and protect them against their just punishment. On this the accused Novomeský said: "After the liberation, I intervened on behalf of the Minister of the Interior of the Slovak State, Alexander Mach, during the trial of Tiso and his accomplices."

By these activities, which were not confined to outstanding representatives of the fascist State, but aimed at sabotaging the punishment of traitors and fascists on the whole territory of Slovakia, the accused deliberately violated the Košice government program and the law of the Republic on the punishment of enemies, traitors, and collaborators. By these activities, the accused at the same time strengthened the position of the fascists and the followers of Hlinka's Populist party in State administration and economy.

In the Sphere of Education and Culture

The Commissariat of Education under the accused Novomeský became, thanks to him, the hideout of collaborators in science, literature and education.

In the Economic Sector

The hostile and anti-State activities of the group of accused bourgeois nationalists were also carried out in the economic field. Their aim was to preserve the economic positions of the fascists and capitalists and to disrupt economic construction in the Republic and in planned economy. In order to foil the confiscation of land in Slovakia the accused prevented the implementation of the decree of the President of the Republic on the confiscation and rapid distribution of agricultural property of traitors and enemies of the Czech and Slovak peoples. As a result of their actions, land reform in Slovakia was nearly entirely sabotaged. With the active support of the reactionary representatives of the Democratic party, the accused members of the bourgeois nationalist group sabotaged the supply of basic foodstuffs and consumer goods for the working people. The main key to this activity was their attempt to maintain as long as possible in Slovakia the supply system of the Slovak State, which aimed at strengthening the black market and aided speculators and kulaks but did not safeguard supplies for the Slovak workers.[8]

Nationality Policy

In all their activity, this group of bourgeois nationalists aimed at creating an atmosphere of hostility between the Czech and Slovak nations. Not only did their activity in the sphere of State administration and economy contribute to this end, but also a number of their speeches and utterances were calculated to engender a feeling of national hatred between the workers of Czech and Slovak nationality.

Crimes Against the Security of the Republic

In 1945 the defendant Horváth, on direct instructions from the prominent member of the leadership of the anti-State conspiratory center and imperialist agent Clementis, entered into contact with Etienne Manac'h, the former French Consul-General in Bratislava, who was engaged in creating important bases in Slovakia for the French espionage network. The defendant Horváth admitted the following about his espionage connections with Manac'h: "Clementis, who introduced me to Manac'h, told me to render every assistance to Manac'h after his arrival in Bratislava and to pass on to him information about conditions in Slovakia for which he would ask."

Holdoš also provided the French espionage service, via Manac'h, with espionage material after 1945. He also provided data to the Cultural Attaché of the French Consulate, Professor Chollet, and Vice-Consul Michelot.

Help to and Organization of Escape Abroad
for Enemies of the State

After February, 1948, the accused bourgeois nationalists enabled their accomplices Lettrich, Fraštacký and others to escape abroad. The defendant Okáli said in this matter: "In my office as Commissioner for the Interior, I failed to investigate the cooperation with the Nazis of certain Zionists who, in Tiso's fascist State, worked in the Jewish Center in Bratislava and who, during World War II, engaged in information service work for the State Security Office and the German Gestapo. I also failed to follow up the subversive activity of the Zionist organization in Bratislava."

On the basis of these facts the defendants Husák, Novomeský, Okáli, Horváth and Holdoš are rightly accused of having conspired with members of the conspiratory center of Vladimír Clementis and others in order to attempt the destruction of the independence and constitutional unity of the Republic and its People's Democratic State system. All defendants violated the duties of their positions with the intention of foiling and harming the execution of a single economic plan, in order to bring about serious disorders in the operation of the State and the economic apparatus. The defendants Horváth and Holdoš conspired with other people, or entered into contact with a foreign power or foreign agents, with the intention of betraying State secrets. Thus all defendants committed the crime of high treason according to Art. 78, 1-A, C, 2-A and 3-B, of the Penal Code; the crime of sabotage according to Art. 85, 1-A, B, 2-A, B, and C, and 3-B of the Penal Code; the defendants Holdoš and Horváth committed the crimes of espionage according to Art. 5, 1 and 2-B, C, D, and Law No. 231-1948.

Sentences of the State Court: Gustav Husák, life imprisonment; Ivan Horváth, twenty-two years; Daniel Okáli, eighteen years; Ladislav Holdoš, thirteen years, and Ladislav Novomeský, ten years. All lost their civic rights and property.

Bibliography

Académie Diplomatique Internationale. *Dictionnaire diplomatique, Tchécoslovaquie*, IV. Paris: 1948.

Address of the Slovak Action Committee to the Council of Foreign Ministers. Bridgeport, Conn.: November, 1946.

Aide-mémoire sur l'existence de la République slovaque et sur la nécessité de conclure le Traité de Paix avec elle. Paris: 1946.

Allix, Leyritz et Merlier. *Géographie pour l'enseignement secondaire: Classe de philosophie*. Paris: 1936.

Appeal of the Slovak Action Committee to the Civilized World Concerning the Deportation of the Slovak Population in Sudeten by the Czechs. Bridgeport, Conn.: February, 1947.

Association Hongroise des Affaires étrangères. *La déportation des Hongrois de Slovaquie*. Budapest: 1947.

Auerbach, B. *Les races et les nationalités en Autriche-Hongrie*. Paris: 1898.

Aulneau, J. *Histoire de l'Europe centrale*. Paris: 1926.

Autonomist. *Slovakia's Plea for Autonomy*. Middletown, Pa.: 1935.

Baník, A. A. *Ján Baltazár Magin a jeho politická, národná i kultúrna obrana Slovákov r. 1728* (*Ján Baltazár Magin and His Defense of the Slovak Nation, Politics and Culture of 1728*). Trnava: 1936.

_____. "Krest'anské idee v slovenskom národnom živote" (Christian Ideas in Slovak National Life) *Kultúra*, XV. Trnava: 1943.

Beis, G. "La nouvelle géographie administrative de la Tchécoslovaquie," *L'information géographique*, (Juillet-Octobre, 1949).

Bél, Mathias. *Notitia Hungariae novae historico-geographica*, I-IV. Vienna: 1735-1742.

Beneš, E. *Czechoslovak Policy for Victory and Peace*. London: 1944.

_____. *Détruisez l'Autriche-Hongrie!* Paris: 1916.

_____. "Discours aux Slovaques sur le présent et l'avenir de notre nation," *Le Monde Slave* (Paris), (Fevrier, 1934).

_____. *Gedanke und Tat. I-II. Vom Bau und Leben des Staates*. Prague: 1937.

_____. *La démocratie aujourd'hui et demain*. Neuchâtel: 1944.

————. La politique extérieure de la République tchécoslovaque, Exposé du 27 Janvier 1921. Prague: 1921.

————. Le problème de l'Autriche et la question tchèque (Thèse). Paris: 1908.

————. Le programme du nouveau Cabinet tchécoslovaque, Exposé du 18 octobre 1921. Prague: 1921.

————. Où vont les Slaves? Paris: 1948.

————. Memoirs. London: 1954.

————. Problème de la Tchécoslovaquie. Prague: 1936.

————.Souvenirs de Guerre et de Révolution 1914-1918, I, II. Paris: 1928.

Bittner, K. "Zur slovakischen Geschichtsschreibung," Geist der Zeit, XVIII. 1940.

Blaško, Š. Slovakia in Blood and Shackles. Passaic, N.J.: 1954.

Blondel, G. "La desagrégation de la Tchécoslovaquie. Paris: 1938.

Bobek, W. Prehľadné dejiny slovenskej literatúry (Historical Outline of Slovak Literature). Bratislava: 1939.

Bokes, Fr. Dejiny Slovákov a Slovenska (History of the Slovaks and Slovakia). Bratislava: 1946.

————. Literarische Uebersicht des geschichtlichen Schaffens in der Slovakei. Leipziger Vierteljahrsschrift für Südosteuropa, IV. Leipzig: 1940.

————. Slovenský životný priestor v minulosti a dnes (Slovak Living Space in the Past and Present. Bratislava: 1943.

————. Vývin predstáv o slovenskom území v 19. storočí (The Evolution of Ideas on Slovak Territory in the Nineteenth Century). Turčiansky Sv. Martin: 1945.

Bokes, Jankovič, and Polla. Bibliografia slovenskej histórie za r. 1939-1942 (Bibliography of Slovak History, 1939 - 1942. Turčiansky Sv. Martin: 1943.

Bokes and Vajcík. Historický atlas k slovenským dejinám (Slovak History Atlas). Bratislava: 1942.

Bonnet, G. De Washington au Quai d'Orsay. Genève: 1946.

Botto, J. Dejiny Matice slovenskej (1863-1875) (History of the "Matica slovenská," [1863-1875]). Turčiansky Sv. Martin: 1923.

————. "Matúš Čák Trenčiansky-Jeho doba" ("Mathias Čák de Trenčín and His Epoch"), Slovenské pohľady (Turčiansky Sv. Martin), XXI, (1901).

_____. *Slováci. Vývin ich národného povedomia (The Slovaks. The Evolution of Their National Consciousness)*, I, II. Turčiansky Sv. Martin: 1906.

Braibant, G. *La planification en Tchécoslovaquie.* Paris: 1948.

Braunias, K. *Die Slowaken.* Stuttgart-Berlin: 1942.

Buc, B. S. *Slovak Nationalism.* Middletown, Pa.: 1960.

Buck, P. *La tragédie tchécoslovaque de septembre 1938 à mars 1939.* Paris: 1939.

Bujnák, P. "Slovník naučný slovenský," (Slovak Encyclopedia), I-III. Praha-Bratislava: 1932.

Carr, E. H. *Nationalism and After.* London: 1945.

Cavalli, F. S. "Caratteristiche della lotta contro la Chiesa in Cecoslovacchia," *Civiltà Cattolica* (Roma), (April 15, 1950).

Čep, J. "La lutte religieuse en Tchécoslovaquie," *Esprit* (Paris), (November, 1949).

Chaloupecký, V. "O znaku Slovenska" ("The Coats of Arms of Slovakia,") *Friedrich's Symposium.* Prague: 1931.

_____. *Staré Slovensko (Ancient Slovakia).* Bratislava: 1923.

_____. *Universita Petra Pázmánya a Slovensko (Peter Pázmány University and Slovakia).* Bratislava: 1935.

_____. *Zápas o Slovensko 1918 (The Struggle for Slovakia in 1918).* Prague: 1930.

Champeaux, G. *La croisade des démocraties,* I-III. Paris: 1943.

Chladný, Hanoš M. *Láska k národu (The Love of the Nation).* Bratislava: 1944.

Chmelař, J. *Les minorités nationales en Europe centrale.* Prague: 1937.

Chudoba, B. "Czechoslovakia. A study in Disintegration," *Thought,* XXV. No. 96.

_____. *Jindy a nyní (Past and Present).* Prague: 1945.

Churchill, W. *The Second World War,* I-VI. Boston: 1948-1953.

Cieker, J. *Slovenská otázka (The Slovak Question).* Bratislava: 1935.

Cincík, J. G. *Ancient Slovak Fibulas and Pseudo-Fibulas.* Whiting, Ind.: 1957.

_____. *Anglo-Saxon and Slovak-Avar Patterns of the Cuthbert Gospel.* Cleveland-Rome: 1958.

Clementis, V. *Medzi nami a Madarmi (Between Us and the Magyars),* London: 1943.

_____. *Odkazy z Londýna (Messages from London).* Bratislava: 1947.

————. *Panslavism, Past and Present.* London: 1943.

————. "Principes de la politique extérieure tchécoslovaque," *Démocratie nouvelle* (Paris), (Février, 1949).

Comité d'action Slovaque. *Aide-mémoire sur la nécessité du plebiscite en Slovaquie.* Paris: 1946.

————. *Pro-memoria adressé au Conseil économique et social des Nations Unies concernant des actes criminels contre l'Humanité et contre les droits fondamentaux de l'Homme commis par les collaborateurs du communisme international en Slovaquie.* New York: 1948.

————. *Demande adressée à l'Assemblée générale des Nations Unies concernant la création d'une commission d'enquête sur le persécution religieuse en Slovaquie et l'exclusion de la Tchécho-Slovaquie des Nations Unies.* Buenos Aires: 1949.

Conseil National Slovaque à l'Etranger. *Aide-mémoire concernant les visées politiques du soi-disant Conseil de la Tchécoslovaquie libre.* Paris: 1949.

————. *Déclaration au sujet du soi-disant Conseil de la Tchécoslovaquie libre.* Rome: June 15, 1949).

Crabites, P. *Beneš, Statesman of Central Europe.* London: 1935.

Craon-Poussy, R. de. "L'Eglise catholique et l'Etat communiste en Tchécoslovaquie," *Etudes* (Paris), (December, 1949).

Čapek, K. *President Masaryk Tells His Story.* London: 1934.

Čulen, K. *Dejiny Slovákov v Amerike (History of the Slovak People in America),* I, II. Bratislava: 1942.

————. *Česi a Slováci v štátnych službách Č.S.R. (Czechs and Slovaks in the Administration of the Czecho-Slovak Republic).* Bratislava: 1944.

————. *Memorandum národa slovenského z r. 1861 (Memorandum of the Slovak Nation of 1861).* Turčiansky Sv. Martin: 1941.

————. *Po Svätoplukovi druhá naša hlava (Biography of Monsignor Tiso).* Middletown, Pa.: 1947.

————. *Pittsburgská dohoda (The Pittsburgh Agreement).* Bratislava: 1937.

————. *Roky slovenských nádejí a sklamaní 1848-1875 (The Years of Slovak Hopes and Disillusions: 1848-1875.* Trnava: 1932.

————. *Zum Slowakisch-Ungarischen Verhältniss.* Bratislava: 1940.

Darras, M. "Onze ans de vie indépendante en Slovaquie," *Le Monde Slave* (Paris), (May-June, 1930).

Daxner, Štefan Marko. *Slovenská otázka od konca 18. stoletia (The Slovak Question from the End of the Eighteenth Century)*. Turčiansky Sv. Martin: 1912.

Denis, E. *La question d'Autriche: Les Slovaques*. Paris: 1917.

Dérer, I. *Tchèques et Slovaques*. Paris: 1938.

Descotes, M. *Aspects de la Tchécoslovaquie*. Paris: 1948.

Diamond, W. *Czechoslovakia between East and West*. London: 1947.

Die Slowakische Republik, Soziale Fürsorge und Kulturleben (*"Blaue Bücherei,"* Nr. 3) Bratislava: 1941.

Dubois, M. "La Tchécoslovaquie," *L'Information géographique* (Paris), (May-June, 1947).

Dulová and Jeršov. *Francúzski bojovníci v slovenskom národnom povstaní (Frenchmen in the Slovak National Uprising)*. Bratislava: 1947.

Durčanský, F. *Der Weg zur slowakischen Freiheit*. Bratislava: 1944.

————. "L'Europe centrale dans le passé et dans l'avenir," *La Revue de Droit International* (Genève), No. 1 (1944).

————. "Le problème de l'existence de la Tchécoslovaquie," *La Revue de Droit International* (Genève), No. 3. (1944).

————. *Pohľad na slovenskú politickú minulosť (A Glance at the Slovak Political Past)*. Bratislava: 1943.

————. *Slovenská Biela kniha (The Slovak White Book)*. Buenos Aires: 1954).

————. *The International Aspects of the Slovak Question*. New York: 1954.

Dvornik, F. *Les Slaves, Byzance et Rome au IXe siècle*. Paris: 1926.

Eisenmann, L. *La Tchécoslovaquie*. Paris: 1921.

————. *Le compromis austro-hongrois de 1867*. Paris: 1904.

————. *Un grand Européen: Edouard Beneš*. Paris: 1934.

European Movement. *Basis for an Eastern European Policy*. London: 1950.

Felix, J. *Červená armáda a S.S.S.R. v. našom boji za slobodu (The Red Army and the U.S.S.R. in Our Fight for Freedom)*. Bratislava: 1945.

Frisch, E. "Spojenci a povstanie" ("The Allies and the Uprising"), *Pravda* (Bratislava), (August 24, 1949).

Gadourek, I. *The Political Control of Czechoslovakia*. Leiden: 1953.

Gašpar, T.J. *Das slowakische nationale Bewusstsein.* Bratislava: 1942.

————. *Der Präsident der Slowakischen Republik.* Bratislava: 1942.

Garin-Michajlovskij, J. *Die Entstehung der Slowakischen Republik als historische Notwendigkeit der Entwicklung Europas.* Bratislava: 1944.

Genet, L. *Histoire contemporaine (1919-1939).* Paris: 1946.

George, P. *Le problème allemand en Tchécoslovaquie.* Paris: 1947.

Gierach, E. *Die Germanen in der Slowakei (Deutschtumsfragen in Nordkarpathen).* Kežmarok: 1943.

Glaser, K. *Czecho-Slovakia: A Critical History.* Caldwell. Idaho: 1961.

Goláň, K. "Príspevok k vývoju slovenskej myšlienky" ("Contribution to the Evolution of Slovak Thought,") *Historica slovaca,* (Turčiansky Sv. Martin), I-II, (1940-1941).

Gottwald, K. *Kupredu, zpátky ni krok (Forward! Events of February, 1948.* Prague: 1949.

————. *Slovensko hladuje (Slovakia Is Hungry).* Bratislava: 1925.

————. *Za socialistický stát, za socialistické právo (For a Socialist State, for a Socialist Law).* Prague: 1950.

Grečo, M. *Martinská deklarácia (The Declaration of Turčiansky Sv. Martin).* Bratislava: 1939.

Grivec, F. *Slovenska apostola Sv. Ciril i Method (The Slav Apostles Saint Cyril and Saint Methodius).* Ljubljana: 1927.

Henderson, N. M. *Failure of a Mission.* New York-London: 1940.

Herben-Hartl-Bláha. *T. G. Masaryk.* Prague: 1923.

Hevesy, A. *L'agonie d'un empire: L'Autriche-Hongrie.* (Paris, 1923).

Historical Section of the Foreign Office. *Slovakia.* London: 1920.

Hitchcock, E. B. *Beneš: The Man and Statesman.* London: 1940.

Hlinka, A. *Mémoire des Slovaques à la Conference de la Paix.* Paris: 1919.

Hodál, J. *Die alte Slowakei.* Bratislava: 1942.

————. *Kostol kniežaťa Pribinu v Nitre (The Church of Prince Pribina at Nitra).* Nitra: 1930.

Hodža, M. "Die Slowakisch-Rumänische Zusammenarbeit im Budapester Parlament," *Prager Rundschau.* (Prague,) V. (1935).

_____. *Česko-Slovenský rozkol (The Czecho-Slovak Schism).* Turčiansky Sv. Martin: 1920.

_____. *Federation in Central Europe.* London: 1942.

_____. *La nouvelle situation de l'Europe et de la Tchécoslovaquie.* Prague: 1938.

Hoch, Charles. *Les partis politiques en Tchécoslovaquie.* Prague: 1935.

Holák, J. *Politické snahy slovenské v rokoch 1848-1849 (Slovak Political Efforts in 1848-1849).* Prague: 1936.

Horanská, E. *Rozpomienky na slovenské národné povstanie (Memories of the Slovak National Uprising).* Turčiansky Sv. Martin: 1945.

Houdek, F. "Československo-maďarské hranice" ("The Frontier between Czecho Slovakia and Hungary"), *Prúdy* (Bratislava), XIV, (1930).

_____. "Kapitulácia Maďarov v r. 1918" ("The Capitulation of the Magyars in 1918"), *Prúdy* (Bratislava), XII, (1928).

_____. *Oslobodenie Slovenska (The Liberation of Slovakia).* Bratislava: 1929.

_____. *Vznik hraníc Slovenska (The Origin of Slovakia's Frontiers).* Bratislava: 1931.

Hrobák, P. A. *"Czechoslovakia": History Made to Order.* Middletown, Pa.: 1958.

Hromádka, J. L. *Mezi Východem a Západem (Between East and West).* Prague: 1947.

Hrušovský, F. "Knieža Pribina" ("Prince Pribina,") *Slovenské pohľady* (Turčiansky Sv. Martin), XLIX, (1933).

_____. *Memorandum národa slovenského z r. 1861 a jeho osud (The Slovak Nation's Memorandum and its Fate).* Turčiansky Sv. Martin: 1941.

_____. *Geschichte der Slowakei.* Bratislava: 1942.

_____. *Slovensko v dejinách Strednej Európy (Slovakia in the History of Central Europe).* Turčiansky Sv. Martin: 1939.

_____. *Slovenskí vladári (The Slovak Princes).* Scranton, Pa.: 1948.

_____. *This is Slovakia.* Scranton, Pa.: 1953.

Hurban, Vajanský S. "Nahľady a výhľady" (Opinions and Perspectives. An Attempt to Describe Contemporary Slovak Spiritual Life with Memories of the Past"), *Complete Works,* XI. Turčiansky Sv. Martin: 1912.

————. *Rok 1847-1848 (The Year 1847 - 1848).* Turčiansky Sv. Martin: 1907.

————. *Život Štefana Moyesa (The Life of Bishop Stephan Moyses).* Turčiansky Sv. Martin: 1935.

Husák, G. *Zápas o zajtrajšok (The Struggle for the Future).* Bratislava: 1948.

Húsek, J. *Hranice mezi zemí Moravskoslezskou a Slovenskem (The Frontier Between Moravia-Silesia and Slovakia).* Prague: 1932.

————. *Národopisná hranice mezi Slováky a Karpatorusy (The Ethnographic Frontier Between the Slovaks and the Carpathian Ruthenians).* Bratislava: 1925.

Huščava, A. "Listina pápeža Jána VII. k Sv. Methodovi a univerzalita svetskej moci pápežskej" ("The Letter from Pope John VIII to Saint Methodius and the Universality of the Temporal Power of the Papacy"), *Sborník Ríša Veľkomoravská.* Prague: 1933.

Ingrim, R. *After Hitler Stalin.* Milwaukee: 1946.

Janin, M. *Général M. R. Štefánik.* Prague: 1929.

Janota, M. *Nápor proti Trianonu (The Opposition to the Trianon Treaty).* Prague: 1933.

Janšák, Š. *Les conditions sociales dans l'ancienne Hongrie et la situation de la Slovaquie.* Prague: 1932.

Jehlicska, F. *André Hlinka à la Conférence de la Paix de Paris.* Genève: 1938.

Jezerník, V. *Západoslovanská federální unie (Federal Union of the Western Slavs).* London-Edinburgh: 1942.

Judgment of the International Military Tribunal for the Trial of German Major War Criminals, (Nuremberg), September 30-October 1, 1946), London: 1946. Cmd 6964.

Jurovský, A. "Slovenská národná povaha" ("The Slovak National Character,"), *Slovenská vlastiveda. (Encyclopedia on Slovakia).* Bratislava: 1943.

Kadlec, K. *Uherské ústavní dějiny* (Constitutional History of Hungary). Prague: 1930.

Kálal, K. *Za ideou (In Pursuit of an Idea: the Czecho-Slovak Problem).* Prague: 1928.

Karpát, J. *Corona Regni Hungariae v dobe arpádovskej (The Crown of the Kingdom of Hungary in Arpad's Time).* Bratislava: 1937.

————. "Dejiny uhorského štátneho pojmu s hľadiska právneho" ("The History of the Conception of the Hungarian State from the Juridical Viewpoint"), *Historica Slovaca* (Turčiansky Sv. Martin), I-II. (1941-1942).

————. *Zákonodárna moc v Uhorsku v rokoch 1525-1604 (The Legislative Power in Hungary from 1525 to 1604)*. Bratislava: 1944.

Kaser, H. *Der Volks und Kulturboden des Slowakeideutschtums.* Breslau: 1934.

Katolícke Slovensko (Catholic Slovakia, 1883-1933). (A Symposium). Trnava: 1933.

Kirschbaum, J. Slovakia: *Nation at the Crossroads of Central Europe.* New York: 1960.

Knappek, L. "Cirkev a štát v boji o rozšírenie kresťanstva v IX, storočí" ("Church and State in the Struggle for the Spread of Christianity in the Ninth Century"), *Sborník Ríša Veľkomoravská.* Prague: 1933.

Kolesár, M. *Zlatá kniha Slovenska (The Golden Book of Slovakia, 1918-1930).* Bratislava: 1929.

Kompánek, A. *Slovák: jeho povaha, vlastnosti a schopnosti (The Slovak: His Character, Qualities and Talents).* Prague: 1921.

Kotátko, J. *La réforme agraire en Tchécoslavaquie.* Prague: May, 1948.

Krajčovič, V. *Die Struktur der slowakischen Wirtschaft.* Bratislava: 1941.

————. "Der Anfang der slowakischen Industrie im Selbständigen Staate," *Slowakische Rundschau* (Batislava) No. 7 (1943).

Kramár, V. *Kulturně-politický program K.S.Č. a výtvarné umění (The Cultural Program of the Czechoslovak Communist Party and Art).* Prague: 1946.

Krčméry, S. *Stopätdesiat rokov slovenskej litertúry (A Hundred and Fifty Years of Slovak Literature).* Turčiansky Sv. Martin: 1943.

Križko, P. "Stredoveké národnostné pomery na Slovensku" ("The Ethnographic Condition of Slovakia in the Middle Ages,") *Sborník Múzeálnej slovenskej spoločnosti,* (Turčiansky Sv. Martin), II. (1897).

Krofta, K. *Československé dějiny (Czechoslovak History).* Prague: 1946.

————. *Čtení o ustavních dějinách slovenských (Course in the Constitutional History of Slovakia).* Prague: 1924.

———. *Histoire de la Tchéchoslovaquie.* Maestricht-Paris-Bruxelles: 1934.

———. *La Tchécoslovaquie en face de la tension internationale.* Prague: 1937.

Kunosi, A. *The Basis of Czechoslovak Unity.* London: 1944.

La Constitution de la République tchécoslovaque. Introduction by J. Hoetzel and V. Joachim. Prague: 1920.

Lades, H. *Die Nationalitätenfrage im Karpathenraum. Der österreichische Ordnungsversuch 1848-1849.* Wien-Leipzig: 1941.

Latu, R. *L'Eglise derrière le Rideau de fer.* Paris: 1949.

Léger, L. *Le Panslavisme et l'Intérêt français.* Paris: 1917.

Lemkin, R. *Axis Rule in Occupied Europe.* Washington: 1944.

Le nouveau régime du travail en Tchécoslovaquie. Prague: 1949.

Le Plan économique biennal tchécoslovaque. (Texte de la loi). Prague: 1949.

Les assurances-pension des mineurs en Tchécoslovaquie. Prague: 1947.

Lettrich, J. *History of Modern Slovakia.* New York: 1955.

Locher, Th. J. *Die nationale Differenzierung und Integrierung der Slowaken und Tschechen in ihrem geschichtlichen Verlauf bis 1848.* Harlem: 1931.

Macartney, C. A. *Hungary and Her Successors.* London-New York-Toronto: 1937.

———. *National States and National Minorities.* London: 1934.

———. *Problems of the Danube Basin.* London: 1942.

Mackenzie, C. *Dr. Beneš.* London: 1946.

Macurek, J. *Dějiny Maďarů a uherského státu (History of the Magyars and the Hungarian State).* Prague: 1934.

Markovič, J. *Slovensko pred prevratom (Slovakia before 1918).* Bratislava: 1924.

Masaryk, J. *Ani opona ani most! (Neither Iron Curtain Nor Bridge!).* Prague: 1947.

———. "La mission de la Tchécoslovaquie," *Cahiers du Monde Nouveau* (Paris), November, 1946.

Masaryk, T. G. *Cesta demokracie (The Way of Democracy),* II. Prague: 1933-1934.

———. *Česká otázka (The Czech Question).* Prague: 1908.

———. *Les Slaves après la guerre.* Prague: 1923.

———. *The Making of a State.* New York: 1927.

———. *Les problèmes de la démocratie.* Paris: 1924.

———. *Palackého idea národa českého (The Idea of the Czech Nation in Palacký).* Prague: 1947.

————. *The New Europe*. London: 1918.

————. *The Problem of Small Nations in the European Crisis*. London: 1915.

Massenon, L. "Edouard Beneš et le slavisme," *Ecrits de Paris*, (October, 1948).

Matejko, Q. *Svätoštefanská myšlienka predtým a dnes (Saint Stephen's Conception of the Unity of Hungary in the Past and Present)*. Prešov-Bratislava: 1943.

————. "Predrevolučné Slovensko-jeho mentálne základy," ("Slovakia before 1918 and the Essence of Its Mentality") *Slovenské pohľady*, (Turčiansky Sv. Martin), LIX, (1943).

Matunák, M. "Slovensko nikdy nepatrilo ani k Česku ani k Poľsku," ("Slovakia Never Belonged to Either Czechia Or Poland"), *Kultúra* (Trnava), II. (1927).

————. *Svätý Cyril i Methód-slovanskí apoštolovia (St. Cyril and St. Methodius, Slav Apostles)*. Trnava: 1926.

Mederly, K. *Ústava Slovenskej Republiky a jej zásadné smernice (The Constitution of the Slovak Republic and Its Principles)*. Bratislava: 1939.

Medvecký, K. *Cirkevné pomery katolíckych Slovákov v niekdajšom Uhorsku (The Position of the Catholic Church among the Slovaks in the Hungary of Yesteryear)*. Ružomberok: 1920.

————. *Slovenský prevrat (The Change-Over in Slovakia)*, I-IV. Trnava: 1930-31.

Memorandum from the Slovak National Council in London to the Rt. Hon. Ernest Bevin, P.C., M.M., His Britannic Majesty's Principal Secretary of State for Foreign Affairs. London: March, 1948.

Mendelssohn, P. *The Nuremberg Documents*. London: 1946.

Mercier, M. *La Formation de l'Etat Tchécoslovaque*. Chartres: 1923.

Mikus, J. A. *La Slovaquie, individualité politique de l'Europe Centrale*. Paris: 1952.

————. *The Three Slovak Bishops*. Passaic, N.J.: 1953.

Miller, D. H. *My Diary at the Paris Peace Conference*. New York: 1924.

Ministère de l'Agriculture. *Le Plan biennal dans l'Agriculture*. Prague: 1948.

Ministère de l'Information et de l'Education populaire. *Du Plan biennal au Plan quinquennal*. Prague: 1949.

Ministère de l'Information et de l'Education populaire. *Le Plan économique quinquennal tchécoslovaque.* Prague: December, 1948.

Ministère de l'Information Tchécoslovaque. *Constitution de la République tchécoslovaque 9 mai 1948.* Prague: 1948.

Ministère des Affaires étrangères. *Le livre jaune français. Documents diplomatiques 1938-1939.* Paris: 1939.

Ministère des Affaires étrangères de l'U.R.S.S. *Documents et matériaux se rapportant à la veille de la Deuxième Guerre mondiale,* I-II. Moscow: 1948.

Ministerstvo informací. *Zahajujeme rozpravu o ustavě (The Ministry of Information's Inquest on the Constitution).* Prague: 1947.

Ministerstvo spravodlivosti. *Proces proti vlastizradným biskupom Vojtaššákovi, Buzalkovi, Gojdičovi (Ministry of Justice: Trial against Bishops Bojtaššák, Buzalka, Gojdič, Traitors to the Country).* Bratislava: 1951.

Ministerstvo vnitra. *Spiknutí proti Republice (Ministry of the Interior: The Conspiracy Against the Republic in Slovakia.* Prague: 1947.

Ministerstvo zemedelstva. *Čo pripravuje ministerstvo zemedelstva pre slovenských roľníkov (What the Ministry of Agriculture is Preparing for the Slovak Peasants).* Prague: 1947.

––––––. *Dvojročný plán v pôdohospodárstve (Ministry of Agriculture: The Two-Year Plan in Agriculture).* Prague: 1946.

Mirkin-Guetzevitch, B. *La Tchécoslovaquie.* Paris: 1930.

Mišík, M. *Husiti na Slovensku (The Hussites in Slovakia). Banská Bystrica:* 1927.

Miškovič, A. *Napravená krivda (An Injustice Redressed).* Turčiansky Sv. Martin: 1940.

Moravec, E. *Das Ende der Benesch Republik.* Prague: 1941.

Mousset, Albert. *Le Monde slave.* Paris: 1946.

Mráz, A. *Die Literatur der Slowaken.* Berlin-Prague-Wien: 1942.

––––––. *Matica slovenská v r. 1863-1875 (The "Matica Slovenská" from 1863 to 1875).* Turčiansky Sv. Martin: 1935.

Němec, L. *Church and State in Czechoslovakia.* New York: 1955.

Niederle, L. *La race slave.* Paris: 1917.

––––––. *Národopisná mapa Slováků v Uhrách (The Ethnographic Map of the Slovaks of Hungary).* Prague: 1900.

Nikolau-Tibal. *Géographie de la Tchécoslovaquie.* Prague: 1926.

Nosko, J. *Vojaci v slovenskom národnom povstaní (The Soldiers in the Slovak National Uprising)*. Bratislava: 1945.

Novák, L. *Jazykovedné glosy k česko-slovenskej otázke (Linguistic Commentaries on the Czecho-Slovak Problem)*. Turčiansky Sv. Martin: 1935.

Novomeský, L. *Kommunizmus v slovenskej narodnej idei (Communism and the Slovak National Idea)*. Bratislava: 1946.

Nowak, R. *Der künstliche Staat. Ostprobleme der Tchecho-Slowakei*. Oldenburg: 1938.

Oddo, G. L. *Slovakia and Its People*. New York: 1960.

Open Letter from the Slovak Action Committee to the Representatives of the Members of the United Nations. New York: 1947.

Opočenský, J. *La fin de l'Autriche et la genèse de l'Etat tchécoslovaque*. Prague: 1928.

Osuský, S. *Beneš and Slovakia*. London: 1943.

Papoušek, J. *La Tchécoslovaquie, l'U.R.S.S. et l'Allemagne*. Prague: 1936.

Partizánske akcie v národnom povstaní (The Partisans in the National Uprising. Bratislava: 1945.

Paučo, J. *Slováci a komunizmus. (The Slovaks and Communism)*. Middletown, Pa.: 1957.

Pekař, J. *Dějiny československé (Czechoslovak History)*. Prague: 1920.

Peška, Z. *Za naše nové státní zřízení (For the New Organization of Our State)*. Prague: 1945.

Peroutka, F. *Budování státu, (The Building of the State)*, I-IV. Prague: 1933-36.

Petition Concerning the Slovak Situation and the Realization of the Plebiscite in Slovakia Presented by the Slovak Action Committee to the General Assembly of the United Nations in Paris, 1948. New York: 1948.

Petition of the Slovak Action Committee to the Security Council of the United Nations. Bridgeport, Conn.: September, 1946.

Petreas, J. O. *Die Slowakei im Umbruch*. Turčiansky Sv. Martin: 1941.

Pic, J. *Der Nationale Kampf gegen das ungarische Staatsrecht*. Leipzig: 1882.

Pietor, A. *Nápor-odpor (Action and Reaction. Study on the Progressive Magyarization in Hungary)*. Turčiansky Sv. Martin: 1905.

378 SLOVAKIA: A Political History

Plea Concerning the Slovak Question Presented by the Slovak Action Committee to His Excellency Rt. Hon. Clement R. Atlee, Prime Minister of His Majesty's Government. Bridgeport, Conn.: March, 1947.

Polakovič, S. K základom slovenského štátu (The Foundations of the Slovak State. Bratislava: 1939.

------. L'évolution des idées fondamentales de la politique slovaque. Bratislava: 1944.

------. Z Tisovho boja (Monsignor Tiso's Struggle). Bratislava: 1941.

Poncet, F. Souvenirs d'une Ambassade à Berlin. Paris: 1949.

Popovici, A. C. Die Vereinigten Staaten von Gross-Österreich. Leipzig: 1906.

Povereníctvo S. N. R. pre informácie, O ľudovom súdnictve (The People's Courts). Bratislava: 1945.

------. Partizánske akcie v národnom povstaní (Partisan Activities in the National Uprising). Turčiansky Sv. Martin: 1946.

------. Rekonštrukcia Slovenska (The Reconstruction of Slovakia). Bratislava: 1945.

------. Vojenské akcie v národnom povstaní (Military Aspect of the Uprising). Turčiansky Sv. Martin: 1946.

Pöstényi, J. Dejiny Spolku Sv. Vojtecha (History of the Association of St. Adalbert). Trnava: 1930.

Pražák, A. Češi a Slováci (Czechs and Slovaks). Prague: 1929.

------. Československý národ (The Czechoslovak Nation). Bratislava: 1925.

------. Duchová podstata slovenské slovesnosti (The Spiritual Essence of Slovak Literature). Prague: 1938.

------. Slovenská svojskosť (Slovak Individuality). Bratislava: 1926.

Prídavok, P. A Good Word to Slovaks Worthy of It. London: 1943.

Puaux, G. "Les illusions de M. Beneš," Revue de Paris (June, 1950).

Radványi, C. Slovenská krv. (Slovak Personalities). Bratislava: 1942.

Rapant, D. K. počiatkom maďarizácie (The beginnings of Magyarization). Bratislava: 1927, 1931.

------. "Národ a československá otázka," ("The Concept of Nation and the Czechoslovak Question"), Prúdy (Bratislava), IX, (1925).

_____. *Slovenské povstanie 1848-1849 (The Slovak Uprising in 1848-1849),* I-II. Liptovský Sv. Mikuláš: 1943.

_____. *Slovenský prestolný prosbopis (The Slovak Petition to the Throne).* Liptovský Sv. Mikuláš: 1944.

_____. *Viedenské memorandum slovenské z r. 1861 (Slovak Memorandum of Vienna, 1861).* Turčiansky Sv. Martin: 1944.

Raschhofer, H. *Die tschechoslowakischen Denkschriften für die Friedenskonferenz von Paris, 1919-1920.* Berlin: 1937.

Rašla, A. *Tiso a povstanie (Monsignor Tiso and the Uprising).* Bratislava: 1947.

Rauscher, R. *Slovenské právní dějiny v rámci dějin práva ve Středni Evropě (The History of Slovak Law within the History of Law in Central Europe).* Bratislava: 1925.

_____. "Ustavní dějiny na Slovensku a v Podkarpatské Rusi" (The Constitutional History of Slovakia and Sub-Carpathian Ruthenia), *Československá vlastivěda (Encyclopaedia on Czechoslovakia),* V. Prague: 1931.

Reed, D. *From Smoke to Smother.* London: 1948.

Report of the International Committee of the Red Cross on Its Activities During the Second World War September 11, 1939-June 30, 1947. I-III. Geneva: 1948.

Révay, S. *Die in Belvedere gezogene ungarisch-slowakische Grenze.* Budapest: 1943.

Ripka, H. *Czechoslovakia Enslaved.* London: 1950.

_____. *East and West.* London: 1944.

_____. "La Tchécoslovaquie comme partenaire commercial," *Cahiers du Monde Nouveau* (Paris), (November, 1946).

_____. *Munich: Before and After.* London: 1939.

_____. *Russians and the West.* London: 1942.

_____. *Small and Great Nations.* London: 1944.

Rízner, K. *Bibliografia písomníctva slovenského od r. 1900 (Bibliography of Slovak Literature after 1900).* Turčiansky Sv. Martin: 1927, 1934.

Romain d'Or. *The Inclined Plane (Some Observations on Russian Expansion).* Stockholm: 1948.

Roquencourt, G. "La question slovaque," *La Revue Politique Internationale,* (Lausanne), (January-February, 1919).

Roux, G. "L'Etat de Slovaquie," *Revue de Paris,* (October 1, 1939).

Rössler, F. *Die Slowakei.* Dresden: 1943.

Rudinský, J. *Revízia Trianonskej smluvy (The Revision of the Trianon Treaty).* Bratislava: 1932.

Sasínek, F. *Slováci v Uhorsku (The Slovaks in Hungary).* Turčiansky Sv. Martin: 1905.

Schlesinger, R. *Federalism in Central and Eastern Europe.* London: 1945.

———. "Slovakia Today and Tomorrow," *Contemporary Review,* (August, 1939).

Schwartz, M. *Untersuchungen über das Mährisch-Slowakische Staatswesen des 9. Jahrhundert.* Berlin-München: 1942.

———. *Die Slowakei.* Leipzig: 1939.

Seton Watson, R. W. *A History of the Czechs and Slovaks.* London: 1943.

———. *Racial Problems in Hungary.* London: 1908.

———. *Slovakia Then and Now.* London-Prague: 1931.

———. *The New Slovakia.* Prague: 1924.

Sharp, S. L. *Nationalisation of Key Industries in Eastern Europe.* Washington, D.C.: 1946.

Sidor, K. *Biography of Monsignor Andrej Hlinka.* Bratislava: 1934.

———. "La Tchéco-Slovaquie n'a pas sa raison d'être," *Journal de Genève,* (December 28, 1948).

———. *Meditazioni di Hlinka a Mirov.* Citta del Vaticano: 1942.

———. *Slováci v zahraničnom odboji (The Slovaks in Their Struggle Against Austria-Hungary).* Bratislava: 1928.

———. *Slovenská politika na pôde pražkého snemu, 1918-1938 (The Slovaks on the Floor of the Parliament of Prague, 1918-1938).* Bratislava: 1943.

———. *Šesť rokov pri Vatikáne (Six Years Minister Plenipotentiary to the Vatican).* Scranton, Pa.: 1947.

———. "Ripka's Version of the Communist Putsch," *Slovak Newsletter* (Middletown, Pa.), (March, 1950).

Slovak Action Committee. *Memoriae sacrae Excellentissimi viri, sacerdotis zelosissimi, hominis status christiani exemplarissimi, Dr. Joseph Tiso qui falso accusatus, occisus, crematus, summam gloriam adeptus est.* Bridgeport, Conn.: 1948.

———. *Déclaration sur les derniers évènements en Tchéco-Slovaquie.* Buenos Aires: April, 1948.

———. *Memorandum Presented to the Peace Conference Concerning the Irrationality of Existence of Czecho-Slovakia.* Paris: 1946.

Slovak National Council Abroad. *Memorandum to H. E. John Foster Dulles, Secretary of State of the U.S.A.* New York: 1953.

Slovenská Liga v Amerike. *Memorandum Slovenskej Ligy v Amerike prijaté XXIX. kongresom 21, októbra 1947 v Cleveland, Ohio (Memorandum of the Slovak League of America Voted in the Twenty-ninth Congress, October 21, 1947, in Cleveland, Ohio).* Springdale, Pa.: 1947.

Slovenská republika, 1939-1949 (The Slovak Republic). Symposium published on the occasion of the tenth anniversary of its founding. Scranton, Pa.: 1949.

Slovenské národné shromaždenie v Turčianskom Sv. Martine, 1861 (The Slovak National Assembly of Turčiansky Sv. Martin, 1861). Turčiansky Sv. Martin: 1941.

Slovenský rozchod s Maďarmi r. 1918 (The Slovaks' Break with the Magyars. Documents Relating to the Negotiations of Dr. Milan Hodža in Budapest). Bratislava: 1929.

Stanislav, J. *Slovenskí apoštoli Cyril a Metód (The Apostles of the Slovaks, Cyril and Methodius).* Bratislava: 1945.

Steier, L. *Ungarns Vergewaltigung. Oberungarn unter tchechischer Herrschaft.* Zurich-Leipzig-Wien: 1929.

Stodola, E. *O jazykovom zákone a menšinových otázkach (The Law on Languages and Minority Questions.* Prague-Prešov: 1936.

―――. *Prelom (The Slovaks' Break with the Past).* Prague: 1933.

Svetoň, J. *Die Slowaken in Ungarn.* Bratislava: 1943.

―――. *Slováci v Europskom zahraničí (The Slovaks in European Countries).* Bratislava: 1943.

―――. *Slováci v Maďarsku (The Slovaks in Hungary. Statistical Contribution to the Study of Magyarization).* Bratislava: 1942.

Svobodný, R. "Les partis politiques slovaques," *Cahiers du Monde Nouveau* (Paris), (November, 1946).

Šepovalov, A. "Geopolitický základ slovenského štátu" ("The Geopolitical Foundation of the Slovak State," *Výročná zpráva S.S.L.O.A.* Tenčín, 1939-1940.

Škultéty, J. "Maďarizmus od konca 18. stoletia" ("Magyarization from the End of the Eighteenth Century"), *Slovenské pohľady,* (Turčiansky Sv. Martin). XXIX. (1909).

―――. *O bývalom Hornom Uhorsku (Former Upper Hungary).* Turčiansky Sv. Martin: 1929.

―――. *O Slovákoch (Considerations on the Slovaks).* Turčiansky Sv. Martin: 1928.

―――. *Slovenské memorandum z r. 1861 (Slovak Memorandum of 1861, Fiftieth Anniversary).* Turčiansky Sv. Martin: 1911.

——. *Zo slovenskej minulosti (The Slovak Past)*. Turčiansky Sv. Martin: 1936.

——. *Stodvadsať päť rokov zo slovenského života (Slovak Life from 1790-1914)*. Turčiansky Sv. Martin: 1920.

Špirko, J. *Cirkevné dejiny s osobitným zreteľom na vývin cirkevných dejín Slovenska (The History of the Church with Considerations on Its Evolution in Slovakia)*. Turčiansky Sv. Martin: 1943.

Šrobár, V. *Oslobodené Slovensko (Slovakia Liberated. Memories of Events from 1918 to 1920)*. Prague: 1928.

Štefánek, A. *Základy sociografie Slovenska (Foundations of the Sociography of Slovakia)*. Bratislava: 1945.

——. *Zur Soziographie der Geistigen Kultur in der Slowakei.* Bratislava: 1944.

Strauss, E. *Tschechoslowakische Aussenpolitik.* Prague: 1936.

Štúr, L. *Hlas k rodákom (Address to Compatriots)*. Turčiansky Sv. Martin: 1943.

——. *Das Slaventhum und die Welt der Zukunft.* Bratislava: 1931.

——. *Starý a nový vek Slovákov (The Slovaks: Ancient and Modern History)*. Bratislava: 1935.

Šujan, J. *Slovenské národné povstanie (The Slovak National Uprising)*. Banská Bystrica: 1945.

Táborsky, E. "Beneš and the Soviets," *Foreign Affairs*, (April, 1949).

——. *The Czechoslovak Cause.* London: 1944.

Tarnowski, A. *Two Polish Attempts to Bring About a Central East European Organization.* London: 1943.

Tchécoslovaquie, Bibliotheque de droit contemporain, MM. Levy-Ullmann et B. Mirkin-Guetzevitch. Paris: 1932.

Tehle, J. *Ukoly R. O. H. v pětiletem plánu (The Tasks of the Revolutionary Trade Union Movement)*. Prague: 1949.

The Trial of German Major War Criminals. II. *December 3-14, 1945.* London: 1946.

Tholt, Velkoštiavický A. *Národ a národnosť (Nation and Nationality)*. Pittsburgh: 1907.

Thomas, L. *Histoire d'un jour. Munich, 29 september 1938.* Paris: 1939.

Thun, L. *Die Stellung der Slowaken in Ungarn.* Prague: 1843.

Tibal, A. *La Tchécoslovaquie. Etude économique.* Paris: 1935.

Tiso, J. *Die Wahrheit über die Slowakei.* München: 1948.

Tobolka, Z. *Politcké dějiny československého národa od r. 1848 až do dnešní doby (The Political History of the Czechoslovak Nation from 1848 to Our Days)*, I-IV. Prague: 1932-37.

Tomsa, B. "Národ a československá otázka" ("The Concept of Nation and the Czechoslovak Question,") *Prúdy* (Bratislava), IX. 1925.

Tourtzer, H. *Louis Štúr et l'idée de l'indépendance slovaque (1815-1856)*, Cahors et Alençon: 1913.

Trnavský sborník (Trnava Symposium. Published on the occasion of the 300th anniversary of the founding of the University of Trnava.) Bratislava: 1935.

Varsík, B. *Die Slowaken und ihr völkischer Lebensraum in der Vergangenheit*. Bratislava: 1942.

———. "Devín a Slováci," ("The Devín Château and the Slovaks"), *Historica Slovaca*. (Turčiansky Sv. Martin), I-II. (1940-1941).

———. *Národnostná hranica slovensko-maďarská v ostatných dvoch storočiach (The Slovak-Magyar Ethnographic Frontier during the Last Two Centuries)*. Bratislava: 1940.

———. "Slováci v Košiciach v posledných dvoch storočiach" ("The Slovaks at Košice during the Last Two Centuries"), *Politika* (Bratislava), X. (1941).

Vietz, C. *Aspects du problème tchécoslovaque. Un corridor soviétique au coeur de l'Europe*. Genève: 1938.

Višňovan, J. (Kirschbaum, J.). *Krvácajúca hranica (The Bloody Frontier. Documents on the Sufferings of the Slovaks Again Bound to Hungary)*. Bratislava: 1940.

Vlček, J. *Dejiny literatúry slovenskej (History of Slovak Literature)*. Turčiansky Sv. Martin: 1923.

———. *Slovensko od reakce Bachovy do zrušení Matice slovenské 1850-1875 (Slovakia from the Bach Regime to the Suppression of the Matica Slovenská, 1850-1875)*. Prague: 1913.

Vondráček, F. S. *The Foreign Policy of Czechoslovakia*. New York: 1937.

Vondrák-Zumann. *Osvobozenská legenda (Legend of the Liberation)*. Prague: 1922.

Votruba, F. "Slovensko v politickej aktivite" ("Slovakia in Political Activity"), *Sborník Milan Hodža*. Prague: 1930.

Weiss-Nägel, A. "Die Aufbaukräfte des Slowakischen Volkscharacters," *Leipziger Vierteljahrsschrift für Südosteuropa*, IV, (1940), Heft 1/2.

Yurchak, P. *The Slovaks.* Whiting, Ind.: 1946.
Woytko, M. G. *Slovakia's Road to Statehood.* Whiting, Ind.: 1957.
Zubek, T. J. *The Church of Silence in Slovakia.* Whiting, Ind.:
  1956.

Index